TRIUMPH TR4

WORKSHOP MANUAL

PART NUMBER 510322

Incorporating Supplement for TR4A Model

Issued by the

SERVICE DIVISION

STANDARD-TRIUMPH SALES LIMITED

A member of the Leyland Motor Corporation

ISBN 0 948207 95 7

INTRODUCTION

This Workshop Manual, which is in loose-leaf form, has been compiled to assist Standard-Triumph Distributors and Dealers throughout the world in the efficient repair and maintenance of Triumph TR4 models from Commission Number (Chassis Number) CT. 1.

The information most frequently required is given in the preliminary pages and includes:—the Introduction, General Specification, Unit reference numbers, Vehicle dimensions, Nut tightening torques, Special tools, Recommended lubricants, Jacking system and a short glossary of part names and alternatives.

Whilst retaining the same grouping system used for Service Information Sheets and previous Workshop Manuals, this book, the first of a new series, introduces an additional group having the designation "0". This describes the position and function of the instruments and controls. Recommendations are also given for "running-in", together with detailed working instructions for carrying out the "Customer Preparation Service", periodical lubrication, and regular maintenance operations listed on the back of vouchers contained in the Maintenance Voucher Booklet accompanying each new vehicle. A lubrication chart is provided at the end of the section.

Dismantling, assembly and adjustment procedures for the complete vehicle are divided into six groups numbered one to six. Each deals with one major unit and associated parts, except group six, which deals exclusively with the electrical system. Each group is preceded by a detailed specification and dimensions.

Special Tools

The use of special tools mentioned in the text, contributes to an efficient and profitable repair. Some operations are, in fact, impracticable without their use, particularly those, for example, which deal with the assembly of the differential unit. Distributors are therefore urged to check their tools and order those necessary.

Numbering Pages and Section

The running headline, at the top of the page, names each section within a group. For example, group one contains four sections, namely : Engine, Cooling, Fuel and Exhaust Systems, these being numbered 1 to 4 respectively.

The group number is shown at the top outer edge of each page and is followed by a decimal point.

Each section number is placed after the decimal point following the group number.

Two numerals placed after the section number are used to identify the pages which comprise a particular section, thus page 5 of the cooling section would appear 1·205.

Service Information and Amendment Procedure

Design modifications, changes in procedure and notice of amendment subsequent to the preparation of this manual are given in Service Information Sheets which are issued regularly to all authorised dealers. Should existing instructions be affected or additional information be warranted, new pages will be included with each consecutively numbered notice of amendment. This will also give details of the pages and groups affected.

To ensure that this manual is kept up to date, Distributors and Dealers are advised to write the amendment number, the page number and the group number in the space provided on the page preceding Group "0" as the amended pages of text are inserted. Any gaps in the sequence of amendment numbers will then be readily apparent and immediate action can be taken to obtain the missing sheets.

Schedule of Repair Operations

The operations listed in the "Schedule of Repair Operation Times" refer to those described in this manual. The time set against each operation in the schedule is evolved by performing the actual operations on a standard vehicle using special tools where stated. The "Schedule of Repair Operation Times", for use with this manual, is issued as a separate publication and may be obtained from the Spares Division under Part Number 511225.

GENERAL SPECIFICATION

Engine

Number of cylinders	4	
Bore of cylinders	3·386″	86 mm.
(Special Order)	3·268″	83 mm.
Stroke of crankshaft	3·622″	92 mm.
Piston area	36·0 sq. in.	232 sq. cm.
(Special Order)	33·5 sq. in.	216 sq. cm.
Cubic capacity	130·5 cu. in.	2138 c.c.
(Special Order)	121·5 cu. in.	1991 c.c.
Compression ratio	9 : 1	
Valve rocker clearances—inlet and exhaust ..	0·010″ (cold)	0·254 mm.
Valve timing with valve rocker clearances set at 0·0165″ (0·42 mm.)	Inlet and exhaust valves to be equally open at T.D.C. on the exhaust stroke.	

Performance Data (Engine)

Nett .. .. 100 B.H.P. at 4,600 r.p.m.
Torque 1,520 lb. in. at 3,350 r.p.m.
(Equivalent to 147 lb/sq. in. B.M.E.P.).

(Special Order) .. .. 100 B.H.P. at 5,000 r.p.m.
Torque 1,410 lb. in. at 3,000 r.p.m.
(Equivalent to 145 lb/sq. in. B.M.E.P.).

Piston speed at 100 m.p.h. (top gear) .. .. 2,850 ft/min. at 4,800 r.p.m. (3·7 : 1 axle).

Lubrication (Engine)

Type of pump .. .. Hobourn-Eaton eccentric rotor.
Oil filter .. .. Purolator ; A.C. Delco ; Tecalemit full flow (replaceable element).
Release pressure .. .. 70 lb/sq. in.   4·921 kg/sq. cm.

Ignition System

Contact breaker gap .. .. 0·015″   0·4 mm.
Spark plugs—Type .. .. Lodge CNY (Normal road use).
    „   HN   (High speed touring).
    „   2HN (Competition use).
    „   CN   (Low octane fuel).
Gap .. .. 0·025″   0·64 mm.
Firing order .. .. 1 : 3 : 4 : 2.
Ignition timing .. .. 4° B.T.D.C. (Basic setting).

Cooling System

Circulation .. .. Pump.
Water pump type .. .. Impeller — incorporating by-pass.
Temperature control .. .. Thermostat.
Opening temperature. 70°C (158°F)
Fully open at 85°C (185°F)
Radiator .. .. Pressurised—finned vertical flat tubes—extended header tank.
Filler cap .. .. A.C. type.
— pressure .. .. 4 lb/sq. in.   0·28 kg/sq. cm.

Fuel System

Fuel tank .. .. Non-pressure type mounted over rear axle.
Carburettors .. .. Twin S.U. H6.
Needle size — SM.
Air cleaners .. .. Wire gauze type.
Fuel pump — type .. .. A.C. mechanical with filter and sediment bowl.
— operating pressure .. .. 1¼ - 2½ lb/sq. in.

Clutch

Type .. .. Borg & Beck 9″ single dry plate.
Operation .. .. Hydraulic.
Adjustment .. .. Push rod at slave cylinder.

Gearbox

Type	4 forward speeds and reverse. Synchromesh on all forward gears.
Control	Centre floor-mounted remote control.

Rear Axle

Type	Hypoid bevel gears ; semi-floating axle shafts. Tapered roller bearings.
Ratio	3·7 or 4·1 : 1.

Gear Ratios

	Overdrive Top	Top	Overdrive 3rd	3rd	Overdrive 2nd	2nd	1st	Rev.
Gearbox Ratios ..	0·82	1·0	1·09	1·325	1·65	2·01	3·139	3·223

3·7 : 1 Axle

	Overdrive Top	Top	Overdrive 3rd	3rd	Overdrive 2nd	2nd	1st	Rev.
Overall Ratios ..	3·034	3·7	4·02	4·9	6·1	7·44	11·61	11·93

4·1 : 1 Axle

	Overdrive Top	Top	Overdrive 3rd	3rd	Overdrive 2nd	2nd	1st	Rev.
Overall Ratios ..	3·36	4·1	4·46	5·44	6·76	8·24	12·87	13·21

Brakes

System	Girling hydraulic. Front — Caliper disc. Rear — Drum (leading and trailing shoes).
Adjustment	Rear brakes only (1 adjuster each wheel).
Dimensions	Rear shoes : 9″ × 1¾″ (22·86 × 4·45 cm.).

TYRE PRESSURE DATA

TYRE PRESSURES

OPERATING CONDITIONS	Goodyear All Weather Rib and Dunlop Gold Seal 5.50/5.90.15 lbs. per sq. in.		Goodyear All Weather Rib Nylon and Dunlop Gold Seal Nylon 5.50/5.90.15 lbs. per sq. in.		Goodyear Motorway Special and Dunlop Road Speed R.S.5 5.50/5.90.15 lbs. per sq. in.		Goodyear D.F.S. (165-380) and Michelin (165/15 X) (165/15 X) lbs. per sq. in.		Dunlop S.P. (Radial Ply) for use with Michelin 'X' 165-15 Type Speedometers (165/15 X) lbs. per sq. in.		Goodyear "Grand Prix" 6.95″ - 15″ (6.95″-15″) lbs. per sq. in.	
	Front	Rear	Front	Rear	Front	Rear	Front	Rear	Front	Rear	Front	Rear
Normal motoring with sustained speeds limited to 85 m.p.h.	20	24	20	24	20	24	24	32	24	28	20	24
Fast motoring on motorways and similar roads with sustained speeds up to 100 m.p.h.	26	30	20	24	20	24	24	32	24	28	20	24
High speed tuning with speeds regularly in excess of 100 m.p.h.	NOT RECOMMENDED		26	30	20	24	24	32	24	28	20	24

Suspension

Front .... Independent suspension with wishbones top and bottom. Patented bottom bush and top ball joint swivels. Coil springs controlled by telescopic dampers. Taper roller hub bearings.

Rear .... Wide semi-elliptic springs, controlled by piston type dampers.

Steering

Type	Rack and pinion unit. Telescopic steering column.	
Caster angle	3°	
Camber angle	2° Static laden.	
King pin inclination	7°	
Front wheel alignment	Parallel to $\frac{1}{8}''$ (3·18 mm.) toe-in.	
	Parallel to $\frac{1}{16}''$ (1·59 mm.) toe-in if fitted with Goodyear D.F.S. or Michelin X tyres.	
Turning circle	33′ 0″	10 metres.

Chassis Data

Wheelbase	7′ 4″	2·236 metres.
Track : Front (Disc wheels)	4′ 1″	1·245 metres.
Rear (Disc wheels)	4′ 0″	1·220 metres.
Front (Wire wheels)	4′ 2″	1·270 metres.
Rear (Wire wheels)	4′ 1″	1·245 metres.
Ground clearance (Static laden)	6″	15·24 cm.

Exterior Dimensions

Overall length	12′ 10″	391 cm.
,, width	4′ 9½″	146 cm.
,, height	4′ 2″	127 cm.

Weight

Dry (excluding extra equipment)	2128 lb.	965 kg.
Complete (including fuel, oil, water and tools) ..	2240 lb.	1015 kg.

Capacities

	Imperial	U.S.	Metric
Engine — from dry	11 pints	13·2 pints	6·25 litres
Drain and refill	10 pints	12 pints	5·7 litres
Gearbox	1½ pints	1·8 pints	0·8 litres
With overdrive from dry	3½ pints	4·2 pints	2·0 litres
Drain and refill	2¾ pints	3·3 pints	1·6 litres
Rear axle	1½ pints	1·8 pints	0·8 litres
Water capacity of cooling system	13 pints	15·7 pints	7·39 litres
With heater fitted	14 pints	16·8 pints	8·0 litres
Fuel capacity	11¾ galls.	14 galls.	53·5 litres

Electrical System

Battery	12 volt, 51 amps. hr.
Control box	Model RB.106-2.
Generator	Model C40-1.

LOCATION OF COMMISSION AND
UNIT NUMBERS

The Body Number is located on the R.H. side of the Scuttle Panel.

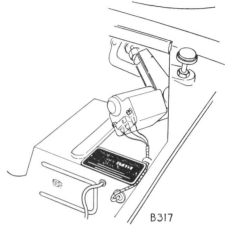

The Commission Number (Chassis Number) is located on the Scuttle Panel adjacent to the windscreen wiper motor and may be seen by lifting the bonnet.

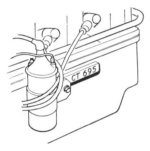

The Engine Serial Number is stamped on the L.H. side of the Cylinder Block.

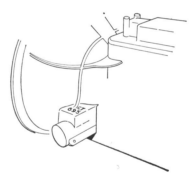

The Gearbox Serial Number is stamped on the L.H. side of the Clutch Housing.

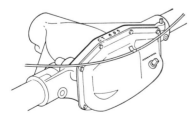

The Rear Axle Serial Number is stamped on the face of the Hypoid Housing Flange.

IMPORTANT

In all communications relating to Service or Spares, please quote the Commission Number (Chassis Number).

VEHICLE DIMENSIONS

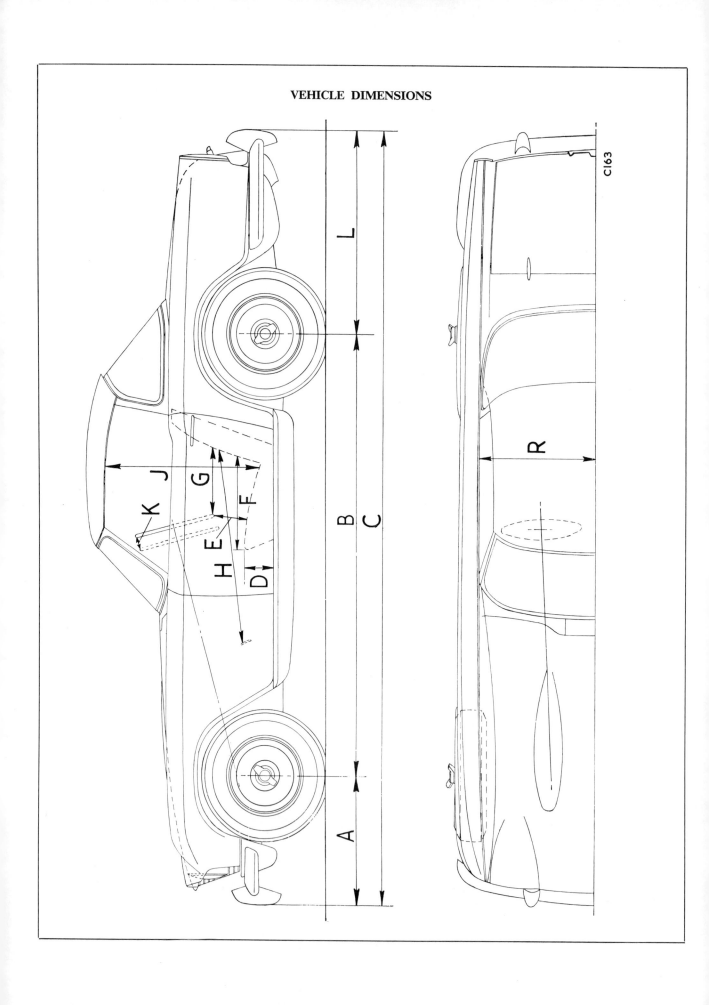

C163

VEHICLE DIMENSIONS

VEHICLE DIMENSIONS

		inches	centimetres
A	... ...	25·5	66·77
B	... ...	88·0	223·52
C	... ...	154·0	391·16
D	... ...	5·5	13·97
E	... ...	6·5	16·51
F	... ...	20·0	52·07
G (min.)	... ...	14·0	35·56
(max.)	... ...	21·5	54·61
H (min.)	... ...	36·5	92·71
(max.)	... ...	44·0	111·76
J	... ...	35·0	88·90
K	... ...	2·0	5·08
L	... ...	40·5	102·87
M	... ...	50·13	127·32
N	... ...	57·25	145·37
P	... ...	49·75	126·37
Q	... ...	60·0	152·40
R	... ...	25·0	63·5
S	... ...	50·0	127·00

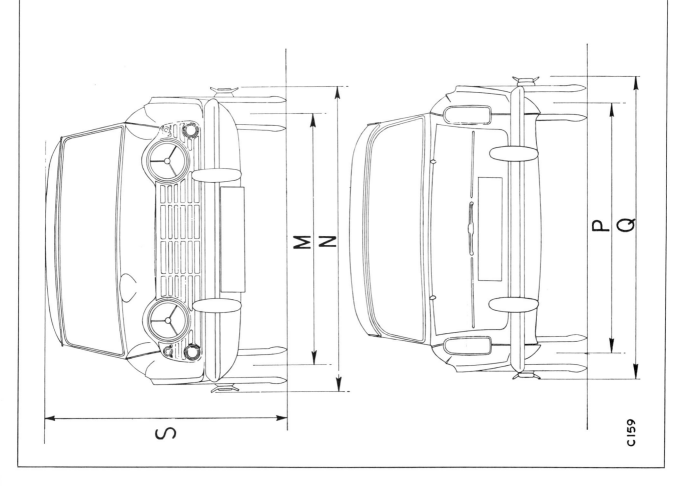

C159

NUT TIGHTENING TORQUES

OPERATION	DESCRIPTION	SPECIFIED TORQUES lbs. ft.	Kgm.
ENGINE			
Cylinder Head	1/2" U.N.F. & B.N.C. Stud	100 - 105	13·826 - 14·520
Connecting Rod Caps	7/16" U.N.F. Bolt	55 - 60	7·604 - 8·293
Clutch Attachment	5/16" × 18 U.N.C. Setscrew	20	2·765
Camshaft Bearing to Block Front	5/16" N.C. Setscrew	16 - 18	2·212 - 2·489
Camshaft Bearing to Block Rear	5/16" U.N.F. Setscrew	12 - 14	1·659 - 1·936
Dynamo Bracket to Block	5/16" × 18 U.N.C. Setscrew	16 - 18	2·212 - 2·489
Dynamo to Bracket and Pedestal	5/16" × 24 U.N.F. Bolt	16 - 18	2·212 - 2·489
Distributor Mounting	1/2" N.F. & N.C. Stud	8 - 10	1·106 - 1·383
Dynamo Adjusting Link to Water Pump Body	5/16" U.N.C. Bolt	16 - 18	2·212 - 2·489
	5/16" U.N.C. Setscrew		
End Plate Attachment	5/16" × 18 U.N.C. Bolt	14 - 16	1·936 - 2·212
Engine Plate and Timing Cover Front ..	5/16" N.F. & U.N.C. Stud	12 - 14	1·659 - 1·936
Flywheel Attachment to Crankshaft	3/8" × 24 N.F. Setscrew	42 - 46	5·807 - 6·360
Fan Attachment	5/16" U.N.F. Bolt	16 - 18	2·212 - 2·489
Manifold Attachment	3/8" N.C. Stud	22 - 24	3·042 - 3·318
Manifold Inlet and Exhaust	5/16" × 24 U.N.F. Stud	12 - 14	1·659 - 1·936
Main Bearing Caps	1/2" U.N.C. Setscrew	85 - 90	11·752 - 12·443
Oil Pump Attachment	5/16" N.F. & N.C. Stud	12 - 14	1·659 - 1·936
Oil Seal Attachment (Rear)	1/4" × 20 U.N.C. Setscrew	8 - 10	1·106 - 1·383
Oil Filter Attachment	5/16" U.N.C. Bolts	22 - 24	3·042 - 3·318
	5/16" N.F. & N.C. Stud		
Oil Gallery Plugs	7/16" × 14 U.N.C. Setscrew	32 - 36	4·424 - 4·977
	3/8" × 16 U.N.C. Setscrew	24 - 26	3·318 - 3·595
Petrol Pump Attachment	5/16" N.F. & N.C. Stud	12 - 14	1·659 - 1·936
Pulley to Water Pump Spindle	5/16" 24 U.N.F. Simmonds Nyloc Nut	16 - 18	2·212 - 2·489
Pulley and Extension to Hub	1/4" U.N.F. Bolt	8 - 10	1·106 - 1·383
Rocker Cover	5/16" N.F. & N.C. Stud	2	0·276
Rocker Pedestal	3/8" U.N.F. & U.N.C. Stud	24 - 26	3·318 - 3·595
Sump Attachment	5/16" × 18 U.N.F. Setscrew	18 - 20	2·489 - 2·765
Starter Motor (Attachment)	3/8" × 24 N.F. Bolt	26 - 28	3·595 - 3·871
Timing Cover	5/16" × 18 & 24 N.C. Setscrew	14 - 16	1·936 - 2·212
Timing Chain Wheel to Camshaft	5/16" × 18 N.C. Setscrew	24 - 26	3·318 - 3·595
Thermostat Assembly to Cylinder Head ..	5/16" × 24 U.N.C. Bolts	16 - 18	2·212 - 2·489
Thermostat Housing	5/16" U.N.F.	12 - 14	1·659 - 1·936
Water Pump Attachment	3/8" × 16 U.N.C. Bolts	26 - 28	3·595 - 3·871
Water Pump Body	3/8" N.F. & N.C. Stud	26 - 28	3·595 - 3·871
Flywheel Ring Gear Attachment	5/16" U.N.F. × 1·25" Bolt	16 - 18	2·212 - 2·489
GEARBOX			
Extension to Gearbox	5/16" × 18 U.N.C. Bolt	14 - 16	1·936 - 2·212
	5/16" × 18 U.N.C. Setscrew	14 - 16	1·936 - 2·212
Gearbox to Engine Attachment	5/16" N.F. & N.C. Setscrew	8 - 10	1·106 - 1·383
Selector Fork Attachment	5/16" U.N.F. Taper Setscrew	8 - 10	1·106 - 1·383
Front Cover to Gearbox	5/16" × 18 N.C. Setscrew	14 - 16	1·936 - 2·212
Propeller Shaft Flange to Mainshaft	3/4" × 16 N.F. Slotted Nut	80 - 120	11·060 - 16·590
Top Cover to Gearbox	5/16" N.C. Setscrew	14 - 16	1·936 - 2·212
	5/16" U.N.C. Bolt	14 - 16	1·936 - 2·212
Mounting Rear to Gearbox Extension ..	1/2" × 20 U.N.F. Bolt	50 - 55	6·913 - 7·604
REAR AXLE			
Bearing Caps to Housing	3/8" × 24 Setscrew	34 - 36	4·701 - 4·977
Backing Plate Attachment	3/8" × 24 Setscrew	26 - 28	3·595 - 3·871
Crown Wheel to Differential Case	3/8" × 24 U.N.F.	35 - 40	4·839 - 5·530
Hypoid Pinion Flange	5/8" × 18 U.N.F.	85 - 100	11·752 - 13·826
Hub to Axle Shaft	5/8" × 18 U.N.F. Nut Slotted	125 - 145	17·282 - 20·047
Rear Cover Attachment	5/16" × 24 U.N.F. Setscrew	16 - 18	2·212 - 2·489

NUT TIGHTENING TORQUES—continued

OPERATION	DESCRIPTION	SPECIFIED TORQUES	
		lbs. ft.	Kgm.
FRONT SUSPENSION			
Back Plate and Tie Rod Levers to Vertical Link	$\frac{3}{8}$″ × 24 U.N.F. Setscrew and Bolts	24 - 26	3·318 - 3·595
Ball Pin to Vertical Link	$\frac{1}{2}$″ × 20 U.N.F. Nut Slotted	55 - 65	7·604 - 8·987
Front Hub to Stub Axle	$\frac{1}{2}$″ × 20 U.N.F. Nut Slotted	See group 4	
Lower Fulcrum Bracket to Chassis	$\frac{5}{16}$″ × 24 U.N.F. Setscrew	16 - 18	2·212 - 2·489
Stub Axle to Vertical Link	$\frac{1}{2}$′ × 20 U.N.F. Stub Axle Thread	55 - 60	7·604 - 8·295
Lower Wishbone to Fulcrum Pin	$\frac{7}{16}$″ × 20 U.N.F. Nyloc Nut	26 - 28	3·595 - 3·871
Spring Pad to Wishbone	$\frac{3}{8}$″ × 24 U.N.F. Stud $\frac{3}{8}$″ × 24 U.N.F. Bolt	26 - 28	3·595 - 3·871
Top Wishbone to Fulcrum Pin	$\frac{7}{16}$″ × 20 U.N.F. Nut Slotted	26 - 40	3·595 - 5·530
Top Inner Fulcrum Pin to Chassis	$\frac{3}{8}$″ × 24 U.N.F. Bolt $\frac{3}{8}$″ × 24 U.N.F. Setscrew	26 - 28	3·595 - 3 871
Outer Tie Rod to Levers	$\frac{3}{8}$″ × 24 U.N.F. Simmonds Nyloc Nut	26 - 28	3·595 - 3·871
Lower Wishbones to Vertical Link Trunnion ..	$\frac{7}{16}$″ U.N.F. Slotted Nut	See group 4	
Hub Extension Studs for Wire Wheel Attachment	$\frac{7}{16}$″ N.F. Stud	65	8·987
Brake Disc Attachment	$\frac{3}{8}$″ N.F. Bolt	32 - 35	4·424 - 4 839
Caliper Attachment	$\frac{7}{16}$″ N.F. Bolt	50 - 55	6·913 - 7·604
Brake Pad Retaining Plate Bolts	$\frac{1}{4}$″ N.F. Bolt	5 - 6	0·691 - 0 830
REAR SUSPENSION			
Rear Road Spring	$\frac{3}{8}$″ Centre Bolt	30 - 35	4·148 - 4·839
Road Spring to Rear Axle	$\frac{3}{8}$″ × 24 U.N.F. Clip Nyloc Nut	28 - 30	3·871 - 4·148
Shock Absorber to Frame Bracket	$\frac{3}{8}$″ × 24 U.N.F. Setscrew $\frac{3}{8}$″ × 24 U.N.F. Nyloc	26 - 28	3·595 - 3·871
Spring Shackle (Nut to Pin)	$\frac{3}{8}$″ × 24 U.N.F. Nut Shackle Pin	26 - 28	3·595 - 3·871
Spring Front End to Frame	$\frac{1}{2}$″ × 20 U.N.F. Bolt	28 - 30	3·871 - 4·148
CHASSIS			
Gearbox Mounting to Crossmember	$\frac{7}{16}$″ U.N.F. Studs	35 - 40	4·839 - 4·530
Gearbox Mounting Crossmember to Chassis ..	$\frac{3}{8}$″ U.N.F. × $\frac{5}{8}$″ Bolts	26 - 28	3·595 - 3·871
Body Mounting Extension to Chassis	$\frac{5}{16}$″ U.N.F. × $\frac{5}{8}$″ Bolts	18 - 20	2·489 - 2·765
Front Cross Tube to Suspension Turrets ..	$\frac{3}{8}$″ U.N.F. × $\frac{3}{4}$″ Bolts	26 - 28	3·595 - 3·871
STEERING UNIT			
Steering Unit to Chassis	$\frac{5}{16}$″ N.F. 'U' Bolts	12 - 14	1·659 - 1·936
Steering Column Coupling	$\frac{5}{16}$″ N.F. Bolts	12 - 14	1·659 - 1·936
Adaptor Column Coupling Unit	$\frac{1}{4}$″ N.F. Bolt	6 - 8	·8295 - 1·106
BODY COMPONENTS			
Seat to Runner Attachment	$\frac{1}{4}$″ U.N.F.	5 - 6	·6913 - ·8295
MISCELLANEOUS			
Wheel Studs and Nuts	$\frac{7}{16}$″ U.N.F.	45 - 55	6·221 7·604

SPECIAL TOOLS

The following special tools, recommended for the efficient servicing of Standard-Triumph vehicles, should be ordered direct from Messrs. V. L. Churchill and Company Limited, Great South West Road, Bedfont, Feltham, Middlesex, England.

Engine Tools

S.138	Cylinder Sleeve Retainers	Desirable
60A	Valve Guide Remover and Replacer (Main Tool)	Desirable
S.60A-2	Valve Guide Remover and Replacer (Adaptors)	Desirable
6056	Valve Seat Insert Cutter	Desirable
MFS.6056-1	Valve Seat Insert Cutter (Adaptors)	Desirable
MFS.6056-2	Valve Seat Insert Cutter (Adaptors)	Desirable
316.X	Valve Seat Cutter Handle	Desirable
316-10	Pilot	Desirable
316-12	Pilot	Desirable
317-22	Cutter 45°, $1\frac{3}{8}''$ dia.	Desirable
317-25	Cutter 45°, $1\frac{9}{16}''$ dia.	Desirable
317.T-22	Cutter 15°, $1\frac{3}{8}''$ dia.	Desirable
317.T-25	Cutter 15°, $1\frac{9}{16}''$ dia.	Desirable
317.P-22	Cutter 75°, $1\frac{3}{8}''$ dia.	Desirable
317.P-25	Cutter 75°, $1\frac{9}{16}''$ dia.	Desirable
6118	Valve Spring Compressor	Desirable
6118-1	Valve Spring Compressor (Adaptor)	Desirable
335	Connecting Rod Aligning Jig	Essential
336	Master Multi-purpose Connecting Rod Arbor	Essential
S.336-2	Arbor Adaptor (2·2325″)	Essential
30A	Bending Bar	Desirable
MFS.127	Water Pump Impeller Remover and Replacer (Adaptors)	Desirable
6312	Universal Pulley Puller	Desirable
20SM. FT.6201	Small End Bush Remover and Replacer	Desirable
6200A	Adjustable Small End Bush Reaming Fixture	Desirable
20SM. FT.6200B	Set of Reamers	Desirable
32	Camshaft Bushes Remover and Replacer (Main Tool)	Essential
S.32-1	Camshaft Bushes Remover and Replacer (Adaptors)	Essential
550	Oil Seal Driver Handle	Desirable
4316F	Fuel Pump Wrench	Desirable
20SM.99	Spark Plug Wrench	Desirable
450	Stud Extractor	Desirable

Clutch and Gearbox Tools

99A	Clutch Assembly Fixture	Essential
20S.72	Clutch Plate Centraliser	Desirable
S.4221A	Multi-purpose Hand Press	Essential
20SM.90	Propeller Shaft Flange Holder	Desirable
20S.63	Gearbox Extension Remover	Desirable
4235	Axle Shaft Remover (Main Tool)	Essential
S.4235A-2	Constant Pinion Shaft Remover (Adaptor)	Essential
20SM.69	Mainshaft Circlip Remover	Desirable
20SM.46	Circlip Installer	Desirable
20SM.76	Gearbox Countershaft Assembly Pilot	Desirable
S.4221-3	Constant Pinion Bearing Removing and Replacing Adaptors	Desirable
20SM.73A	Gearbox Front Cover Oil Seal Driver	Desirable
20SM.47	Gearbox Front Oil Seal Installer	Desirable
7065	2-way Circlip Pliers	Desirable
S.314	Mainshaft Ball Bearing Replacer	Essential
S.4221A-15	Mainshaft Ball Race Remover	Essential

Overdrive Tools

L.188	Hydraulic Test Equipment	Essential
L.176A	Drive Shaft Oil Seal Remover (Adaptor)	Essential
7657	Mainshaft Oil Seal Remover	Essential
L.177A	Drive Shaft Oil Seal Replacer Cone Clutch and Spring Thrust Housing Dismantling Tool	Essential
L.178	Freewheel Assembly Ring	Essential
L.179	Piston Ring Fitting Tool, 1⅛″ dia.	Essential
L.181	Accumulator "O" Ring Replacer	Essential
L.182	Accumulator Piston Housing Remover	Essential
L.183	Pump Barrel Remover	Essential
L.184	Pump Barrel Replacer	Essential
L.185A	Dummy Drive Shaft	Essential
L.180	Piston Ring Fitting Tool, 1⅜″ dia.	Essential
L.186	Mainshaft Bearing Replacer	Essential
L.187	Annulus and Tail Shaft Bearing Remover and Replacer	Essential
L.190A	Tail Shaft End Float Gauge	Essential

Rear Axle Tools

M.86A	Hub Remover	Essential
S.4235A-3	Half Shaft Remover (Adaptor)	Essential
S.4221-2	Half Shaft Bearing Remover (Taper Roller Bearing Type—Adaptors)	Desirable
20S.92	Half Shaft Bearing and Rear Hub Oil Seal Driver	Desirable
S.101	Differential Case Spreader	Essential
S.103	Differential Bearing Removal Ring	Essential
TS.1	Pinion Head Bearing Inner Cone Remover/Replacer	Essential
M.100A	Pinion Oil Seal Replacer (Adaptor)	Desirable
M.84	Pinion Bearing Setting Gauge	Essential
20SM.98	Pre-load Tester	Essential
20SM.90	Propeller Shaft Flange Holder	Desirable

Front Suspension and Steering Tools

S.3600	Steering Wheel Remover	Essential
S.160	Tie Rod Ball Joint Separator	Desirable
S.166	Vertical Link Ball Joint Separator	Desirable
S.112	I.F.S. Coil Spring Compressor	Essential
S.112-1	I.F.S. Coil Spring Compressor (Adaptor)	Essential

RECOMMENDED LUBRICANTS—BRITISH ISLES (All seasons)

COMPONENT	MOBIL	SHELL	ESSO	B.P.	CASTROL	DUCKHAM'S	REGENT
ENGINE SUMP*	Mobiloil Arctic or Mobiloil Special	Shell X-100 20W or X-100 Multigrade 10W/30	Esso Extra Motor Oil	Visco Static or Energol Motor Oil 20W or Visco Static Longlife	Castrolite	Duckham's No1 'Twenty' or Duckham's Q20/50	Havoline 20/20W or Havoline Special 10W/30
CARBURETTOR DASHPOTS — SUMMER	Mobiloil A	X-100 30	Essolube 30	Energol Motor Oil 30	Castrol XL	No1 'Thirty'	Havoline 30
CARBURETTOR DASHPOTS — WINTER	Mobiloil Arctic	X-100 20W	Essolube 20	Energol Motor Oil 20W	Castrolite	No1 'Twenty'	Havoline 20/20W
GEARBOX AND OVERDRIVE REAR AXLE	Mobilube GX.90	Shell Spirax 90 E.P.	Esso Gear Oil GP.90/140	Energol S.A.E. 90 E.P.	Castrol Hypoy	Duckham's Hypoid 90	Universal Thuban 90
STEERING UNIT GREASE GUN FRONT WHEEL HUBS	Mobilgrease M.P.	Shell Retinax A	Esso Multi-Purpose Grease H	Energrease L.2	Castrolease L.M.	Duckham's LB.10	Marfak Multipurpose 2
OIL CAN	Mobil Handy Oil	Shell X-100 20W	Engine Oil	Energol S.A.E. 20W	Everyman Oil	Duckham's General Purpose Oil	Havoline 20/20W
REAR ROAD SPRINGS	OLD REAR AXLE OR ENGINE OIL						
BRAKE CABLES	Mobilgrease Special or Mobilgrease M.P.	Shell Retinax A	Esso Multi-Purpose Grease H	Energrease L.2	Castrolease Brake Cable Grease	Duckham's Keenol K.G.16	Marfak Multi-Purpose 2
CLUTCH AND BRAKE RESERVOIR — GIRLING SYSTEM	CASTROL GIRLING BRAKE AND CLUTCH FLUID TO S.A.E. 70 R3 SPECIFICATION				WHERE THE PROPRIETARY BRAND IS NOT AVAILABLE, OTHER FLUIDS WHICH MEET THE S.A.E. 70 R3 SPECIFICATION MAY BE USED		
CLUTCH AND BRAKE RESERVOIR — LOCKHEED SYSTEM	LOCKHEED SUPER HEAVY DUTY BRAKE FLUID						

*Where circuit or other severe competitions are contemplated it is advisable to use oils of high viscosity in view of the increased temperature encountered.

APPROVED ANTI-FREEZE SOLUTIONS	Mobil Permazone	Shell Anti-Freeze	Esso Anti-Freeze	B.P. Anti-Frost	Castrol Anti-Freeze	Duckham's Anti-Freeze	Regent P.T. Anti-Freeze / Smith's Bluecol

Where these proprietary solutions are not available, others which meet B.S.I. 3151 or 3152 Specification may be used.

RECOMMENDED LUBRICANTS—OVERSEAS COUNTRIES

Component	Air Temp. °C.	Air Temp. °F.	Mobil	Shell	Esso	B.P.	Castrol	Duckham's	Caltex Texaco	S.A.E. & A.P.I. Designation
ENGINE*	Over 20°	Over 70°	Mobiloil A.F.	Shell X-100 40	Esso Motor Oil 40	Energol S.A.E. 40	Castrol XXL	Duckham's Nol 'Forty'	Havoline 40	S.A.E. 40 M.M.
	0° to 20°	40° to 70°	Mobiloil A	Shell X-100 30	Esso Motor Oil 30	Energol S.A.E. 30	Castrol XL	Duckham's Nol 'Thirty'	Havoline 30	S.A.E. 30 M.M.
	−10° to 0°	10° to 40°	Mobiloil Arctic	Shell X-100 20W	Esso Motor Oil 20	Energol S.A.E. 20W	Castrolite	Duckham's Nol 'Twenty'	Havoline 20/20W	S.A.E. 20W M.M.
	Below −10°	Below 10°	Mobiloil 10W	Shell X-100 10W	Esso Motor Oil 10W	Energol Motor Oil 10W	Castrol Z	Duckham's Nol 'Ten'	Havoline 10W	S.A.E. 10W M.M.
			MOBILOIL SPECIAL	MULTIGRADE X-100 10W/30 · X-100 Multigrade 20W/40	ESSO EXTRA MOTOR OIL 10W/30 · ESSOEXTRA MOTOR OIL 20W/40	VISCO-STATIC · VISCO-STATIC LONGLIFE	Q.5500 · Q.20/50		HAVOLINE SPECIAL 10W/30 · HAVOLINE SPECIAL 20W/40	
CARBURETTOR DASHPOTS			USE APPROPRIATE CURRENT SINGLE GRADE ENGINE OIL							
GEARBOX REAR AXLE	Over 0°	Over 30°	Mobilube GX.90	Shell Spirax 90 E.P.	Esso Gear Oil GP.90	Energol S.A.E. 90 EP.	Castrol Hypoy	Duckham's Hypoid 90	Universal Thuban 90	G.L.4 Hypoid 90
	Below 0°	Below 30°	Mobilube GX.80	Shell Spirax 80 E.P.	Esso Gear Oil GP.80	Energol S.A.E. 80 EP.	Castrol Hypoy Light	Duckham's Hypoid 80	Universal Thuban 80	G.L.4 Hypoid 80
STEERING UNIT GREASE GUN FRONT WHEEL HUBS			Mobilgrease M.P.	Shell Retinax A	Esso Multi-Purpose Grease H	Energrease L.2	Castrolease L.M.	Duckham's L.B.10	Marfak Multi-Purpose 2	
OIL CAN			Mobil Handy Oil	Shell X-100 20W	Engine Oil	Energol S.A.E. 20W	Everyman Oil	Duckham's General Purpose Oil	Home Lubricant	
REAR ROAD SPRINGS			OLD REAR AXLE OR ENGINE OIL							
BRAKE CABLES			Mobilgrease Special or Mobilgrease M.P.	Shell Retinax A	Esso Multi-Purpose Grease H	Energrease L.2	Castrolease Brake Cable Grease	Duckham's Keenol K.G.16	Marfak Multi-Purpose 2	
CLUTCH & BRAKE RESERVOIR — GIRLING SYSTEM			CASTROL GIRLING BRAKE AND CLUTCH FLUID TO S.A.E. 70 R.3 SPECIFICATION							
CLUTCH & BRAKE RESERVOIR — LOCKHEED SYSTEM			LOCKHEED SUPER HEAVY DUTY BRAKE FLUID		WHERE THE PROPRIETARY BRAND IS NOT AVAILABLE, OTHER FLUIDS WHICH MEET THE S.A.E. 70 R.3 SPECIFICATION MAY BE USED					

*Where circuit or other severe competitions are contemplated it is advisable to use oils of high viscosity in view of the increased oil temperature encountered.

APPROVED ANTI-FREEZE SOLUTIONS	Mobil	Shell	Esso	B.P.	Castrol	Duckham's	Caltex/Smith
	Regent P.T. Anti-Freeze / Mobil Permazone	B.P. Anti-Frost / Shell Anti-Freeze	Shell Anti-Freeze / Esso Anti-Freeze	Esso Anti-Freeze / Mobil Permazone	Castrol Anti-Freeze	Duckham's Anti-Freeze	Smith Bluecol

Where these proprietary solutions are not available, others which meet B.S.I. 3151 or 3152 specification may be used

Jacking (Fig. 3)

Using the jack provided in the tool kit, raise either side of the vehicle for road wheel removal, as follows :—

1. Ensure that the handbrake is applied and one of the wheels remaining on the ground is chocked.
2. Lift the floor covering adjacent to the door sill and remove the rubber grommet from the aperture in the floor panel.
3. Lower the jack through the aperture and engage the jack lug with the slotted bracket on the chassis frame.
4. Using the ratchet jack handle included in the tool kit, rotate the hexagonal shank of the jack clockwise to raise the vehicle.
5. To lower the jack, reverse the position of the ratchet handle and turn it counter-clockwise.

Front End (Fig. 1)

When raising the front end for servicing, place a hydraulically operated trolley jack under the front crossmember centrally between the front wheels, and place chassis stands under the chassis side members rearward of the front suspension.

Rear End (Fig. 2)

Raise the rear end using a trolley jack under the centre of the rear axle and place chassis stands under the chassis side members forward of the rear springs.

Towing

One or two methods of towing may be employed when moving the car.

(a) A towing ambulance, which may be placed under the front crossmember, or under the rear axle, depending upon the tow required.
(b) A towing rope secured to the front crossmember.

NOTE : Do NOT jack up or tow the vehicle using the radiator cradle.

Fig. 1. Using an hydraulic trolley jack under the front cross-member

Fig. 2. Jacking under the rear axle

Fig. 3. The car jack located in the chassis lifting bracket

GLOSSARY OF PART NAMES AND ALTERNATIVES

ENGINE ..

Gudgeon Pin	Piston pin. Small-end pin. Wrist pin.
Inlet Valve	Intake valve.
Piston Oil Control Ring ..	Piston scraper ring.
Induction Manifold	Inlet manifold. Intake manifold.
Oil Sump	Oil pan. Oil reservoir. Sump tray.
Core Plug	Expansion plug. Welch plug. Sealing disc.
Dipstick	Oil dipper rod. Oil level gauge rod. Oil level indicator
Silencer	Muffler, expansion box, diffuser.

FUEL .. ..

Carburettor Choke	Carburettor Venturi.
Slow Running Jet	Low speed jet. Idler jet.
Volume Control Screw.. ..	Idling mixture screw.
Fuel Pump	Petrol Pump. Fuel lift pump.
Air Cleaner	Air silencer, muffler.
Fuel Tank	Petrol tank.
Accelerator	Throttle.

CLUTCH ..

Clutch Release Bearing ..	Throwout bearing. Thrust bearing.
Clutch Lining	Disc facing. Friction ring.
Spigot Bearing	Clutch pilot bearing.
Clutch Housing..	Bell housing.

GEARBOX ..

	Transmission.
Gear Lever	Change speed lever, gearshift lever.
Selector Fork	Change speed fork. Shift fork.
Input Shaft	Constant motion shaft. First motion shaft, drive gear. First reduction pinion. Main drive pinion. Clutch shaft. Clutch gear.
Countershaft	Layshaft.
Synchro Cone	Synchronizing ring.
Reverse Idler Gear	Reverse Pinion.

REAR AXLE ..

	Final Drive Unit.
Crown Wheel	Ring gear, final drive gear, spiral drive gear.
Bevel Pinion	Small pinion, spiral drive pinion.
'U' Bolts	Spring clips.
Axle Shaft	Half-shaft. Hub driving shaft. Jack driving shaft.
Differential Gear	Sun wheel.
Differential Pinion	Planet wheel.

ELECTRICAL..

Generator	Dynamo.
Control Box	Cut-out, voltage regulator, voltage control, circuit breaker.
Capacitor	Condenser.
Interior Light	Dome lamp.
Lens	Glass
Head Lamp Rim	Head lamp surround. Head lamp moulding.
Direction Indicators	Signal lamps, flashers.
Micrometer Adjustment ..	Octane selector.
Rear Lamps	Tail lamps.

GLOSSARY OF PART NAMES AND ALTERNATIVES — continued

STEERING	..	**Drop Arm**	..	..	..	Pitman arm.
		Rocker Shaft	..	..	..	Pitman shaft. Drop arm shaft.
		Swivel Pin	..	..	..	Pivot pin. King pin. Steering pin.
		Stub Axle	..	..	..	Swivel axle.
		Track Rod	..	..	..	Cross tube. Tie rod.
		Draglink ..	..	..	..	Side tube. Steering connecting rod.
		Steering Column		..	..	Steering gear shaft.
		Steering Column Bearing			..	Mast jacket bearing.
		Steering Arm ..	..	..	..	Steering knuckle arm.
		Starter Tube	..	..	..	Control tube.
BRAKES	..	**Master Cylinder**		..	..	Main cylinder.
		Brake Shoe Lining		..	..	Brake shoe facing.
BODY	..	**Bonnet** ..	..	..	..	Hood.
		Luggage Locker		..	..	Boot. Luggage compartment.
		Luggage Locker Lid	..		..	Boot lid. Rear deck.
		Mudguards	..	..	..	Quarter panels. Fenders. Mud wings. Wings.
		Roof ..	..	..	..	Canopy.
		Nave Plate	..	..	..	Wheel disc. Hub cap.
		Finishing Strip ..	..	..		Moulding. Chromed strip.
		Windscreen	..	..	..	Windshield.
		Rear Window ..	..	..		Rear windscreen. Rear windshield. Backlight.
		Quarter Vent ..	..	..		(N.D.V.). No draught ventilator.

Abbreviations

L.H.S. — Left-hand side (viewed from driver's seat).

R.H.S. — Right-hand side (viewed from driver's seat.)

GENERAL SPECIFICATION

The general specification for the TR.4A is the same as that for the TR.4 except where listed below:

Performance Data (Engine)

Nett	104 B.H.P. at 4,700 r.p.m.
	Torque 1,590 lb. in. at 3,000 r.p.m.
	(Equivalent to 154 lb/sq. in. B.M.E.P.).
Piston Speed at 100 m.p.h. (top gear)	2,898 ft/min. at 4,800 r.p.m.

Cooling System

Radiator	Pressurised—finned vertical flat tubes. No-loss system.

Fuel System

Carburettors	Twin Stromberg 175 C.D. Horizontal.
	Needle size—2E up to CTC 54939.
	2H from CTC 54940.
Air Cleaners	Replaceable paper elements.

Clutch

Type	Borg & Beck Diaphragm spring type, 8½″ diameter.

Rear Axle

Type	Hypoid bevel gears, taper roller bearings.
Live axle	Semi-floating axle shafts, three-piece casing.
I.R.S.	Final-drive unit rubber mounted.
Ratio	3·7 or 4·1 : 1.

TYRE PRESSURE DATA

TYRE PRESSURES

TYRE	Revs./Mile at 30 m.p.h.	ROLLING RADIUS Inches	Independent rear suspension vehicles PRESSURE—lbs/sq. in. Front	Rear	Rigid rear axle vehicles PRESSURE—lbs/sq. in. Front	Rear
Goodyear 6.95 × 15 G.P. ..	820	12·3	17	21	19	23
Dunlop 165/6.5 × 15 S.P. ..	820	12·3	24	28	24	28
Michelin .. .. .. 165 × 15 'X'	808	12·48	17	21	17	25

NOTE: The tyre pressures given in the above table are suitable for speeds up to 110 m.p.h. Where cars are to be used for racing, consult the respective Tyre Company regarding the need for tyres of full racing construction.

Suspension

Front	Low periodicity independent suspension system. Patented bottom bush and top ball-joint swivels. Coil springs controlled by telescopic dampers. Taper roller hub bearings.
Rear—Live axle	Wide semi-elliptic springs, controlled by piston dampers.
I.R.S.	Semi-trailing arm independent suspension with coil springs controlled by piston dampers. Mounted onto frame through rubber-bushed pivots and with rubber insulation of spring.

Steering

Type	Rack and pinion unit. Telescopic steering column.	
Castor Angle	$2° 40' \pm \frac{1}{2}°$	
Camber Angle	$0° \pm \frac{1}{2}°$	
Kingpin inclination	$9° \pm \frac{3}{4}°$	
Front wheel alignment	Parallel to $\frac{1}{16}''$ (1·59 mm.) toe-in.	
Turning circle	33′ 0″	10 metres.

Chassis Data

Wheelbase	7′ 4″	223·6 cm.
Track: Front—Disc Wheels	4′ 1″	124·5 cm.
Wire Wheels	4′ $1\frac{3}{4}''$	126·3 cm.
Rear—		
I.R.S. Disc Wheels	4′ $0\frac{1}{2}''$	123·2 cm.
Wire Wheels	4′ $1\frac{1}{4}''$	125·1 cm.
Live Axle Disc Wheels	4′ 0″	122·0 cm.
Wire Wheels	4′ $0\frac{3}{4}''$	123·9 cm.
Ground Clearance (Static laden)	6″	15·24 cm.

Exterior Dimensions

Overall length	13′ 0″	396 cm.
″ width	4′ 10″	147 cm.
″ height (unladen)		
Hood erect	4′ 2″	127 cm.
Top of screen	3′ 10″	117 cm.
Hood folded and screen		
removed	3′ 4″	102 cm.

Capacities

	Imperial	U.S.	Metric
Water capacity of cooling system	10 pints	12 pints	5·7 litres
with heater fitted	11 pints	13·2 pints	6·25 litres

NUT TIGHTENING TORQUES

The nut tightening torques for the TR.4A are as those for the TR.4 with the addition of those listed below:

OPERATION	DESCRIPTION	SPECIFIED TORQUES	
		lbs. ft.	Kg.m.
REAR AXLE			
Crown Wheel to Differential Case	⅜″ × 24 U.N.F. Bolt	40 - 45	5·530 - 6·221
Rear Cover Attachment	⁵⁄₁₆″ × 24 U.N.F. Setscrew	18 - 20	2·489 - 2·765
Inner Driving Flange to Inner Axle	⅝″ × 18 U.N.F. Nyloc nut	100 - 110	13·826 - 15·209
Mounting Plate to Hypoid Housing Rear ..	⅜″ × 24 U.N.F. Stud	26 - 28	3·595 - 3·871
Mounting Plate to Hypoid Housing Front ..	⅜″ × 24 U.N.F. Bolt	35	4·839
Oil Seal Housing to Hypoid Housing ..	⁵⁄₁₆″ × 24 U.N.F. Setscrew	16 - 18	2·212 - 2·489
REAR SUSPENSION (Live Axle)			
Front Spring Eye to Brackets	⅝″ × 18 U.N.F. Bolt	28 - 30	3·871 - 4·148
Front Spring Eye Brackets to Frame ..	⅜″ × 24 U.N.F. Bolt	28 - 30	3·871 - 4·148
Damper to Frame Brackets	⁷⁄₁₆″ × 20 U.N.F. Setscrew	55 - 60	7·604 - 8·293
Spring to Axle 'U' Bolts..	⅜″ × 24 U.N.F. 'U' Bolt	26 - 28	3·595 - 3·871
Damper Link Attachment	⁷⁄₁₆″ × 20 U.N.F.	40 - 45	5·530 - 6·221
	⅜″ × 24 U.N.F. Link	18 - 20	2·489 - 2·765
Bump Rubber Attachments	⅜″ × 24 U.N.F.	18 - 20	2·489 - 2·765
Extension Studs for Wire Wheels	⁷⁄₁₆″ × 20 U.N.F. Stud	65	8·987
Wheel Attachment	⁷⁄₁₆″ × 20 U.N.F. Nut	55 - 60	7·604 - 8·293
REAR SUSPENSION (I.R.S.)			
Damper to Frame Mounting Brackets.. ..	⁷⁄₁₆″ × 20 U.N.F. Setscrew	55 - 60	7·604 - 8·293
Damper Link Attachment	⅜″ × 24 U.N.F. Link	18 - 20	2·489 - 2·765
Inner Driving Flange to Rear Hub and Axle Shaft	⅜″ × 24 U.N.F. Bolt	28 - 30	3·871 - 4·148
Rear Hub Assembly	⅝″ × 18 U.N.F. Stub Axle	100 - 110	13·826 - 15·209
Trailing Arm to Mounting Bracket ..	⁷⁄₁₆″ × 20 U.N.F. Bolt	45 - 50	6·221 - 6·913
Trailing Arm Mounting Brackets to Frame ..	⅜″ × 24 U.N.F. Bolt	28 - 30	3·871 - 4·148
Trailing Arm to Brake Back Plate	⁵⁄₁₆″ × 24 U.N.F. Stud	12 - 14	1·652 - 1·936

SPECIAL TOOLS

The special tools required for the TR.4A are the same as those for the TR.4 with the addition of those listed below:

SUSPENSION
S.112A	I.F.S. Coil Spring Compressor
S.112A—1A	I.F.S. Coil Spring Compressor Adaptor

REAR AXLE
S.101—1	Differential Case Spreader Adaptors
S.317	Rear Hub Adjusting Nut Wrench
S.318	Halfshaft Assembly Holding Jig
S.4221A—16	Outer Hub Taper Bearing Remover/Replacer Adaptor

TRIUMPH TR4
WORKSHOP MANUAL

GROUP 0

Comprising:

TR4 WORKSHOP MANUAL

GROUP 0

CONTENTS

INSTRUMENTS

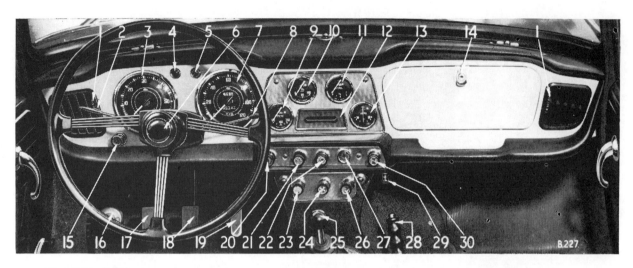

1	Fresh air vent controls	11	Fuel gauge	21	Windscreen washer control
2	Overdrive switch (Special Accessory)	12	Ash tray	22	Windscreen wiper switch
3	Tachometer	13	Ammeter	23	Heat control
4	Turn signal indicator	14	Facia locker	24	Heater blower switch
5	Ignition warning light	15	Panel illumination rheostat	25	Gear shift lever
6	Horn button	16	Headlamp dipper switch	26	Heat distribution control
7	Speedometer	17	Clutch pedal	27	Ignition/Starter switch
8	Turn signal control	18	Brake pedal	28	Handbrake lever
9	Water temperature gauge	19	Accelerator pedal	29	Scuttle ventilator control
10	Oil pressure gauge	20	Parking and headlamp switch	30	Choke control

Fig. 1.   Arrangement of Instruments, Switches and Controls (L.H.D.)

Fig. 2.   Tachometer (left) and Speedometer (right)
L.H.D.

Viewed left to right from the driving position, each instrument and indicator within the left-hand group performs the following function :—

Tachometer

The tachometer, which is the large instrument on the left, indicates the engine speed in revolutions per minute and is calibrated in divisions of 100, extending to 6,000.   The speed range within the red segment is subject to special precautions.   These are given on page 0·108.

Turn Signal Indicator

The green flashing indicator monitor light, at the right-hand side of the tachometer, glows intermittently when the direction control is operated and the ignition is switched on.   See "Turn Signal Control" on page 0·105.

Ignition Warning Light

The small red warning light at the left of the speedometer glows when the ignition is switched on and is extinguished when the engine is accelerated.   If the indicator glows when driving, this indicates an electrical fault which should be traced and rectified without delay.

Speedometer

The speedometer indicates the road speed of the vehicle in miles per hour and is calibrated in divisions of 2, extending to 120.

The figures within the aperture above the centre of the dial may be used to record individual journeys, provided that the figures are re-set to zero at the beginning. This is achieved by pushing up and turning anti-clockwise the knob which extends downwards from behind the instrument.

The figures within the aperture below the centre of the dial show the total mileage of the vehicle and may be used as a guide for periodic lubrication and maintenance.

The High Beam indicator near the bottom of the dial glows only when the headlamp main beams are in use. When the dipper switch is operated the indicator is extinguished.

Tachometer and Speedometer Illumination

Illumination of the tachometer and speedometer is controlled by a switch at the left side of the tachometer. Turn the switch knob clockwise to switch on, and further clockwise to dim the illumination. Turn fully anti-clockwise to switch off.

1 Trip indicator
2 Total mileage indicator
3 High beam indicator

Fig. 3. Speedometer

Water Temperature Gauge

The gauge is calibrated in degrees Fahrenheit and indicates the temperature of water leaving the cylinder head. The normal operating temperature is reached when the needle registers in the central sector of the dial.

Oil Pressure Gauge

Calibrated in lbs. per sq. in., the oil gauge registers the pressure of oil fed to the bearings. At speeds exceeding 30 m.p.h., when the oil is hot, the gauge needle should register between 65 and 75. A low pressure is normal when idling or running at a lower speed.

Fuel Gauge

The fuel gauge is calibrated relative to the fuel tank and registers the approximate contents only. When the ignition is switched on the needle moves slowly across its scale, taking up to one minute to reach a true reading. The needle then maintains a steady reading regardless of vehicle movement.

Ammeter

The ammeter is calibrated in amperes and indicates the rate of battery charge and discharge. The charging rate is indicated when the pointer moves to the right-hand side of "zero", and discharge, by movement to the left.

1 Water temperature gauge
2 Oil pressure gauge
3 Ashtray
4 Fuel contents gauge
5 Ammeter

Fig. 4. Centre instrument group

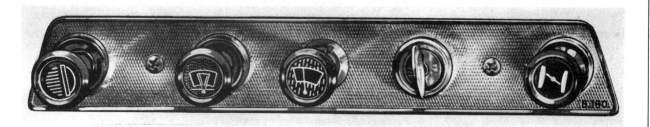

Fig. 5. Upper Central Controls

Lighting Switch

Mounted on the central switch panel and identified by a "Headlamp" sign, the lighting switch is on the extreme left. Pull this out to the first position to illuminate the side, rear, number plate and centre instrument panel lights. In addition to these, twist the switch slightly clockwise and pull out to the second position to illuminate the headlamps. See "Dipper Switch".

Windscreen Washer

The windscreen washer control, on the right of the lighting switch, should be used in conjunction with the windscreen wiper. Operate by pushing the control to spray clean fluid on to the screen as the wiper blades disperse the mud. If the washer has remained unused for some time, depress the control a few times to charge the system.

Windscreen Wiper

The windscreen wiper switch is located in the centre of the panel and to the left of the ignition switch. Pull the switch knob to operate, and push to switch off, when the wipers will automatically return to the parked position at the base of the windscreen. The wipers can only be operated when the ignition switch is turned to the "ignition" or auxiliary positions.

Choke Control

The choke control is located on the extreme right of the panel and is used to enrich the fuel mixture for easier starting from cold. The control should not be used if the engine is warm, and may not be necessary in warm climates.

Ignition and Starter Switch

Operated by a separate key, the combined ignition and starter switch has four positions. These are : 1, "Off", in which position the key may be withdrawn ; 2, "Ignition"; 3, Start ; 4, Auxiliary. (See Fig. 6).

With the key in the "Off" position (vertical), turn the key clockwise to switch on the ignition and auxiliary circuits.

To operate the starter motor, turn the key further clockwise against spring pressure and when the engine fires, release the key, which will return to the "Ignition" position. If the engine has failed to start, wait until the starter motor has come to rest before returning the key to the "Start" position.

To select "Auxiliary" turn the key anti-clockwise from the vertical position. This will enable, for example, the radio to be used with the ignition switched off and, since the key must be withdrawn from the switch to lock the vehicle, accessories cannot continue to function.

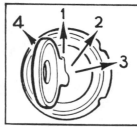

1. OFF
2. IGNITION
3. START
4. AUXILIARY

B185

Fig. 6. Ignition Switch positions

Headlamp Dipper Switch

A foot operated dipper switch, located on the toeboard to the left of the clutch pedal, enables the driver to quickly lower his headlamp beams whilst maintaining full control of the steering and other hand controls.

When the headlamps are illuminated, see lighting switch on page 0·104, the main beams may be lowered by pressing the dipper switch and releasing it. To return to the main beam position, again press the dipper switch and release it. The main beam position is indicated by a red warning light near the bottom of the speedometer dial.

Horns

Operate the horns by pressing the button in the centre of the steering wheel.

Overdrive Control

When an overdrive is fitted, the control is mounted on the right-hand side of the steering column cowl. Move the lever down to engage overdrive, and up to release it. Before using the control, see "Recommended speed limits" on page 0·108.

Turn Signal Control

The turn signal lamps are controlled by a lever mounted on the left-hand side of the steering column cowl. Before making a right-hand turn, move the lever upwards. Move it downwards before turning left. When either left- or right-hand turn signal lamps are operating, this is indicated by the intermittent flashing of a green indicator light on the facia.

Clutch, Brake and Accelerator Pedals

These are conventional items which do not need further explanation.

Gear Shift Lever

All forward gears have synchromesh engagement. See Fig. 10 for the gear shift positions. Reverse is engaged by moving the gear shift lever to the right, lifting it and then moving it rearwards.

Handbrake

To apply the rear wheel brakes, pull the handbrake lever and retain it in position by pressing the button on top of the lever. Release the handbrake by pulling it slightly rearwards to free the pawl, then allow the lever to move forward to the "OFF" position.

Seat Adjustment

The driver's and passenger's seats are adjustable for leg reach by lifting the lever at the outer side of each seat and sliding the seat to the desired position, allowing the lever to re-engage in the nearest adjustment notch. The passenger's seat backrest hinges forward to provide access to the rear compartment. Do not forget to move the driver's seat forward before lowering or raising the "Soft Top". See group 5.

Radio Controls

For operating instructions see the radio leaflet provided with the set. This is protected against electrical damage by a 5 amp. fuse housed in the main lead union.

1	Headlamp dipper switch	2	Clutch pedal
3	Footbrake	4	Accelerator pedal

Fig. 7. Foot controls

Fig. 8.
Turn signal control

Fig. 9.
Overdrive control

**Fig. 10. Change speed
lever positions**

Fig. 11.
Handbrake lever

Left—Heater control   Centre—Blower switch   Right—Distribution control

Fig. 12.   Heater controls

Fig. 13.   Scuttle ventilator and control
shown on inset

Fig. 14.   Facia
vent control

HEATING AND VENTILATION

The heater is designed to heat and distribute incoming fresh air, or if dust and exhaust fumes are being admitted, the heater may be used to recirculate air already in the vehicle.

Fresh air is admitted to the heater duct through the open scuttle ventilator. This is opened by pulling the ventilator lever rearwards and closed by pushing it forwards.

When the scuttle ventilator is closed, air is drawn in through the open facia vents and recirculated by the heater unit. The facia vents are opened by turning the handwheel, at the side of each vent, forward.

When the scuttle ventilator is open, cool fresh air is blown out of the open facia vents and may be directed up or down, or may be cut-off by adjusting the handwheel. There is no provision for heating the air blown from the facia vents.

The degree of heat given out by the heater unit is controlled by the left-hand control on the heater control panel. Pull the control fully out for maximum heat, or push it fully in for cold. Intermediate positions give varying degrees of heat.

The blower switch on the centre of the panel controls a motor-driven fan which stimulates the flow of fresh air from outside when the vehicle is stationary, and boosts the air circulation when the vehicle is moving. The blower is operated by pulling the control to switch on, and pushing it to switch off.

The distribution of warmed air is effected by the right-hand control. Pulling the control fully out directs air to the interior of the vehicle. Pushing the control fully in directs air to the windscreen only. Intermediate positions direct air to the screen and interior in varying proportions.

LOCKS

Locks and Keys

Two sets of keys are provided, one for operating the ignition switch and door locks, and the other for locking the facia locker and luggage compartment.

Fig. 15.   Facia locker

Facia Locker (Fig. 15)

The facia cubby box may be unlocked by turning the key a quarter turn clockwise and opened by depressing the locking barrel and pulling on the lipped plate.

Luggage Compartment (Fig. 16)

To open the luggage compartment lid, turn the unlocked handle counter-clockwise to a vertical position and raise the lid to its limit before engaging the stay in the slot provided.

To close the lid, raise it slightly to release the stay which can then be engaged in its rubber retainer on the boot lid support assembly. Lower the lid and turn the handle, which may be locked by turning the key a half turn counter-clockwise.

Fuel Filler Cap (Fig. 17)

The fuel filler cap, located forward of the luggage locker lid, is opened by depressing a small lever at the side of the cap. Press the cap to close.

Fig. 16.   Luggage locker showing hinged
spare wheel cover

Bonnet Release

To open the bonnet, pull the control situated below the right-hand side of the facia. The bonnet will rise sufficiently to enable the fingers to be inserted under the rear edge to raise it to a near vertical position, where it will be supported by a stay. Disengage the stay from its recess before closing the bonnet.

Door Locks

Either door may be locked from inside or outside irrespective of which door was last used as an exit. The mechanism automatically prevents the inside handle being set in the locked position whilst the door is open. This eliminates the possibility of being locked out of the car in the event of the key being inadvertently left inside.

Fig. 17.   Fuel filler cap

RUNNING-IN FROM NEW

Running-in

The importance of correct running-in cannot be too strongly emphasized, for during the first 500 miles of motoring, the working surfaces of a new engine are bedding down. Power and performance will improve only if during this vital period the engine receives careful treatment.

Whilst no specific speeds are recommended during the running-in period. avoid placing heavy loads upon the engine, such as using full throttle at low speeds or when the engine is cold. Running-in should be progressive and no harm will result from the engine being allowed to "rev." fairly fast provided that it is thoroughly warm and not pulling hard. Always select a lower gear if necessary to relieve the engine of load.

Full power should not be used until at least 500 miles have been covered and even then, it should be used only for short periods at a time. These periods can be extended as the engine becomes more responsive.

After 1,000 miles running, the engine can be considered as fully run-in.

To prevent possible damage to a valve seat as the metal stabilizes during the running-in period, valve grinding is recommended early in the life of the engine.

Recommended Speed Limits

Avoid over-revving, particularly in the lower gears. The driver is advised not to drive the car continuously at engine speeds above 4,500 r.p.m. in any gear. However, whilst accelerating through the gears it is permissible to attain 5,000 r.p.m. for short periods, this speed being indicated by a red segment on the tachometer.

When an overdrive is fitted, do not change from overdrive to normal 3rd or 2nd gears at engine speed exceeding 3,500 r.p.m., otherwise damage may result from "over-revving".

SUPPLEMENT TO GROUP "0" SECTION 1.

The instruments, switches and controls used in TR.4A models are mounted in a walnut facia.   They are similarly positioned and function as those described for TR.4 models, except for the following details:-

Panel Illumination Rheostat

The panel illumination rheostat switch (item 15, Fig. 1) is positioned in place of the lighting switch (item 20, Fig. 1).

Windscreen Wiper Switch

The windscreen wipers have two speeds, these being controlled by a two-position pull switch positioned as item 22, Fig. 1.   When the switch is pulled to its first position, the wipers operate at fast speed, when the switch is pulled to its second position, the wipers operate at slow speed.

Handbrake

The handbrake has been re-positioned and is mounted on the propeller shaft tunnel.

Recommended Speed Limits

The recommended speed limits stated on page 0·108 apply to TR.4 models.   The following figures apply to TR.4A models.

Avoid over-revving, particularly in the lower gears.   The driver is advised not to drive the car continuously at engine speeds above 5,000 r.p.m. in any gear.   However, whilst accelerating through the gears it is permissible to attain 5,500 r.p.m. for short periods, these speeds being indicated by the beginning and the end of the red segment on the tachometer.

When an overdrive is fitted, do not change from overdrive to normal 3rd or 2nd gears at engine speed exceeding 4,500 r.p.m., otherwise damage may result from "over-revving".

Suggested minimum engagement speeds are:—

Top gear	40 m.p.h.
Third gear	30 m.p.h.

Maximum disengagement speeds are:—

	3·7 AXLE	4·1 AXLE
Top gear	At driver's discretion	At driver's discretion
3rd gear	82 m.p.h.	74 m.p.h.
2nd gear	54 m.p.h.	49 m.p.h.

The above disengagement speeds correspond approximately to peak revs. in normal gear.   Disengagement of the O/D at speeds higher than those stated may cause damage from "over-revving".

CUSTOMER PREPARATION SERVICE

For Triumph Passenger Vehicles, Vans, and Leyland Light Commercial Vehicles

Commission Number..   Engine Number........................   Date ....

Owner's Name..

Address..   Registration Number........................   Speedometer Reading........................

Every precaution has been taken at the factory to ensure that the car reaches the customer in the best possible condition. A few preparatory operations remain, however, which in the best interests of all, must be carefully carried out by the selling Distributor or Dealer before the car is handed to the customer.

Details of the preparation service are as follows :—

MECHANICAL

☐ 1   Check cooling system for leaks and top up radiator level and windscreen washer bottle as necessary.

☐ 2.   Check the fuel system for leaks.

☐ 3.   Check brake/clutch master cylinders fluid level and top up as necessary. **Investigate if levels are low.**

☐ 4.   Check and adjust tyre pressures.

☐ 5.   Check tightness of wheel nuts.

ELECTRICAL

☐ 1.   Top up battery with distilled water as necessary.

☐ 2.   Check operation of windscreen wiper **and Screen washer.**

☐ 3.   Check operation of horn.

☐ 4.   Check all instruments for operation.

☐ 5.   Check flasher operation.

☐ 6.   Check lamps for operation.

LUBRICATION

☐ 1.   Check engine for correct oil level.

COACH

☐ 1.   Fit front carpets and retainer strips, where applicable.

☐ 2.   Ensure that the carpet does not restrict dip switch operation or prevent full throttle.

☐ 3.   Check operation of all locks and windows.

☐ 4.   Check front seats for squab and slide operation, as applicable.

GENERAL FINISH

☐ 1.   Examine paintwork, touching-up as necessary.

☐ 2.   Check interior trim and seats for cleanliness.

☐ 3.   Remove all masking tape and anti-corrosive preparation from chromium plating.

☐ 4.   Wash the vehicle and examine for leaks.

☐ 5.   Dry off vehicles finished in primer paint, and polish finish-painted vehicles.

☐ 6.   Check tool kit and ensure that all literature and spare fuses are present.

ROAD TEST

☐ 1.   Road test the vehicle.

☐ 2.   Check for oil and water leakage.

☐ 3.   Check for rattles.

IMPORTANT

To avoid possible errors, mark the appropriate square as each operation is completed and record on the back of this form any points requiring special attention.

Issue 2

Fig. 1. Under Bonnet View

DAILY ATTENTION

Engine

Daily, or every 250 miles (500 km.), withdraw the dipstick (1), wipe clean and push fully home before withdrawing it for reading ; if the reading corresponds with the lower mark, 4 pints (4·8 U.S.A.) (2·27 litres) will be required for topping up via the cap (3).

Radiator

Top up the radiator with clean rain water until the level is one inch below the filler neck. This will allow for expansion of the coolant as the engine warms up and is particularly important if an anti-freeze mixture is being used, since the expansion allowance will prevent unnecessary loss of fluid and consequent dilution as further topping up takes place. (See page 1·206).

CAUTION   If the engine is hot, turn the filler cap (2) a half-turn and allow pressure to be fully released before completely removing it.

WEEKLY ATTENTION

Tyres

Adjust the tyre pressures in accordance with conditions and pressure schedules given on page 7. Additional information is given in group 3.

Battery

Examine the level of the electrolyte in the cells and, if necessary, add distilled water via the plugs (4), Fig. 1, to bring the level up to the top of the separators.

Examine the battery terminals and, if necessary, clean and coat them with petroleum jelly. Wipe away any foreign matter or moisture from the top of the battery and ensure that the connections and fixings are clean and tight.

IMPORTANT
Never use a naked light when examining the battery, as the mixture of oxygen and hydrogen given off by the battery can be dangerously explosive.

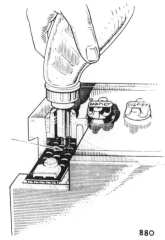

Fig. 2. Topping up the battery cells

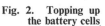

1,000 MILES (FREE SERVICE)

Many of the components, including gaskets, bolts and studs, inevitably settle down during the first 1,000 miles (2,000 km.) of use. Therefore, at the completion of this mileage, the vehicle should receive the following attention :—

1. Thoroughly lubricate all chassis points, door hinges, luggage locker and bonnet hinges, locks and striker plates, pedal pivots, throttle controls, handbrake cable and rear hubs.

2. Change oil in engine, gearbox and rear axle.

3. Examine and top up if necessary :—
   (a) Water level in radiator.
   (b) Electrolyte level in battery.
   (c) Hydraulic fluid levels in brake and clutch systems.
   (d) S.U. Carburettor dashpots (if fitted).

4. Tighten all nuts where required, particularly those securing the cylinder head, exhaust manifold, exhaust pipe and silencer attachments, steering unit, tie-rods and levers, differential unit, universal couplings, rear springs and body mountings.

5. Check oil filter attachments for tightness.

6. Check and if necessary adjust :—
   (a) Ignition timing.
   (b) Fan belt.
   (c) Carburettor and controls for slow running.
   (d) Front wheel track alignment.
   (e) Front hubs, wheel nuts and tyre pressures.
   (f) Valve clearances.
   (g) Ignition distributor and sparking plug points.

7. Clean the air filter and fuel pump bowl.

8. Adjust brakes and clutch if required.

9. Check operation of all electrical equipment and focus headlamps.

10. Clean battery terminals, smear with petroleum jelly and check battery mounting but do not over-tighten holding down clamps.

11. Check and tighten starter and generator attachment bolts and terminals.

12. Check all hydraulic pipe connections for tightness and all flexible hoses for clearance.

13. Road test car and report any defects.

14. Wipe clean door handles, controls and windscreen.

Fig. 3.
1 Brake master cylinder.
2 Clutch master cylinder.

Fig. 4. Steering and Front Suspension Greasing Points

Fig. 5. Propeller Shaft Greasing Points

IMPORTANT: See revised schedule on pages 0·213 and 0·214.

EVERY 1,500 MILES

Engine Compartment

1. Check the levels and if necessary top up the engine oil sump and radiator header tank.
2. Wipe the master cylinder caps clean, remove them and check the fluid level in the clutch and brake master cylinder reservoirs. If necessary, top up the fluid until it is level with the arrow on the side of the reservoirs. Ensure that the breather hole in each cap is unobstructed before refitting the caps to the master cylinders.

NOTE. As the brake pads wear, the level of fluid in the master cylinder falls. The addition of fluid to compensate for pad wear is unnecessary. Should the level have fallen appreciably, check the condition of the pads. If their condition is satisfactory, establish the cause of loss and rectify the defect immediately. Refer to group 3, "Bleeding the Brake and Clutch Hydraulic System".

Car Hoisted

1. **Front Suspension and Steering Tie Rods**—take the weight off the front suspension by jacking up the front of the chassis until the road wheels are clear of the ground. Using good quality grease, pressure lubricate the nipples 1-5 on both sides of the vehicle. Wipe away all surplus grease to prevent contamination of the disc brakes and tyres.

NOTE. The inner ends of the upper and lower wishbones are mounted on nylon bushes which sometimes develop a pronounced squeak when dry. This can be rectified by occasionally forcing each rubber dust seal to one side and injecting a few drops of thin oil.

2. **Propeller Shaft**—Apply the grease gun to nipples A and B.
3. **Gearbox and Rear Axle**—Check each unit for leakage. Rectify and replenish lubricant if required.

Car on Ground

1. **Tyre pressure**—Adjust (See page 7).
2. Check tightness of road wheel nuts.
3. Wipe clean door handles, steering wheel, gear lever, handbrake lever and windscreen.

IMPORTANT: See revised schedule on pages 0·213 and 0·214.

3,000 MILES

At 3,000 mile intervals, carry out the work listed under 1,500 miles and the following additional work:—

Change Engine Oil

For average driving conditions, defined below, drain the oil sump by removing the plug shown arrowed, refit the plug and refill with the appropriate grade of oil at the end of each 3,000 mile period. This period should be reduced for unfavourable conditions or may be extended for those more favourable.

Favourable	Long distance journeys with little or no engine idling, on well-surfaced roads, reasonably free from dust.
Average	Medium length journeys on well-surfaced roads with a small proportion of stop/start operation.
Unfavourable	Either of the following :—

    (a) Operating during cold weather, especially when frequent engine idling is involved.

    (b) Extremely dusty conditions.

If the vehicle is used for competition or sustained high speed work, use of higher viscosity oils is advised because of the increased oil temperature. Additives which dilute the oil or impair its efficiency must not be used.

An upper cylinder lubricant, mixed with the fuel in the proportions given on the container, may be used with advantage throughout the life of the vehicle, particularly during the running-in period and when the weather is wintry.

Top-up Gearbox

With the vehicle standing on level ground, remove the oil level plug (2) and, using a suitable dispenser such as a pump type oil can with flexible nozzle, filled with an extreme pressure (Hypoid) lubricant, top up the gearbox until the oil is level with the bottom of the filler plug threads.

Allow surplus oil to drain away before refitting the level plug and wiping clean. Avoid overfilling as this may result in the oil leaking into the clutch housing with consequent ill-effects to the clutch facings.

Top-up Rear Axle

Remove the oil level plug (1) and, using the same dispenser as used for topping-up the gearbox, and the same oil, i.e., extreme pressure (Hypoid) lubricant, top up the rear axle until the oil is level with the bottom of the filler plug threads.

Allow surplus oil to drain away before refitting the level plug and wiping clean. Avoid overfilling and if an excessive amount of oil is required, check for leakage around the driving flange seal and rear cover.

Fig. 6.
Engine oil filler

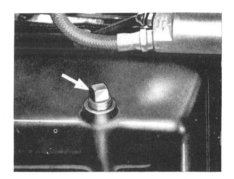

Fig. 7.
Engine sump
drain plug

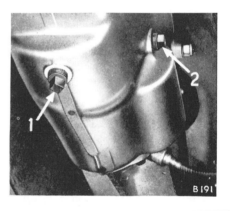

1 Drain plug.
2 Filler plug.

Fig. 8.
Gearbox drain
and filler plugs

1 Filler plug.
2 Drain plug.

Fig. 9.
Rear Axle drain
and filler plugs

Fig. 10.   Filling Carburettor Dashpots (S.U.)

1	Bleed nipple	3	Locknut	5	Cross-shaft
2	Adjusting rod	4	Clevis		greaser

Fig. 11.   Clutch Linkage

1	Brake adjuster	2	Hub greaser
	3 Bleed nipple		

Fig. 12.   Rear Hub and Backing Plate

Carburettor Dash Pots

Unscrew the hexagon plug from the top of each carburettor and withdraw the plug and damper assembly. Top up the damper chambers with the current grade of engine oil. The oil level is correct when, utilizing the damper as a dipstick, its threaded plug is $\frac{1}{4}''$ (6·3 mm.) above the dash pots when resistance is felt. Refit the damper and hexagonal plug. Using an oil can, apply oil to the throttle and choke control linkages.

NOTE: For Zenith and Stromberg carburettors see page 1·311. (Fig 22).

Clutch Adjustment

Check, and if necessary, adjust the clearance between the clutch operating piston and the push rod (2). The correct clearance is 0·1″ (2·5 mm.). To adjust :—
1. Slacken the nut (3) and unscrew the push rod (2) until all clearance between the push rod and the cupped end of the operating piston (inside slave cylinder) is taken up.
2. Adjust the position of the locknut (3) until a feeler gauge of 0·1″ (2·5 mm.) thickness may be inserted between the locknut face and the clevis fork (4).
3. Without disturbing the locknut on the push rod, screw the push rod into the clevis until the nut contacts the clevis face, then lock up the nut (3).

Front Brake Adjustment

The disc brakes, fitted to the front wheels, are self-adjusting and should only need replacement shoe pads when the linings are reduced to approximately $\frac{1}{8}''$ (3 mm.) thickness.

Rear Brake Adjustment

Check the travel of the foot brake and hand brake.

Each rear brake is provided with a smaller adjuster, (1), Fig. 12, which is positioned on the brake backing plate, above the axle case, and accessible with the road wheel removed. To adjust the shoes, turn the adjuster clockwise until the shoes are hard against the drum ; then slacken the adjuster by one notch. If the drum is not free to rotate slacken the adjuster still further.

Hand Brake Adjustment

Adjustment of the rear brake shoes automatically re-adjusts the hand brake mechanism.

IMPORTANT: See revised schedule on pages 0·213 and 0·214.

6,000 MILES

At 6,000 mile intervals, carry out the work listed under 3,000 miles and the following additional work:—

Ignition Distributor

Release the clips and remove the distributor cap and rotor arm. Detach the contact breaker points and clean their contact faces with a fine carborundum stone. If all trace of pitting cannot be removed, fit new contacts. Using a small screwdriver in the slot (2), adjust the moving contact so that when the contact heel is on the peak of the cam a 0·015″ (0·38 mm.) feeler gauge may be inserted between the contact faces (7); then tighten the screw (8).

Apply a few drops of thin oil around the edge of the screw (3) to lubricate the cam bearings and distributor spindle. Place a single drop of clean engine oil on the pivot (6). Smear the cam (4) with engine oil. A squeak may occur when the cam is dry.

Refit the rotor arm and ensure that the distributor cap is clean and the central carbon brush is free in its housing. Refit the cap and secure it to the distributor.

Sparking Plugs

Remove the sparking plugs for cleaning and re-set the gaps to 0·025″ (0·63 mm.). Clean the ceramic insulators and examine them for cracks or other damage likely to cause "H.T." tracking. Test the plugs before refitting and renew those which are suspect.

Water Pump

Apply a grease gun to the grease nipple and inject grease until it exudes from a hole in the side of the pump.

Fuel Pump Bowl

Clean the sediment bowl as follows:—

Disconnect the fuel pipe (1) from the suction side of the pump and to prevent loss of fuel, fit a tapered rubber or wood plug into the pipe bore (¼″ I.D.). (6·35 mm.). Alternatively, attach one end of a length of rubber tube over the end of the fuel pipe and tie the opposite end of the tube above the fuel tank level.

Unscrew the stirrup nut (2) under the bowl, swing the stirrup to one side and remove the bowl. Swill out the sediment bowl and wipe it clean.

To avoid damaging the glass sediment bowl when refitting it, tighten the stirrup nut only sufficiently to ensure a fuel-tight joint. Reconnect the fuel pipe and prime the carburettors.

Air Cleaners

Remove and wash the air cleaners in fuel. Soak the gauzes in engine oil and allow to drain before wiping them clean. When refitting the cleaners, ensure that the holes above the carburettor flange setscrew holes are correctly aligned with corresponding holes in the air cleaner and gaskets. (See Fig. 16).

If the engine is operating under dusty conditions, clean the filters more frequently.

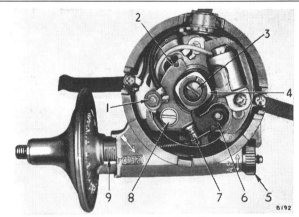

Fig. 13. Ignition Distributor

Fig. 14. Water Pump Greaser

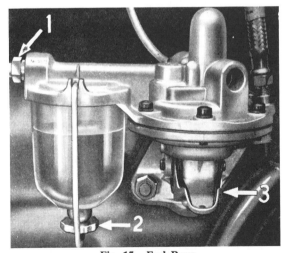

Fig. 15. Fuel Pump

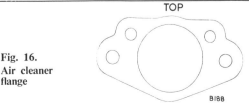

Fig. 16. Air cleaner flange

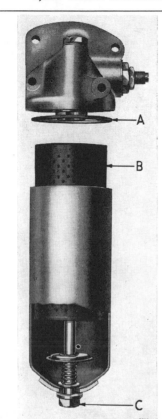

A. Washer.
B. Element.
C. Securing bolt.

Fig. 17.
Oil Filter

Oil Filter Element (Fig. 17)

To renew the element, unscrew the securing bolt 'C', remove the container and withdraw the element. Wash the container to remove foreign matter trapped by the filter and discard the old washer 'A', replacing it by a new one each time the element is renewed.

When re-assembling the container and a new element, ensure that the washer 'A' is correctly positioned in its groove in the filter body. Do not tighten the bolt 'C' more than is necessary to effect an oil-tight joint.

Before restarting the engine, make sure that the sump is filled to the correct level with clean fresh oil.

Fan Belt Tension (Fig. 18)

The fan belt should be sufficiently tight to drive the generator without unduly loading the bearings.

Adjust the belt by slackening the adjusting bolt (5) and the generator pivots (3 and 4). Pivot the generator until the belt can be moved ¾″ to 1″ (19 to 25 mm.) at its longest run (6). Maintaining the generator in this position, securely tighten the adjusting bolt and the two pivots.

Generator

Use an oil can to pour a few drops of engine oil through the hole in the centre of the rear end cap.

Oil Filler Cap (Fig. 1)

Remove and swill the cap (3) in fuel, allow to drain before refitting.

Valve Rocker Clearances (Fig. 19)

Check and, if necessary, adjust the inlet and exhaust valve clearances to 0·010″ (0·25 mm.) when cold. These settings, which are correct for all operating conditions, are obtained as follows :—

1. Turn the crankshaft until No. 1 push rod has reached its highest point, then rotate the crankshaft a further complete revolution.
2. To adjust No. 1 rocker, slacken the locknut and insert a 0·010″ (0·25 mm.) feeler gauge between the rocker and valve stem. Turn the adjuster with a screwdriver until slight resistance is felt as the gauge is moved across the valve stem ; then re-tighten the locknut.
3. After tightening the locknut, re-check the clearance and, if satisfactory, deal with the remaining rockers in a similar manner, ensuring that each rocker is correctly positioned before attempting to adjust it.

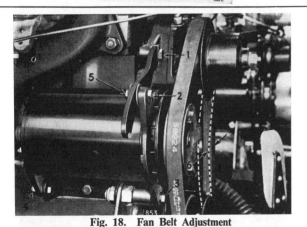

Fig. 18. Fan Belt Adjustment

Fig. 19. Adjusting Valve Rocker Clearances

Rear Hub Bearings (Fig. 12)

Lubricate the rear hub bearings by applying the grease gun and giving 5 strokes to a nipple (2) situated behind the rear brake backing plate.

Front Hub Bearings (Fig. 20)

Adjust the front hub bearings as follows :

Remove the split pin, tighten the hub nut until slight resistance to hub rotation is felt ; then slacken off the nut by one-half flat and insert the split pin through one of the two holes provided.

De-Dust Rear Brake Linings (Fig. 21)

Jack up the rear of the car and remove both road wheels and brake drums. Examine the brake linings for wear and freedom from oil or grease. Renew worn or contaminated linings.

Using a high pressure air line, or a foot pump, blow all loose dust from the mechanism and, using a clean dry cloth, wipe the dust from the inside of the drums. Avoid touching the braking surfaces with greasy hands.

Refit the brake drums and road wheels, re-adjust the brakes and remove the jack.

Interchange Road Wheels (Fig. 22)

Uneven tyre wear may be caused by road conditions, traffic conditions, driving methods and certain features of design which are essential to the control, steering and driving of a vehicle. Close attention to inflation pressures and the mechanical condition of the vehicle will not always prevent irregular wear. It is therefore recommended that front tyres be interchanged with rear tyres at least every 3,000 miles. Diagonal interchanging between near front and off rear and between off front and near rear provides the most satisfactory first change because it reverses the direction of rotation.

Subsequent interchanging of front and rear tyres should be as indicated by the appearance of the tyres, with the object of keeping the wear of all tyres even and uniform.

When interchanging the wheels, examine each tyre and remove flints or other road matter which may have become embedded in the tread. Remove oil or grease with a petrol- (gasoline)- moistened cloth.

Adjust all tyres to the correct pressure. (See page 7).

Overdrive Filter

If an overdrive is fitted, unscrew the large knurled drain plug under the overdrive unit and withdraw the gauze filter for cleaning. Refit the filter and tighten the drain plug.

Replenish the unit with oil, and after a short run using the overdrive, re-check and adjust the oil level if necessary.

The same oil is used both for the overdrive unit and the gearbox, an internal transfer hole allows oil to flow from the gearbox into the overdrive unit until a common level is attained. *Do not use additives ; their use may be detrimental to the proper operation of the unit.*

Fig. 20. Adjusting the front hubs

Fig. 21. Rear wheel brakes

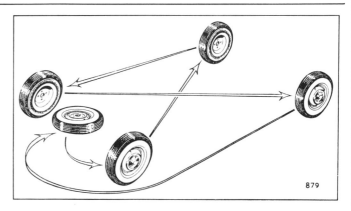

879

Fig. 22. Diagram of wheel interchanging

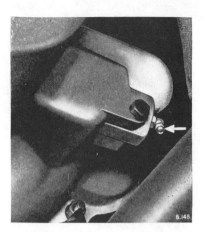

Fig. 23.   Clutch Cross-shaft Grease Nipple

Clutch Cross Shaft Bearings (Fig. 23)

Inject a small amount of grease through a nipple located at each end of the clutch cross shaft and accessible from beneath the vehicle.

Clutch and Brake Pedal Bearings

Use an oil can to lubricate the clutch and brake pedal bearings and their linkages. These are accessible from within the driving compartment.

Fig. 24. Hand Brake Cable and Compensator Grease Nipples

Hand Brake Cable Conduit (Fig. 24)

Inject grease through a nipple (1) on the hand brake conduit until grease exudes from both ends of the conduit. During winter months, frequent greasing at this point will prevent a frozen hand brake cable.

Hand Brake Compensator (Fig. 24)

Inject grease through two nipples (2 and 3) on the hand brake compensator. Apply oil to all pivot pins.

Fig. 25.   Steering Unit Filler

Steering Unit

Remove a sealing plug from the top of the steering unit and replace it by a grease nipple. Apply the grease gun and give 5 strokes only. Remove the nipple and refit the plug. Over-greasing can cause damage to the rubber bellows.

Check the tightness of all bolts and nuts, particularly the front and rear suspension, the steering and the wheel nuts.

IMPORTANT: See revised schedule on pages 0·213 and 0·214.

12,000 MILES

At 12,000 mile intervals, carry out the work listed under 6,000 miles, and the following additional work:—

Front Hub Lubrication (Fig. 26)

If the car is being used for competition work, re-pack the front hubs with grease every 12,000 miles. This period may be extended to 24,000 miles for normal use.

To pack the hubs with grease:—

Jack up the front of the car and remove one front road wheel. Without disturbing the hydraulic pipe unions, unscrew the caliper securing bolts (1) and lift the caliper from the disc, tying it to a convenient point to prevent it hanging by the attached hydraulic pipe. Note the number of shims fitted between the caliper and vertical link.

When wire-spoked wheels are fitted, remove the splined hub extensions by detaching the nuts shown on Fig. 27.

To remove the hub grease cap, screw the No. 10 A.F. setscrew provided in the tool kit into the tapped hole in the grease cap.

Withdraw the split pin and remove the slotted nut and "D" washer. Detach the hub assembly and outer race from the stub axle Wash all trace of grease from the hub and bearings. Pack the hub and bearings with new grease, working it well into the rollers.

Re-assemble the hub and races to the stub axle, securing them with the "D" washer and slotted nut. Spin the hub and tighten the nut until resistance is felt to hub rotation, then slacken off the nut one-half flat and fit a new split pin. Re-assemble the brake caliper unit to the vertical link, refitting any shims removed during dismantling. Re-assemble the splined hub extension (if fitted). Refit the road wheel and lower the jack. See "Warning" on page 3·401.

Repeat the above operations with the opposite wheel hub.

Sparking Plugs (Fig. 28)

Renew the sparking plugs at 12,000 miles. When replacing the plugs, make sure that they are the correct type and the gaps are set to 0·025". The types recommended are given on page 6.

Re-connect the plug leads as shown.

Gearbox Oil Change

Drain and refill the gearbox. See page 0·205.

Rear Axle Oil Change

Drain and refill the rear axle. See page 0·205.

Rear Road Springs

Periodically, relieve the weight of the vehicle from the rear springs and apply oil to the spring leaves with a brush or spray. Ensure that the oil penetrates between the spring leaves, but avoid contaminating the rubber bushes at the end of the spring.

Hydraulic Dampers

Remove the plugs from the rear dampers and top up with Armstrong Shock Absorber Fluid to the level of the bottom of the plug hole. Take care to prevent foreign matter falling into the damper. Refit the plugs to the damper.

1   Caliper attachments   2   Bleed nipple
Fig. 26.   Disc Brake Caliper

Fig. 27.   Wire Wheel Nut Extension

Fig. 28.   Arrangement of H.T. Cables

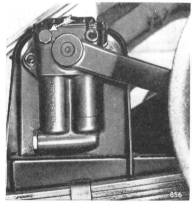

Fig. 29.   Rear Damper Filler Plug

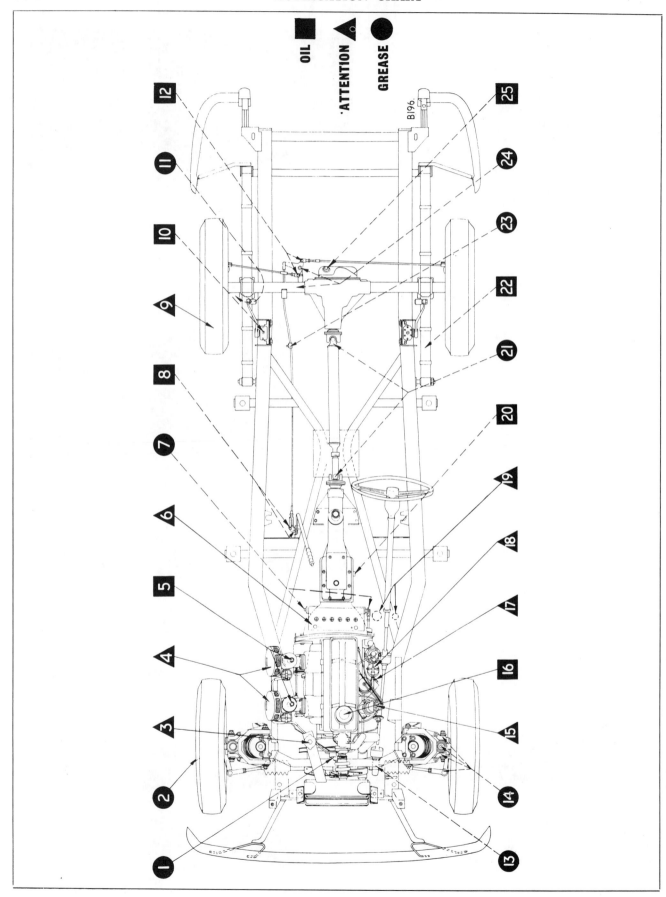

Ref.	Items		Details	Page Ref.	Mileage Intervals
9	Tyre Pressures			0·202	Weekly
3	Radiator Water Level		Top up	0·202	Weekly
6	Battery		Top up	0·202	Monthly
14	Steering Swivels (4 nipples)			0·204	3,000
14	Steering	Outer Tie Rod Ball Joints (4 nipples)	Grease Gun	0·204	3,000
		Slave Drop Arm Pivot		0·204	3,000
14	Lower Wishbone Outer Bushes (4 nipples)			0·204	3,000
21	Propeller Shaft	Splines (1 nipple)	Gun Three or Four Strokes	0·204	3,000
		Universal Joints (2 nipples)		0·204	3,000
19	Hydraulic Brake and Clutch Reservoirs		Top up Fluid Level	0·204	3,000
5	Carburettor Dashpots and Control Linkages		Oil as Recommended Oil Can	0·206	3,000
16	Engine ...... 250 Miles		Top up Oil Level Drain and Refill with New Oil	0·204 0·205	6,000
20	Gearbox		Top up Oil Level	0·205	6,000
23	Handbrake	Cable (1 nipple)	Grease Gun	0·210	3,000
24		Compensator (2 nipples)		0·210	3,000
7	Clutch Cross Shaft Bearings (2 nipples)			0·210	3,000
1	Engine Water Pump (1 nipple)		Grease Gun	0·207	6,000
11	Hubs—Rear (2 nipples)			0·209	12,000
15	Ignition Distributor			0·207	6,000
8	Handbrake Lever		Oil Can	0·210	6,000
	Door Locks, Hinges, Bonnet Safety-Catch, Boot and Wheel Locks				6,000
	Generator			0·208	12,000
	Oil Filler Cap		Wash	0·208	6,000
25	Rear Axle		Drain and Refill with New Oil	0·205	6,000
13	Steering Unit		Grease Five Strokes	0·210	6,000
4	Air Cleaners		Oil as Recommended	0·207	6,000
17	Oil Filter		Renew Cartridge	0·208	6,000
18	Fuel Pump		Clean out Filter Bowl	0·207	6,000
2	Hubs—Front		Remove and Re-pack	0·211	12,000 or 24,000
22	Rear Road Springs		Clean and Oil	0·211	12,000

IMPORTANT

AMENDMENT TO 500 MILE SERVICE AND LUBRICATION RECOMMENDATIONS

Since the first edition of the TR.4 Manual was issued, a revised Schedule of Lubrication and Maintenance has been introduced.

ENGINE

Experience has revealed that bedding-in of engine components, particularly the piston rings, is incomplete at the end of 500 miles motoring. To facilitate running-in, engines of new cars contain a special running-in oil which should be retained until 1,000 miles have been completed. Although the level of this oil may not reach the high mark on the dipstick, the quantity is sufficient for the running-in period and, providing that the level is maintained between the high and low marks, topping-up is unnecessary. Draining the oil at an earlier period delays the attainment of maximum compression and oil control. **The period for the free service has therefore been extended from 500 miles to 1,000 miles.**

GEARBOX, OVERDRIVE AND REAR AXLE

Rear axles, gearboxes and overdrive units fitted to new cars are filled with a special oil formulated to give all necessary protection to new gears. **This oil should not be drained,** but may be topped-up with any of the approved oils.

Any reference to draining, contained in the manual, should therefore be ignored.

MILEAGE INTERVALS

A revised Lubrication Chart, Page 0·213, bearing Issue 2, has been incorporated, and states the revised intervals at which specific operations should be performed. The revised mileages supersede those quoted in the text, which should be amended accordingly.

Interchanging of wheel assemblies is no longer recommended, and reference to this should be deleted.

RADIATOR

The remotely mounted radiator header tank, incorporating a filler neck, has been deleted, the header tank and filler now being integral with the radiator.

SUPPLEMENT TO GROUP "0" SECTION 2.

Experience and design improvements incorporated in TR.4A models have permitted servicing intervals and operations to be revised.   The revised schedules, which apply to TR.4A models are listed below.

SCHEDULE OF OPERATIONS RELATING TO "FREE SERVICE"

At the completion of 1,000 miles (1,600 km.) or as near to this figure as possible, perform the following operations:

ENGINE
Coolant—Check level
Sump—Drain and refill
Cylinder head—Check tightness
Carburettor—Top up carburettor dash pots and adjust engine idling speed
Accelerator control linkage and pedal fulcrum—Oil
Fan belt—Adjust tension
Valves—Adjust clearances
Mounting bolts—Check tightness
Manifolds—Check tightness
Oil filter—Check for oil leaks
Fuel pump—Clean filter

CLUTCH AND CONTROLS
Pedal pivot bushes—Lubricate
Master cylinder—Top up
Hydraulic pipes—Check for leakage

TRANSMISSION
Gearbox, Overdrive—Check level and top up
Rear axle—Check level and top up
Universal joint coupling bolts—Check tightness

STEERING AND SUSPENSION
Lower steering swivels—Lubricate
Wheel alignment—Check by condition of tyre tread
Steering unit attachments and "U" bolts—Check for tightness
Tie rods and levers—Check for tightness

BRAKES AND CONTROLS
Handbrake cable and linkage—Lubricate
Hydraulic pipes—Check for leaks, chafing and for hose clearance
Master cylinder—Check level and top up
Pedal pivot bush—Lubricate
Brake shoes and handbrake cable—Adjust as necessary

ELECTRICAL EQUIPMENT
Battery—Check and adjust level
    Check charging rate
Dynamo and starter motor—Check fixing bolts for tightness
Distributor—Lubricate and adjust points
Headlamp—Check alignment and adjust if required
Lights, heater, screen washer, wipers and warning equipment—Check operation

WHEELS AND TYRES
Wheel nuts—Check tightness
Tyres—Check and adjust pressures

BODY
Door strikers, locks and hinges— Oil and check operation
Body mounting bolts—Check tightness
Door handles, controls and windshield—Wipe clean
Road test—Test vehicle on road

SCHEDULE OF OPERATIONS RELATING TO "A" VOUCHERS

Carry out the following operations every 6,000 miles (10,000 km.) or every six months, whichever is the earlier.

ENGINE
Sump—Drain and refill
Air cleaner—Remove element, clean and replace
Carburettor dash-pots—Top up
Carburettor idling controls—Adjust
Accelerator controls and pedal fulcrum—Oil
Fan belt—Adjust tension
Valves—Adjust clearances

CLUTCH AND CONTROLS
Pedal pivot bushes—Lubricate
Hydraulic pipes—Check for leakage

TRANSMISSION
Propeller shaft—Lubricate (if nipples are provided)

STEERING AND SUSPENSION
Upper steering swivels—Lubricate
Lower steering swivels—Lubricate
Wheel alignment (Front and Rear independent suspension models)—Check by condition of tyre tread

BRAKES AND CONTROLS
Handbrake cable and linkage—Lubricate
Hydraulic pipes—Check for leaks, chafing and hose
    clearance
Pedal pivot bushes—Lubricate
Brakes—Adjust shoes

ELECTRICAL EQUIPMENT
Distributor—Lubricate and adjust points
Sparking plugs—Clean, re-set gaps, test and refit
**Lights, heater, screen washer, wipers and warning
    equipment**—Check operation

WHEELS AND TYRES
Wheel nuts—Check for tightness
Tyres—Check and adjust tyre pressures

BODY
Door strikers, locks and hinges—Oil and check
    operation
Door handles, controls and windshield—Wipe clean
Test vehicle on road

SCHEDULE OF OPERATIONS RELATING TO "B" VOUCHERS

Every 12,000 miles (20,000 km.) or every twelve months, whichever is the earlier, carry out the work listed for "A" vouchers and perform the following additional operations:

ENGINE
Oil filter—Renew
Fuel pump—Clean the filter and sediment chamber
Exhaust system—Examine and report condition
Crankcase breather valve—Dismantle, clean and re-
    assemble. Ensure breather hole in oil filler cap is
    free from obstruction
Water pump—Grease

TRANSMISSION
Gearbox, Overdrive—Check level and top up
Rear axle—Check level and top up
Universal joint coupling bolts—Check tightness

STEERING AND SUSPENSION
Steering unit attachments and "U" bolts—Check
    tightness
Tie rods and levers—Check tightness
Steering unit—Grease

BRAKES AND CONTROLS
Brake drums and caliper pads—Remove, de-dust and
    examine brake shoes, pads, drums, and wheel
    cylinders

ELECTRICAL EQUIPMENT
Generator—Lubricate rear bearing
Sparking plugs—Renew

WHEELS AND TYRES
Front hubs—Check and adjust if necessary
Rear hubs (fitted with Live axle)—Lubricate
Test vehicle on road

TRIUMPH TR4
WORKSHOP MANUAL

GROUP 1

Comprising:

TR4 WORKSHOP MANUAL

GROUP 1

CONTENTS

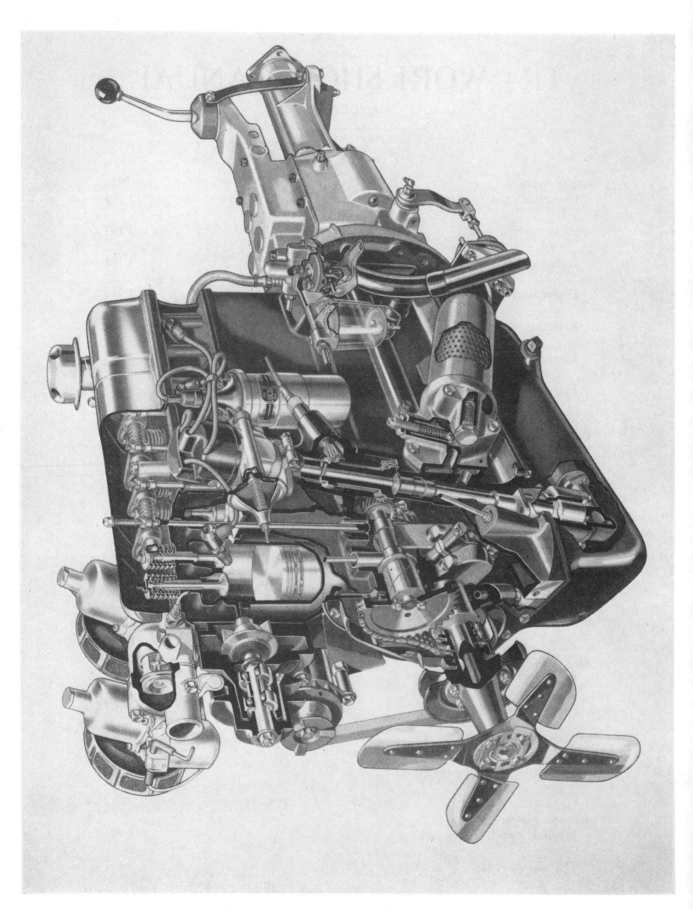

Cut-away view of the engine unit

Dimensions and Tolerances

Parts and Description	ins.	mm.	Remarks
CYLINDER BLOCK			
Block bore in liners	3·6245 — 3·6260	(92·062 — 92·1004)	

PISTON AND CYLINDER LINERS

GRADING DIMENSIONS FOR STANDARD BORE SIZE ONLY (Fig. 33)

GRADE	F		G		H	
	mm.	ins.	mm.	ins.	mm.	ins.
Cylinder Liner Bore ..	85·997	3·3857	86·007	3·3861	86·017	3·3865
	85·989	3·3854	85·999	3·3858	86·009	3·3862
Major Top Dia. 'BB' ..	85·870	3·3807	85·880	3·3811	85·890	3·3815
	85·860	3·3803	85·870	3·3807	85·880	3·3811
Major Bottom Dia. 'AA'	85·908	3·3822	85·918	3·3826	85·928	3·3830
	85·898	3·3818	85·908	3·3822	85·918	3·3826

	ins.	mm.	Remarks
Number of rings			2 compression, 1 scraper
Ring groove width :			
Top	0·0635 — 0·0645	(1·6129 — 1·638)	
Centre	0·0635 — 0·0645	(1·6129 — 1·638)	
Scraper	0·1572 — 0·1582	(3·993 — 4·018)	
Piston pin bore	0·87505 — 0·87530	(22·226 — 22·233)	
Piston removal			From top of block
PISTON PIN			
Length	2·916 — 2·920	(74·06 — 74·168)	
Diameter	0·87485 — 0·87510	(22·187 — 22·227)	
Clearance in piston	0·00005 — 0·00045	(0·00127 — 0·01029)	
PISTON RINGS			
Width :			
Top	0·0615 — 0·0625	(1·562 — 1·5875)	
Centre	0·0615 — 0·0625	(1·562 — 1·5875)	
Scraper	0·1552 — 0·1562	(3·942 — 3·967)	
Ring to groove clearance, all rings :			
Mfg.	0·0010 — 0·0030	(0·0254 — 0·0762)	
Wear limit	0·0038	(0·0965)	
Gaps (in position) all rings ..	0·010 — 0·015	(0·254 — 0·381)	
VALVE SPRINGS			
No. of Springs per valve :			
Inlet	2		
Exhaust	3		
Free length :			
Auxiliary inner (Exhaust only)	1·55 — 1·57	(39·37 — 39·878)	
Inner	1·88 — 1·90	(47·752 — 48·360)	
Outer	1·94 — 1·96	(49·276 — 49·784)	
Valve clearance (cold) :			
Inlet and Exhaust	0·010	(·254)	

Dimensions and Tolerances

Parts and Description	ins.	mm.	Remarks
CONNECTING RODS			
Type	Big end offset, will pass through liner bore		
Length (centre to centre) ..	6·248 — 6·252	(158·7 — 158·8)	
Big end — Bore	2·2327 — 2·2335	(56·71 — 56·73)	
— Width	1·1775 — 1·1795	(29·90 — 29·96)	
Big end bearing clearances :			
Mfg.	0·0028 — 0·0040	(0·071 — 0·1016)	
Wear limit	0·005	(0·127)	
Big end bearing width	0·965 — 0·975	(24·511 — 24·765)	
Small end bearing bore when			
reamed	0·8742 — 0·8758	(22·208 — 22·252)	
Width	1·070 — 1·090	(27·178 — 27·686)	
Connecting rod end float, on			
crankpin	0·007 — 0·014	(·1778 — ·3556)	
Undersize big end bearings avail-			
able	0·010, 0·020, 0·030	(·254, ·508, ·762)	
Max. connecting rod bend and			
twist	0·002	(·0508)	
CRANKSHAFT			
Crankpin diameter	2·0861 — 2·0866	(52·9689 — 52·9964)	
Crankpin width	1·1865 — 1·1915	(30·1971 — 30·3241)	
Main journal diameter	2·4790 — 2·4795	(62·966 — 62·9793)	
Undersize main bearings available	0·010, 0·020, 0·030,		
		(·254, ·508, ·762)	
Main journal length :			
Front	1·776 — 1·786	(45·1104 — 45·3644)	
Centre	1·7498 — 1·7507	(44·4549 — 44·4678)	
Rear	1·808 — 1·818	(45·9232 — 46·1772)	
Main bearing wall thickness ..	0·0720 — 0·07225	(1·8288 — 1·83400)	
Main bearing housing dia. ..	2·6250 — 2·6255	(66·675 — 66·6877)	
Main bearing clearance :			
Mfg.	0·0015 — 0·0025	(·0381 — ·0635)	
Wear limit	0·0031	(·0787)	
Crankshaft end float	0·004 — 0·006	(·1016 — ·1524)	
	(desirable)		
Mfg.	0·0048 — 0·0117	(·12192 — ·28118)	
Wear limit	0·015	(·381)	
OIL PUMP			
Outer Rotor :			
External diameter	1·5965 — 1·5975	(40·5511 — 40·5765)	
Housing internal diameter ..	1·603 — 1·604	(40·7162 — 40·7416)	
Depth of rotor	1·4985 — 1·4995	(38·0619 — 38·0873)	
Housing depth	1·500 — 1·501	(38·1 — 38·1254)	
Inner Rotor :			
Major diameter	1·171 — 1·172	(29·7434 — 29·7688)	
Minor diameter	0·729 — 0·731	(18·5166 — 18·5674)	
Rotor depth	1·4985 — 1·4995	(38·0619 — 38·0873)	
Spindle diameter	0·4980 — 0·4985	(12·6492 — 12·6619)	
Bore in housing for spindle ..	0·4995 — 0·5010	(12·6873 — 12·7254)	
Spindle clearance in housing ..	0·001 — 0·003	(·0254 — ·0762)	

Dimensions and Tolerances

Parts and Description	ins.	mm.
CAMSHAFT		
Number of bearings	4	
Front journal diameter	1·871 — 1·872	(47·5234 — 47·5488)
Centre intermediate and rear journal diameter	1·7153 — 1·7158	(43·637 — 43·6624)
Front bearing length	1·870 — 1·872	(47·4984 — 47·5488)
Centre and rear bearing length ..	1·190 — 1·210	(30·226 — 30·734)
Intermediate bearing length ..	0·740 — 0·760	(18·796 — 19·304)
Journal length :		
Front	1·8760 — 1·8775	(47·6304 — 47·6685)
Centre	1·115 — 1·135	(28·321 — 28·829)
Intermediate	0·740 — 0·760	(18·796 — 19·304)
Rear	1·3025 — 1·3225	(33·0835 — 33·5915)
Front bearing internal dia. ..	1·8748 — 1·8757	(47·7199 — 47·7428)
Centre, intermediate and rear bearing internal diameter ..	1·71725 — 1·71825	(43·61815 — 43·64355)
Clearance between front bearing and journal :		
Mfg.	0·0028 — 0·0047	(·07112 — ·11938)
Wear limit	0·0059	(·14986)
Clearance between centre, inter-mediate, rear bearings and journals :		
Mfg.	0·0015 — 0·0029	(·0381 — 0·766)
Wear limit	0·0037	(·09398)
Cam. lift (max.)	0·260	(6·604)
Camshaft end float	0·0040 — 0·0075	(·1016 — ·1905)
TAPPETS		
Length	1·969 — 1·971	(39·8069 — 39·8119)
Stem diameter	0·9367 — 0·9371	(23·7922 — 23·8023)
Block bore for tappet	0·9373 — 0·9380	(23·8074 — 23·8252)
Clearance in block — Mfg. ..	0·0002 — 0·0013	(·00508 — ·03302)
— Wear limit	0·0016	(·04064)
VALVES		
Head diameter — Inlet ..	1·558 — 1·562	(39·5732 — 39·6748)
— Exhaust ..	1·299 — 1·303	(32·9955 — 33·0962)
Angle of seat (Valves)	45°	
Angle of seat (Cylinder Head) ..	44½°	
Valve stem diameter :		
Inlet	0·310 — 0·311	(7·864 — 7·8994)
Exhaust	0·3705 — 0·3715	(9·4107 — 9·4361)
Valve guide bore :		
Inlet	0·312 — 0·313	(7·9248 — 7·9502)
Exhaust	0·3745 — 0·3755	(9·5123 — 9·5377)
Stem to guide clearance :		
Inlet — Mfg.	0·001 — 0·003	(·0254 -— ·0762)
— Wear limit ..	0·0038	(·0965)
Exhaust — Mfg. ..	0·003 — 0·005	(·0762 — ·127)
Exhaust — Mfg. ..	0·003 — 0·005	(·0762 — ·127)
— Wear limit ..	0·0063	(·16002)

VALVE SEAT INSERTS
Refer to page 1·125 for details

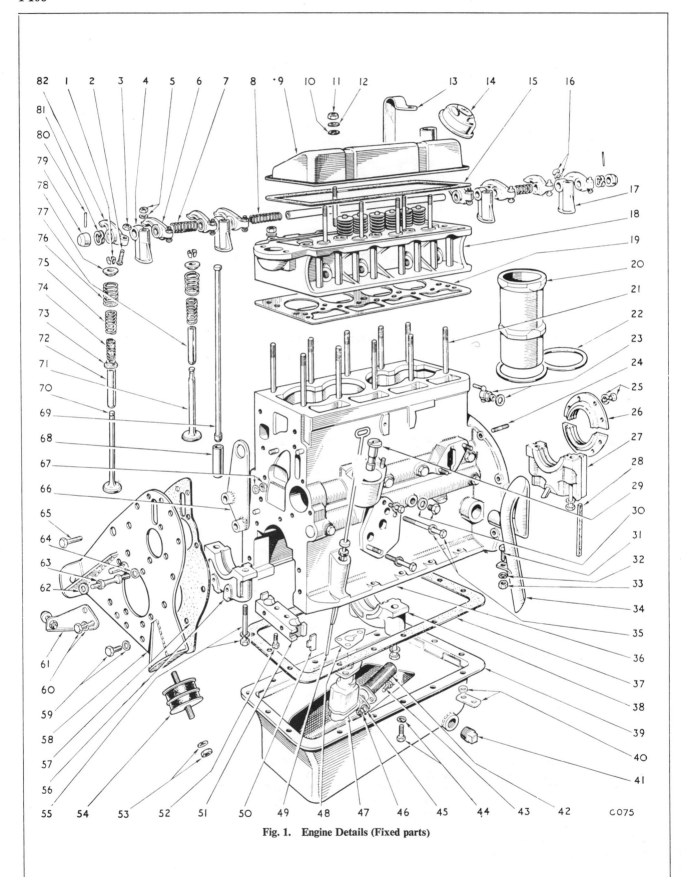

Fig. 1. Engine Details (Fixed parts)

C075

Key to Fig. 1

1	Split collets	42	Oil pump filter gauze
2	Adjusting screw	43	Bolt
3	Nut	44	Setscrew and spring washer
4	Rocker pedestal	45	Spring washer
5	Nut and spring washer	46	Nut
6	Rocker, R.H.	47	Oil pump
7	Spring	48	Oil pump gasket
8	Spring—centre	49	Dipstick
9	Rocker cover	50	Sealing piece
10	Fibre washer	51	Front sealing block
11	Nyloc nut	52	Screw
12	Plain washer	53	Nut and spring washer
13	Lifting eye	54	Engine mounting
14	Filler cap	55	Main bearing cap bolt and spring washer
15	Rocker cover gasket	56	Front main bearing cap
16	Screw and shakeproof washer	57	Gasket
17	Rear rocker pedestal	58	Front bearer plate
18	Cylinder head	59	Setscrew and spring washer
19	Cylinder head gasket	60	Setscrew and spring washer
20	Cylinder liner	61	Torque reaction arm and buffer
21	Cylinder head stud	62	Fibre washer
22	Liner gasket	63	Shouldered stud
23	Drain tap and fibre washer	64	Spring washer
24	Stud	65	Bolt
25	Setscrew and spring washer	66	Lifting eye
26	Rear oil seal	67	Nut and spring washer
27	Rear main bearing cap	68	Tappet
28	Sealing felt	69	Pushrod
29	Distributor drive gear bush	70	Exhaust valve
30	Oil gallery plug and copper washer	71	Inlet valve
31	Setscrew	72	Exhaust valve guide
32	Spring washer	73	Collar
33	Nut	74	Auxiliary valve spring
34	Breather pipe	75	Inner valve spring
35	Oil filter attachment bolt and spring washer	76	Outer valve spring
36	Cylinder block	77	Inlet valve guide
37	Sump gasket	78	Valve collar
38	Centre main bearing cap	79	Rocker shaft end cap
39	Sump	80	Mills pin
40	Breather pipe bracket and distance piece	81	Spring
41	Sump plug	82	Rocker, L.H.

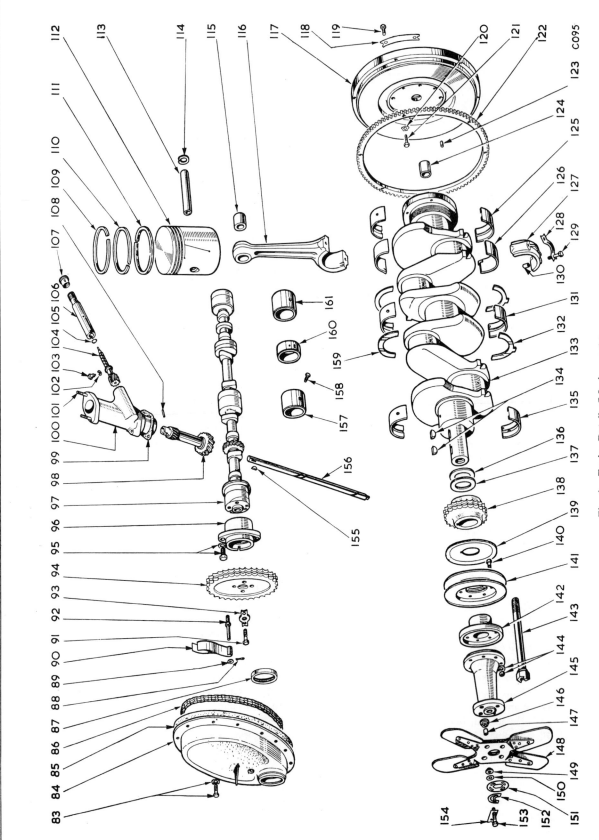

Fig. 4. Engine Details (Moving parts)

Key to Fig. 4

83 Bolt and spring washer
84 Timing cover
85 Gasket
86 Timing chain
87 Oil seal
88 Split pin
89 Washer
90 Tensioner blade
91 Bolt
92 Tensioner pin
93 Lockplate
94 Camshaft sprocket
95 Bolt and spring washer
96 Front camshaft bearing
97 Camshaft
98 Distributor drive gear
99 Gasket
100 Distributor pedestal
101 Stud
102 Spring washer
103 Peg bolt
104 Tachometer drive gear
105 Rubber 'O' ring
106 Drive gear housing
107 Cap
108 Mills pin

109 Compression ring (taper)
110 Compression ring (parallel)
111 Oil control ring
112 Piston
113 Gudgeon pin
114 Circlip
115 Gudgeon pin bush
116 Connecting rod
117 Flywheel
118 Lockplate
119 Bolt
120 Tab washer
121 Bolt
122 Starter ring gear
123 Dowel
124 Spigot bearing
125 Rear main bearing shell
126 Con-rod bearing shell
127 Con-rod cap
128 Lockplate
129 Con-rod bolt
130 Dowel
131 Centre main bearing shell
132 Lower thrust washer
133 Crankshaft
134 Woodruff keys

135 Front main bearing shell
136 Shim washer 0·004" (0·1 mm.)
137 Shim washer 0·006" (0·15 mm.)
138 Crankshaft sprocket
139 Oil thrower disc
140 Bolt
141 Pulley
142 Pulley hub
143 Starting handle dog bolt
144 Washer and nut
145 Fan extension
146 Rubber bush
147 Distance tube
148 Fan
149 Rubber bush
150 Plain washer
151 Plate
152 Balancer
153 Bolt
154 Lockplate
155 Woodruff key
156 Oil pump drive shaft
157 Intermediate front camshaft bearing
158 Peg bolt
159 Upper thrust washer
160 Intermediate rear camshaft bearing
161 Rear camshaft bearing

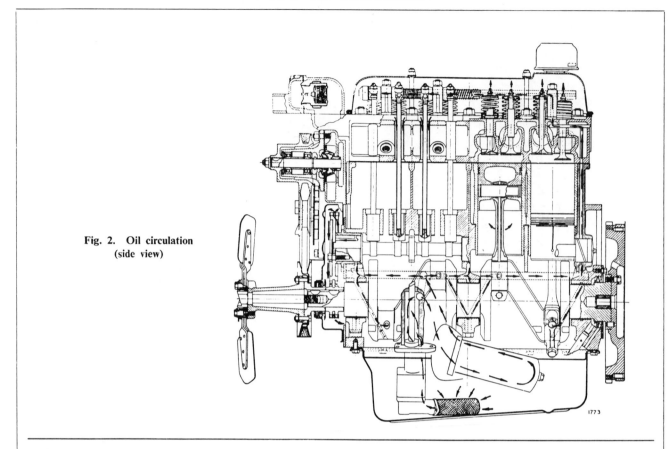

Fig. 2. Oil circulation
(side view)

Fig. 3. Oil circulation
(end view)

ENGINE AND GEARBOX REMOVAL

Remove the battery and drain the cooling system, engine and gearbox.

Refer to Fig. 5 and disconnect:
— oil pressure pipe (6).
— fuel pipe (5).
— tachometer drive cable (7).
— fuel pipe (2).
— vacuum pipe (8).
— coil S.W. cable (4).
— temperature transmitter cable (3).
— horns (1).
— fan belt.
— engine earthing strap.   (Not shown).

Fig. 5.   Left-hand view of Engine

Refer to Fig. 6 and disconnect:
— heater valve control (12).
— hoses (13) and (14).
— mixture control cable (10).
— accelerator rod (11) and remove the carburettors (9).
— exhaust pipe flange (not shown).

Fig. 6.   Right-hand view of Engine

Referring to Fig. 7:
— remove the coupling bolt (1).
— release two 'U' bolts (2).
— move the steering unit (3) as far forward as possible.
— remove the front cross tube (4).

Fig. 7.   Steering unit attachment

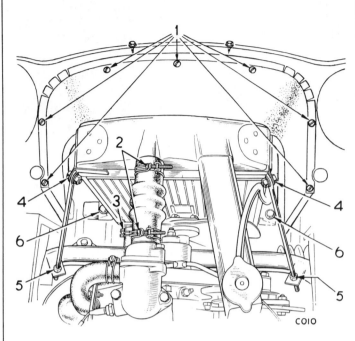

1 Air deflector attachment screws
2 Top hose clips
3 Bottom hose clips
4 Radiator stay attachments
5 Adjusting nuts
6 Radiator attachments

Fig. 8.   Radiator and air deflector attachment

ENGINE AND GEARBOX REMOVAL (cont'd.)

Remove :

— starter motor (not shown).
— bonnet (see group 5).
— radiator and air deflector by detaching items in the order shown on Fig. 8.
— engine torque reaction arm (item 61, Fig. 1).
— clutch slave cylinder (accessible from under vehicle) and allow it to hang on hose.

Working inside the vehicle and referring to Fig. 12, remove :

— seat cushions and carpets.
— attachments 'B' and 'C', and facia support.
— attachments 'A' and centre floor cover.
— speedometer cable.
— front end of propeller shaft.
— overdrive solenoid cables (if fitted).

Remove the gearbox top cover and fit a temporary cardboard cover to prevent the entry of foreign matter.

Attach a lifting cable to the engine lifting eyes and, supporting the engine unit on a hoist, release :

— front engine mounting (6), Fig. 10.
— rear mounting (10), Fig. 9.
— crossmember (8), Fig. 9.

Lift the engine and gearbox unit, tilting it rearwards at an angle of 35 - 40° as shown on Fig. 11. Manoeuvre the unit clear of the vehicle.

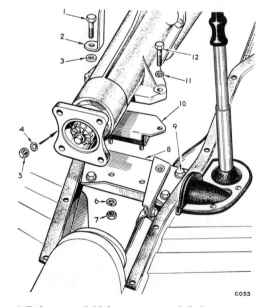

1 Bolt	5 Nyloc nut	9 Bolt
2 Stay	6 Washer	10 Rear mounting
3 Washer	7 Nut	11 Washer
4 Washer	8 Crossmember	12 Bolt

Fig. 9.   Rear Engine Mounting

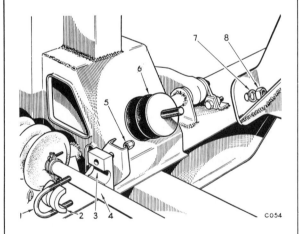

1 'U' bolt	5 Nyloc nut
2 Clamp (outer)	6 Engine mounting
3 Clamp (inner)	7 Lockwasher
4 Steering unit	8 Nut

Fig. 10.   Front Engine Mounting

ENGINE INSTALLATION

Refit the clutch unit and gearbox to the engine.

Using a wire sling and hoist, tilt the engine 35-40° rearwards and manoeuvre it into position.

Refit:
— crossmember (8) and rear mounting (10), Fig. 9.
— front mounting (6), Fig. 10.
— torque reaction arm (61), Fig. 1, and adjust to take up clearance between buffer and chassis.
— gearbox cover, propeller shaft, speedometer drive and overdrive solenoid cables (if fitted).
— centre floor cover attachments 'A', facia support and attachments 'B' and 'C', Fig. 12.
— seat cushions and carpets.
— clutch slave cylinder and adjust as described on page 2·106.
— steering unit (3) and tighten the 'U' bolts (2) and coupling bolt (1), Fig. 7.
— front crossmember (4), Fig. 7.
— starter motor.
— air deflector and radiator (see page 1·110).
— exhaust pipe flange.

Refer to Fig. 5 and refit:
— engine earthing strap.
— fan belt and adjust (see page 0·208).
— horn cables (1).
— temperature transmitter cable (3).
— vacuum pipe (8).
— fuel pipe (2).
— tachometer drive cable (7).
— fuel pipe (5).
— oil pressure pipe (6).
— coil, S.W. cable (4).

Refer to Fig. 6 and refit:
— carburettors (9).
— accelerator rod (11).
— mixture control cable (10).
— heater hoses (13) and (14).
— heater valve control (12).
— exhaust pipe.

Refit the bonnet (see group 5), re-connect the battery, refill the radiator, engine oil sump and gearbox to the correct levels.

Prime the carburettors, start the engine and tune the carburettors as described on page 1·305.

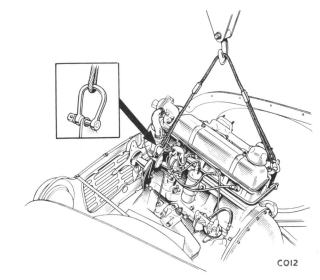

Fig. 11. Removing engine unit

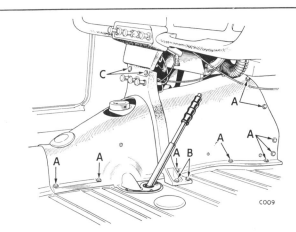

Fig. 12. Centre floor cover attachments

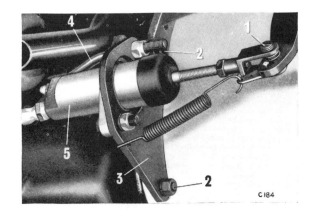

1	Pin	4	Stay
2	Bolt	5	Slave cylinder
3	Mounting bracket		

Fig. 13. Clutch slave cylinder attachment

Fig. 14. Left-hand view of reconditioned engine as supplied under the Unit Exchange Plan

Fig. 15. Right-hand view of reconditioned engine as supplied under the Unit Exchange Plan

Removing Auxiliary Equipment

Before returning an engine for reconditioning, drain the sump and remove the following items:—

1 Gearbox and clutch unit
2 Generator and fan belt
3 Water pump
4 Fuel pump
5 Distributor
6 Coil
7 Inlet and exhaust manifold
8 Starter motor
9 Temperature transmitter
10 Top water elbow and thermostat
11 Sparking plugs

Refitting Auxiliary Equipment

Remove all masking tape from the apertures in the reconditioned unit and ensure that all joint faces are clean. Using new gaskets, fit the following items:—

1 Clutch unit and gearbox
2 Water pump
3 Generator and fan belt
4 Distributor. For timing see page 1·131
5 Fuel pump
6 Coil. Ensure a good earth to the cylinder block
7 Inlet and exhaust manifolds
8 Top water elbow and thermostat
9 Temperature transmitter
10 Starter motor
11 Sparking plugs

ENGINE DISMANTLING

Remove the gearbox and clutch assembly. Place the engine on a stand or bench and dismantle as follows :—

Refer to Fig. 16 and from L.H.S. remove :
— heater pipe (2).
— by-pass hose (1).
— coil (6).
— oil filter (5) and pipe (3).
— fuel pump (4).
— H.T. leads, distributor (7) and pedestal.
— breather pipe (8).

Refer to Fig. 17 and from R.H.S. remove :
— fan belt (10).
— adjusting link (11).
— water pump (9).
— generator and mounting bracket (12).
— manifolds (13) and gasket.
— thermostat housing (14).

To complete the dismantling, refer to Figs. 1 and 2 when carrying out the following operations. Note that items 1 to 82 are shown on Fig. 1, and items 83 to 161 are shown on Fig. 4.

Remove :
— rocker cover (9).
— rocker shaft assembly and push rods (69).
— cylinder head nuts, lifting eye (13), plain washers, cylinder head (18) and gasket (19).

Using a valve spring compressor, remove :
— split collets (1).
— inner, outer and auxiliary springs (75), (76) and (74).
— upper and lower spring caps (78) and (73).

Mark the valves, 1 to 8 from the front, to identify them, and remove them from the cylinder head.

Withdraw the distributor driving gear (98), shaft (156), tappets (68) and dipstick (49).

Release the lockplates (118), remove the bolts (119) and detach the flywheel (117).

Remove the dog bolt (143), withdraw the fan and pulley assembly. If necessary, strip the assembly as follows :—
— release the lockplates (154), unscrew four bolts (153) and remove items (152), (151), (150), (149), (148), (147), (146).
— unscrew six nuts (144), withdraw the bolts (140) and detach items (145), (142) and (141).

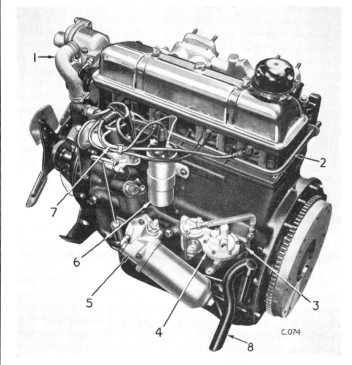

1 By-pass hose	5 Oil filter
2 Heater pipe	6 Ignition coil
3 Oil pressure pipe	7 Distributor
4 Fuel pump	8 Breather pipe

Fig. 16. Left-hand view of engine unit

9 Water pump	12 Generator
10 Fan belt	13 Exhaust manifold
11 Adjusting link	14 Thermostat housing

Fig. 17. Right-hand view of engine unit

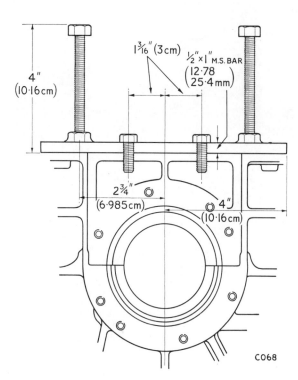

Fig. 18. Removing rear main bearing cap

Unscrew the bolts (83) and remove the timing cover (84) and gasket (85).

Release the lockplates (93), unscrew two bolts (91) and remove sprockets (94), chain (86), disc (139), sprocket (138), shims (136), (137), and keys (134).

Unscrew two bolts (95) and withdraw bearing (96) and camshaft (97).

Unscrew the attachment details (59), (60), (63) and remove the bearer plate (58).

Remove :

— oil sump (39), gasket (37), oil pump (47) and gasket (48).

— connecting rod caps (127) and bearing shells (126).

— cylinder liners (20) complete with pistons; then withdraw pistons from liners.

— circlips (114) and eject the gudgeon pins (113).

— front sealing block (51), main bearing caps (27), (38), (56).

— thrust washers (132) and lower oil scroll (26).

— crankshaft (133), bearing shells (125), (131), (135), thrust washers (159) and upper oil scroll (26).

— remaining plugs, copper washers, studs and bearings.

ENGINE RECONDITIONING

General Recommendations

Scrape old gasket material from the joint faces and clean all engine components, preferably in a trichlorethylene degreasing plant, giving particular attention to oilways.

Assess the serviceability of all components by careful examination and by checking the measurements of worn surfaces against the maximum worn tolerances given on pages 1·103-4-5.

When rebuilding the engine, use new gaskets, lockplates, and renew damaged studs, nuts, bolts, spring washers and leaking core plugs.

Use Hylomar, Wellseal or Hermatite jointing compounds for all gasket joints and sealing block faces.

Tighten all nuts, bolts and studs to the appropriate torque figures listed on pages 12 and 13.

Crankshaft Regrinding

Measure the diameter of the crankshaft journals and crankpins at various points to determine maximum wear, taper and ovality. If the wear exceeds the worn tolerance quoted on page 1·104 regrind the crankshaft to the nearest undersize dimension.

Undersize Bearings

Dimensions of undersize bearings are given on page 1·104.

Camshaft Bearings

Remove three shouldered setscrews 'A' (Fig. 20). Drift the sealing disc from the rear camshaft bearing. Use the extractor, Tool No. S.32-1, to withdraw the worn bearings from the cylinder block. When fitting each new bearing, align its oil feed and location holes with those in the block and ensure that the bearing does not turn whilst pulling it into position. Refit the locating setscrews, using $\frac{1}{16}''$ (1·6 mm.) thickness plain steel washers under the setscrew heads.

Renew the rear sealing disc.

1 Handle
2 Thrust piece
3 Centraliser
4 Shaft
5 Camshaft bearing
6 Guide and remover
7 Lock
8 Guide pin

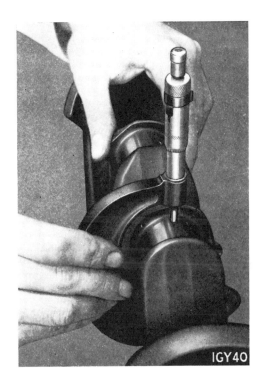

Fig. 19. Measuring Crankpins

Fig. 20. Showing camshaft bearing locating screws "A", and oil gallery sealing plugs "B"

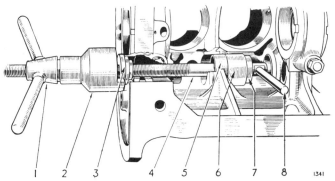

Fig. 21. Using tool No. S.32-1 to fit camshaft bearings

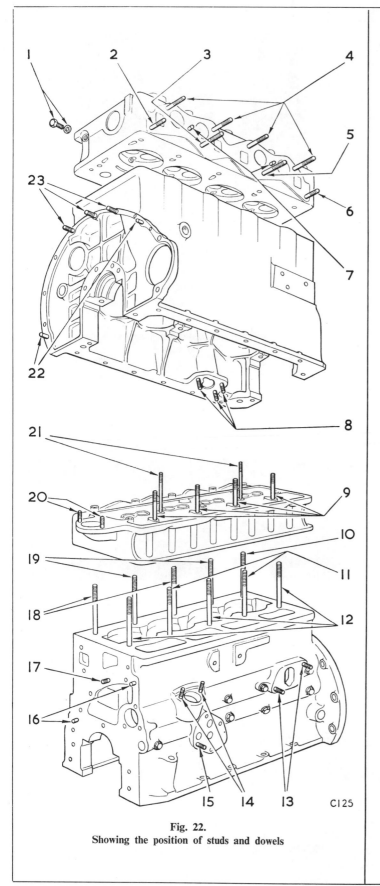

Fig. 22.
Showing the position of studs and dowels

Studs

Refit all studs and dowels to the cylinder block as shown on Fig. 22.

POSITIONS OF STUDS AND DOWELS

1 $\frac{3}{8}''$ U.N.C. $\times \frac{3}{8}''$ (9·525 mm.) setscrew and copper washer

2 $\frac{3}{8}''$ U.N.C. $\times 1\frac{15}{16}''$ (49·21 mm.) stud

3 $\frac{3}{8}''$ U.N.C. $\times 2\frac{3}{8}''$ (60·33 mm.) stud

4 $\frac{3}{8}''$ U.N.C. $\times 2\frac{1}{16}''$ (52·39 mm.) stud

5 $\frac{3}{8}''$ U.N.C. $\times 2\frac{3}{8}''$ (60·33 mm.) stud

6 $\frac{3}{8}''$ U.N.C. $\times 1\frac{11}{16}''$ (42·86 mm.) stud

7 $\frac{5}{16}'' \times \frac{3}{4}''$ (7·94 mm. $\times$ 19·05 mm.) dowel

8 $\frac{5}{16}''$ U.N.C./N.F. $\times 1\frac{5}{16}''$ (33·34 mm.) stud

9 $\frac{3}{8}''$ U.N.C./N.F. $\times 3\frac{1}{8}''$ (79·38 mm.) stud

10 $\frac{1}{2}''$ U.N.C./N.F. $\times 5\frac{1}{2}''$ (139·7 mm.) stud

11 $\frac{1}{2}''$ U.N.C./N.F. $\times 9''$ (228·6 mm.) stud

12 $\frac{1}{2}''$ U.N.C./N.F. $\times 5''$ (127 mm.) stud

13 $\frac{5}{16}''$ U.N.C./N.F. $\times 1\frac{5}{16}''$ (33·34 mm.) stud

14 $\frac{5}{16}''$ U.N.C./N.F. $\times 1\frac{5}{16}''$ (33·34 mm.) stud

15 $\frac{5}{16}''$ U.N.C./N.F. $\times 2\frac{3}{16}''$ (55·56 mm.) stud

16 $\frac{5}{16}'' \times \frac{3}{4}''$ (7·94 mm. $\times$ 19·05 mm.) dowel

17 $\frac{5}{16}''$ U.N.C./N.F. $\times 1\frac{5}{16}''$ (33·34 mm.) stud

18 $\frac{1}{2}''$ U.N.C./N.F. $\times 5\frac{5}{8}''$ (142·87 mm.) stud

19 $\frac{1}{2}''$ U.N.C./N.F. $\times 9\frac{1}{2}''$ (241·3 mm.) stud

20 $\frac{5}{16}''$ U.N.C. $\times 2''$ (50·8 mm.) bolt

21 $\frac{5}{16}''$ U.N.C./N.F. $\times 3\frac{11}{16}''$ (93·66 mm.) stud

22 $\frac{5}{16}'' \times \frac{3}{4}''$ (7·94 mm. $\times$ 19·05 mm.) dowel

23 $\frac{5}{16}''$ U.N.C./N.F. $\times 1\frac{5}{16}''$ (33·34 mm.) stud

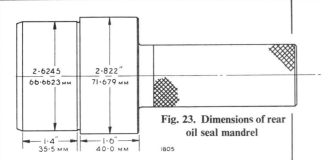

Fig. 23. Dimensions of rear oil seal mandrel

Rear Oil Seal

Ensure that both halves of the rear oil seal bear the same serial numbers.

Apply jointing compound to the contacting faces and loosely attach one half of the seal to the cylinder block, and the other half to the rear bearing cap.

Lay the mandrel (Fig. 24) into the rear bearing housing (without shell bearings). Fit the rear bearing cap (without shell bearing) and tighten the cap bolts sufficiently to nip the mandrel.

Tighten the oil seal securing bolts and remove the bearing cap and mandrel.

Crankshaft and Bearings

Fit the bearing shells in the crankcase. Ensure that the locating tags register in the recesses provided. Lubricate the journals and install the crankshaft.

Placing the white metal faces of the thrust washers against the thrust faces of the crankshaft, slide the thrust washers into position.

Similarly, assemble the bearing shell and thrust washers to the centre main bearing cap, and the bearing shells to the outer caps. Fit the bearing cap assemblies in position, ensuring that the markings on the caps are placed adjacent to identical markings on the crankcase, as shown in Fig. 26.

Fit the main bearing cap bolts (55) with spring washers and, ensuring that the rear face of the rear bearing cap is aligned with the rear face of the crankcase, securely tighten the cap bolts.

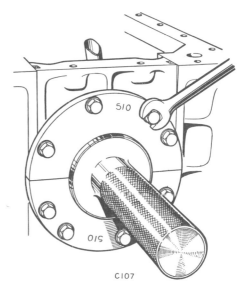

Fig. 24. Using a mandrel to centralise the rear oil seal

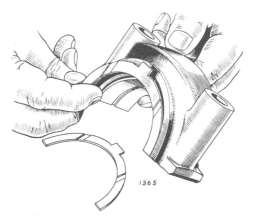

Fig. 25. Fitting thrust washers to centre main bearing cap

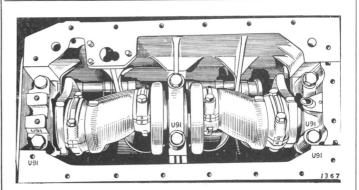

Fig. 26. Disposition of bearing cap numbers relative to the cylinder block

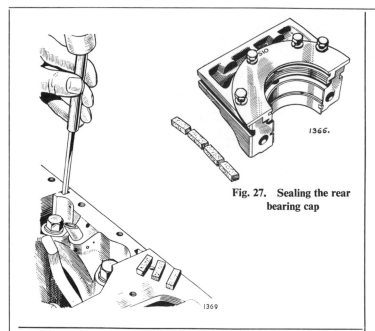

Fig. 27.   Sealing the rear
bearing cap

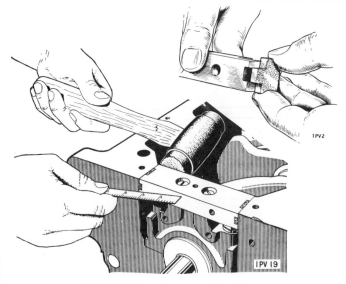

Fig. 28. Fitting "T" packings
and aligning the front sealing
block

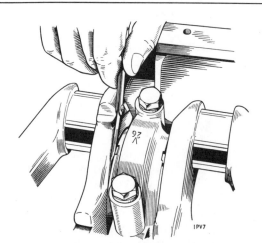

Fig. 29.   Using feeler gauges to check crankshaft end float

Rear Sealing Block

Ram lengths of felt, soaked in jointing compound, into the rear bearing cap slots, as shown in Fig. 27. Trim off the excess felt with a sharp knife.

Front Sealing Block

Coat the two 'T'-shaped packings with jointing compound and position them in the end recesses of the front sealing block. Align the block with the front face of the crankcase and secure it with two cheese-headed screws.

Crankshaft End Float

Check the end float by moving the crankshaft endwise, as shown. The correct end float is 0·004″ - 0·006″ (0·1 - 0·15 mm.).

Excess end float can be reduced by fitting 0·005″ (0·127 mm.) oversize thrust washers.

Connecting Rods

Small End Bush

Use Tool No. 20SM. FT.6201 to renew small end bush. Ensure that the small end bush oil feed holes are aligned.

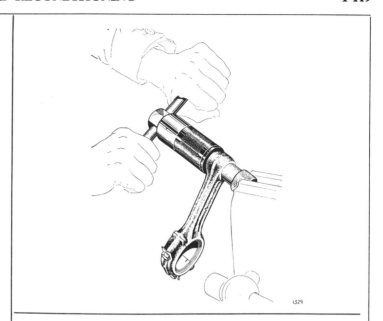

Fig. 30. Simultaneously removing the old bush and fitting a new one in a single operation

Reaming the Gudgeon Pin Bush

Use Tool No. 6200.A. to ream the gudgeon pin bushes as shown.

A. Pilot bush
C. Positioning plate
B. Centralising tool
D. Steady pin

Fig. 31. Gudgeon pin bush reaming fixture

Connecting Rod Alignment

Use connecting rod alignment jig No. 335, with adaptor No. 336-2, to check twist 'A' and bend 'B'. Determine amount of misalignment by inserting feeler gauges between the face of the fixture and one of the buttons.

Correct misalignment with a bending iron and re-check.

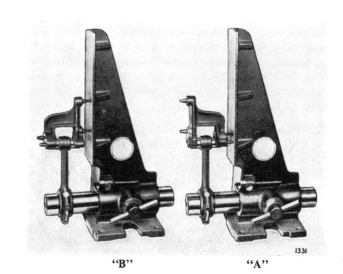

"B"   "A"

Fig. 32. Checking for bend at "B", and twist at "A"

Cylinder Liners

The cylinder liners are of the wet type with flanged upper faces, on the sides of which are machined two pairs of flats, 90° to one another. These flats provide alternative fitting positions to overcome wear along the axis of thrust.

The lower portion of each liner is provided externally with a reduced diameter, surmounted by a flanged face for spigoting into a machined recess in the cylinder block. This spigot also accommodates the liner gasket which is used for water sealing.

Pistons and Liners

Pistons and liners are graded "F", "G" or "H" according to their dimensions. The appropriate symbol is stamped on the top face of each piston and liner. When fitting new pistons and liners, ensure that they are both of the same grade, for example, "F" piston to "F" liner. Dimensions are given on page 1·103.

Piston Measurement The piston dimensions given on page 1·103 are the maximum when measured across the thrust faces at the top of the skirt 'BB' and bottom of the skirt 'AA' (Fig. 33).

Piston Weight The maximum variation in weight between four pistons comprising a "set" must not exceed 4 drams (7·09 grams).

Piston Rings (Fig. 34)

Rings are fitted to each piston as follows :

1. Compression ring (plain).
2. Taper faced compression ring. Fit with taper towards top and "T" or "Top" marking on upper face.
3. Oil control ring.

Gaps First insert the ring into the liner, then use a piston to push the ring squarely down the bore to a point ¼″ (6 mm.) from the top. Measure the gap with feeler gauges (Fig. 35).

Ring to Groove Clearance Piston ring thickness, width of ring groove in the piston and recommended clearances are given on page 1·103.

Fitting Connecting Rods to Pistons

Ensure that the oil feed holes and cross drillings are unobstructed. Heat the piston in boiling water and assemble to the connecting rod as shown. Secure the gudgeon pin with circlips.

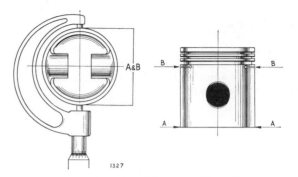

Fig. 33. Measuring piston across thrust face

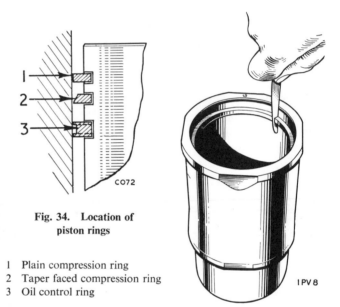

Fig. 34. Location of piston rings

1   Plain compression ring
2   Taper faced compression ring
3   Oil control ring

Fig. 35. Measuring ring gaps

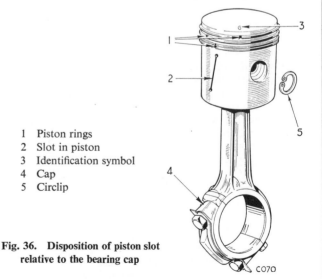

1   Piston rings
2   Slot in piston
3   Identification symbol
4   Cap
5   Circlip

Fig. 36. Disposition of piston slot relative to the bearing cap

Measuring Cylinder Liners

Check the cylinder liner bore diameters with a cylinder gauge or comparator such as the Mercer dial gauge shown on Fig. 37. Select an extension piece of suitable length, screw it into the instrument and lock it with the knurled locking ring. Using a new liner of known bore diameter or a 3″ to 4″ micrometer, set the feeler foot and extension piece to the correct bore diameter, rotate the dial to zero the needle, and tighten the locking screw.

Insert the gauge into the cylinder liner bore and, by taking readings at different positions, determine the maximum bore wear which normally occurs towards the top of the bore across its thrust axis. Replace liners worn in excess of the limits given on page 1·103 either with new standard-sized liners and pistons or with re-bored liners and oversize pistons.

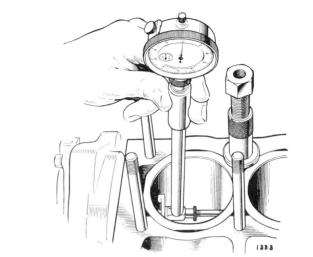

Fig. 37. Measuring cylinder bores

Fitting Pistons to Liners

Using a piston ring clamp, compress the piston rings and insert each piston into its liner. Fit new Figure "8" gaskets coated with jointing compound. Lower each liner and piston assembly into the block. Ensure that the connecting rod offset is towards the camshaft side of the engine. Secure each pair of liners with a clamp, as shown on Fig. 56.

Fit the bearing shells to the connecting rods and caps, locating the bearing tags in the recesses provided. Fit the connecting rods to the crankpins, and assemble the caps. Fit new lockplates, and securely tighten the connecting rod bolts and turn up the lockplate tabs.

From engine Commission Number CT.34072, connecting rod bolts have been replaced by "place bolts", thus dispensing with the need for tab washers. These new bolts have been re-designed to ensure that correct torque tightening loads are maintained, thus preventing bolts from becoming loose.

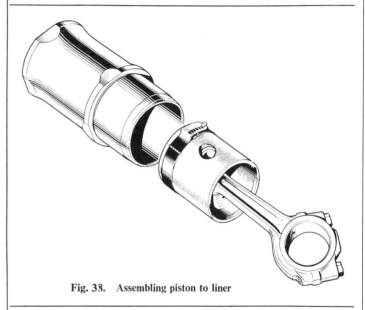

Fig. 38. Assembling piston to liner

Measuring Liner Protrusion

Place a straight edge across the top of the liner and measure its protrusion above the cylinder block.

Liner protrusion — ·003″/·005″ (0·08 mm./ 0·13 mm.)

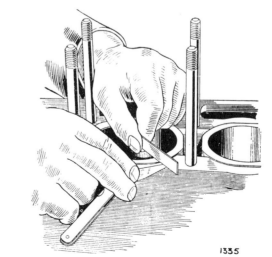

Fig. 39. Measuring liner protrusion

Fig. 40. Measuring clearance between rotors

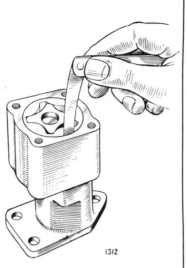

Fig. 41. Measuring clearance between outer rotor and body

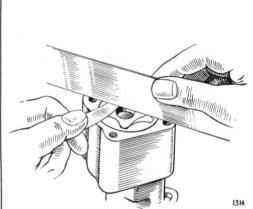

Fig. 42. Measuring rotor end clearance

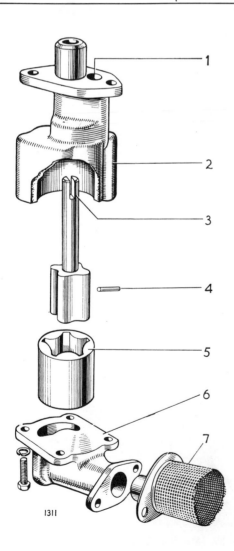

Oil Pump

Measure clearance between inner and outer rotors.

This must not exceed 0·010″ (·254 mm.).

Measure clearance between outer rotor and body.

This must not exceed 0·010″ (·254 mm.).

Measure the rotor end clearance.

This should not exceed 0·004″ (0·102 mm.).

Re-face the end plate face if worn.

Re-assemble the pump as shown and attach it to the cylinder block.

1 Oil pump outlet
2 Oil pump body
3 Shaft and inner rotor
4 Securing pin
5 Outer rotor
6 End plate
7 Filter

Fig. 43. Arrangement of oil pump components

Flywheel

Flywheel Clutch Face

If the flywheel clutch face is deeply scored, renew the flywheel, or alternatively, skim the face in a lathe, maintaining the following tolerances :
Max. flywheel face run-out
relative to spigot face = ·003″ (·0762 mm.)
at a radius of 5″.
Balance = 1 dram.

Starter Ring Gear

The four compressions invariably cause the crankshaft to stop at one of two positions. This concentrates wear on the leading edge of the starter ring gear teeth at the two points of starter pinion engagement.

Provided that the teeth are not sufficiently worn to cause jamming, the life of the starter ring may be extended by rotating the ring gear 60° or 120° around the flywheel and re-bolting in position, or by refitting the flywheel to the crankshaft on its second dowel hole.

When the second method is chosen, obliterate the original T.D.C. arrow on the flywheel and re-mark at the appropriate position.

To Remove the Starter Ring Gear

Remove the six bolts and place short lengths of ¼″ dia. (6·35 mm.) M.S. rod in the tapped holes in the clutch face of the flywheel. Refit the bolts and force the ring gear from the flywheel by progressively tightening the bolts.

To Refit the Ring Gear

Pull the ring gear onto its spigot by progressively tightening the bolts.

Fitting the Flywheel to the Crankshaft

Ensure that the flywheel attachment flange on the crankshaft and the corresponding spigot and face on the flywheel are clean. Screw a ⅜″ U.N.F. stud into one of the crankshaft holes as a pilot and fit the flywheel to the crankshaft flange, ensuring that the dowel and dowel hole correspond. Tighten the flywheel attachment bolts and secure them with the lockplates. Using a dial indicator gauge as shown on Fig. 46, measure the flywheel face for run-out.

Maximum run-out must not exceed ·003″ (·0762 mm.).

Engines are now being serviced under a new condition as follows:
Flywheel bolts have been replaced by place bolts, thus dispensing with the need for tab washers. These new bolts have been re-designed to ensure that correct torque tightening loads are maintained, thus preventing bolts from becoming loose.

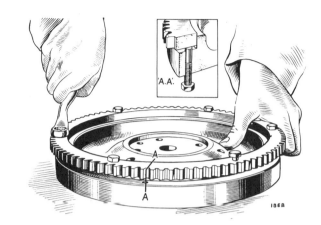

Fig. 44. Fitting ring gear to flywheel. Inset shows method of removing ring gear

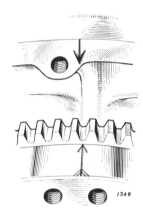

Fig. 45. T.D.C. marks on flywheel and cylinder block

Fig. 46. Checking flywheel clutch face for run-out

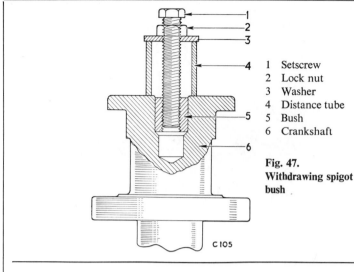

1 Setscrew
2 Lock nut
3 Washer
4 Distance tube
5 Bush
6 Crankshaft

**Fig. 47.
Withdrawing spigot
bush**

Crankshaft Spigot Bush

If it is necessary to renew the spigot bush and its removal is found difficult, cut a $\frac{9}{16}''$ (14·5 mm.) diameter thread in the bush and, using a distance tube and plain washer, withdraw the bush, as shown.

Drive a new spigot bush into the crankshaft bore.

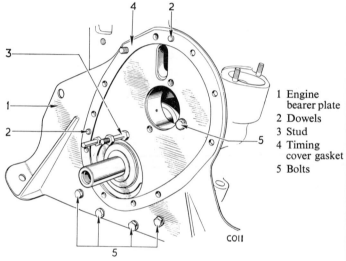

1 Engine
  bearer plate
2 Dowels
3 Stud
4 Timing
  cover gasket
5 Bolts

Fig. 48.   Front bearer plate attachments

Engine Bearer Plate

Using a straight edge, check the face of the bearer plate for flatness, and correct any irregularities.

Locate the gasket and bearer plate (1) on two dowels (2) and secure with five bolts (5), stud (3) and spring washers, as shown on Fig. 48.

Oil Sump

Using a straight edge, check the sump flanges for distortion and rectify as necessary.

When fitting the oil sump, note that a long bolt is used to secure the breather pipe bracket and two short bolts are fitted to the front sealing block.

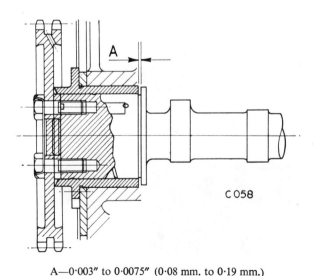

A—0·003″ to 0·0075″ (0·08 mm. to 0·19 mm.)

Fig. 49.   Camshaft end-float

Camshaft

End Float

Assemble the camshaft front bearing to the camshaft and temporarily attach the camshaft sprocket.

Measure the end float of the front bearing on the camshaft journal as shown on Fig. 49.   End float should be 0·003″ to 0·0075″ (0·08 mm.- 0·19 mm.).

Installation

Lubricate the camshaft bearings and insert the camshaft into the cylinder block.   Fit the front camshaft bearing and secure it with two bolts and spring washers.

Tappets

Lubricate each tappet and insert it into the cylinder block, making sure that it rotates freely.

Cylinder Head Assembly

Examination

Remove carbon from the cylinder head and examine the valve seats for scores, burns and wear.

Inspect the valve springs for cracks or distortion and check the fitted load. Check the cylinder head welch plug for evidence of leakage and, renew it if necessary.

Valve Guides

Check valve guide wear by inserting a new valve, lifting it ⅛″ (3·2 mm.) from its seat and rocking it sideways. Movement of the valve head across its seat must not exceed 0·020″ (0·5 mm.). If required, renew the guide by using Churchill Tool No. S.60A-2.

Valve guide protrusion above top face of the cylinder head — 0·78″ (19·84 mm.).

Valve Seats

When re-cutting the valve seats, ensure that the pilot of the cutter is a close fit in the valve guide. Should it be necessary to use a 15° cutter for reducing the seat width, do not exceed dimension 'B'.

Valve seat angle — 45°.

Valve Seat Inserts

When the original valve seat cannot be rectified by re-cutting, use Churchill Tool No. 6056 with adaptors to bore out the old seats.

If both inlet and exhaust seat inserts are required, bore out the inlet seat recess first, fit the insert and then bore the exhaust recess, cutting into the edge of the inlet insert.

Remove all swarf from the cylinder head and, drive the insert squarely into its bore. Secure it by peening the edges of the combustion chamber.

Cut a new seat on each valve insert as described under "Valve Seats".

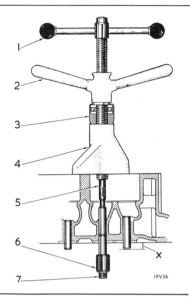

1 Tommy bar
2 Wing nut
3 Bearing assembly
4 Tool body
5 Centre spindle
6 Distance piece
7 Knurled nut
X 0·78″ (19·84 mm.)

Fig. 50. Fitting new valve guides

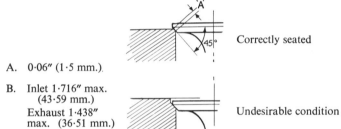

A. 0·06″ (1·5 mm.)

B. Inlet 1·716″ max. (43·59 mm.)
   Exhaust 1·438″ max. (36·51 mm.)

C. 0·10″ max. (2·5 mm.)

Correctly seated

Undesirable condition

Method of rectification

Fig. 51. Valve seat conditions

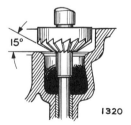

Fig. 52. Using a 15° cutter to remove valve seat "steps"

1 0·25″—0·253″ (6·35—6·43 mm.)

2 0·044″ × 89° included (1·12 mm. × 89° included)

3 1·717″—1·716″ (43·61—43·59 mm.)

4 1·439″—1·438″ (36·53—36·51 mm.)

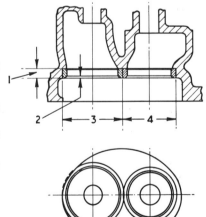

Fig. 53. Valve seat insert dimensions

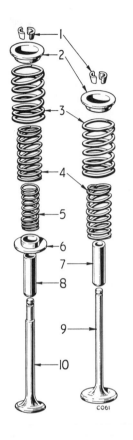

1 Split collets
2 Upper collars
3 Outer valve springs
4 Inner valve springs
5 Auxiliary valve spring
6 Lower collars
7 Inlet valve guide
8 Exhaust valve guide
9 Inlet valve
10 Exhaust valve

Fig. 55.　Valve details

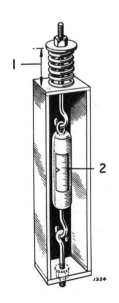

1 Fitted length
2 Fitted load

**Fig. 57.　Using spring balance
to check valve springs**

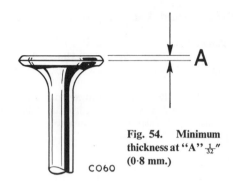

**Fig. 54.　Minimum
thickness at "A" $\frac{1}{32}$"
(0·8 mm.)**

Valves

Check valve stems for wear and distortion. Examine the condition of each valve face and re-face, or renew the valve as required. Remove the minimum necessary to clean up the face. Reject valve if its head thickness is less than $\frac{1}{32}$" (0·8 mm.).

Valve Seat Grinding

Grind the valves into their respective seatings in the cylinder head.

Test each seating by lightly smearing the valve face with engineer's marking blue. Insert the valve into its seating and rotate it not more than $\frac{1}{8}$" (3 mm.) in each direction. A complete circle should appear on the valve seating, indicating satisfactory seating.

Valve Springs

If a spring testing machine is not available, use a spring balance as shown on Fig. 57 to check the valve springs. Valve spring data is given on page 1·103.

Assembly

Remove all trace of grinding paste, lubricate the valve stems and fit them to the guides. Assemble the valve springs, collars and split collets as shown on Fig. 55. Ensure that closed coils of the valve springs are nearest the cylinder head.

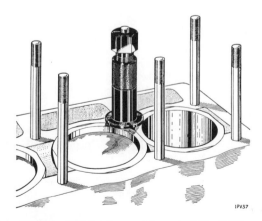

Fig. 56.　Cylinder liner retainers, tool No. S.138

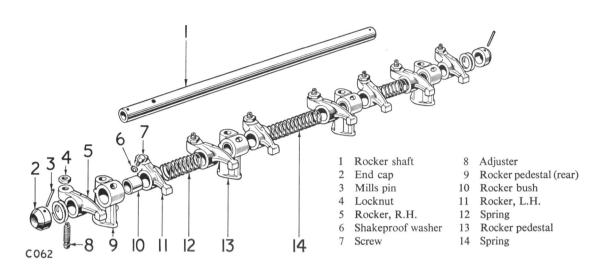

1	Rocker shaft	8	Adjuster
2	End cap	9	Rocker pedestal (rear)
3	Mills pin	10	Rocker bush
4	Locknut	11	Rocker, L.H.
5	Rocker, R.H.	12	Spring
6	Shakeproof washer	13	Rocker pedestal
7	Screw	14	Spring

Fig. 58. Rocker shaft details

Cylinder Head Re-assembly

Remove the cylinder liner retainers S.138, coat a new cylinder head gasket with jointing compound and fit this over the cylinder head studs.

Lower the cylinder head onto the block, and fit the lifting eye, plain washers and nuts. Tighten the nuts in the order shown in Fig. 59.

Insert the eight push rods, ensuring that their lower ends engage correctly in the tappets.

Lubricate and assemble the components onto the rocker shaft as shown on Fig. 58. Note that each pair of rockers are offset and that a shouldered screw and shakeproof washer are used to locate the rear pedestal on the shaft. Slacken off the locknuts (4) and screw in the adjusters (8) to avoid bending the pushrods. Lower the rocker shaft assembly over the four studs simultaneously locating the rocker adjusters in the push rod cups.

Fit and progressively tighten the four rocker shaft nuts.

Rocker Clearance

Check and if necessary adjust the rocker clearances when the tappet is resting on the back of the cam. To obtain this position, turn the camshaft until number one push rod has reached its highest point, then turn a further full revolution to ensure that the push rod is fully down and the tappet is resting on the back of the cam.

If adjustment is necessary, slacken off the locknut and turn the adjusting screw until the correct clearance is obtained. (Fig. 60).

Tighten the locknut and re-check the clearance. Treat each rocker similarly.

Rocker clearances 0·01″ (0·25 mm.) cold.

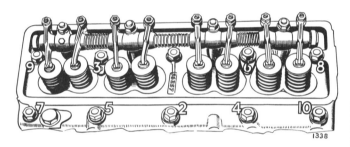

Fig. 59. Cylinder head nut tightening sequence

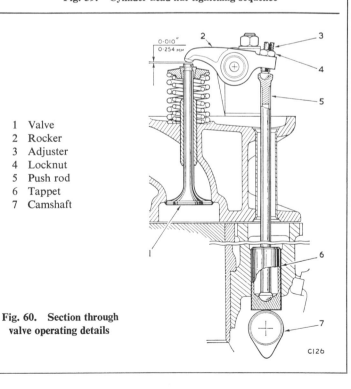

1	Valve
2	Rocker
3	Adjuster
4	Locknut
5	Push rod
6	Tappet
7	Camshaft

Fig. 60. Section through valve operating details

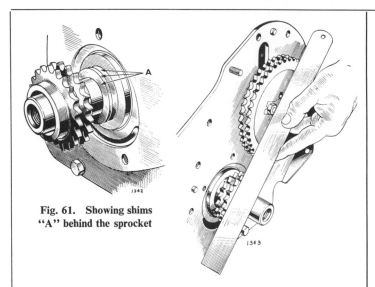

Fig. 61.   Showing shims "A" behind the sprocket

Fig. 62.   Checking sprocket alignment

Alignment of Timing Sprockets

Timing sprocket alignment is controlled by shims interposed between the rear face of the crankshaft sprocket and a shoulder on the crankshaft.

To align the sprockets, temporarily fit the camshaft sprocket and check the alignment by placing a straight edge across both sprockets. Remove or fit shims as required.

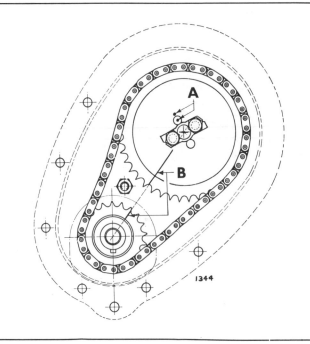

Valve Timing with Marked Sprockets

If the original sprockets are being refitted, set the valve timing by utilizing the timing marks on the sprockets as shown on Fig. 63.

A.   Punch marks
B.   Scribed lines

Fig. 63.   Relative position of timing marks when No. 1 piston is at T.D.C. (compression stroke)

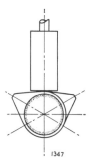

Fig. 64.   Position of cams at the point of balance

Valve Timing with Unmarked Sprockets

Temporarily attach the camshaft sprocket and turn the camshaft until number one push-rod has reached its highest point.   In this position, adjust number eight rocker clearance to ·040″ (1 mm.).

Repeat the procedure with number two push-rod and adjust number seven rocker until its clearance is identical to that of number eight rocker.

Again turn the camshaft until numbers seven and eight valves have reached the point of balance, that is, where one valve is about to open and the other about to close. Fig. 64 illustrates the position of the cams at this point.

Move the camshaft slowly to a point where the clearances between the rockers and valve stems are exactly equal, this is the point of balance.

Turn the crankshaft to bring numbers one and four pistons to T.D.C.

Fitting Timing Chain

Exercising the greatest care, remove the timing sprocket without disturbing the camshaft. Encircle both sprockets with the timing chain and offer up the camshaft sprocket to the camshaft. Manoeuvre the sprocket by slipping a link at a time or by reversing the sprocket until a pair of holes exactly coincide with those of the camshaft.

NOTE : The camshaft timing sprocket is provided with four holes which are equally spaced but offset from a tooth centre. Half tooth adjustment is obtained by rotating the sprocket 90 degrees from its original position.

A quarter tooth adjustment may be obtained by turning the sprocket "back to front". By rotating it 90 degrees in this reversed position, three-quarters of a tooth variation is obtained.

After securing the sprocket, re-check the timing to ensure that the camshaft has not been disturbed during this operation. With number one piston at T.D.C., numbers seven and eight rocker clearances should be identical.

Adjust the rocker clearances to 0·010″ (0·254 mm.).

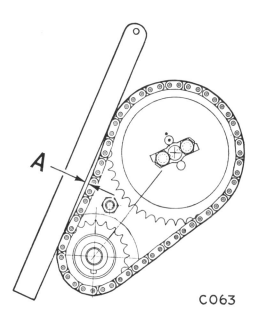

Fig. 65. Checking the timing chain for wear. Dimension "A" should not exceed 0·4″ (10 mm.)

VALVE TIMING

Inlet opens 17° B.T.D.C.

Inlet closes 57° A.B.D.C.

Exhaust opens 57° B.B.D.C.

Exhaust closes 17° A.T.D.C.

Inlet and exhaust cam period 127° at 0·0093″ (0·236 mm.) tappet clearance

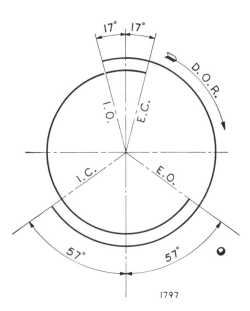

Fig. 66. Valve timing. (Theoretical reference only)

Fig. 67.   A small hole in the fan pulley is aligned with a pointer when No. 1 piston is at T.D.C.

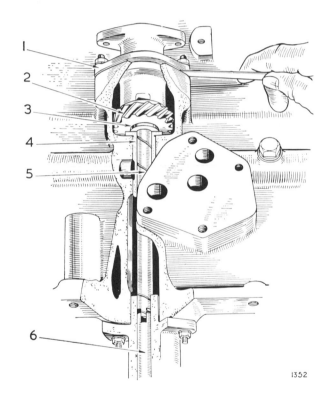

1   Distributor pedestal
2   Distributor drive gear
3   0·5″ (12·7 mm.) I.D. washer
4   Oil pump drive shaft bush
5   Oil pump drive shaft
6   Oil pump rotor shaft

Fig. 68.   Measuring distributor drive gear end float

Timing Cover (Figs. 1 and 4)

Renew a worn or damaged oil seal.

Remove a worn tensioner by opening the blade sufficiently to spring it over the pin.   Fit a new blade by reversing this procedure.

Fit a fibre washer (62) to the extended centre attachment stud (63).   Position the oil thrower (139), dished face outwards, adjacent to the sprocket on the crankshaft and insert a Woodruff key (134) into the keyway.

Fit a new gasket (85) on the dowels and stud. Compress the chain tensioner (90) and fit the timing cover (84), releasing the tensioner when it engages the edge of the cover.   Secure the timing cover with the bolts (83).

Fan Pulley Assembly

Assemble the hub (142) and extension (145) to the pulley (141), placing the hub keyway 180° away from the small T.D.C. indicator in the pulley flange.   (See Fig. 67).

Fit the shouldered rubber bushes (146) to the fan, (four front and four rear) and insert a distance sleeve (147) through each pair of bushes. Assemble the fan to the extension.

NOTE :   A $\frac{1}{16}$″ (1·6 mm.) diameter hole is drilled through the balancer (152), plate (151), fan (148) and extension (145); these components are correctly positioned when the shank of a $\frac{1}{16}$″ (1·6 mm.) drill can be pushed through the aligned holes.

Fit the fan pulley assembly to the crankshaft and secure it with the dog bolt (143).   When fully tightened, the position of the "starter dogs" should be equivalent to "ten minutes to four" (No. 1 piston at T.D.C.).   Adjust if necessary by altering the thickness of shims between the extension and dog bolt.

Rocker Cover

Apply jointing compound to the cover flange face and fit a new cork gasket.   Leave to dry on a flat surface with a weight on top of the cover. Fit the rocker cover to the cylinder head and secure it, using a fibre washer, plain washer and nyloc nut on each attachment stud.

Distributor Drive Gear End Float (Fig. 68)

Determine the requisite amount of packing under the distributor pedestal to give 0·003″ to 0·007″ (0·076 to 0·178 mm.) distributor drive gear end float by the following procedure :-

Insert the oil pump drive shaft (5) through the bush (4) and rotate the shaft to engage its driving tongue with the oil pump driving slot. Measure the thickness of a plain washer having an internal diameter of $\frac{1}{2}$″ (12·7 mm.).   Slide the washer (3) and gear (2) over the shaft and fit the distributor pedestal.

Measure the gap between the pedestal and cylinder block as shown.   Subtract this dimension from the washer thickness to determine the end float of the gear.

Example 1

If the washer thickness is 0·062″ 1·57 mm.
and the width of the gap is 0·060″ 1·52 mm.

Then the gear float
will be + 0·002″ 0·05 mm.
The float of 0·002″ (0·0508 mm.) is insufficient and requires packing of 0·003″ (0·08 mm.) thickness to produce an end float of 0·005″ (0·12 mm.) (mean tolerance).

Example 2

Thickness of washer 0·062″ 1·57 mm.
Width of gaps 0·065″ 1·65 mm.

Gear interference 0·003″ 0·08 mm.

In this example, the interference of 0·003″ (0·08 mm.) requires packing of 0·008″ thickness (0·2 mm.) to give an end float of 0·005″ (0·12 mm.).

Remove the pedestal, gear and drive shaft, and withdraw the ½″ I.D. washer from the shaft.

To Position Timing Gear

Position the crankshaft at T.D.C. with No. 1 piston on the compression stroke.

Fit the Woodruff key to the oil pump drive shaft and lower the shaft into the bush, engaging the driving tongue with the oil pump driving slot. Rotate the shaft so that the key is pointing outwards at right angles to the cylinder block.

Lower the distributor drive gear onto the shaft, allowing it to turn as it meshes with the camshaft gear.

With the gear resting on the bush, the distributor drive slots must be in the position shown on Fig. 69.

Fit the paper packing washers and secure the distributor pedestal.

Distributor Timing

Adjust the distributor points to 0·015″ (0·4 mm.). Secure the clamp plate to the pedestal and lower the distributor into the pedestal, engaging its driving dog with the slot of the gear. With the crankshaft at T.D.C. and firing on No. 1 cylinder, the rotor arm must be positioned as shown in Fig. 70.

Set the vernier adjustment (2) in the centre of its scale and adjust the distributor in a clockwise direction until the C.B. points are commencing to open. Tighten the clamp bolt (1) and rotate the screw (4) until one extra division appears on the scale (2). One division is equal to 4° crankshaft angle.

NOTE : These settings are nominal and should be adjusted to give the best road test performance.

Distributor rotation — anti-clockwise.
Firing order — 1, 3, 4, 2.

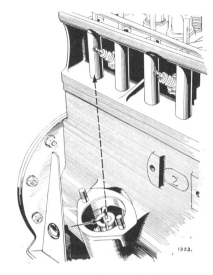

Fig. 69. Driving slot aligned with No. 1 push rod tube when No. 1 piston is at T.D.C. compression stroke. Note the offset shown arrowed

1 Clamp bolt
2 Adjusting scale
3 Rotor arm
4 Thumb-screw

Fig. 70. Ignition distributor

Fig. 71. H.T. Cables

| Correct grade | Too hot running | Too cool running | Mixture too rich | Worn out plug |

Fig. 72. Guide to sparking plug conditions

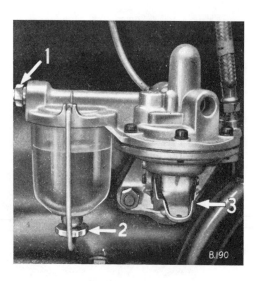

Fig. 73. Fuel pump

Fig. 74. Water pump

Sparking Plugs

The life of spark plugs and the periods at which they should be cleaned varies with the condition of the engine and the work it performs. As a general recommendation, adjust electrode gaps to 0·025″ (·635 mm.) every 3,000 miles, and renew plugs every 12,000 miles.

Fig. 72 provides an easy guide for identifying the various plug conditions.

Smear the threads of new plugs with graphite grease to prevent the possibility of seizure and damage to the cylinder head.

Coil and H.T. Cables

Secure the coil to the cylinder block and connect the H.T. cables as shown on Fig. 71. These cables are of special construction and must under no circumstances be replaced by tinned copper cored cables.

FUEL PUMP
Installation

Service the fuel pump as described on page 1·301 and assemble it to the engine. The rear nut is also used to secure the oil pressure pipe clip.

Water Pump

Service the water pump as described on page 1·204 and assemble it to the engine as shown on Fig. 74.

Generator

Service the generator as described in Group 6, assemble it to the engine as shown, and adjust the fan belt as described on page 0·208.

Fig. 75. Generator attachments

Manifolds

Assemble the inlet and exhaust manifolds and attach them to the engine. The details are shown on page 1·401.

Carburettors

To avoid damage, fit the carburettors after the engine has been installed in the chassis. Connect the controls, pipes and attach the air cleaners (Fig. 76). Service the carburettors as described on page 1·303.

Fig. 76. Manifolds and carburettor assembly

Oil Filter

Renew the element as described on page 0·208 and secure the unit to the crankcase. Connect the oil pressure pipe as shown on Fig. 77.

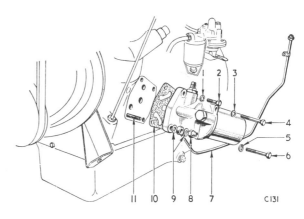

1	Spring washer	7	Oil pressure pipe
2	Bolt	8	Cap nut
3	Spring washer	9	Copper washers
4	Bolt	10	Gasket
5	Spring washer	11	Stud
6	Bolt		

Fig. 77. Oil pressure pipe attachment

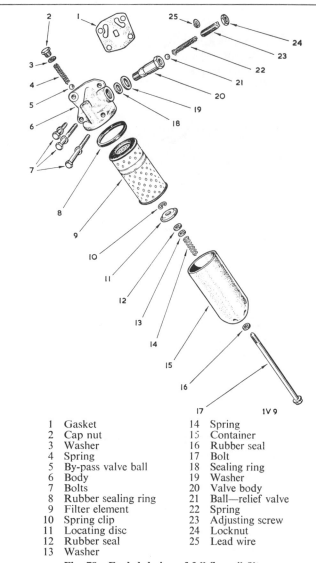

1	Gasket	14	Spring
2	Cap nut	15	Container
3	Washer	16	Rubber seal
4	Spring	17	Bolt
5	By-pass valve ball	18	Sealing ring
6	Body	19	Washer
7	Bolts	20	Valve body
8	Rubber sealing ring	21	Ball—relief valve
9	Filter element	22	Spring
10	Spring clip	23	Adjusting screw
11	Locating disc	24	Locknut
12	Rubber seal	25	Lead wire
13	Washer		

Fig. 78. Exploded view of full-flow oil filter

Pressure Relief Valve Adjustment

To test relief valve operation, proceed as follows :—

1. Run the engine until normal operating temperature is attained.
2. Slowly increase the engine speed to approximately 2,000 r.p.m. and observe the oil pressure gauge. Pressure should rise steadily to 75 lb./sq. in. (5·273 kg./cm.^{2}) and at 2,000 r.p.m. fall to 70 lb./sq. in. (4·921 kg./cm.^{2}).
3. If necessary, adjust the relief valve pressure by slackening the locknut (24). Rotate the screw (23) clockwise to increase the relief valve opening pressure and counter clockwise to reduce it. When correct adjustment is obtained, tighten the nut (24).

Fig. 79. Closed circuit breathing

Closed Circuit Breathing

A closed circuit breathing system has been introduced to prevent fumes entering the atmosphere from crankcase blow-by. A pipe from the air cleaners to the rocker cover draws these fumes from the crankcase up the push-rod tubes, and passes them to the carburettor air intake where they are then returned by incoming air for re-combustion.

A simple flame-trap device is incorporated in the system as a safeguard against back-fire.

Modified Rocker Cover Assembly, Part Number 306527, and Oil Filler Cap, Part Number 138176, are also embodied.

COOLING SYSTEM

Description

Circulation of water in the pressurized cooling system shown on Fig. 1, is assisted by a belt driven water pump of the impeller type and controlled by a thermostat.

Filling

Close the drain taps (1 and 2) and set the heater control in the hot position.

Remove the filler cap (3), fill with clean soft water, and refit the cap. Warm up the engine and replenish the water level if necessary.

Draining

Remove the filler cap, set the heater control in the hot position and open the radiator and cylinder block drain taps.

Flushing

Periodically flush the cooling system, using a proprietary flushing compound and follow the instructions supplied.

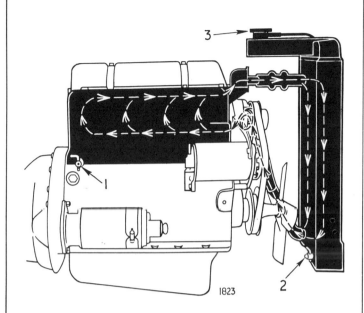

Fig. 1. Water circulation

Pressure Testing

Use an A.C. pressure tester to test the cooling system as follows:

With the engine warm, remove the filler cap, and top up the water level. Using an adaptor, fit the pressure tester to the filler neck and pump up to a pressure of 4 lb. sq. in. (0·281 kg/cm²).

The cooling system should maintain this pressure for 10 seconds.

A more severe test may be applied by following the above procedure with the engine running. Absence of external leaks accompanied by pressure fluctuations usually indicates a leaking cylinder head gasket.

Filler Cap

Use an A.C. pressure tester to check the operation of the filler pressure cap as follows:

1. Rinse the cap in water to remove sediment and fit the cap to the tester whilst wet, as shown on Fig. 2.
2. Pump up the pressure until the gauge pointer stops rising.
3. Reject the cap if it will not register and maintain 4 lb. sq. in. (0·281 kg./cm²) for 10 seconds without additional pumping.

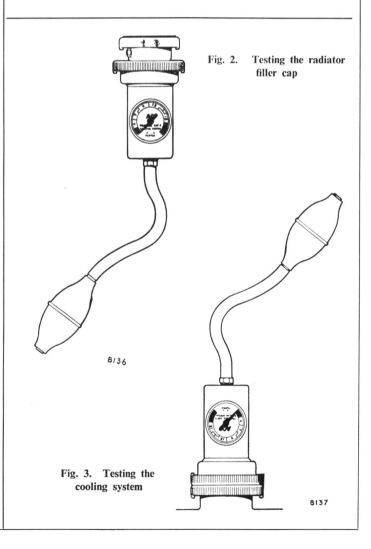

Fig. 2. Testing the radiator filler cap

Fig. 3. Testing the cooling system

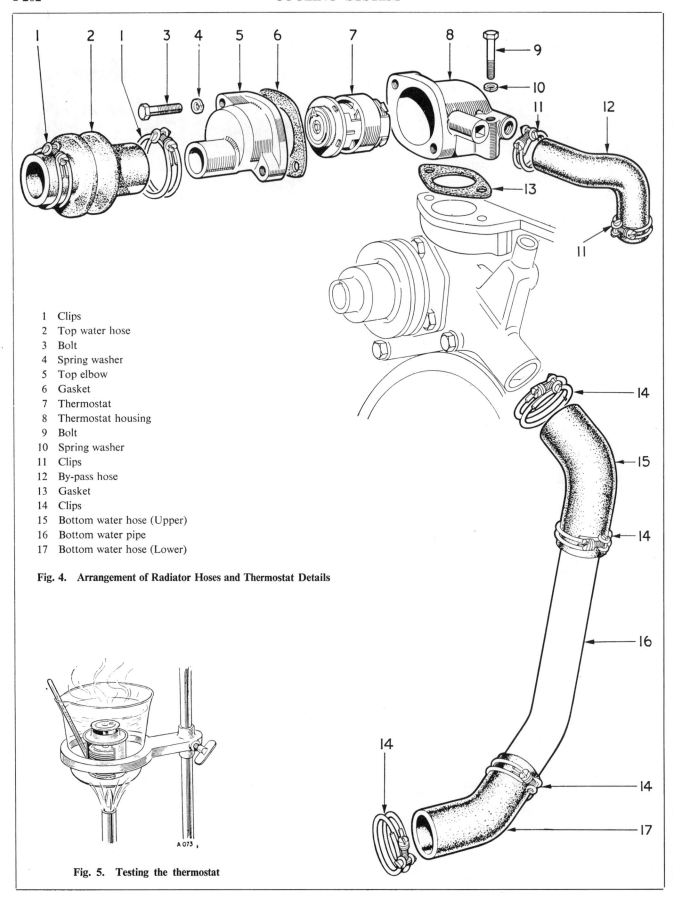

1 Clips
2 Top water hose
3 Bolt
4 Spring washer
5 Top elbow
6 Gasket
7 Thermostat
8 Thermostat housing
9 Bolt
10 Spring washer
11 Clips
12 By-pass hose
13 Gasket
14 Clips
15 Bottom water hose (Upper)
16 Bottom water pipe
17 Bottom water hose (Lower)

Fig. 4.   Arrangement of Radiator Hoses and Thermostat Details

A 073

Fig. 5.   Testing the thermostat

Anti-freeze Mixtures

To protect the cooling system during frosty weather, use an inhibited Glycol base anti-freeze solution. Because of the searching effect of these solutions, check the system for leaks before adding the anti-freeze.

Approved brands of anti-freeze are given on page 16. For quantities of anti-freeze mixtures required to safeguard the system at specific temperatures, consult the manufacturer's recommendations.

It is recommended that fresh anti-freeze is used each year, since the inhibitor becomes exhausted and the components in contact with the cooling water may corrode. When topping up the coolant, use a mixture of anti-freeze and water.

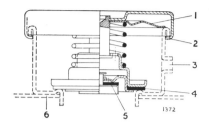

1 Spring friction plate	4 Pressure valve seal
2 Retaining lugs	5 Vacuum valve seal
3 Pressure release pipe	6 Header tank

Fig. 6. Section through radiator filler cap

Thermostat

To remove the thermostat, drain the cooling system, detach the bolts (3) (Fig. 4), spring washers (4) and swing the outlet cover (5) sideways on the flexible hose (2). Detach the gasket (6) and remove the thermostat (7) from its housing (8).

Testing the Thermostat

Test the thermostat by heating it in water together with a thermometer as shown on Fig. 5. Note the temperatures at which the valve starts to open.

Opening temperatures - 70°C. (158° F.).
Maximum Valve Lift - 0·281″/0·407″
(7·137/10·337 mm.).

To Refit

Reverse the removal procedure.

Radiator

Removal

Drain the cooling system and remove or disconnect items in the order shown on Fig. 7.

Lift out the radiator.

Refitting

Reverse the sequence of operations shown on Fig. 7.

NOTE: Composition packings are fitted between the lower radiator attachment points and the chassis brackets.

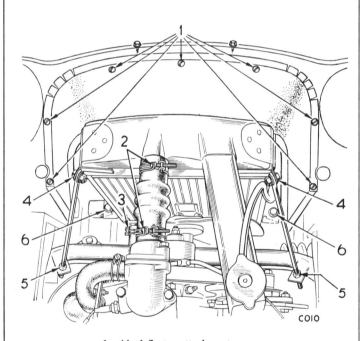

1 Air deflector attachment screws
2 Top hose clips
3 Bottom hose clips
4 Radiator stay attachment
5 Adjusting nuts
6 Radiator attachments

Fig. 7. Radiator and air deflector attachments

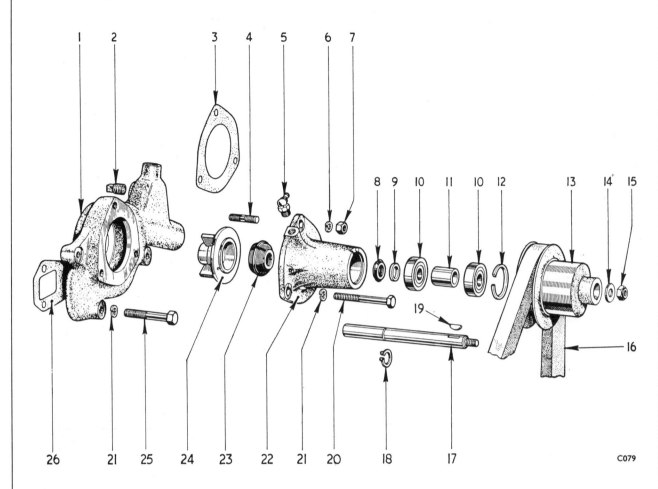

Fig. 8. Arrangement of Water Pump Details

1	Body	10	Ball race	19	Woodruff key
2	Heater return pipe blanking plug	11	Distance tube	20	Bolt
3	Gasket	12	Circlip	21	Spring washer
4	Stud	13	Pulley	22	Bearing housing
5	Grease nipple	14	Plain washer	23	Seal and bellows assembly
6	Spring washer	15	Nyloc nut	24	Impeller
7	Nut	16	Driving belt	25	Bolt
8	Spinner	17	Shaft	26	Gasket
9	Distance washer	18	Circlip		

Water Pump (Fig. 8)

Removal

1. Disconnect the battery and drain the cooling system.
2. Slacken the generator attachments, swing the generator inwards and remove the driving belt.
3. Disconnect the lower radiator hose (15), Fig. 4, and by-pass hose (12).

4. Remove three bolts (25) and spring washers and detach the water pump from the cylinder block.

To remove the bearing housing only, remove nut (7), spring washer (6) and unscrew two bolts (20). Remove the housing (22) and gasket (3) from the pump body (1).

To Refit

Reverse the removal procedure and tension the driving belt. (See page 0·208).

Bearing Housing Assembly (Fig. 8)

To Dismantle
1. Remove items (14) and (15) and detach the pulley (13).
2. Use Churchill Tool No. FTS.127 with Press S.4221.A to remove the impeller (24) and seal assembly (23). (See Fig. 9).
3. Remove the circlip (12) and drift out shaft and ball race assembly.
4. Remove the spinner (8), circlip (18), washer (9) and Woodruff key (19) from the shaft (17), and press off items (10) and (11).

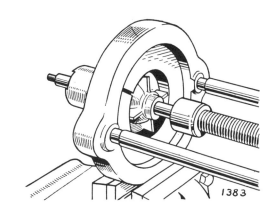

Fig. 9.   Removing impeller from pump spindle

Re-Cutting the Sealing Gland Face (Fig. 10)
Use Churchill Tool No. S.126 as follows :
1. Insert the pilot of the tool from the gland side of the housing.
2. Fit the bush (small diameter leading), tool bearing and knurled nut on the protruding pilot.
3. Turn the knurled nut to bring the cutters into contact with the seal face. Rotate the tommy bar and simultaneously tighten the knurled nut to maintain a light cut until the gland face is free from score lines. Periodically remove and clean the tool whilst carrying out the cutting operation. The depth of the gland face from the housing mounting face must not exceed 0·3″ (7·6 mm.).

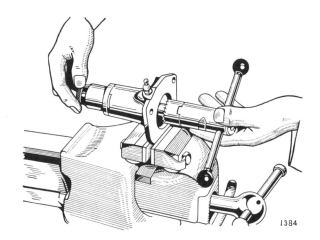

Fig. 10.   Re-cutting sealing gland face

Re-Assembly (Fig. 8)
1. Fit items (9), (18) and (8) to the shaft (17). Pack the ball races (10) with grease and press them onto the shaft with their sealed faces outwards and the spacer (11) between them.
2. Using a tubular drift, drive the bearings with the shaft (17) into the housing and secure with the circlip (12). Press the seal assembly (23) into the impeller (24).
3. Using an 0·085″ (2·159 mm.) thick spacer, press the impeller (24) onto the shaft (17) as shown on Fig. 11. Solder the impeller to the end of the shaft to prevent leakage.
4. Fit the Woodruff key (9) and pulley (13) to the shaft (17), securing with a Nyloc nut (15) and plain washer (14).

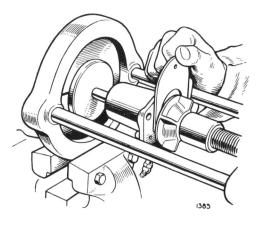

Fig. 11.   Utilising gauge to obtain correct clearance between impeller and housing face

Fig. 12. Modified Radiator

Radiator Type (TR.4)

The previous type radiator having a remote header tank incorporating a filler cap has been superseded by a radiator having an integral header tank incorporating the filler cap.

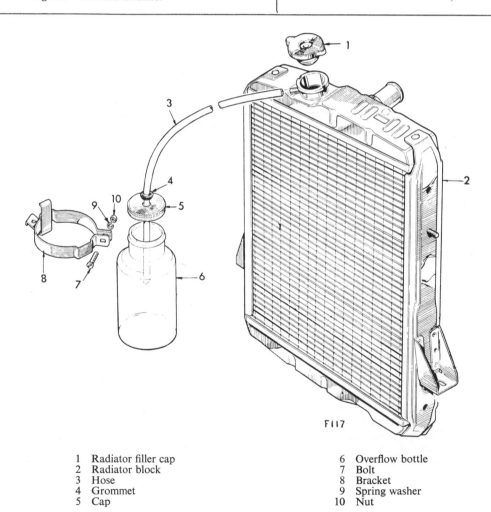

1	Radiator filler cap	6	Overflow bottle
2	Radiator block	7	Bolt
3	Hose	8	Bracket
4	Grommet	9	Spring washer
5	Cap	10	Nut

Fig. 13. Details of overflow bottle (Sealed cooling system) (TR.4A)

FUEL PUMP

To Clean the Pump Filter

Loosen the thumb nut below the glass sediment bowl. Swing the wire frame to one side and remove the sediment chamber, cork gasket and gauze filter for cleaning.

When re-assembling, renew the cork washer if damaged.

Run the engine and check for leakage.

To Dismantle Fuel Pump

(a) Clean the exterior of the pump and file a mark across both flanges to facilitate re-assembly.

(b) Dismantle in the sequence given on Fig. 2. Re-assemble by reversing the sequence.

(c) To remove the diaphragm assembly (12) first turn it through 90° in an anti-clockwise direction and lift out of engagement with link lever (24).

NOTATION FOR FIG. 2

Ref.
No.   Description
1   Stirrup
2   Glass sediment bowl
3   Cork seal
4   Gauze filter
5   Securing screw
6   Lock washer
7   Upper body
8   Screw for retaining plate
9   Valve retaining plate
10* Inlet and outlet valve assemblies
11   Valve gasket
12   Diaphragm assembly
13   Diaphragm spring
14   Oil seal retainer
15   Oil seal
16   Primer lever
17   Cork washer
18   Primer lever shaft
19   Hand primer spring
20   Circlip
21   Rocker arm pin
22   Washer
23   Rocker arm
24   Link lever
25   Rocker arm spring
26   Lower body

* These valves are identical, but on fitting them to the upper body the spring of the inlet valve is pointing towards the diaphragm and the spring of the outlet valve away from the diaphragm, as shown in the illustration.

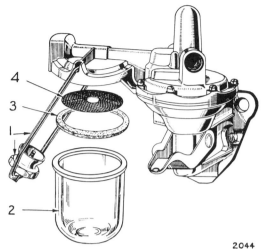

| 1 | Retaining stirrup | 2 | Glass sediment bowl |
| 3 | Cork seal | 4 | Gauze filter |

Fig. 1. Fuel pump

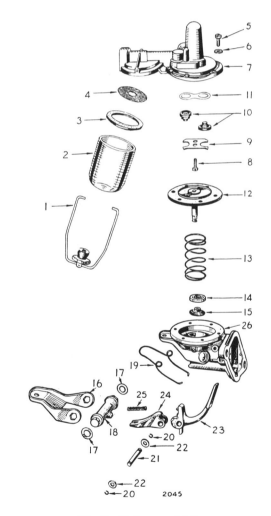

Fig. 2. Fuel pump details

CARBURETTOR DETAILS

CARBURETTORS

Replenishing Dampers

Every 3,000 miles (5,000 km.) remove the dampers and replenish the dashpots with thin engine oil, grade SAE20 (but no thicker than SAE30). The oil level is correct when the damper is approximately ¼″ (6 mm.) above the dashpots when resistance is felt. The function of the damper assembly is to provide the appropriate degree of enrichment for acceleration and starting from cold.

Cleaning Suction Chamber and Piston

At approximate intervals of twelve months, detach the piston unit. Clean the piston and the inside bore of the suction chamber. Re-assemble dry except for a few spots of thin oil on the piston rod.

Replenish the damper reservoir.

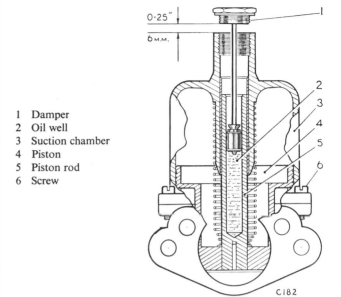

1 Damper
2 Oil well
3 Suction chamber
4 Piston
5 Piston rod
6 Screw

Fig. 4. Replenishing the dampers

Jet and Throttle Interconnection Adjustment

With the choke control fully 'in', the engine warm and idling on a closed throttle, adjust the screw (77) to give a clearance of $\frac{1}{16}$″ (1·5 mm.) between the end of the screw and rocker lever (70).

Always check this adjustment when the throttle stop screw "A" is altered.

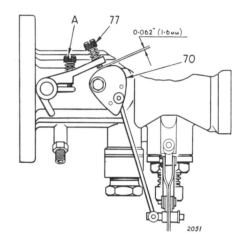

Fig. 5.   Jet and throttle interconnection adjustment

Float-chamber Fuel Level

The level of fuel in the float-chamber is adjusted by setting the fork lever in the float-chamber lid as follows :

1. Disconnect the fuel feed pipe from the float-chamber lid, remove the cap nut (17) and lift the lid from the float-chamber.
2. Invert the lid of the float-chamber and with the shank of the forked lever resting on the needle of the delivery valve, pass a $\frac{7}{16}$″ (11 mm.) diameter gauge between the inside radius of the forked lever and the face of the float-chamber lid as shown.

    If the forked lever does not contact both the needle valve and gauge, bend the lever at the start of the forked section as required, taking care to keep both prongs of the fork level with each other.
3. Re-assemble the carburettor and connect the fuel pipe.

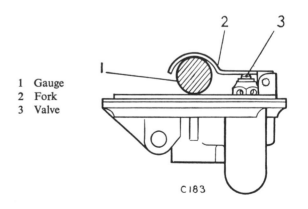

1 Gauge
2 Fork
3 Valve

Fig. 6. Adjusting the float-chamber fuel level

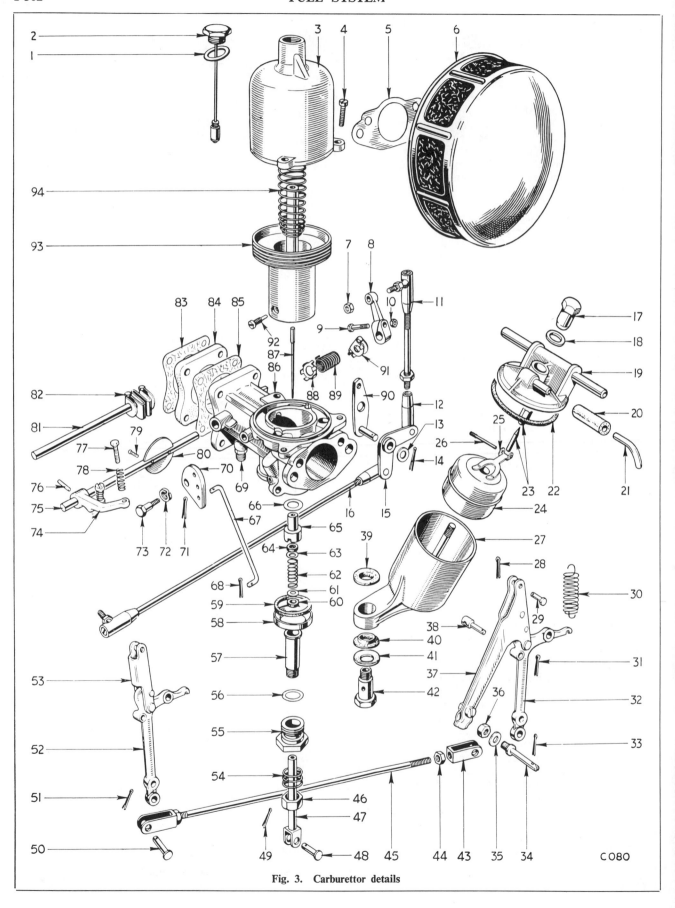

Fig. 3.   Carburettor details

C080

Key to Fig. 3

1	Fibre washer	33	Split pin	64	Cork gland washer
2	Damper assembly	34	Choke cable connector	65	Top half jet bearing
3	Suction chamber	35	Washer	66	Washer
4	Screw	36	Nut	67	Choke/throttle interconnecting link
5	Gasket	37	Jet link and choke cable support	68	Split pin
6	Air cleaner	38	Clevis pin	69	Vacuum union
7	Nut	39	Washer	70	Lever cam
8	Throttle lever	40	Shouldered washer	71	Split pin
9	Pinch bolt	41	Washer	72	Double spring washer
10	Nut	42	Float chamber attachment bolt	73	Shouldered bolt
11	Link rod coupling	43	Fork end	74	Throttle stop
12	Link rod coupling	44	Nut	75	Throttle spindle
13	Plain washer	45	Jet control connecting link	76	Pin
14	Split pin	46	Jet adjusting nut	77	Stop adjusting screw
15	Relay lever	47	Jet head	78	Spring
16	Link rod assembly	48	Clevis pin	79	Throttle butterfly screw
17	Cap nut	49	Split pin	80	Butterfly
18	Washer	50	Clevis pin	81	Throttle connecting rod
19	Front chamber cover	51	Split pin	82	Coupling
20	Fuel pipe coupling	52	Jet lever	83	Gasket
21	Fuel pipe	53	Jet lever link	84	Insulator
22	Joint washer	54	Loading spring	85	Gasket
23	Needle valve	55	Jet locking nut	86	Carburettor body
24	Float	56	Washer	87	Needle
25	Fork	57	Bottom half jet bearing	88	Anchor plate
26	Hinge pin	58	Sealing ring	89	Return spring
27	Float chamber	59	Cork washer	90	Pivot lever
28	Split pin	60	Cork gland washer	91	End clip
29	Clevis pin	61	Copper gland washer	92	Needle locking screw
30	Jet lever return spring	62	Spring between gland washer	93	Piston
31	Split pin	63	Copper gland washer	94	Piston spring
32	Jet lever				

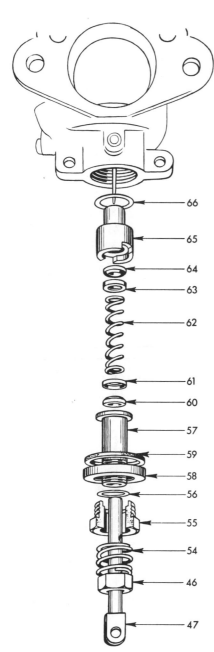

66
65
64
63
62
61
60
57
59
58
56
55
54
46
47

Fig. 7. Carburettor jet details
(The key to annotations is given on Page 1·302)

Jet Gland Replacement (Figs. 3 and 7)

If persistent slow leakage is observed at the base of the jet unit (a mere surface dampness can generally be disregarded) it is probable that the three cork gland washers (59), (60) and (64) require replacement.

To Remove

1. Remove air cleaner (6).
2. Remove return spring (30), pivot pins (48), (50), and swing linkage to one side.
3. Withdraw jet (47), unscrew adjusting nut (46) and remove spring (54).
4. Remove gland nut (55), sealing ring (58), gland washer (59), copper washer (56), jet bearing assembly (57), spring (62) and jet bearing assembly (65).
5. Remove the copper washer (66) and washers (63) and (64) from the jet bearing (65).
6. Remove the washers (60) and (61) from jet bearing (57).

To Replace

Using new cork washers (59), (60), (64), copper washers (56) and (66), and brass washers (61) and (63) proceed as follows :

1. Fit the cork washer (60) and brass washer (61) to the jet bearing (57). Ensure that the concave side of the brass washer contacts the cork washer.
2. Insert the spring (62) into the jet bearing (57).
3. Fit the cork washer (64) and brass washer (63) into the jet bearing (65).
4. Fit the sealing ring (58) and gland washer (59) over the gland nut (55). Ensure that the concave side of the sealing ring contacts the gland washer.
5. Fit the washer (56) to jet bearing (57) and insert jet bearing through the gland nut (55).
6. Fit the washer (66) to the bearing (65) and place the assembly on the spring (62).
7. Insert the jet bearing assembly into the carburettor, leaving the gland nut slack.
8. Centralise the jet as follows :

Jet Centralising

If the suction piston is lifted by hand and released, it should fall freely and hit the inside "jet bridge" with a soft metallic click when the jet adjusting nut (26) (Fig. 8) is screwed to its topmost position.

If a click is audible, only when the jet is in the fully lowered position, the jet should be centralised as follows :

Holding the jet (47) in its upper position, move the jet assembly laterally until the jet is concentric with the needle (87), then tighten gland nut (55). The piston should now fall freely and hit the jet bridge with a soft metallic click.

Withdraw the jet and again lift and release the piston, noting any difference in the sound of impact. If a sharper impact sound results, repeat the centralising operation to achieve identical sounds with and without the jet.

Re-connect the jet lever (52), replenish the dampers and tune the carburettors before replacing the air cleaner.

TUNING CARBURETTORS

Twin carburettor installations cannot be successfully tuned unless the general condition of the engine, ignition and the fuel system is satisfactory.

Tuning procedure is as follows:

1. Warm up the engine, remove air cleaners and disconnect choke cable. Slacken clamping bolts (82) on throttle spindle (81) and detach connecting rod (45). Ensure that the screw (77) is clear of its abutment during subsequent adjustments.

2. With the engine idling at approximately 500 r.p.m., check the hiss of air at carburettor intakes with a piece of tubing approximately 0·3″ (7·5 mm.) bore.

3. Maintaining this idling speed, set both throttle adjusting screws to equalise the level of hiss at the carburettor intakes.
   To reduce hiss, UNSCREW the adjusting screw.

4. When adjustment is satisfactory, re-tighten the throttle spindle clamping bolt and re-check hiss.

5. Check mixture at each carburettor by lifting the piston approximately ⅛″ (3 mm.) with a pen-knife blade.
   If the engine speed increases, the mixture is too rich and the nut (26) (Fig. 8) should be screwed up one flat. If the engine speed decreases unscrew nut (26) one flat.

6. Continue adjustment on each carburettor until, when the piston is lifted, no increase, or a very slight increase followed by a fall in engine speed is noticed. The mixture is then satisfactory and the exhaust note should be regular and even.

7. Re-connect the choke controls and reset the screw (77) to give 0·062″ (1·6 mm.) clearance between the end of the screw and rocker lever (70).

8. Refit air cleaners.

Fig. 8. Checking jet setting

Fig. 9. Relay lever connections

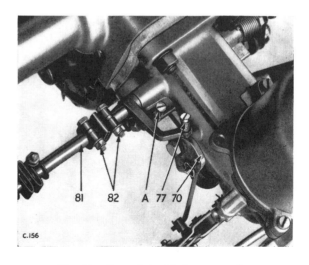

Fig. 10. Jet and throttle interconnection

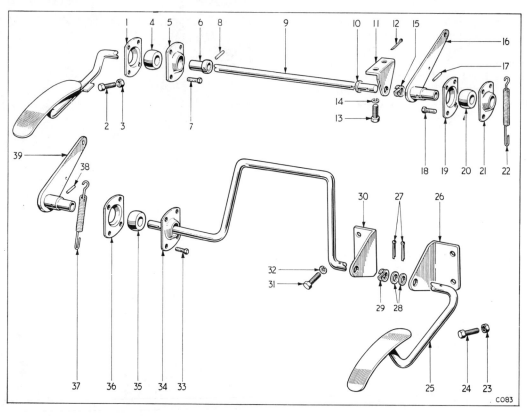

Fig. 11.   Arrangement of accelerator pedal details (L.H. and R.H. drive)

1	Bearing housing (half)	21	Bearing housing (half)
2	Screw (pedal limit stop)	22	Return spring
3	Nut	23	Nut ⎫ Accelerator pedal
4	Self-aligning bearing	24	Setscrew ⎭ limit stop
5	Bearing housing (half)	25	Accelerator pedal shaft
6	Pedal bush	26	Fulcrum bracket (pedal to toe-board)
7	Self-tapping screw (bearing housing attachment)	27	Split pin (locating pedal shaft in fulcrum bracket)
8	Mills pin	28	Plain washer (between split pin and bracket)
9	Cross shaft	29	Double spring washer (pedal shaft)
10	Plain washer	30	Fulcrum bracket (pedal to toe-board)
11	Mounting bracket	31	Setscrew ⎫ Fulcrum bracket
12	Split pin	32	Spring washer ⎭ to bulkhead
13	Setscrew ⎫ Bracket	33	Self-tapping screw (bearing housing attachment)
14	Lock washer ⎭ attachment	34	Bearing housing (half)
15	Spring washer (between lever and bracket)	35	Self-aligning bearing (on pedal shaft)
16	Lever assembly	36	Bearing housing (half)
17	Mills pin (securing lever)	37	Return spring
18	Self-tapping screw (bearing housing attachment)	38	Mills pin (securing lever to pedal shaft)
19	Bearing housing (half)	39	Lever assembly
20	Self-aligning bearing		

Instructions for removing and refitting the following items are given in the Body Section (Group 5) :—

Fuel tank and gauge.   Fuel gauge (facia).

ZENITH-STROMBERG CARBURETTORS
(SERIES 175.CD)

Starting from Cold (Fig. 12)

The mixture is enriched for cold starting when the choke control is pulled. This operates a lever (6) which rotates the starter bar (20) to lift the air valve (18) and needle (29), thus increasing the area of the annulus between needle and jet orifice. Simultaneously, a cam on the lever (6) opens the throttle beyond its normal idle position to provide increased idling speed, according to the setting of the screw (4).

When the motor fires the increased depression will lift the air valve (18) to weaken the initial starting mixture and prevent the engine stalling through over richness.

While the choke remains in action the car may be driven away, but the control knob should be released or pushed in gradually as the engine attains normal working temperature. This will progressively decrease the extent of enrichment and the degree of throttle opening for fast-idle to the point where the screw (4) is out of contact with the cam on the choke lever, and the throttle is permitted to return to the normal idle position as determined by the setting of the throttle stop screw (3).

NOTE: The accelerator pedal should not be depressed when starting from cold.

Normal Running

With the opening of the butterfly throttle, manifold depression is transferred, via a drilling (25) in the air valve, to the chamber (24) which is sealed from the main body by the diaphragm (16).

The pressure difference between chamber (24) and that existing in the bore (26) causes the air valve to lift, thus any increase in engine speed or load will enlarge the effective choke area since the air valve lift is proportional to the weight of air passing the throttle (27). By this means, air velocity and pressure drop across the jet orifice remain approximately constant at all speeds.

As the air valve (18) rises it withdraws a tapered metering needle (29), held in the base of the air valve by the screw (10), from the jet orifice (19) so that fuel flow is increased relative to the greater air flow.

Acceleration

At any point in the throttle range a temporarily richer mixture is needed at the moment of further throttle opening. To provide this, a dashpot and hydraulic damper is arranged inside the hollow guide rod (17) of the air valve.

The rod is filled with S.A.E. 20 oil to within a $\frac{1}{4}''$ of the end of the rod in which the damper (14) operates, when the throttle is opened, the immediate upward motion of the air valve is resisted by the damper during which time the suction or depression at the jet orifice is increased to enrich the mixture.

The downward movement of the air valve (18) is assisted by the coil spring (15).

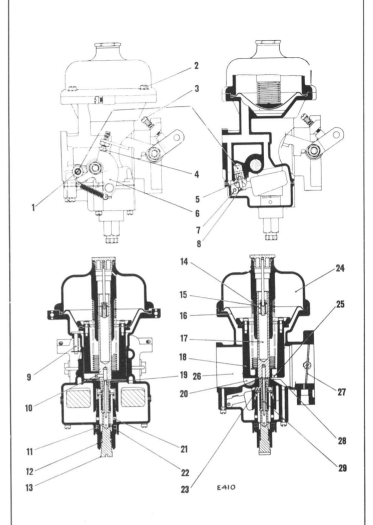

Key to Fig. 12

1	Petrol inlet	16	Diaphragm
2	Screws	17	Guide rod
3	Throttle stop screw	18	Air valve
4	Screw	19	Jet orifice
5	Needle seating	20	Starter bar
6	Lever	21	Inlet hole
7	Float arm	22	Inlet hole
8	Needle	23	Orifice bush
9	Spring-loaded pin	24	Chamber
10	Locking screw	25	Air valve drilling
11	"O" ring	26	Bore
12	Jet assembly	27	Throttle
13	Jet adjusting screw	28	Bridge
14	Damper	29	Metering needle
15	Coil spring		

Fig. 12. Functional diagram

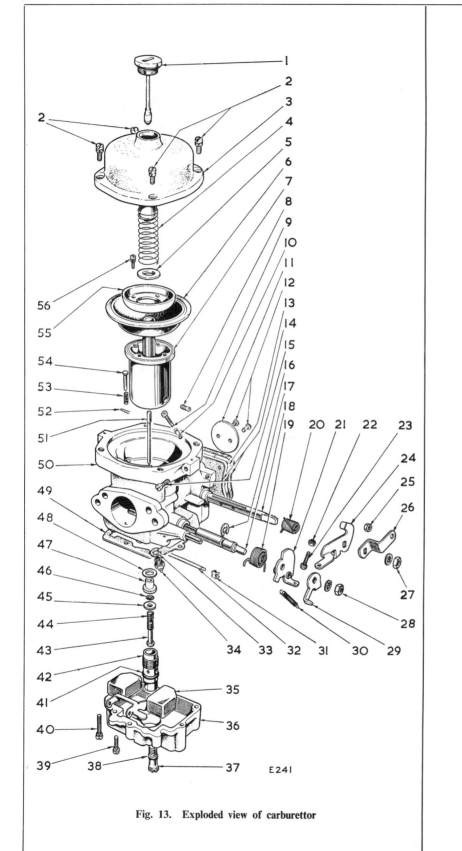

Fig. 13.   Exploded view of carburettor

E241

CARBURETTOR DETAILS

1	Damper
2	Screw
3	Cover
4	Return spring
5	Washer
6	Diaphragm air valve
7	Air valve
8	Locking screw
9	Clamping screw
10	Spring
11	Butterfly
12	Screw
13	Insulating washer
14	Joint
15	Screw
16	Retaining ring
17	Starter bar
18	Spindle
19	Spring
20	Spring
21	Lever
22	Nut
23	Screw
24	Lever
25	Nut
26	Lever
27	Nut
28	Nut
29	Lever
30	Spring
31	Clip
32	Fulcrum pin
33	Washer seating
34	Needle valve
35	Float assembly
36	Float chamber
37	Adjusting screw
38	"O" ring
39	Screw (short)
40	Screw (long)
41	"O" ring
42	Bushing screw
43	Jet
44	Spring
45	Washer
46	"O" ring
47	Jet bush
48	Washer
49	Gasket
50	Body
51	Needle
52	Clip
53	Spring
54	Pin
55	Retaining ring
56	Screw

DISMANTLING
CARBURETTOR ASSEMBLY

First clean off surfaces of carburettor with paraffin. Remove all connecting linkage and pipes from carburettor.

Unscrew damper (1) from suction chamber. Remove four screws from cover (3) and take cover from main body (50). Remove return spring (4), washer (5), diaphragm (6), retaining ring (55) and air valve (7).

If it is necessary to renew the diaphragm, remove four screws (56) securing diaphragm to air valve.

Take out adjusting screw (37), (a coin will suffice), and bushing screw (42) from base of carburettor. Remove eight screws (39) and (40), three short and five long (float chamber to main body), and take off base unit of carburettor (float chamber (36), together with float gasket (49).

Take out jet (43) and spring (44), washer (45), "O" ring (46). Remove needle valve (34).

Examine the butterfly assembly for wear.

Clean and check all dismantled components, and renew unserviceable items.

Re-assembly

Re-assemble the carburettor by reversing the above procedure.

Float Chamber Fuel Level (Fig. 15)

To check the float level, remove the carburettor from the engine and remove the float chamber. Invert the carburettor. Check that the highest point of the float, when the needle is against its seating, is 0·73″ (18·5 mm.) above the face of the main body. Reset the level by carefully bending the tag which contacts the end of the needle. The addition of a thin fibre washer under the needle valve seat will effectively lower the fuel level.

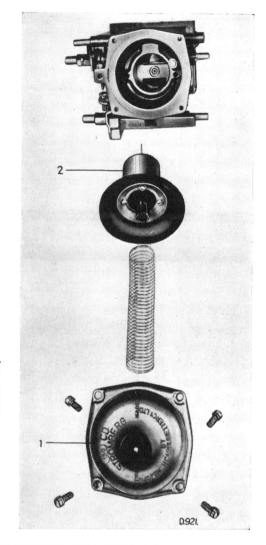

**Fig. 14.
Top view of carburettor with cover (1) and air valve assembly (2) removed**

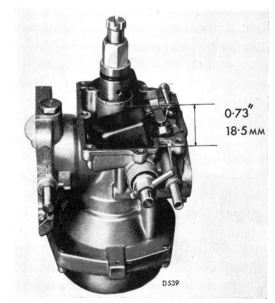

0·73″
18·5 MM

**Fig. 15.
Checking float chamber**

Fig. 16. Diaphragm location point

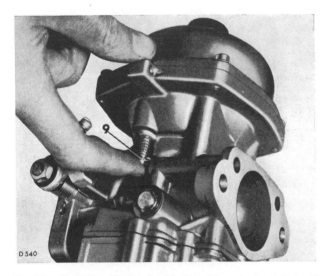

Fig. 17. Checking air valve for freedom with spring-loaded pin (9)

Fig. 18. Jet assembly (12) and adjusting screw (13)

Jet Centralisation

Efficient operation of the carburettor depends upon a freely moving air valve and a correctly centred needle in the jet orifice. The air valve may be checked for freedom by lifting the valve with the spring-loaded pin (9) (Fig. 17). A valve failing to fall freely indicates a sticking valve, or an off-centred jet, and/or the needle (29) fouling the jet orifice. Rectify by removing and cleaning the valve and bore in paraffin, or by re-centralising the needle in the jet.

NOTE: When required, the jet needle must be renewed by one bearing the same code number. The shoulder of the needle must be fitted flush with the lower face of the air valve.

Procedure (Fig. 12)

1. Lift the air valve (18) and fully tighten the jet assembly (12).

2. Screw up the orifice adjuster until the top of the orifice (19) is just above the bridge (28).

3. Slacken off the jet assembly (12) approximately one half turn to release the orifice bush (23).

4. Allow the air valve (18) to fall; the needle will then enter the orifice and thus centralise it.

5. Slowly tighten the assembly (12), checking frequently that the needle remains free in the orifice. Check by raising the air valve approximately $\frac{1}{4}''$ (6·35 mm.) and allowing it to fall freely. The piston should then stop firmly on the bridge.

6. Reset the engine idling.

Adjustment

Setting the Idle (Fig. 19)

Two adjustment screws are used to regulate the idle speed and mixture. The throttle stop screw (3) controls the speed, and the jet adjusting screw (13) determines the quality of air-fuel mixture entering the cylinders. Turning the jet adjusting screw **clockwise** decreases the mixture strength; **anti-clockwise** will enrich.

Fig. 19. Idle speed and mixture adjustment screw

With the engine at normal working temperature, remove the air cleaner and hold the air valve down on to the bridge in the throttle bore. Screw up the jet adjustment screw (13)—a coin is ideal for this purpose—until the jet contacts the underside of the air valve. From this position turn down the jet adjusting screw three turns. This establishes an approximate jet position from which to work.

Fig. 20. Filter removal

Run the engine until it is thoroughly warm and adjust the stop screw (3) to give an idle speed of 600/650 r.p.m.

The idle mixture is correct when the engine beat is smooth and regular and the air intake "hiss" is equal on both carburettors (Fig. 21).

Fig. 21. Checking "hiss"

As a check, lift the air valve a very small amount ($\frac{1}{32}''$) (·794 mm.) with a long thin screwdriver, and listen to the effect on the engine. If the engine speed rises appreciably, the mixture is too rich and, conversely, if the engine stops, the mixture is too weak. Properly adjusted, the engine speed will either remain constant or fall slightly on lifting the air valve.

Reset the screw (4) Fig. 24, to give 0·062″ (1·587 mm.) clearance between the end of the screw and the rocker lever (6).

Refit the air cleaners and re-connect the choke cable.

Fig. 22. Topping up dampers

Fig. 23. Twin carburettor installation

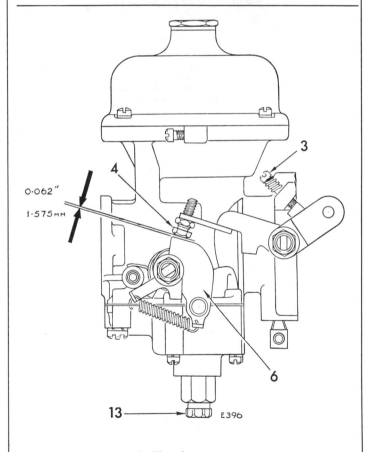

3 Throttle stop screw
4 Screw
6 Lever
13 Jet adjusting screw

Fig. 24. Carburettor linkage

Adjusting and Synchronising Twin Carburettor Installation (Fig. 23)

Loosen the clamping bolts (30) on the throttle spindle couplings between the two instruments. Next, unscrew the throttle stop screw (3) to permit the throttle in each carburettor to close completely, and tighten the clamping bolts on the couplings between the spindles of the two carburettors.

Screw in the throttle stop screws (3) to the point where the end of the screw is just contacting the stop lever attached to each throttle spindle. From this point, rotate the stop screw in each carburettor one complete turn to open the throttles an equal amount to provide a basis from which final speed of idle can be set.

Having re-connected the throttles and set each open an equal amount, regulate the jet adjusting screws (13) in the instruments as detailed under the heading "Setting the Idle", *i.e.*, three turns down from the point where the jet orifice comes into contact with the base of the air valve (18).

Jet and Throttle Interconnection Adjustment (Fig. 24)

With the choke control fully "in", the engine warm and idling on a closed throttle, adjust the screw (4) to give a clearance of $\frac{1}{16}$" (1·587 mm.) between the end of the screw and the rocker lever (6).

Always check this adjustment when the throttle stop screw (3) is altered.

NOTE: Remember that the idle quality depends to a large extent upon the general engine condition, and such points as tappet adjustment, spark plugs, and ignition timing should be inspected if idling is not stable. It is also important to eliminate any leaks in the induction system.

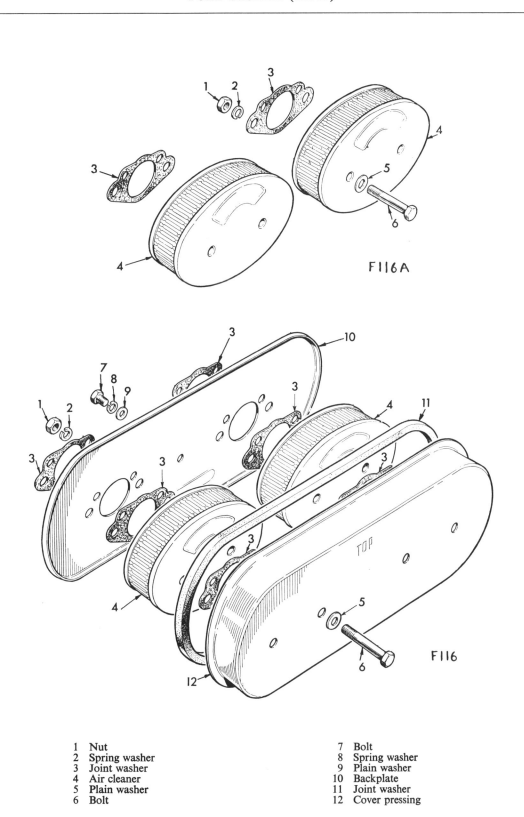

1	Nut	7	Bolt
2	Spring washer	8	Spring washer
3	Joint washer	9	Plain washer
4	Air cleaner	10	Backplate
5	Plain washer	11	Joint washer
6	Bolt	12	Cover pressing

Fig. 25. Alternative air cleaner details   (TR.4A)

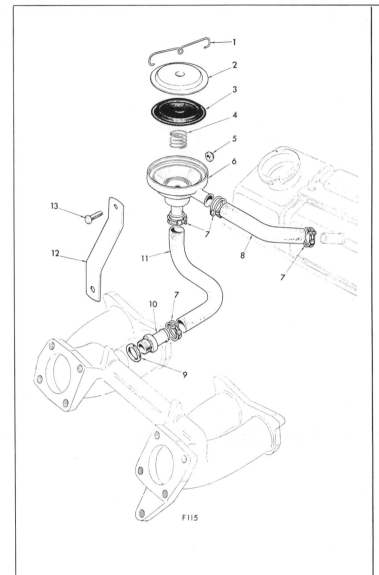

F115

1   Clip
2   Cap
3   Diaphragm
4   Spring
5   Nut
6   Regulator valve body
7   Clip
8   Hose
9   Cork washer
10   Adaptor
11   Hose
12   Bracket
13   Bolt

**Fig. 26.   Crankcase breather regulator valve
details (TR.4A)**

Crankcase breather valve (Fig. 26)

At 12,000 mile intervals, slacken the pipe clips (7) and remove the breather pipes (8) and (11). Remove the nut (5) and bolt (13) and lift off the valve assembly. Disengage the clip (1) from the valve body and lift out the diaphragm (3) and spring (4). Clean the components by swilling them in methylated spirits (denatured alcohol). Ensure that the breather pipes are clean and serviceable.

Reverse the dismantling sequence to re-assemble.

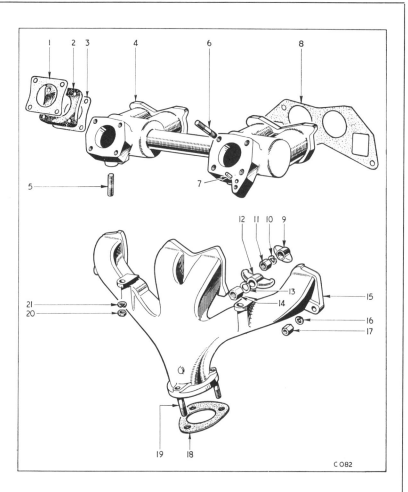

1 Carburettor gasket
2 Insulating washer
3 Carburettor gasket
4 Induction manifold
5 Stud—induction to exhaust manifold
6 Stud—induction manifold to carburettor
7 Dowel—accelerator relay lever
8 Manifold gasket
9 Bridge clamp securing manifold
10 Lockwasher
11 Nut
12 Bridge clamp securing manifold
13 Lockwasher
14 Nut
15 Exhaust manifold
16 Lockwasher
17 Nut
18 Gasket—front exhaust pipe to manifold
19 Studs—manifold to front exhaust pipe
20 Nut
21 Lockwasher

Fig. 1. Arrangement of manifold details

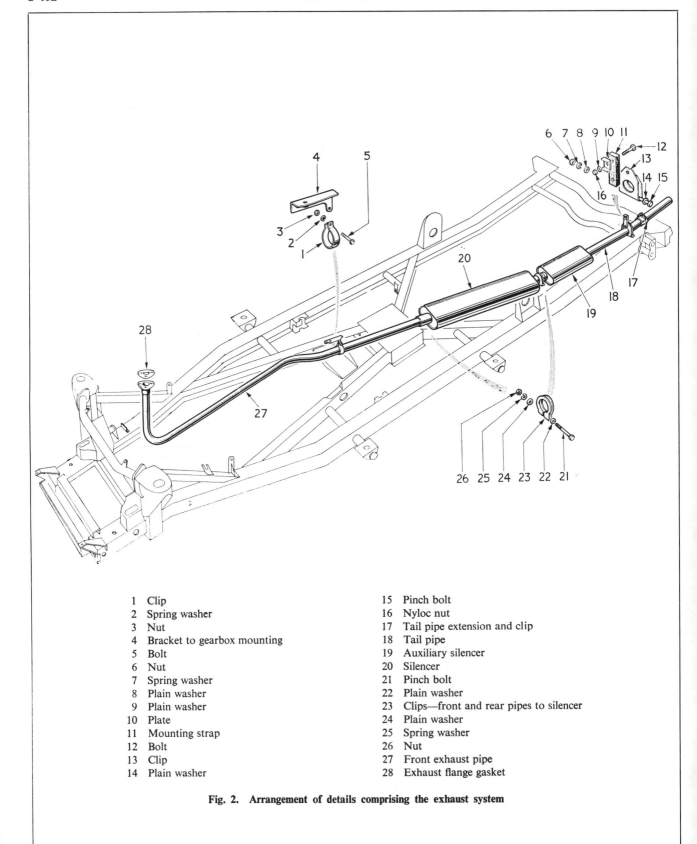

1 Clip	15 Pinch bolt
2 Spring washer	16 Nyloc nut
3 Nut	17 Tail pipe extension and clip
4 Bracket to gearbox mounting	18 Tail pipe
5 Bolt	19 Auxiliary silencer
6 Nut	20 Silencer
7 Spring washer	21 Pinch bolt
8 Plain washer	22 Plain washer
9 Plain washer	23 Clips—front and rear pipes to silencer
10 Plate	24 Plain washer
11 Mounting strap	25 Spring washer
12 Bolt	26 Nut
13 Clip	27 Front exhaust pipe
14 Plain washer	28 Exhaust flange gasket

Fig. 2. Arrangement of details comprising the exhaust system

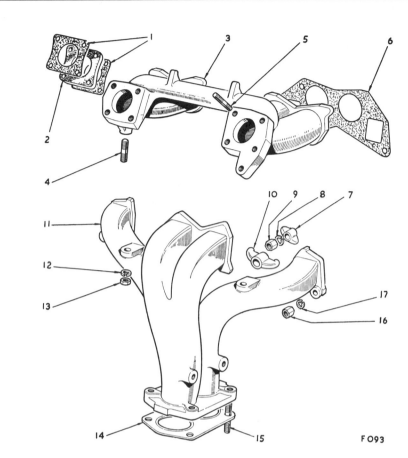

1 Carburettor joint washer
2 Insulating washer
3 Induction manifold
4 Stud — induction to exhaust manifold
5 Stud — carburettor attachment
6 Manifold gasket
7 Bridge clamp
8 Lockwasher
9 Nut
10 Bridge
11 Exhaust manifold
12 Lockwasher
13 Nut
14 Gasket — manifold to downpipe
15 Stud — manifold to downpipe
16 Nut
17 Lockwasher

Fig. 3.   Arrangement of manifold details   (TR.4A)

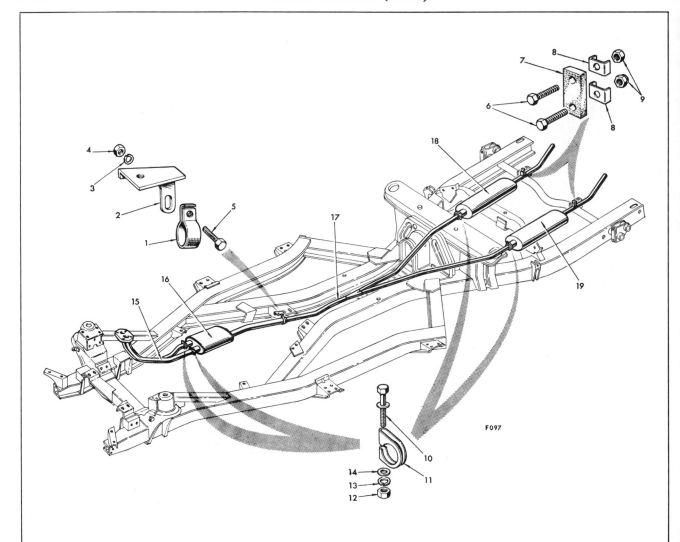

F 097

1	Clip	11	Clip
2	Bracket	12	Nut
3	Spring washer	13	Spring washer
4	Nut	14	Plain washer
5	Bolt	15	Front exhaust pipes
6	Bolt	16	Front silencer
7	Flexible strap	17	Intermediate pipes
8	Plate	18	Tail pipe and silencer R.H.
9	Nut	19	Tail pipe and silencer L.H.
10	Bolt		

Fig. 4.   Arrangement of details comprising the exhaust system   (TR.4A)

TRIUMPH TR4

WORKSHOP MANUAL

GROUP 2

Comprising:

TR4 WORKSHOP MANUAL

GROUP 2

CONTENTS

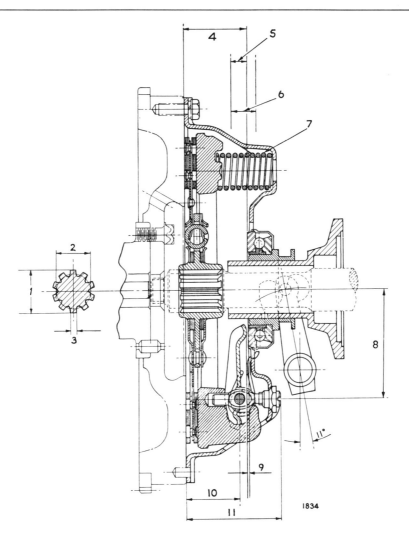

CLUTCH DATA

TYPE — 9A6. "Single Dry Plate".

OPERATION — Hydraulic.

ADJUSTMENT — Slave cylinder push-rod.

DRIVEN PLATE — Belleville washer type, cushioned by White/Light Green Springs.

FACINGS — Wound yarn (R.Y.Z.).

1	Spline diameter (O/D)	... ...	1·247″/1·245″	(31·7/31·6 mm.)
2	Spline diameter (I/D)	... ...	1·010″/1·005″	(25·65/25·53 mm.)
3	Splines	... ...	1·25″ (31·75 mm.) × 10 S.A.E. Splines	
4	Release lever height ...	... ...	1·895″	(48·13 mm.)
			(using 0·33″ (8·38 mm.) gauge plate in place of driven plate)	
5	Minimum travel to release ...	... ...	0·38″	(9·65 mm.)
6	Maximum travel available ...	... ...	0·47″	(11·94 mm.)
7	Thrust springs—9 cream ...	... ...	120 - 130 lbs.	(54·4 - 59·0 kg.)
8	Release lever pivot centres ...	... ...	3·19″	(81·0 mm.)
9	Bearing to lever top clearance ...	... ...	0·1″	(2·54 mm.)
10	Release lever pivot centres ...	... ...	1·55″ approx.	(39·4 mm.)
11	Maximum height of adjusters ...	... ...	2·9″	(73·7 mm.)

Fig. 1. **Sectional view of the clutch**

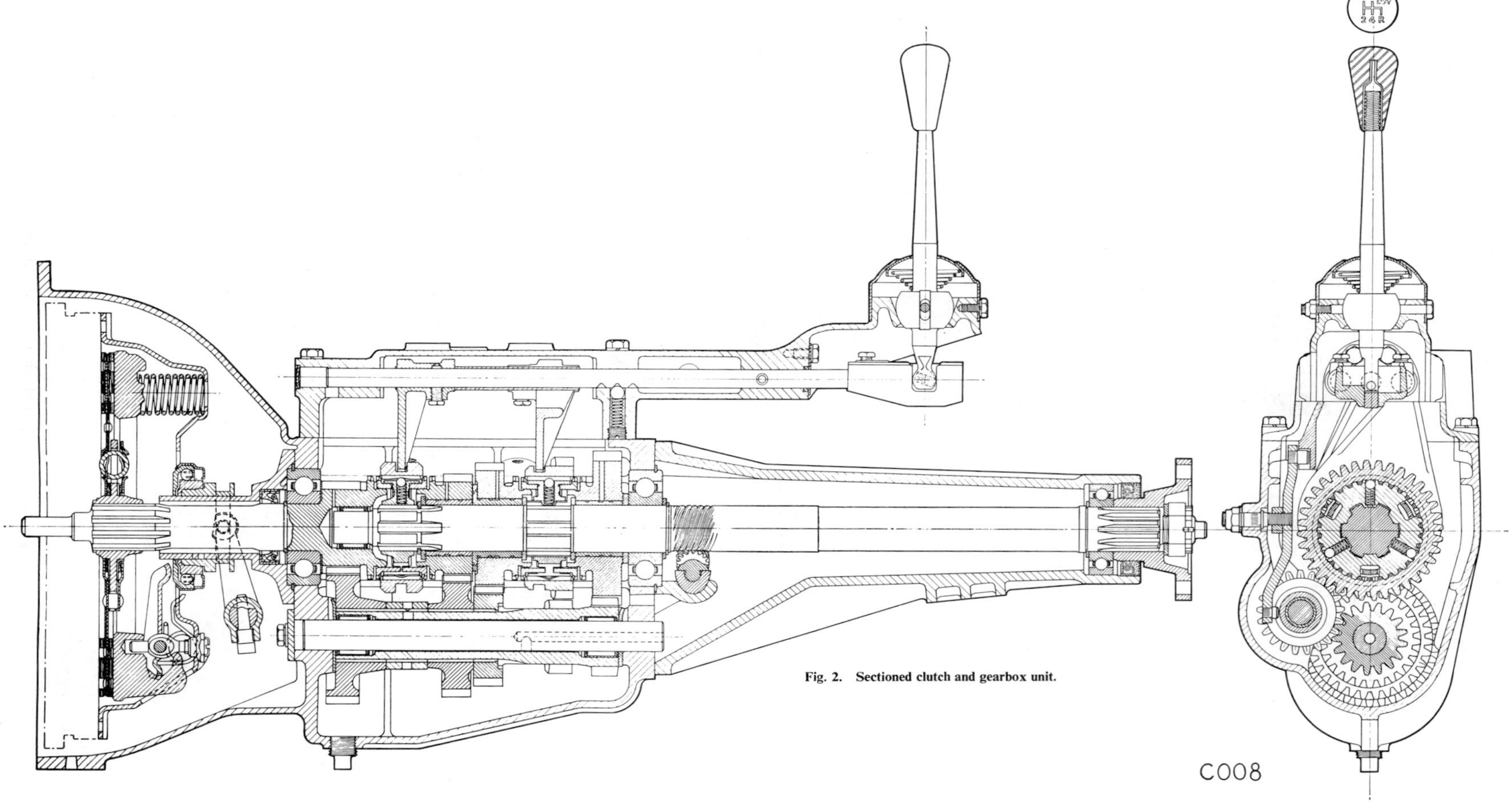

C008

Fig. 2. Sectioned clutch and gearbox unit.

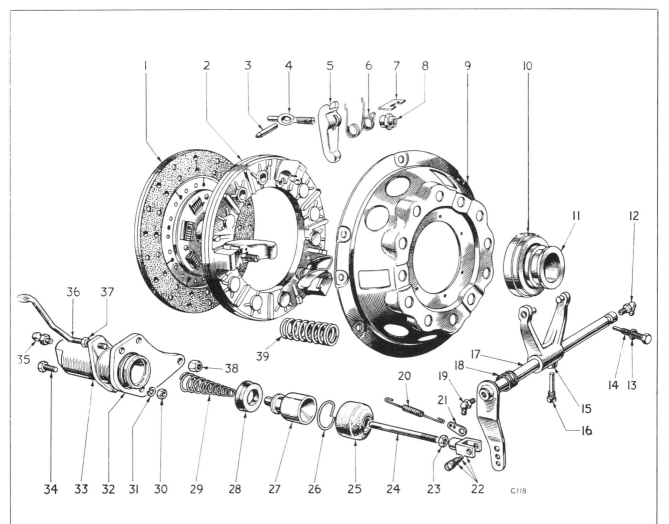

1	Driven plate assembly	21	Spring anchor plate
2	Pressure plate	22	Clevis fork, spring and pin
3	Release lever pin	23	Locknut
4	Eyebolt	24	Push rod
5	Release lever	25	Rubber end cover
6	Anti-rattle spring	26	Circlip
7	Strut	27	Piston
8	Adjusting nut	28	Piston seal
9	Clutch cover	29	Piston return spring
10	Release bearing	30	Nut
11	Bearing sleeve	31	Spring washer
12	Grease nipple	32	Slave cylinder bracket
13	Washer	33	Slave cylinder
14	Shaft locating bolt	34	Bolt
15	Clutch operating fork	35	Bleed nipple
16	Screwed taper pin	36	Stay
17	Clutch operating shaft	37	Nut
18	Fork return spring	38	Nut
19	Grease nipple	39	Clutch thrust spring
20	Push rod return spring		

Fig. 3.   Clutch and slave cylinder details

MASTER CYLINDER

A. Clutch Driving Condition

When the clutch pedal is released, the push rod (9) is returned to its stop (12) by the pedal return spring. This permits the plunger (7) to move rearwards under pressure of the spring (5). The flange on the end of the valve shank (4) contacts the spring retainer (6) and as the plunger continues to move rearwards, the valve shank (4) lifts the seal (1) from its seat on the end of the cylinder bore and compresses the spring (2). Hydraulic fluid can then flow past the three legged distance piece (3) and seal (1) either to or from the reservoir.

B. Clutch Released Condition

Initial movement of the push rod (9) and plunger (7) releases the valve shank (4) and permits the spring (2) to press the valve shank (4) and seal (1) against its seat. This cuts off communication between the cylinder and reservoir. Continued movement of the plunger displaces fluid through the hydraulic pipelines and releases the clutch.

Maximum stroke available—
      1·38″ (35·05 mm.).

Stroke position at maximum cut off—
      0·099″ (2·5 mm.).

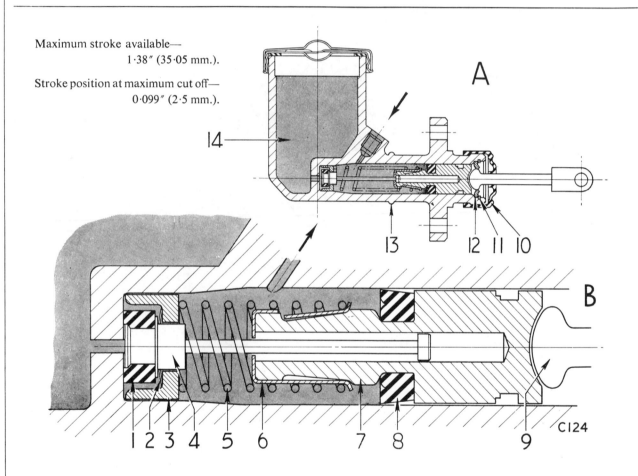

Fig. 4. Section through clutch master cylinder

1 Valve seal	6 Spring retainer	11 Circlip
2 Spring (valve seal)	7 Plunger	12 Push rod stop
3 Distance piece	8 Plunger seal	13 Identification ring
4 Valve shank	9 Push rod	14 Fluid reservoir
5 Plunger return spring	10 Dust cover	

Clutch Master Cylinder (Fig. 5)

Removal

Clutch and brake master cylinders cannot be removed individually, but only as an assembly, therefore:
1. Empty the clutch and brake hydraulic systems.
2. Detach the fluid pipes from the master cylinders.
3. Remove the brake and clutch pedal clevis pins (1).
4. Remove setscrews (4) from the cylinder support bracket (11) and lift the bracket, complete with cylinders, from the scuttle.
5. Remove the master cylinders from the support bracket.

Dismantling
1. Remove the dust cover (10). Depress the push rod (9), remove the circlip (11) and withdraw the push rod (9) together with items (10), (11) and (12).
2. Shake out the plunger, spring and valve assembly. If necessary, apply low pressure compressed air to the outlet union to eject the plunger assembly.
3. Lift the locating clip on the spring retainer (6) and remove the retainer from the plunger (7) with the valve and spring assembly.
4. Detach the valve shank (4) by passing it through the offset hole in the retainer (6). Remove the spring (5), distance piece (3) and spring (2) from the valve shank (4). Using fingers, detach the seal (1) from item (4) and the seal (8) from item (7).

Inspection
Clean and examine all components for deterioration, renewing items as necessary.

Re-Assembly
1. Refit the seals (1) and (8) to items (4) and (7) as shown on Fig. 4.
2. Fit the spring (2), distance piece (3) and spring (5) to the valve shank (4), attach the spring retainer (6) and fit the assembly to the plunger (7). Lubricate the components with clean hydraulic fluid and fit them to the master cylinder bore. Fit the push rod (9) with stop plate (12), circlip (11) and dust cover (10).

To Refit
Re-assemble the master cylinder to the bracket and secure this to the bulkhead as shown on Fig. 5. Re-connect the clutch and brake pedals to the push rods, using new split pins to secure the clevis pins (1). Refill and bleed the clutch and brake hydraulic systems.

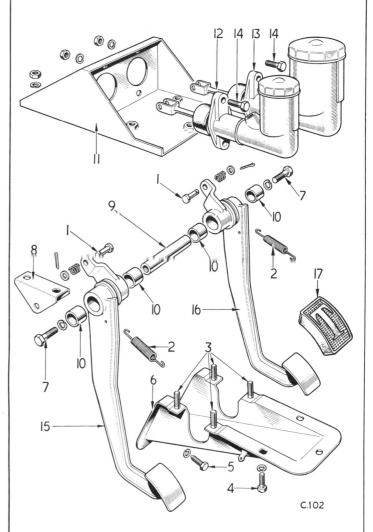

C.102

1 Clevis pin
2 Pedal return spring
3 Bolts ⎫ Pedal shaft cover assembly to
4 Bolts ⎰ master cylinder support bracket
5 Setscrew (pedal shaft cover assembly to bulkhead)
6 Pedal shaft cover assembly
7 Setscrew (pedal stay to pedal shaft support bracket)
8 Pedal shaft support bracket
9 Pedal shaft
10 Pedal pivot bush
11 Master cylinder support bracket
12 Push rod
13 Bracket master cylinder
14 Setscrew (master cylinder to support bracket)
15 Clutch pedal
16 Bracket pedal
17 Pedal pad

Fig. 5. Master cylinder support and pedal details

1 Bleed nipple
2 Push-rod
3 Locknut
4 Clevis fork
5 Grease nipple

Fig. 6.   Clutch slave cylinder linkage

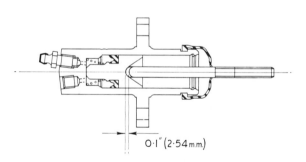

0·1″ (2·54 m.m.)

Fig. 7.   Sectioned slave cylinder and push-rod

Clutch Adjustment (Fig. 6)

Check, and if necessary, adjust the clearance between the clutch operating piston and the push rod (2). The correct clearance is 0·1″. To adjust:—

1. Slacken the nut (3) and unscrew the push rod (2) until all clearance between the push rod and the cupped end of the operating piston (inside slave cylinder) is taken up.

2. Adjust the position of the locknut (3) until a feeler gauge of 0·1″ thickness may be inserted between the locknut face and the clevis fork (4).

3. Without disturbing the locknut on the push rod, screw the push rod into the clevis until the nut contacts the clevis face, then lock up the nut (3).

Bleeding the Hydraulic System

The clutch hydraulic system is bled in a similar manner to that described for the brakes in Group 3.

Slave Cylinder (Fig. 3)

To Remove

1. Drain the hydraulic system by attaching a tube to the bleed nipple (35) and pumping the clutch pedal.

2. Detach the stay (36), bolt (34), nut (30) and spring washer (31). Detach the rubber end cover.

3. Withdraw the slave cylinder from its bracket and disconnect the flexible hose by holding the hose union with a spanner whilst rotating the slave cylinder.   AVOID TWISTING THE HOSE.

To Refit

Reverse the removal procedure, refill and bleed the clutch hydraulic system.

To Dismantle

Remove the circlip (26) and using low pressure compressed air, eject the piston and spring (29). Detach the seal (28) from the piston (27). Clean the components with hydraulic fluid.

To Re-Assemble

Fit the seal (28), with its lip facing inwards, to the piston (27).   Assemble the piston and spring (29) to the cylinder bore and secure with the circlip (26).

Clutch Release Bearing (Fig. 8)
To Remove:

With the gearbox removed from the vehicle, remove the grease nipple (12), locating bolt (13) and taper bolt (10). Withdraw the cross shaft (8) and remove the release bearing (1) and sleeve (2). Press the sleeve from the bearing.

To Re-assemble:

Reverse the removal procedure and wire lock the bolt (10).

Servicing the Clutch Unit

Removal

Remove the gearbox as detailed on page 2·205 and progressively unscrew the clutch attachment setscrews. Lift the cover assembly and driven plate from the flywheel face.

Dismantling

A Churchill clutch fixture, No. 99A, is recommended for dismantling and re-assembling the clutch unit.

Before dismantling, mark the following parts to facilitate re-assembly and maintain the original degree of balance.

    (a) Cover pressing.
    (b) Lugs on the pressure plate.
    (c) Release levers.

1. Clean the top of the base plate and place three (number 3) spacers on the positions marked 'D'.
2. Place the cover assembly on the base plate so that the release levers are directly above the spacers, and the bolt holes of the cover are in line with tapped holes in the base plate.
3. Screw the actuator into the centre hole and press the handle down to clamp the cover housing to the base plate.
4. Use six bolts to secure the cover pressing to base plate. Remove the actuator.
5. Remove three adjusting nuts. Considerable torque may be necessary.
6. Release the cover pressing from base plate, lift nine thrust springs from the pressure plate and remove three anti-rattle springs from the cover.
7. Lift up inner end of each release lever and disengage the strut.
8. Gripping the tip of the release lever and the eye bolt, lift out the assembly from the pressure plate. Repeat procedure for 2nd and 3rd levers.
9. Remove the eye bolts from release levers and take out pins. Remove the struts from pressure plate.

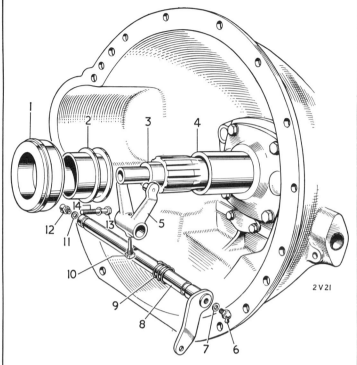

1	Release bearing	8	Cross-shaft
2	Bearing sleeve	9	Anti-rattle spring
3	Input shaft	10	Tapered locking bolt
4	Front cover	11	Fibre washer
5	Fork	12	Grease nipple
6	Grease nipple	13	Locating bolt
7	Fibre washer	14	Lockwasher

Fig. 8. Clutch release details

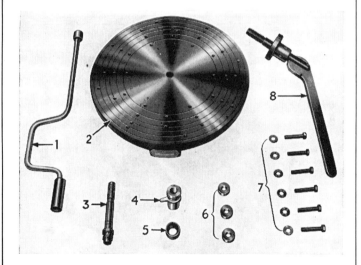

1	Brace	5	Adaptor
2	Base plate	6	Spacers
3	Pillar	7	Washers and setscrews
4	Gauge finger	8	Actuator

Fig. 9. Clutch assembly fixture No. 99A

Fig. 10. Securing cover assembly to base plate

Fig. 11. Adjusting the release levers

Fig. 12. Using Tool No. 20S.72 to centralize the clutch driven plate

Assembly

Before assembling, lubricate all bearing surfaces and arrange the components with strict regard to the markings made previously.

1. Place strut in position in lug of pressure plate.

2. Assemble pin to eye bolt and feed threaded portion through release lever.

3. By holding the strut in the pressure plate to one side, feed the plain end of the eye bolt (assembled to release lever) into the pressure plate.

4. Place the strut into groove in the outer end of the release lever.

5. Repeat with remaining release levers.

6. Place the pressure plate and the assembled release levers, with the latter over the spacers, on the base plate of the Churchill Fixture.

7. Assemble the springs to their seats on the pressure plate. Fit the anti-rattle springs and place the cover pressing over the pressure plate, allowing the lugs to protrude through the cover.

8. Secure cover pressing to base plate.

9. Screw on adjuster nuts until their heads are flush with the tops of the eye bolts.

10. Fit the actuator into the centre hole of the base plate and pump handle up and down half a dozen times to settle the components. Remove actuator.

11. Secure pillar firmly into centre of base plate and to it assemble adaptor No. 7, recessed side downwards, and gauge finger.

12. Adjust nuts to raise or lower the release levers sufficiently to just contact the finger gauge.

13. Remove pillar, refit actuator and operate the clutch a dozen or so times. Re-check with finger gauge and make any adjustments necessary.

14. Lock the adjusting nuts by peening over the collars into the nuts of the eye bolts.

15. Remove completed assembly from base plate.

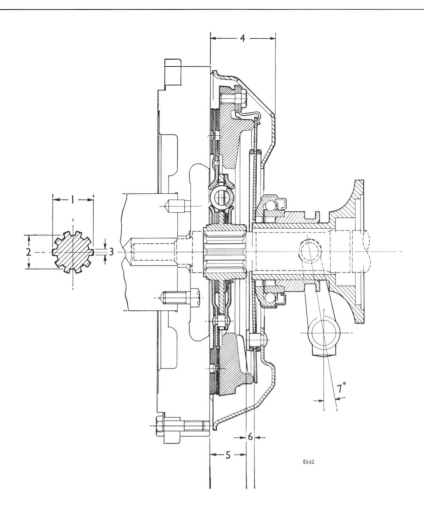

E 662

CLUTCH DATA

TYPE — Borg & Beck 8½″ dia. TYPE DS.

OPERATION — Hydraulic.

ADJUSTMENT — Non adjustable.

DRIVEN PLATE — Belleville washer type cushioned by Yellow/Lt. Green Springs.

FACINGS — Wound Yarn.

1. Spline diameter (O/D)	1·247″/1·245″	(31·7/31·6 mm.)
2. Spline diameter (I/D)	1·010″/1·005″	(25·65/25·53 mm.)
3. Splines	1·25″ (31·75 mm.) × 10 S.A.E. Splines	
4. Flywheel face to cover	2·10″ (51·05 mm.)	
5. Flywheel face to spring tips (fully released position)	1·15″/1·29″ (29·21/32·77 mm.)	
6. Maximum travel	0·27″/0·29″ (6·76/7·37 mm.)	

Fig. 13.   Sectioned view of the clutch   (TR.4A)

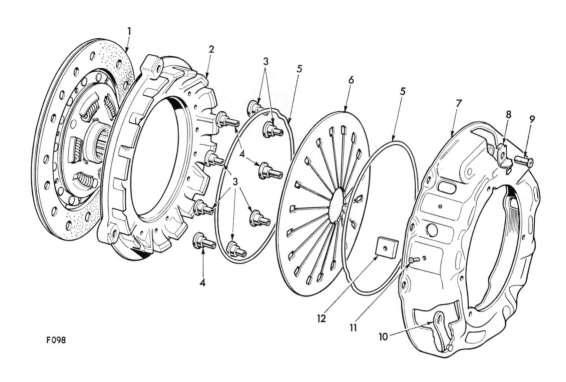

F098

1   Driven plate
2   Pressure plate
3   Rivets
4   Locating pins
5   Fulcrum rings
6   Diaphragm spring
7   Cover pressing
8   Retractor clips
9   Rivet
10 Pressure plate strap
11 Rivet
12 Balance weight

Fig. 14.   Clutch details   (TR.4A)

CLUTCH UNIT

The diaphragm spring clutch unit fitted to TR.4A models must not be dismantled for any reason.

Should any fault develop in the unit, a complete replacement assembly must be fitted.

GEARBOX

DIMENSIONS AND TOLERANCES

	Ins.	mm.	Remarks
Input Shaft Spline Size .. .. Bore for Torrington Needle Roller Bearing	10 × 1¼″ S.A.E.		
Mainshaft 1st, 2nd and 3rd Gear .. .. Journal Diameter	1·2505″ 1·2500″	31·7627 31·75	
Overall End Float of 2nd and 3rd Gear Bushes and Thrust Washers on Mainshaft	0·003″ to 0·009″	0·0762 to 0·2286	Obtained by selective use of thrust washers below.
Overall End Float of 1st Speed Gear Bushes and Thrust Washers on Mainshaft	0·003″ to 0·009″	0·0762 to 0·2286	Obtained by selective use of Thrust Washers, Part Numbers 129941-4.
Inside Diameter of 1st, 2nd and 3rd Gear Bushes	1·251″ 1·252″	31·7754 31·8008	
Outside Diameter of 1st and 3rd Gear Bushes	1·4983″ 1·4978″	38·057 38·044	
End Float of 1st, 2nd and 3rd Gear on Bushes	0·004″ to 0·008″	0·1016 to 0·2032	0·004″ 0·1016 to to 0·006″ 0·1524 Recommended
Mainshaft Spigot Bearing Outside Diameter	0·8750″ 0·8745″	22·225 22·2123	

1ST AND 2ND/3RD SPEED GEAR THRUST WASHERS

Part No.	Colour	Thickness Ins.	mm.
129941	Self-finish	0·120″/0·118″	3·048/2·997
129942	Green	0·123″/0·121″	3·124/3·0734
129943	Blue	0·126″/0·124″	3·200/3·1496
129944	Orange	0·129″/0·127″	3·2766/3·2258
134670	Yellow	0·134″/0·132″	3·4036/3·3528

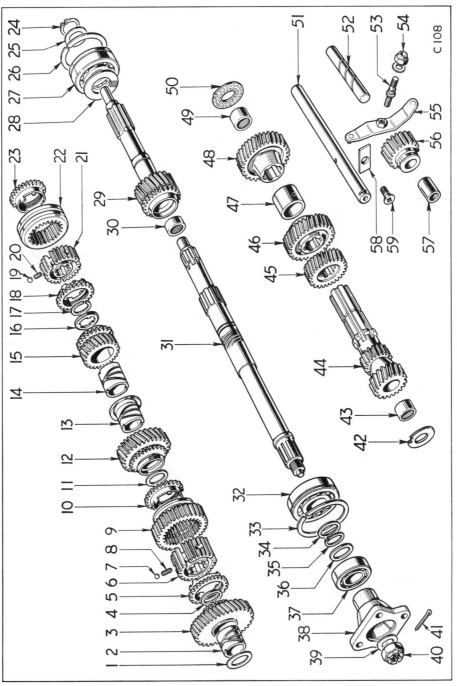

Fig. 1.　Gearbox Details (Moving Parts)

Key to Fig. 1

1 Thrust washer
2 Bush—1st speed gear
3 1st speed gear
4 Thrust washer
5 1st speed synchro cup
6 1st/2nd speed synchro hub
7 Synchro ball
8 Spring
9 Reverse mainshaft gear and synchro outer sleeve
10 2nd speed synchro cup
11 Thrust washer
12 2nd speed gear
13 Bush—2nd speed gear
14 Bush—3rd speed gear
15 3rd speed gear
16 Thrust washer
17 Circlip
18 3rd speed synchro cup
19 Synchro ball

20 Spring
21 3rd/top synchro hub
22 Synchro sleeve
23 Top gear synchro cup
24 Circlip
25 Distance washer
26 Circlip
27 Ball race
28 Oil deflector plate
29 Input shaft
30 Needle roller bearing
31 Mainshaft
32 Ball race
33 Circlip
34 Distance washer
35 Circlip
36 Distance washer
37 Rear ball race
38 Flange
39 Plain washer

40 Slotted nut
41 Split pin
42 Rear thrust washer
43 Needle roller bearing
44 Countershaft hub
45 2nd speed countershaft gear
46 3rd speed countershaft gear
47 Distance piece
48 Countershaft gear
49 Needle roller bearing
50 Front thrust washer
51 Countershaft
52 Reverse gear shaft
53 Pivot stud
54 Nyloc nut and washer
55 Reverse gear operating lever
56 Reverse gear
57 Reverse gear bush
58 Locating plate
59 Screw

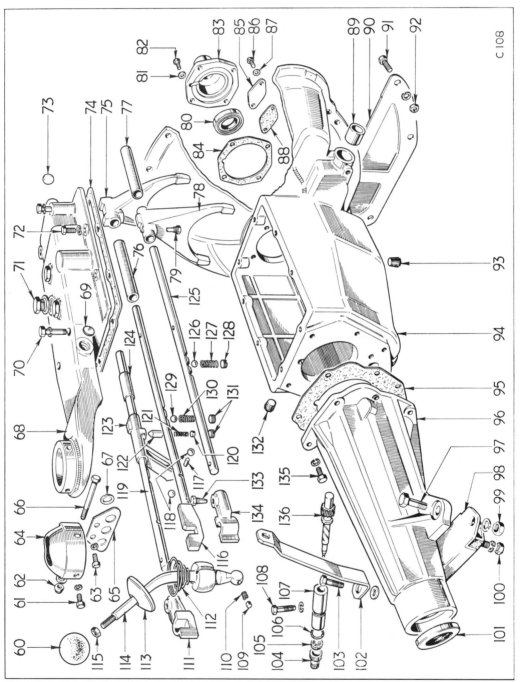

Fig. 2.　Gearbox Details (Fixed Parts)

C 108

Key to Fig. 2

60 Knob
61 Setscrew
62 Nyloc nut
63 Setscrew
64 Cap
65 End plate
66 Cross bolt
67 Rubber 'O' ring
68 Top cover
69 Welch plug
70 Bolt
71 Plug
72 Bolt
73 Welch plug
74 Gasket
75 Top/3rd selector fork
76 Distance tube
77 Distance tube
78 2nd/1st selector fork
79 Peg bolt
80 Oil seal
81 Copper washer
82 Bolt
83 Front cover
84 Gasket
85 Countershaft end plate

86 Setscrew
87 Copper washer
88 Gasket
89 Bush
90 Cover plate
91 Setscrew
92 Nut
93 Drain plug
94 Casing
95 Gasket
96 Extension housing
97 Bolt
98 Silentbloc mounting
99 Nut
100 Nut
101 Oil seal
102 Stay
103 Bolt
104 Speedometer cable adaptor
105 Seal
106 Rubber 'O' ring
107 Housing
108 Peg bolt
109 Plunger—anti-rattle
110 Spring
111 Selector—reverse

112 Spring
113 Cap disc
114 Lever
115 Nut
116 Top/3rd selector shaft
117 Interlock plunger
118 Balls—interlock
119 Reverse selector shaft
120 Shim
121 Spring
122 Plunger
123 Reverse actuator
124 Distance piece
125 2nd/1st selector shaft
126 Ball—detent
127 Spring
128 Plug
129 Ball—detent
130 Spring
131 Plug
132 Level/filler plug
133 Peg bolt
134 Selector 1st/2nd
135 Bolt
136 Speedo drive gear

GEARBOX — continued

	Ins.	mm.	
Bore of 1st Speed Gear	1·5005″ 1·4995″	38·1127 38·087	
Bore of 2nd Speed Gear ..	1·5672″ 1·5680″	39·807 39·827	
Bore of 3rd Speed Gear	1·5005″ 1·4995″	38·1127 38·087	
Countershaft Countershaft Diameter	0·8125″ 0·8120″	20·637 20·625	
Bore of Countershaft Hub for Needle Rollers	1·063″ 1·062″	27·000 26·975	
Thickness of Front Thrust Washer	0·068″ 0·066″	1·7272 1·6764	
Thickness of Rear Thrust Washer	0·105″ 0·107″	2·667 2·718	
Recommended Countershaft End Float	0·007″ 0·012″	0·1778 0·3048	
Synchromesh Release Loads 1st and 2nd Gear Synchro. Unit ..	25 lbs. to 27 lbs.	11·34 kg. to 12·247 kg.	
3rd and Top Gear Synchro. Unit ..	19 lbs. to 21 lbs.	8·618 kg. to 9·525 kg.	
Selector Shaft Release Loads 1st/2nd	32 lbs. to 34 lbs.	14·515 kg. to 15·422 kg.	
3rd/Top	26 lbs. to 28 lbs.	11·793 kg. to 12·701 kg.	From gearbox number CT9899, 3rd/Top selector shaft release load became identical to the reverse selector shaft release load. See note on page 2·214.
Reverse	26 lbs. to 28 lbs.	11·793 kg. to 12·701 kg.	

GEARBOX REMOVAL

To Remove Gearbox Leaving Engine in Position

Raise the vehicle on a ramp or support it on axle stands.

Disconnect the battery, drain the gearbox and remove the seat cushions and front carpets.

Referring to Fig. 3, disconnect:
— cables (1) (3) from heater control switch.
— control cable (2) from heater unit.
— control cable (4) from control panel.

Remove:
— facia support (two bolts (7) top, two bolts (8) each side bottom).
— dipper switch (leave cables attached).
— centre floor cover (17 bolts and washers).
— propeller shaft.

Referring to Fig. 4, remove:
— clevis pin (1).
— two bolts (2).
— stay (4).
— clutch slave cylinder (5), (allowing it to hang by its flexible hose).
— clutch cover plate from lower portion of clutch housing.

Disconnect the speedometer cable, and overdrive connectors (if fitted). See page 2·304.

Using a block of wood to protect the sump, take the weight of the engine and gearbox with a jack placed as far as possible towards the rear of the sump.

Referring to Fig. 5, release the exhaust pipe bracket (9) and detach the rear mounting (10) from the gearbox and crossmember (8). Raise the engine and gearbox and remove the crossmember by sliding it forwards.

Remove the bolts, nuts and spring washers securing the clutch housing flange to the engine. Withdraw the gearbox rearwards until clear of the clutch; then manoeuvre the clutch housing to the right and the rear end to the left, tilting the box to permit the clutch operating lever to clear the floor aperture.

Lift the gearbox from the vehicle.

To Refit

Reverse the removal procedure.

IMPORTANT : Do not allow the gearbox to hang on the clutch spigot shaft whilst fitting it to the engine.

Refill the gearbox with oil.

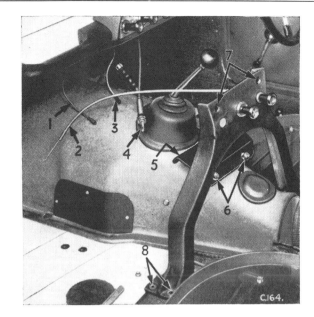

Fig. 3. Facia support and heater controls

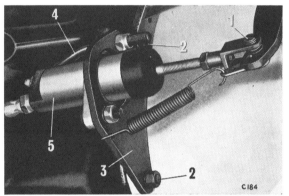

Fig. 4. Clutch slave cylinder

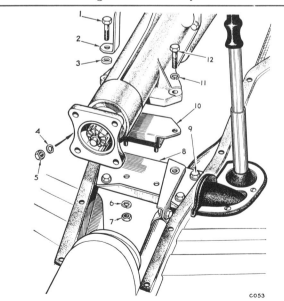

Fig. 5. Gearbox rear mounting

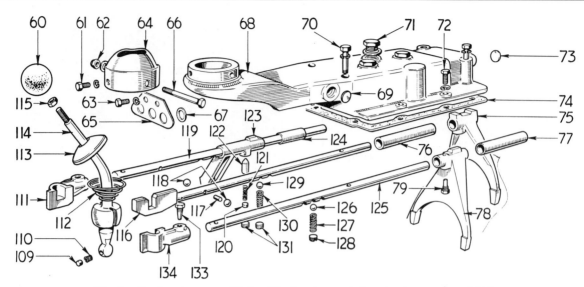

Fig. 6. Gearbox top cover details. The key to annotations is given on page 2·204

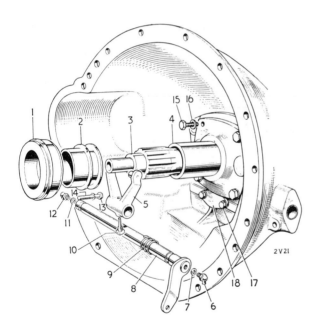

Fig. 7. Clutch release details

1 Release bearing	10 Screwed taper pin
2 Sleeve	11 Fibre washer
3 Input shaft	12 Grease nipple
4 Front cover	13 Cross-shaft locating bolt
5 Fork	14 Spring washer
6 Grease nipple	15 Wedglok bolts
7 Fibre washer	16 Washers
8 Cross-shaft	17 Bolts
9 Anti-rattle spring	18 Plate

GEARBOX

Dismantling

Top Cover (Fig. 6)

Remove the bolts (70) and (72), spring washers, top cover (68) and paper gasket (74).

Remove the nut (62), cross pin (66), cover (64) and withdraw the gear lever assembly from the top cover.

Invert the cover and remove the plugs (128), (131), distance piece (120), springs (130), (121) and (127), plunger (122) and balls (126), (129).

Detach the peg bolts (79).

With the selector shafts in the neutral position, withdraw the 3rd/Top gear selector shaft, (116) taking care to remove the interlock plunger (117) and balls (118) as they are released. Lift the 3rd/Top selector fork and distance tube from the top cover. Repeat this operation on the 1st/2nd and reverse gear selector shafts.

Remove the screws (63), spring washers and detach the retaining plate (65). Remove sealing rings (67) from recesses in the casing.

If necessary, remove the peg bolts (133) and detach the selectors (111) and (134) from their respective shafts.

Front Cover Details (Fig. 7)

Remove grease nipple (12), taper bolt (10), bolt (13), spring washer (14).

Withdraw cross-shaft (8) and release spring (9), release bearing (1), sleeve (2) and fork (5). Remove Wedglok bolts (15), washers (16) and detach front cover (4), bolts (17) and plate (18).

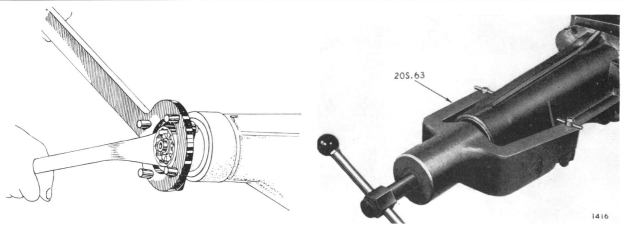

Fig. 8. Using Tool 20.SM.90 to remove the driving flange

Fig. 10. Using Tool 20S.63 to remove rear extension

Rear Extension (Figs. 1 and 2)

Remove the peg bolt (108), spring washer, and withdraw the speedometer drive gear assembly (104) - (107).

Remove split pin (41), slotted nut (40), plain washer (39), and withdraw flange (38).

Remove bolts (135), spring washers, and detach the rear extension (96) using Churchill extractor No. 20.S/63.

Countershaft (Fig. 11)

Using a Phillips screwdriver, remove the screw (59) and retaining plate (58).

Withdraw the countershaft (51) and reverse pinion shaft (52).

Input Shaft (Fig. 1)

Using Churchill Tool No. S.4235.A, withdraw the input shaft assembly from the gearbox.

Remove the circlips (24) and (26), spacer washer (25) and withdraw the race (27) using Churchill Tool No. S.4221-2. Detach the disc (28). If necessary, extract the needle roller bearing (30).

Fig. 11. Countershaft and reverse pinion shaft locating plate

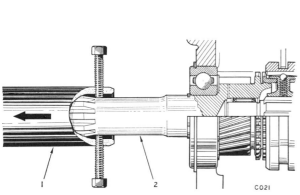

Fig. 9. Using Tool S.4235A with adaptor to remove the input shaft assembly

Fig. 12. Using Tool S.4221-2 to remove the input shaft ball race

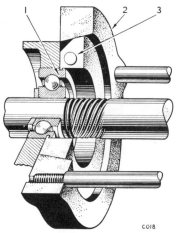

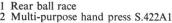

1 Rear ball race
2 Multi-purpose hand press S.422A1
3 Adaptor No. S.4221A-15

Fig. 13. Removing mainshaft rear bearing. The sectioned view on the left shows the adaptor gripping the ball race groove

Fig. 14. Removing the mainshaft assembly

Mainshaft (Fig. 1)

Remove items (35), (34), (33) and detach the mainshaft rear race (32) using Churchill Tool No. S.4221A/15, as shown on Fig. 13.

Manoeuvre the mainshaft assembly out through the gearbox top cover aperture. Lift out the countershaft assembly, thrust washers (42) and (50) and reverse gear (56).

Remove the countershaft gears from the hub, and, if necessary, extract the needle roller assemblies from the hub bore.

Using Churchill Tool No. 20.SM.69, remove the circlip (17) by driving the tool beneath the circlip and levering the 3rd speed gear forward to dislodge the circlip from its groove. Remove all components from the mainshaft.

Remove the 1st/2nd and 3rd/4th synchro inner hubs from the outer sleeves, taking care to catch the springs (8) and (20), and balls (7) and (19).

Fig. 15. Using Tool No. 20.SM.69 to remove the mainshaft circlip

Re-assembly (Fig. 1)

Reverse Gear

Install the reverse gear (56) in the gearbox, placing the selector groove rearwards. Fit the reverse gear shaft (52) and secure it with string to prevent the shaft from sliding into the gearbox.

Countershaft

Using a stepped drift, drive a new needle roller bearing (lettered face outwards) into each end of the countershaft hub.

Fit the gears (45), (46), distance piece (47) and gear (48) to the countershaft hub as shown on Fig. 17.

Using grease to retain them, locate the countershaft thrust washers (42) and (50) in the gearbox and lower the gear cluster into position. Temporarily fit the countershaft (51) and measure the gear end float. This should be 0·007″-0·012″. Reduce excessive end float by selective assembly of available thrust washers and distance pieces.

Remove countershaft (51) and drop the gears to the bottom of the casing.

Synchro Units

1. Assemble synchro springs (20), balls (19) and shims to the 3rd/Top synchro hub (21). Fit the outer sleeve (22).
2. Repeat with 2nd/1st synchro unit.
3. Test the axial release load which should be :
   3rd/Top. 19/21 lbs. 8·618/9·525 kg.
   2nd/1st. 25/27 lbs. 11·34/12·247 kg.
   NOTE : If the actual release loads differ from those specified, adjust the number of shims beneath each synchro spring to give the correct loading.

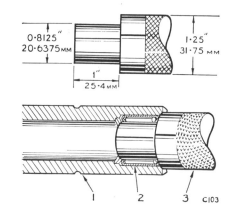

1 Countershaft 2 Bearing 3 Tool

Fig. 16. Details of tool required for installing new countershaft bearings

Fig. 17. Countershaft and reverse gear assembly

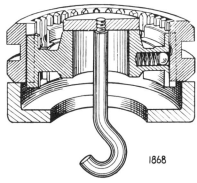

Fig. 19. Showing a simple method of checking synchro release loads. A spring balance is attached to the hook and the pull pressure increased to the point of release

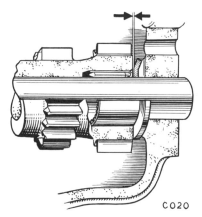

Fig. 18. Countershaft rear thrust washer Clearance 0·007″ - 0·012″ (0·18 - 0·3 mm.)

Fig. 20. Measuring gear end-float

1st, 2nd and 3rd Mainshaft Gear End Float on Bushes

Measure the end float of each gear on its respective bush as shown on Fig. 20. This should be 0·004″ to 0·006″ (0·1 to 0·15 mm.). Fit a new bush to increase float ; decrease float by reducing bush length.

CAUTION : Reduced bush length will increase end float of bushes on mainshaft.

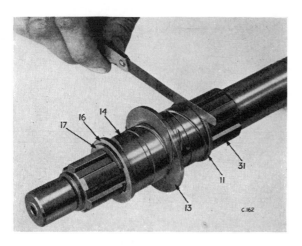

Fig. 21. Measuring bush end-float

Overall End Float of Bushes (Mainshaft)

Assemble the thrust washer (11), bush (13), bush (14) and thrust washer (16) to the mainshaft. Secure the assembly with a discarded half-circlip (17) and measure the total end float of the bushes and thrust washers on the mainshaft. If necessary, adjust the end float by selective use of thrust washers (11) to give 0·003″ to 0·009″ (0·08 to 0·23 mm.). Thrust washers are available in the following thicknesses :

Part Number	Colour	Thickness	
		ins.	mm.
129941	Self-finish	0·119	3·02
129942	Green	0·122	3·10
129943	Blue	0·125	3·18
129944	Orange	0·128	3·25
134670	Yellow	0·133	3·38

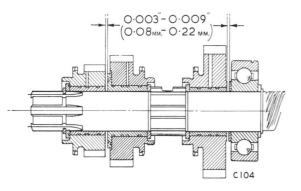

Fig. 22. Section through mainshaft assembly showing end-float of mainshaft bushes

1st Speed Gear End Float

Assemble the thrust washer (4), bush (2) and thrust washer (1) to the mainshaft. Using the Churchill driver (S. 314), drift the race (32) into position and fit the washer (34), circlip (35). Drive the race rearwards to ensure that it is hard against the circlip.

Measure the distance between the washer (1) and bush (2). This should be 0·003″ to 0·009″. Adjust by selective use of above thrust washers.

Remove all components from the mainshaft prior to final assembly.

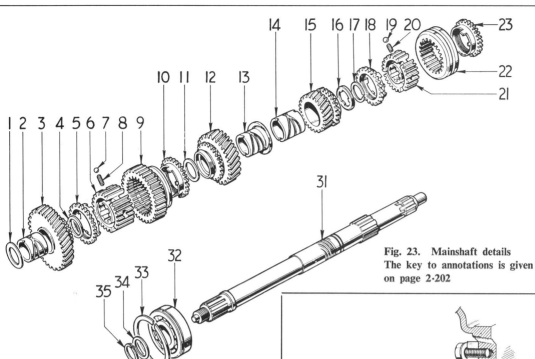

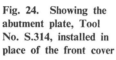

Fig. 23. Mainshaft details
The key to annotations is given
on page 2·202

Mainshaft Assembly

Place the components as shown on Fig. 23 and assemble to the front of the mainshaft in the following order :
— thrust washer (11).
— gear and bush (12), (13).
— gear and bush (14), (15).
— thrust washer (16).
— new circlip (17).
— 3rd/Top synchro unit with baulk ring (18) and (23) at each side.

With a baulk ring (5), (10) assembled to each side of the 2nd/1st synchro unit, slide this over the rear of the mainshaft and locate on the larger splines.

To the rear of the mainshaft assemble :
— washer (4).
— gear and bush (2), (3).
— washer (1).

Enter the rear of the mainshaft through the rear bearing housing and manoeuvre the shaft into position. Fit Churchill abutment plate (S.314) to gearbox front face.

Fit circlip (33) to bearing (32) and use Churchill driver S.314 to drift the bearing into position. Fit washer (34) and circlip (35) behind the bearing.

Strike rear end of mainshaft with a copper mallet to take up clearance between circlip (35), washer (34) and bearing (32).

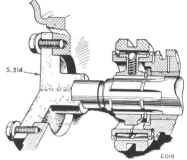

Fig. 24. Showing the abutment plate, Tool No. S.314, installed in place of the front cover

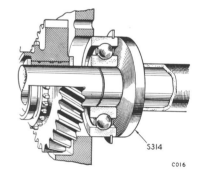

Fig. 25. Using driver, Tool No. S.314, to drift the rear bearing into position

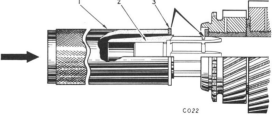

1 Driver S.145   2 Circlip expander   3 Circlip

Fig. 26. Installing the front circlip to the mainshaft

Fig. 27.   Fitting the input shaft bearing

Fig. 28.   Fitting the front cover

Fig. 29.   Mainshaft assembled

Fig. 30.   Using tapered pilot, Tool No. 20.SM.76, to align the countershaft prior to installing the layshaft

Input Shaft Assembly (Figs. 1 and 27)

Assemble to the input shaft (29) :
— disc (28).
— bearing (27), circlip groove to front.
— washer (25).
— circlip (24).

If necessary, fit a new bearing (30) into the input shaft bore, positioning the lettered face outwards.

Fit circlip (26) to the bearing (27) and drift the assembly into position.

Front Cover (Figs. 2 and 28)

Placing the lip of seal towards the gears, use Tool No. 20.SM.73.A to drive a new seal (80) into the front cover (83).

Using Tool No. 20.SM.47 to protect the oil seal, fit gasket (84) and cover. Secure with washers (81) and Wedglok bolts (82).

Countershaft (Figs. 1, 2 and 30)

Insert a tapered pilot tool 20.SM.76, as shown in Fig. 30, to align the countershaft and thrust washers. Insert countershaft (51) and eject the pilot tool. Engage the end of the countershaft and reverse gear shafts with the keeper plate (58) and secure with the screw (59). Fit and secure the countershaft cover gasket (88) and cover plate (85) with washers (87) and bolts (86).

Rear Extension (Figs. 1 and 2)

Attach a gasket (95) and rear extension (96) to the gearbox and secure with spring washers and bolts (135).

Fit a distance washer (36) to the mainshaft, and drive the extension ball race (37) into position. Fit a new oil seal (101) with its sealing face facing forwards. Position the driving flange (38) on the mainshaft and fit the washer (39) and slotted nut (40). Tighten the nut to the specified torque before fitting a new split pin (41).

Fit the speedometer drive gear assembly (104 - 107) and secure it with the peg bolt (108).

Top Cover

Re-assembly (Fig. 32)

Assemble the selectors (111) and (134) to their respective shafts and secure with peg bolts (133).

Fit new 'O' rings (67) to recesses in the rear of the top cover and fit the retaining plate (65), securing with screws (63) and spring washers.

Position the interlock plunger (117) in the 3rd/Top selector shaft and insert the shaft in the top cover. Engage the selector fork (75), distance tube and secure the fork with a peg bolt.

Fit the interlock ball (118) between the reverse and 3rd/Top selector shaft bores, retaining the ball with grease.

Slide the reverse selector shaft (119) into the top cover, engaging it with the reverse selector fork (123) and distance tube. Fit the peg bolt to the selector fork (123).

Ensuring that the reverse and 3rd/Top selector shafts are in the neutral position, fit the second interlock ball (118), securing it with grease.

Insert the 1st/2nd selector shaft into the top cover, passing the shaft through the 1st/2nd selector fork (78) and distance tube.

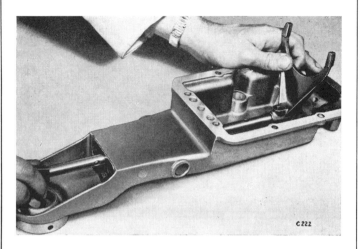

Fig. 31. Installing the Top/3rd selector shaft

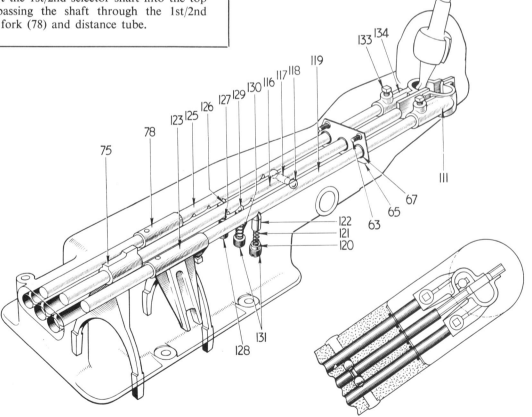

Fig. 32. Top cover details
The key to annotations is given on page 2·204

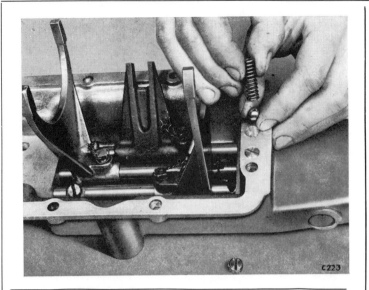

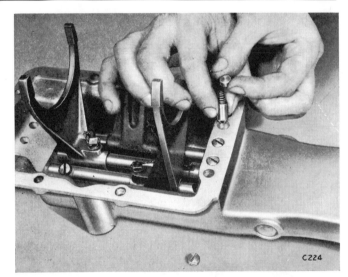

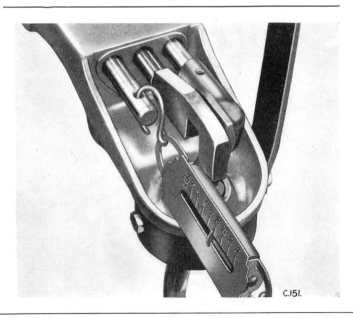

Top Cover—Reassembly (cont'd.)

Fit the balls (126 - 129) and long springs (127 - 130) to the 1st/2nd and 3rd/Top selector shaft detents, retaining the springs by screwing the plugs (128 - 131) in flush with the machined lower face of the top cover. See note below.

Similarly, fit the plunger (122), short spring (121) and shim (120) to the reverse selector shaft detent, retaining the assembly with the plug (131).

Using a spring balance as shown on Fig. 35, check the selector shaft release loads and compare them with those quoted on page 2·203. If necessary, adjust the spring loads by grinding the end of the spring to reduce the release load or by fitting shims between the spring and plug to increase the load.

Referring to Fig. 2 refit the spring (110) and plunger (109) to the lever (114), then assemble the lever, spring (112) and plate (113) to the top cover, depressing the plunger (109) with a screwdriver as the lever end is engaged in the selectors. Secure the lever by fitting the cap (64), cross pin (66) and nut (62).

Using a new gasket (74), refit the top cover assembly to the gearbox, ensuring that the reverse selector fork engages with the actuating lever (55).

Fit the strap (102) beneath the head of the rear mounting bolt.

Note: From gearbox number CT.9899, the 3rd/Top selector shaft ball and long spring were replaced by a plunger and short spring identical to the reverse selector shaft plunger and short spring.

Fig. 33.   **Fitting a ball and spring to the 1st/2nd and 3rd/Top selector shafts. See note above.**

Fig. 34.   **Fitting a plunger, spring and distance piece to the reverse selector shaft**

Fig. 35.   **Using a spring balance to check the selector shaft release loads**

OVERDRIVE DETAILS

OVERDRIVE UNIT — DIMENSIONS AND TOLERANCES

PARTS AND DESCRIPTION	DIMENSIONS NEW	CLEARANCE NEW
PUMP		
Plunger Diameter	0·375″ — ·004″ — ·0008″	
Bore for Plunger in Pump Body	0·375″ ± ·0008″ — ·002″	+ ·0016″ + ·0002″
Plunger Spring Fitted Load at top of Stroke ..	9 lbs. 12¾ ozs.	
Valve Spring Load	4 lbs. at $\frac{17}{32}$″ long	
Pin for Roller	0·25″ ± ·00025″	
Bore for Pin in Roller	0·25″ + ·002″ + ·001″	·00225″ ·00075″
GEARBOX MAINSHAFT		
Shaft Diameter at Steady Bushes	1·15625″ — ·0009″ — ·0018″	
Steady Bush Internal Diameter	1·15625″ + ·003″ + ·002″	+ ·0048″ + ·0029″
Shaft Diameter at Sun Wheel	1·15625″ — ·0009″ — ·0018″	
Sun Wheel Bush Internal	1·15625″ + ·003″ + ·002″	+ ·0048″ + ·0029″
Shaft Diameter at Rear Steady Bush	0·625″ — ·0008″ — ·0015″	
Rear Steady Bush Internal Diameter	0·625″ — ·001″ — ·000″	+ ·0025″ + ·0008″
GEAR TRAIN		
Planet Pinion Bush Internal Diameter	0·4375″ + ·0020″ + ·0012″	
Planet Bearing Shaft External Diameter	0·4375″ + ·0000″ — ·0005″	+ ·0025″ + ·0012″
End Float of Sun Wheel	0·008″ to ·014″	
PISTON BORES		
Accumulator Bore	1·125″ ± ·0005″	
Operating Piston Bore	1·125″ ± ·0005″	
MISCELLANEOUS		
Clutch Movement from Direct to Overdrive ..	0·080″ - ·120″ allowance for ¼″ wear of direct drive clutch	Allowance for wear ⅛″ overdrive clutch

Fig. 2. Overdrive thrust springs
1 Long springs 2 Short springs

Fig. 3. Showing the wire locking of adaptor plate bolts

Overdrive Assembly to Gearbox

1. Dismantle the gearbox as described on page 2·206 and replace the existing mainshaft with a shorter overdrive mainshaft. Re-assemble the gearbox and in place of the normal gearbox rear extension fit the over-drive adaptor and gasket as shown on Fig. 3. Coat a paper gasket on both sides with jointing compound and fit it over the studs on the overdrive mounting flange.

2. Assemble the pump eccentric to the gearbox mainshaft. Mount the overdrive vertically in a vice with its driving flange downwards and, using a spare overdrive mainshaft, align the splines in the overdrive, easing the cone clutch bridge pieces with a screwdriver to facilitate spline alignment.

3. Lower the gearbox onto the overdrive, engaging the gearbox mainshaft splines with those in the overdrive and ensuring that the clutch springs engage with their corresponding locations in the adaptor plate. Tie the reverse gear operating lever in the neutral position and engage top gear to permit rotation of the mainshaft to assist spline alignment whilst lowering the gearbox onto the overdrive.

4. Using one screwdriver to depress the hydraulic pump plunger and a second screwdriver to push the cam into alignment with the plunger roller, engage the pump plunger with the cam face as shown on Fig. 4.

5. Fit and progressively tighten the two nuts on the long studs, compressing the thrust springs and pulling the gearbox adaptor plate against the overdrive unit. Finally secure the two units together by fitting nuts and spring washers to the remaining four studs.

Fig. 4. Assembling the gearbox to the overdrive unit

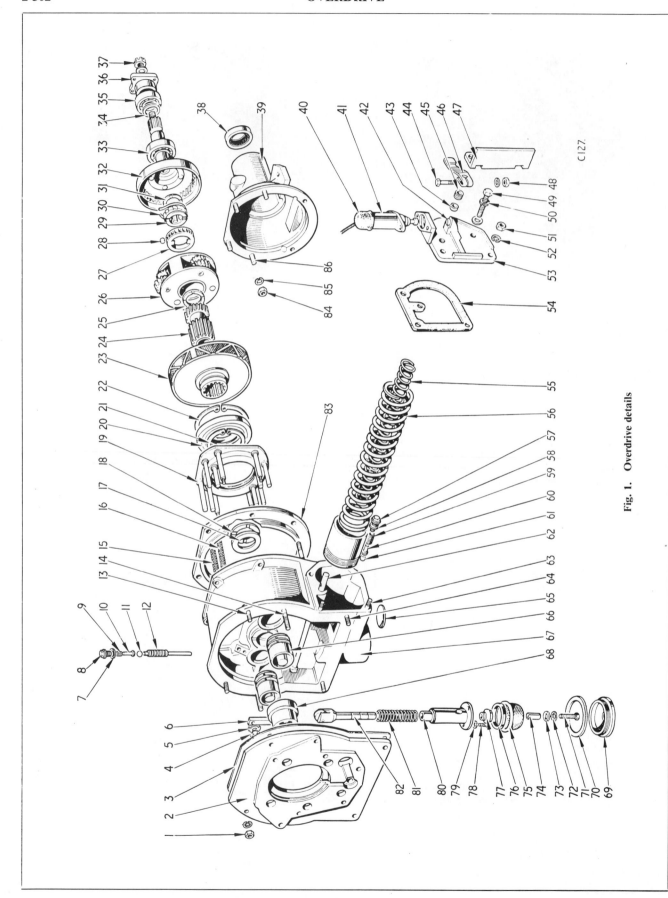

Fig. 1. Overdrive details

Key to Fig. 1

EXPLODED VIEW OF OVERDRIVE UNIT

1 Nut
2 Adaptor plate
3 Gasket
4 Nut
5 Tab washer
6 Bridge piece
7 Washer
8 Plug
9 Spring
10 Plunger
11 Ball
12 Valve
13 Stud (short)
14 Stud (long)
15 Spring (long)
16 Spring (short)
17 Thrust washer (steel)
18 Thrust washer (bronze)
19 Thrust ring assembly
20 Thrust race
21 Circlip
22 Circlip
23 Clutch sliding member
24 Sun wheel
25 Thrust washer
26 Planet carrier assembly
27 Roller cage
28 Clutch roller
29 Uni-directional clutch inner member

30 Spring—inner member to cage
31 Thrust washer
32 Annulus and output shaft
33 Ball race (front)
34 Distance washer
35 Ball race (rear)
36 Driving flange
37 Slotted nut
38 Oil seal
39 Rear housing
40 Rubber cover
41 Solenoid
42 Rubber stop button
43 Seal
44 Pinch bolt
45 Collar
46 Operating lever
47 Dust shield
48 Nut
49 Setscrew
50 Spring washer
51 Nut
52 Spring washer
53 Cover plate
54 Gasket
55 Inner accumulator spring
56 Outer accumulator spring
57 Plug
58 Sealing washer

59 Spring
60 Plunger
61 Ball
62 Operating valve cross shaft
63 Stud
64 Stud
65 Welch plug
66 Piston
67 Body
68 Pump eccentric
69 Drain plug
70 Sealing washer
71 Setscrew
72 Spring washer
73 Plain washer
74 Distance tube
75 Filter gauze
76 Seal
77 Pump end plug
78 Screw
79 Spring washer
80 Pump body
81 Pump return spring
82 Pump plunger
83 Brake ring
84 Nut
85 Spring washer
86 Stud

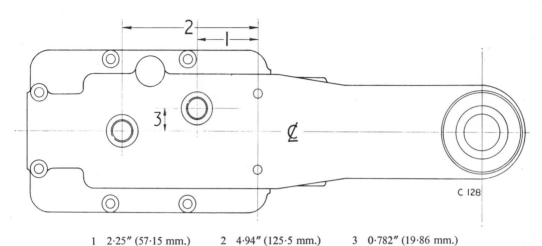

1　2·25″ (57·15 mm.)　　　2　4·94″ (125·5 mm.)　　　3　0·782″ (19·86 mm.)

Fig. 5.　Showing the position of the isolator switches

Fig. 6.　Cover removed to gain access to
the solenoid operating lever

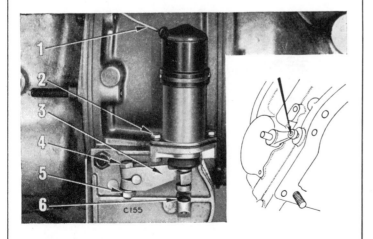

Fig. 7.　Overdrive solenoid and operating lever

Overdrive Isolator Switches

Fit the isolator switches and washers to the top cover supplied in the kit. Alternatively, drill and tap two 16 mm. × 2 mm. pitch holes in the existing cover as shown on Fig. 5.

Dismantle the original top cover and transfer the components to the new cover or re-assemble after tapping the old cover.

Using a new paper gasket, fit the top cover to the gearbox.

Valve Adjustment (Fig. 7)

Remove the cover plate (Fig. 6) and release the operating lever (3) by slackening the bolt (4). Lock the valve operating shaft by inserting a $\frac{3}{16}$″ diameter pin through the setting lever and into a corresponding hole in the casting as shown on Fig. 7 (inset).

Operate the solenoid and while the plunger is drawn into the solenoid, hold the lever against the head of the plunger and tighten the clamp bolt (4).

Switch off the solenoid, remove the pin from the setting lever and refit the cover plate.

1　Electrical lead to solenoid
2　Securing screws
3　Operating lever
4　Clamp bolt
5　Nut and spring washer
6　Rubber stop

OVERDRIVE 2·305

OVERDRIVE SERVICING

Hydraulic Pressure

A working oil pressure of 380 - 400 lb. per sq. in. (26·72 - 28·12 Kg.cm.^{2}) is required. This is checked by a special pressure gauge connected to an adaptor which screws into the operating valve chamber in place of the normal plug. Low pressure indicates leakage at the pump valve seat, a broken accumulator spring or faulty piston rings.

The Operating Valve

To Remove (Fig. 9)

Remove the carpet and take out the rubber plug in the gearbox cover giving access to the valve retaining plug (Fig. 1). Unscrew the plug (1) and remove the spring (2) and plunger (3) to expose the ball (4), which should lift $\frac{1}{32}''$ (0·8 mm.) off its seat when the operating switch is moved to the overdrive position. If the ball does not lift by this amount, reset the lever as described on page 2·304.

To remove the valve for examination use a magnet to extract the ball (4) and withdraw the valve (9), avoiding damage to the ball seat.

Ensure that the restrictor jet (8) at the lower end of the valve is not blocked. If the ball (4) does not seat correctly, gently tap the ball onto its seating with a copper drift and hammer.

The Pump

If the valve is satisfactory and the unit fails to operate, check the pump operation as follows:

Jack up the rear wheels of the car, remove the valve plug and ball, and with the engine ticking over engage top gear. If the valve chamber remains dry, the pump is not functioning.

The pump shown on Fig. 10 delivers oil via a non-return valve to the accumulator. Possible sources of trouble are (1) ineffective non-return valve due to foreign matter on the seat or (2) a choked air bleed causing air to be trapped inside the pump. If this occurs, remove the pump and clean the flat of the pump body and the bore of the casting into which it fits.

The Pump Valve (Fig. 1)

Access to the pump valve is as follows:
1. Remove drain plug and drain oil.
2. Remove the operating lever (46).
3. Remove the nuts (51), spring washers (52), and gradually slacken the setscrews (49). Remove the end plate (53), gasket (54) and springs (55) and (56). Unscrew the plug (57), washer (58) and withdraw spring (59), plunger (60) and ball (61).

Fig. 8. Using a pressure gauge to check hydraulic pressure

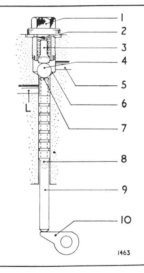

1 Plug
2 Spring
3 Plunger
4 Ball
5 Passage to accumulator
6 Ball seat
7 Valve seat
8 Restrictor hole
9 Valve
10 Operating cam

Fig. 9. Cross section of operating valve

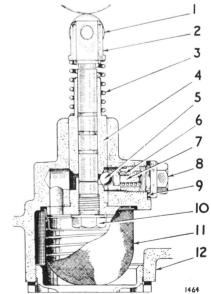

1 Cam roller
2 Plunger
3 Return spring
4 Pump cylinder
5 Ball
6 Spring
7 Plunger
8 Plug
9 Washer
10 End plug
11 Gauze filter
12 Casing

Fig. 10. Cross section of pump

Fig. 11. Showing Tool No. L.183A prior to screwing item 1 into the pump body

Fig. 12. Extracting the pump

1 Guide pins
2 Pump body

Fig. 13. Using Tool No. L.184 to replace the pump body

Re-Assembly (Fig. 1)
1. Refit items (61), (60), (59), (58) and (57), tightening the plug to prevent oil leakage.
2. Refit the springs (55) and (56), a new gasket (54) and end plate (53). Tighten the setscrews (49) and fit the nuts (51) and spring washers (52).
3. Fit and reset the operating lever as instructed on page 2·304.

To Remove Pump
Proceed as follows :
1. Remove pump valve as described previously.
2. Unscrew the securing bolt (71) and remove the filter (75).
3. Remove two screws (78) securing the pump body flange and using Churchill Extractor No. L.183A, extract the pump body (80).

To Refit the Pump
Refit the plug in the bottom of the pump body. Line up the pump body so that the inlet port and holes for securing screws register with the corresponding holes in the housing and drive in the pump body.

The pump plunger is prevented from rotating by a guide peg carried in the front casing. When assembling the pump, insert the plunger with the flat of its head facing the rear of the unit. Guide it past the guide peg with a screwdriver inserted through the side of the casing.

To Remove the Accumulator Piston
Screw a $\frac{3}{8}''$ U.N.F. bolt into the piston and extract the piston by pulling the bolt.

Dismantling the Unit

Should additional dismantling be necessary, remove the unit from the car as directed on page 2·205.

The unit is attached to the gearbox casing by nuts and six $\frac{5}{16}$" studs, two of which are extra long. Remove the nuts (Fig. 1) from the short studs (13), then progressively unscrew the nuts from the longer studs (14) and withdraw the unit from the mainshaft.

Remove the eight clutch springs (15), (16) from their pins and the two bridge pieces (6). If necessary, withdraw the two operating pistons (66). Remove the pump valve as described on page 2·305. Remove the nuts (84) securing the two halves of the housing and separate them, removing the brake ring (83). Lift out the planet carrier assembly (26). Remove the clutch sliding member (23) complete with the thrust ring (19), bearing (20), sun wheel (24) and thrust washers (17), (18) and (25).

Take out the inner member of the unidirectional clutch (29), the rollers (28) and cage (27), spring (30) and thrust washer (31).

If necessary, dismantle the planet carrier by extracting the Mills pins from the carrier and drifting out the shafts.

Remove the flange (36) and speedo gear assembly. Drift the output shaft and annulus from the rear. Extract the front bearing (33) and drift the bearing (35) from the housing.

Inspection

Clean and inspect each part after the unit has been dismantled to assess which components require renewal. It is important to appreciate the difference between parts which are worn sufficiently to affect the operation of the unit and those which are merely "bedded in".

Re-Assembly of Overdrive (Fig. 1)

Press the front ball race (33) onto the annulus shaft (32) and insert the assembly into the rear housing (39). Fit a distance washer (34) to the annulus shaft (32) and press the rear ball race (35) into the rear housing. Fit the driving flange (36) and secure it with the slotted nut (37). To prevent bearing pre-load, end float of the annulus shaft when assembled in the rear housing should be 0·005" - 0·010" (0·13 - 0·25 mm.).

Adjust by selective use of the following distance washers.

XN.657E	..	0·146"±0·0005"	(3·71 mm.)
XN.657F	..	0·151"±0·0005"	(3·83 mm.)
XN.657G	..	0·156"±0·0005"	(3·96 mm.)
XN.657H	..	0·161"±0·0005"	(4·09 mm.)

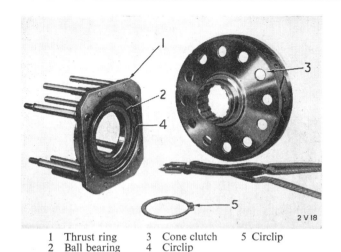

1 Thrust ring	3 Cone clutch	5 Circlip
2 Ball bearing	4 Circlip	

Fig. 14. Sliding clutch member

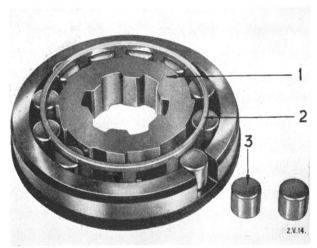

1 Inner member   2 Cage   3 Rollers

Fig. 15. Using Tool No. L.178 to assemble roller clutch

Fig. 16. Transferring the roller clutch to the annulus
Note the thrust washer (1)

Fig. 17.   Rear housing with roller clutch assembled

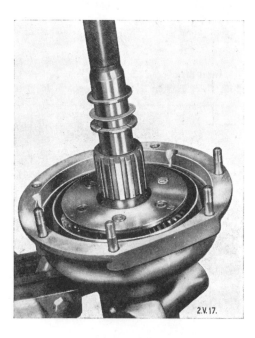

Fig. 18.   Fitting sun wheel thrust washers
Note extra thrust washer of known thickness

Placing its sealing lip inwards, fit a new oil seal (38) to the rear housing. Refit the driving flange (36), slotted nut (37) and secure the nut with a split pin. Fit the speedometer drive gear assembly.

Refit the thrust washer (31) and uni-directional clutch inner member (29) with its rollers (28), cage (27) and spring (30). The "Free Wheel Assembly Ring" and "Transfer Ring" shown on Fig. 15, are ideal for assembling the uni-directional clutch, but where these fixtures are not available, assemble the rollers and hold them in place with a strong elastic band.

Ensure that the spring is fitted correctly, i.e., so that the cage urges the rollers up the ramps on the inner member. If an elastic band is being used to assemble the clutch, the assembly should be installed by holding the cage whilst the inner member is rotated against the spring. This causes the rollers to roll down the ramps and so enables the assembly to be inserted into the outer ring. Remove the elastic band.

Prepare the main casing assembly by fitting the oil pump, valve and accumulator assemblies as described on page 2·306.

Utilizing Churchill Tool No. L.179, fit the two operating pistons. Fit the operating valve assembly as shown in Fig. 9.

Assemble the brake ring (83) to the main casing (67). *Do not use jointing compound.*

Sun Gear End Float

To determine the amount of sun gear end float, which should be 0·008″ to 0·014″ (0·2 - 0·35 mm.) proceed as follows :

Holding the rear housing (39) in a vice as shown in Fig. 18, insert the dummy mainshaft, tool No. L.185A, through the roller clutch and temporarily assemble the following items in the order given:

— thrust washer (25).
— planet carrier (26) and sun wheel (24), placing the marked teeth of the planets radially outwards as shown in Fig. 19.
— thrust washers (18) and (17) plus an additional washer of known thickness.
— brake ring (83).
— front housing assembly (67).

Measure the gap between the flanges of the brake ring (83) and rear casing (39) as shown on Fig. 20.

This gap will be equal to the thickness of the extra washer less the amount of the sun wheel end float.   Example :

Thickness of extra washer ..	= 0·078″
Gap between rear casing and brake ring	= 0·062″
Sun wheel end float	= 0·016″

Separate the two casings and leaving the planet carrier in situ, remove the extra thrust washer. If required, replace the steel thrust washer (17) at the front of the sun wheel by one of greater or lesser thickness as required to produce the correct end-float. Ensure that the steel washer is fitted adjacent to the bronze transfer bush.

Washers are available for this purpose in the following sizes :—

Part Number	Size	
	ins.	mm.
SN.667A	0·114	2·9
SN.667B	0·108	2·7
SN.667C	0·102	2·59
SN.667D	0·096	2·44
SN.667E	0·090	2·29
SN.667F	0·084	2·13
SN.667G	0·078	1·98

Sliding Clutch Member (Fig. 1)

Assemble the sliding clutch components as follows :—

Press the ball bearing (20), into the thrust ring (19), and secure with the circlip (22). Press the thrust ring and bearing onto the sliding clutch member (23) and secure the bearing with the circlip (21).

Assemble the sliding clutch unit to the sun gear splines and fit the main casing and brake ring to the rear casing, securing this with spring washers and nuts.

Fit the bridge pieces (6) to the pull rods and secure them with nuts (4) and locking plate (5).

Assemble the clutch thrust springs (15) and (16), ensuring that the four long springs are fitted on the outer guide pegs and the short springs on the inner pegs.

Refit the unit to the gearbox as described on page 2·303.

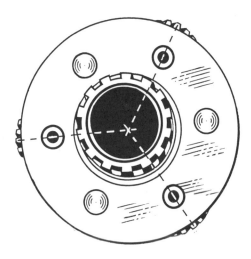

Fig. 19. Showing the position of markings on the planet wheels when assembled to the sun wheel

Fig. 20. Measuring sun wheel end float

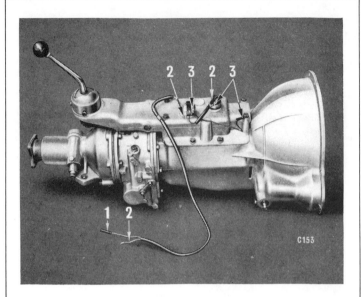

Fig. 21.   Colour coding of overdrive cables

1   Yellow and purple
2   Yellow
3   Black (earth)

Refitting the Gearbox

1. Pass the gearbox through the near side door of the vehicle. Ensure that the clutch driving plate is centralized on the flywheel by passing a dummy clutch spigot shaft or centralizing tool through the spline centre of the clutch plate. Remove the centralizing tool and manoeuvre the gearbox into position, entering the clutch release lever past the edge of the floor aperture, and slide the unit forward into engagement with the clutch splines. Engaging top gear and rotating the gearbox driving flange will assist in engaging the gearbox input shaft splines with those of the clutch driven plate. Ensure that the clutch flange is fully home against the rear face of the engine before fitting and tightening the flange bolts and nuts.

2. Fit the rear crossmember and mounting to the chassis, lower the engine and gearbox onto the silentbloc rear mounting, and tighten the bolts, engaging the R.H. bolt with the exhaust pipe mounting bracket.

3. Refit the starter motor and clutch cover plate, fit the propeller shaft and fit the longer speedometer cable supplied in the kit. Fit the clutch slave cylinder to the clutch housing flange, securing the slave cylinder stay to the sump bolt. Refit the slave cylinder push rod, securing it with a new split pin. Check and if necessary adjust the clutch release bearing clearance. See page 2·106.

4. Fit the overdrive switch to the steering column, secure the relay unit beneath the facia and, using the cable harness supplied in the kit, make the necessary electrical connections as described in the electrical section.

5. Refill the gearbox and overdrive with oil. Refit the gearbox casing, passing the overdrive operating cables through the grommetted hole in the casing, bridge piece, heater controls, carpets and seats.
Re-connect the battery.

Fig. 22.   Overdrive installation

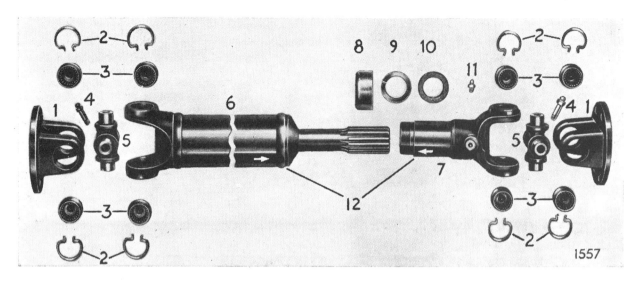

1 Flange yoke	5 Spider	9 Steel washer
2 Circlips	6 Propeller shaft	10 Washer
3 Cups	7 Sliding yoke	11 Grease nipple
4 Grease nipple	8 Dust cap	

Fig. 1. Propeller shaft details

PROPELLER SHAFT

Universal Joints

Individual parts of the needle roller bearing assemblies should not be renewed. If replacements are necessary, fit the complete set of bearing parts which comprise : journal complete with oil seals, and retainers, needle bearing assemblies and snap rings.

Renew the bearings as follows :—

Disconnect the propeller shaft and remove it from the vehicle.

Remove circlip (2), pinching the ends together with a pair of circlip pliers. If the circlip does not readily snap out of the groove, remove enamel from the yoke holes and lightly tap the ends of the bearing cup (3) which will relieve pressure against the circlip.

Holding the joint in one hand, tap lightly with a soft hammer on the radius of the lug of the yoke, as shown in Fig. 2. The needle bearing will gradually emerge and can finally be withdrawn using grips. If necessary, tap the bearing race from inside.

Repeat this operation for the opposite bearing and remove the yoke as shown in Fig. 3. Rest the two exposed trunnions on wood or lead blocks and tap the ears of the flange yoke to remove the remaining needle rollers. Remove the rear universal joint by repeating this procedure. Wash all the parts in petrol or paraffin.

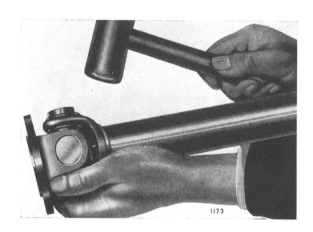

Fig. 2. Tapping bearing cap cups from yoke

Fig. 3. Removing spider from yoke

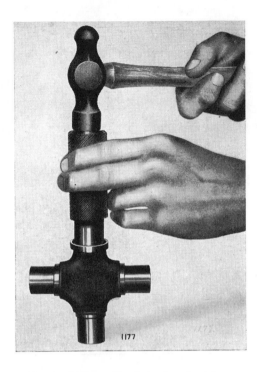

Fig. 4. Fitting spider journal seal retainers

Fig. 5. Sliding yoke alignment

Assembly

Apply jointing compound to the spider journal shoulders and fit the oil seals and the retainers on the trunnion by using a tubular drift as shown on Fig. 4.

Insert the spider journal (5), Fig. 1, into the flange yoke and, using a soft drift, tap the bearing into position. Repeat with the remaining bearings.

Fit new circlips and ensure that these are firmly located in the grooves. If, when assembled, the joint tends to bind, tap the yoke lightly with a wooden mallet to relieve pressure. Re-assemble the other universal joint by repeating the procedure.

To Detach the Sliding Yoke

Unscrew the dust cap (8), steel washer (9) and washer (10).

Withdraw the sliding yoke (7).

To Refit Sliding Splines

Align the arrows (Fig. 5) so that the front and rear universal joints are in the same plane.

TRIUMPH TR4
WORKSHOP MANUAL

GROUP 3

Comprising:

TR4 WORKSHOP MANUAL

GROUP 3

CONTENTS

REAR AXLE

Parts and Description	Dimensions when new	Clearances when new	Remarks
Axle Ratio Track Width between Spring Centres	3·7 or 4·1 : 1 4′ 0″ 2′ 11″		4′ 1″ with wire wheels.
Crown Wheel Number of Teeth Locating Diameter Maximum permissible Run-out	37 (41) 4·3750″/4·3760″ 0·003″	0·0010″/0·0030″	4·1 crown wheel is identified by two grooves on its periphery. Diameter of location on carrier—4·373″/4·374″. When bolted to differential carrier.

Pinion
Number of Teeth
 	
Diameter of Journal—
    for Pinion Head Bearing
 	
    for Pinion Tail Bearing
 	
Spline Diameters—Maximum
          —Minimum
Thread Dimensions
	10
	
	1·2506″/1·2511″
	
	1·0004″/1·0009″
	
	0·9900″/0·9940″
	0·8460″/0·8475″
	$\frac{5}{8}$″—18 U.N.F.
			4·1 pinion identified by two annular grooves on the splines.
			
			Bearing press-fit. Interference of —0·000″/0·0011″.
			Bearing light drive fit. Limits allow clearance of 0·0002″ to an interference of 0·0009″.
			
			Driving flange locating diameter.

Axle Casing
Internal Diameter for :
    Pinion Head Bearing Outer Ring
 	
    Pinion Nose Bearing Outer Ring
 	
    Differential Bearing Outer Rings
 	
Width between Differential Bearing Outer Ring Abutments
Maximum Spreading Load for entry of Assembled Differential Unit
	
	2·8578″/2·8588″
	
	2·4395″/2·4405″
	
	2·8445″/2·8455″
	
	7·2550″/7·2630″
	
	3250 lbs.
			Ring is press fit in bore. Interference of 0·0005″/0·0021″.
			Ring is press fit in bore. Interference of 0·0005″/0·0019″.
			With bearing caps tightened, limits allow clearance of 0·0015″ to an interference of 0·0001″.
			
			Load applied between reaction points 30″ apart.

Axle Shafts Overall Length Hub Bearing Journal Diameter External Diameter of Serrations Number of Serrations Thread Dimensions Keyway Width Driving Key Dimensions Axle Shaft End Float	26·31″ 1·3135″/1·3140″ 1·0377″/1·0417″ 24 $\frac{3}{4}$″×16 T.P.I. U.N.F. 0·2500″/0·2510″ 1$\frac{7}{16}$″ × $\frac{1}{4}$″ × $\frac{1}{4}$″ 0·0040″/0·0060″	 Class 2A	Bearing press fit on shaft. Interference of 0·0004″/0·0015″. End float controlled by shim thickness between end of axle casing and brake backing plate. See remarks concerning "Thrust Button".
Hub Bearing Housing Internal Diameter for Bearing Outer Ring	 2·7485″/2·7495″		Ring is press fit in housing. Interference of 0·0005″/0·0019″.

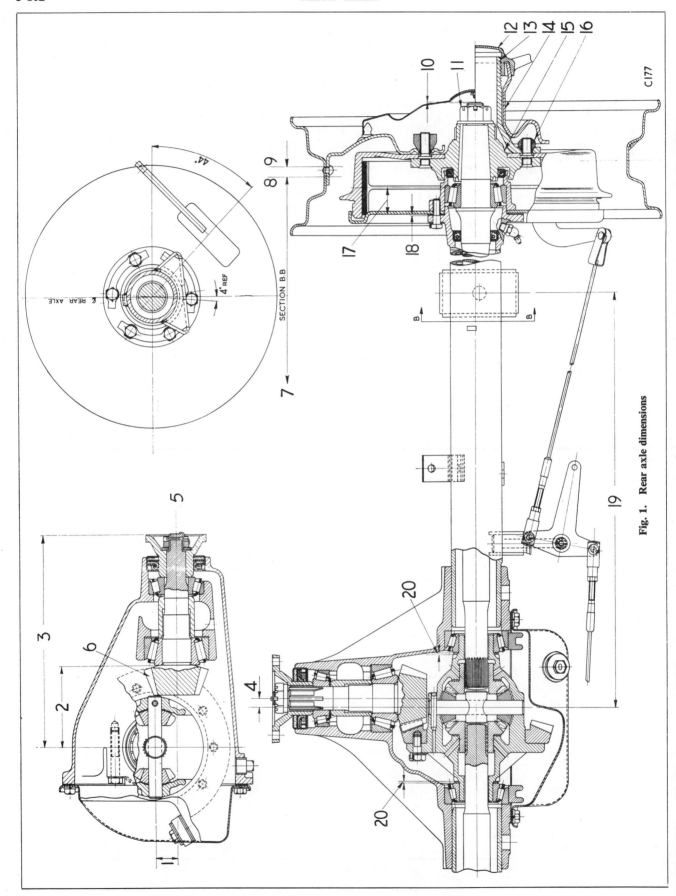

Fig. 1. Rear axle dimensions

C177

Key to Fig. 1

REAR AXLE DIMENSIONS

1 Pinion height below crown wheel centre line = 1" (25·4 mm.)

2 Pinion front face to crown wheel centre line = 3·44" (87·38 mm.) ; 3·437" (87·3 mm.)

3 Driving flange to crown wheel centre line = 8·94" (227·07 mm.)

4 Pinion offset from axle centre line = 0·38" (9·65 mm.)

5 Pinion pre-load 15 - 18 lb. in. (0·1728 - 0·207 m.k.g.) without oil seal

6 Pinion and crown wheel backlash 0·004" - 0·006" 0·1016 - 0·1524 mm.)

7 24·04" (61·07 cm.) to centre line of axle

8 Centre line to disc wheel

9 Centre line of wire spoke wheel

10 0·004" - 0·006" (0·1016 - 0·1524 mm.) hub end float

11 Axle shaft nut — tighten to 125 - 145 lb. ft. (17·28 - 20·05 k.g.m.) torque

12 Centre lock wheel nut (wire spoked wheels)

13 Hub extension (wire spoked wheels)

14 Wire spoked wheel centre

15 Hub

16 Hub extension nut (wire spoked wheels)

17 1·13" (28·7 mm.)

18 Total thickness of shims in both sides of axle 0·016" (0·406 mm.) min. to 0·108" (2·74 mm.) max.

19 Axle centre line to spring mounting 17·5" (444·5 mm.)

20 Differential bearing pre-load to be shimmed 0·002" - 0·004" (0·0508 mm. - 0·1016 mm.) measured over both bearings

REAR AXLE — continued

Parts and Description	Dimensions when new	Clearances when new	Remarks
Pinion Setting Dimensions			
Distance from Head Bearing Abutment Face on Pinion to Centre of Crown Wheel Bearings	3·4375″		
Pinion Centre Line 'Offset' below Crown Wheel Centre Line	0·9990″/1·0010″		
Pinion Bearing Pre-load (without Oil Seal)	15/18 lb. ins.		Controlled by shim thickness between bearing spacer and nose bearing inner cone.
Backlash between Pinion and Crown Wheel	0·0040″/0·0060″		Controlled by shim thickness behind differential bearings.
Differential Unit			
Differential Sun Gear :			
Number of Teeth	16		
Journal Diameter	1·4985″/1·4993″	0·002″/0·004″	Clearance of gear in gear carrier.
Number of Internal Serrations	24		
Internal Diameter	0·9750″/0·9790″		
Thrust Washer Thickness	0·0470″/0·0490″		
Planet Gear :			
Number of Teeth	10		
Internal Diameter	0·6250″/0·6265″	0·0008″/0·0028″	Clearance between gear and cross-pin.
Thrust Washer Thickness	0·0470″/0·0490″		
Cross-pin :			
Diameter	0·6237″/0·6242″	0·0003″/0·0020″	Clearance of pin in differential housing.
Length	4·19″		
Thrust Button :			
Length between Thrust Faces	1·3700″/1·3800″		Arrange hub bearing adjusting shims to permit the thrust button to assume a central position in relation to cross-pin.
Differential Casing :			
Diameter of Journal for Differential Bearings	1·5012″/1·5018″		Bearing press fit. Interference of 0·0006″/0·0018″.
Width of Case between Differential Bearing Abutments	5·3120″/5·3170″		
Dimension between Bearing Abutment and Crown Wheel Locating Face	1·5620″/1·5680″		
Internal Diameter for Differential Sun Gear Journals	1·5013″/1·5025″	0·002″/0·004″	Clearance of gear in gear carrier.
Width between Differential Side Gear Thrust Faces	2·3620″/2·3660″		
Diameter of Cross-pin Bore	0·6245″/0·6257″	0·0003″/0·0020″	Clearance of cross-pin in housing.
Differential Bearing Pre-Load (measured over both bearings)	0·0020″/0·0040″		Controlled by thickness of shims.
Hubs (Rear)			
Thread Dimensions for Withdrawal Purposes	1⅞″ × 8 T.P.I. S.A.E.		

REAR AXLE

To Remove

1. Jack up the rear of the vehicle and lower onto stands positioned beneath the chassis frame adjacent to the forward spring eyes. Remove road wheels and drain axle oil.
2. Disconnect propeller shaft at the rear end.
3. Disconnect the handbrake primary cable from the compensator lever (2) and release the cable from its abutment (3) on the axle tube.
4. Drain the brake system and disconnect the flexible brake hose (4).

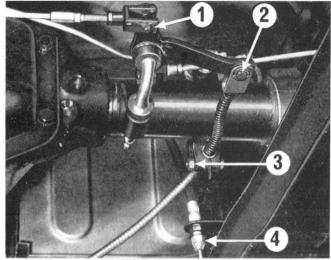

Fig. 2. Handbrake compensator connections

5. Release the brake pipe assembly (7) from the axle and the handbrake cables from the wheel cylinder levers (4).
6. Release the lock tabs, remove six bolts (5) and detach the hubs, axle shafts, brake drums and backplates as a unit. Keep the two shim packs separate.
7. Remove the axle bump straps (9).
8. Jack up each spring until the axle rebound rubbers are clear of the chassis frame. Remove the U-bolts (6) allowing the plates to hang on the damper links (8).
   Remove the jacks from the springs.

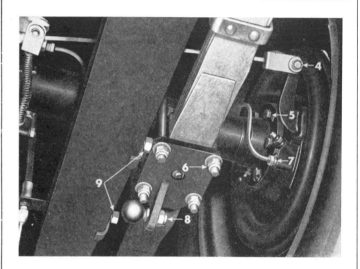

Fig. 3. Axle attachments

9. Release the exhaust tail pipe mounting from the chassis.
10. Feed the axle over the L.H. side of the chassis frame. Lower the R.H. side of the axle and move rearwards to allow the axle tube to pass beneath the chassis frame.
11. Manoeuvre the axle clear of the chassis.

To Refit

To refit, reverse the removal procedure, noting that on L.H. steering cars, a $\frac{3}{16}''$ thick packing piece must be fitted between the spring and the axle tube mounting platform on the passenger side of the car.

Fill the axle with oil and bleed the brake hydraulic system.

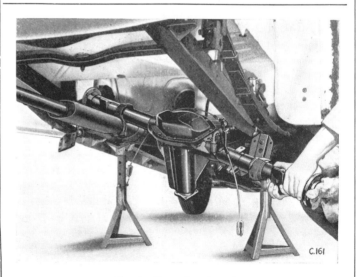

Fig. 4. Removing the axle

Fig. 5. Using Tool No. 20S.93 to remove hub bearing outer rings

Fig. 6. Using Tool No. S.4221-2 to withdraw hub bearing from axle shaft

Fig. 7. Using Tool No. 20S.92 to fit oil seal in axle tube

Fig. 8. Using Tool No. 20S.93 to fit hub bearing outer rings

Fig. 9. Using Tool No. M.86A to remove rear hub

Axle Shaft, Hub Bearing and Oil Seals

To Remove and Dismantle (Fig. 13)

Jack up the rear of vehicle and place on stands : remove road wheel, hub extension (if fitted) and brake drum. Drain the brake hydraulic system and uncouple the brake pipe and handbrake cable from the backplate.

Withdraw split pin (48) and remove the slotted nut (46) and plain washer (47). Extract rear hub using Tool No. M86.A.

Release lock plates (41), remove six setscrews (42) and detach the bearing housing (38), shims (40) and brake assembly.

Tap out the oil seal (39) and extract the bearing outer ring (37) from the housing, using Tool No. 20S.93.

Withdraw the axle shaft, remove the key (45) and extract the bearing (37) using Tool No. S.4221-2.

Extract the oil seal (51) from the axle casing.

To Re-Assemble

Placing the sealing lip inwards, install a new seal (51) into the axle casing.

Using Tool No. 20S.92, drive the hub bearing (37) onto the axle shaft and refit key (45).

Draw the bearing outer ring into the housing (Tool No. 20S.93) and install a new oil seal (39), its lip facing inwards. Pack the hub bearing with grease.

Thread the bearing housing (38) onto the shaft (36) and refit hub (43), plain washer (47) and slotted nut (46), which must be tightened to a torque of 125 to 145 lbs. ft. (17·28 to 20·05 kilogrammetres) and secured with a split pin (48).

Insert the assembled axle shaft into the axle casing. Locate the shaft serrations in the sun wheel and secure the bearing housing with six setscrews (42) and lockplates (41).

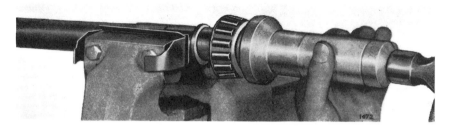

Fig. 10. Using Tool No. 20S.92 to drive bearing
onto half shaft

Axle Shaft End Float

Check the axle shaft end float as shown on
Fig. 11. This should be 0·004″ to 0·006″ (0·1 to
0·15 mm.). Adjust by altering the thickness of
the shim pack interposed between axle sleeve
and backing plate.

IMPORTANT: To ensure centralisation of the
thrust block with the cross pin
(see Fig. 12) equalize the thickness of the shim packs behind
both backing plates.

Replace the brake drum and road wheel,
then remove the axle stands and lifting jack.

Fig. 11. Measuring axle shaft end float

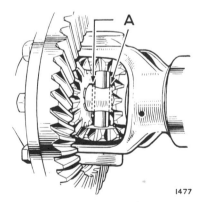

Fig. 12. Showing position of differential cross-pin
in relation to the thrust block
Clearances A should be equal

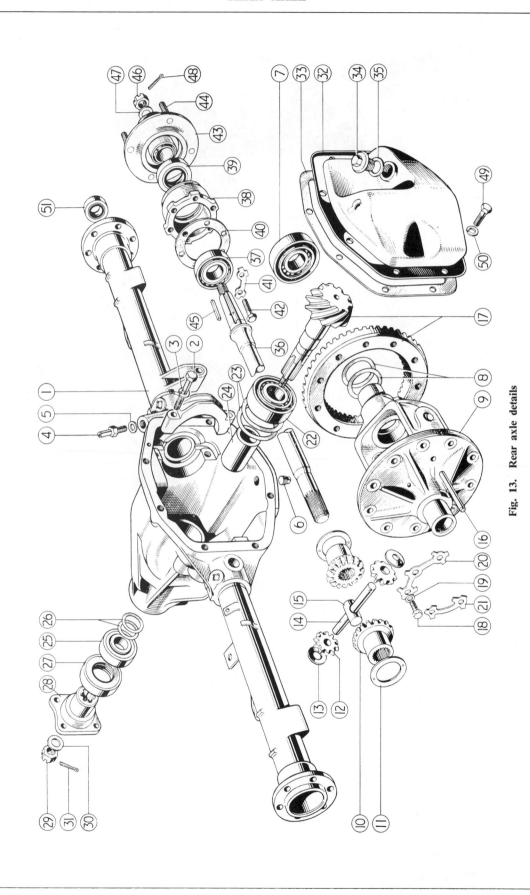

Fig. 13. Rear axle details

Key to Fig. 13

1   Axle casing assembly
2   Bearing cap setscrew
3   Spring washer
4   Axle case breather
5   Fibre washer
6   Drain plug
7   Differential bearing
8   Adjusting shims for (7)
9   Differential carrier
10 Differential sun gear
11 Thrust washer for (10)
12 Differential planet gear
13 Thrust washer for (12)
14 Cross pin
15 Thrust block
16 Lock pin for securing (14)
17 Crown wheel and pinion

18 Crown wheel securing bolt
19 Spring washer for (18)
*20 Three hole lockplate
*21 Two hole lockplate
22 Pinion head bearing
23 Adjusting shims for (22)
24 Bearing spacer
25 Pinion tail bearing
26 Adjusting shims for (25)
27 Pinion shaft oil seal
28 Pinion driving flange
29 Driving flange securing nut
30 Plain washer for (29)
31 Split pin for (29)
32 Rear cover
33 Joint washer for (32)
34 Oil filler plug

*35 Fibre washer
36   Axle shaft
37   Hub bearing
38   Hub bearing housing
39   Oil seal for hub bearing housing
40   Adjusting shims for hub bearing
41   Lockplate
42   Setscrew for securing housing
43   Hub
44   Road wheel attachment stud
45   Hub driving key
46   Hub securing nut
47   Plain washer for (46)
48   Split pin for (46)
49   Cover plate securing setscrew
50   Spring washer for (49)
51   Axle tube oil seal

*Now Deleted

Differential Unit—To Remove (Fig. 13)

Remove the axle shafts as described on page 3·106.

Remove setscrews (49), lockwashers (50), cover plate (32) and joint (33). Unscrew the four securing bolts (2) and remove the bearing caps.

Assemble the axle spreading tool as shown on Fig. 14. Turn the double ended tensioner screw until it is hand tight, then a further half turn with a spanner.

IMPORTANT: OVER-SPREAD WILL DAM-
AGE THE AXLE CASING.

Lift the differential unit from the casing.

If the bearings are likely to be re-used, tie the bearing outer rings to their respective inner races.

Differential Unit—To Dismantle

Remove the fixing bolts (18) and detach the crown wheel (17) from the carrier (9).

Drive out the lock pin (16), withdraw the pinion cross shaft (14) and remove the thrust block (15).

Rotate the sun wheels and remove the gears (12), (10) and the thrust washers (13), (11).

Preliminary Check for Run-out of the Differential Carrier

Before removing the bearings (7) from the carrier (9) check the crown wheel mounting face of the carrier for run-out as follows :—

Re-install the carrier into the centre casing.

Mount a dial indicator gauge on the casing as shown in Fig. 15 and rotate the carrier.

Maximum amount of run-out should not exceed 0·003″ (0·08 mm.).

Readings in excess of this figure indicate defective bearings, or carrier.

Remove the differential carrier from the casing and extract the bearings (7) and shims (8).

Remove the spreading tool from the rear axle case.

Removing Pinion and Bearings

Remove split pin (31), slotted nut (29), washer (30) and withdraw the flange (28).

Using a soft drift, drive the pinion (17) from the casing.

Remove the shims (26), spacer (24) and extract the pinion head bearing (22) as shown in Fig. 17.

Drive out the tail bearings (25) and seal (27) ; the pinion head bearing outer ring and shims (23).

Fig. 14. Using axle spreading tool, No. S.101, to remove differential unit

Fig. 15. Checking the differential carrier for run-out

Fig. 16. Using Tool No. S.103 and Press No. S.4221A to remove differential bearings

Fig. 17. Using Tool No. TS.1 and Press No. S.4221A to remove pinion head bearing

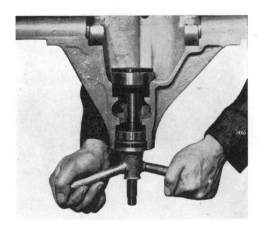

Fig. 18. Using
Tool No. M.70
to install the
pinion head and
tail bearing outer
rings

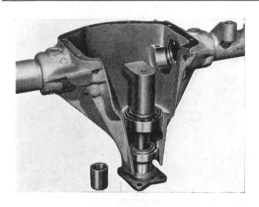

Fig. 19. Showing
the dummy
pinion installed

Setting gauge,
Tool No. M.84

Fig. 20. Using
a special ground
button to zero
the gauge

Fig. 21. Using
setting gauge to
calculate thick-
ness of shims
required under
pinion head
bearing outer
ring

AXLE RE-ASSEMBLY

Before re-assembling the axle components, check the bearing housing for burrs or other damage caused by driving the bearing rings from the casing. Incorrectly seated bearings will prevent accurate measurement of shim requirements and may result in premature loss of pre-load, rapid wear and pinion failure.

Carefully examine all components for serviceability. If the crown wheel or pinion is worn or damaged, discard both items and fit a new matched pair. These gears are machined together and etched with identical markings to identify them as a pair ; therefore, before fitting, ensure that each is identically marked.

Keep the component parts of each bearing together, and when renewal becomes necessary replace the complete bearing assembly.

Pinion Assembly

Using Tool No. M.70, pull the outer rings of bearings (25) and (22) into position as shown in Fig. 18. Shims are not fitted at this stage.

Fit the pinion head bearing (22) on the dummy pinion (Tool No. M.84) and assemble to casing. Fit the tail bearing (25), driving flange (28), washer (30) and nut (29), Fig. 19. Tighten the flange nut to give a pre-load of 15 to 18 lb. ins. (Fig. 25).

The bearing spacer and oil seal are not fitted at this stage.

Zero the pinion setting gauge and determine the required shim thickness as follows:

Using the ground button, depress the dial gauge plunger to its maximum and zero the gauge as shown in Fig. 20.

Place the gauge in the axle casing with the plunger contacting the dummy pinion (Fig. 21).

Exerting downward pressure on the gauge, centralize it by slightly rocking to show maximum reading. This indicates the thickness of shims required under the pinion head bearing outer ring.

Remove the gauge, dummy pinion and the bearing outer rings.

Place a shim pack of the required thickness on the pinion head bearing abutment face (Fig. 23) and fit both bearing outer rings, as shown on Fig. 18.

Assemble the bearing (22), spacer (24) and shims (26) to the pinion shaft.

NOTE : The thickness of shim pack (26) may require re-adjustment to give correct pre-loading.

Drive the bearing (25) onto the pinion shaft. Fit the driving flange (28), washer (30) and nut (29) which should be securely tightened.

Pinion Pre-load

Attach a pre-load gauge on the driving flange as shown on Fig. 25. Slowly move the weight along the graduated scale and note the point at which it falls. This should be 15 to 18 lb. ins.

Higher readings indicate the need for a thicker shim pack between the tail bearing and spacer, lower readings require a thinner shim pack.

When the pre-load is correct, remove the driving flange and fit the oil seal. Replace the flange, plain washer and nut, tighten the nut to the specified torque and secure with a split pin.

Fig. 22. Using Tool No. S.123A to remove pinion bearing outer rings

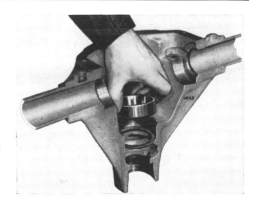

Fig. 23. Placing a shim pack under the pinion head bearing outer ring

Fig. 24. Using Tool No. S.103 and Press S.4221A to fit pinion head bearing

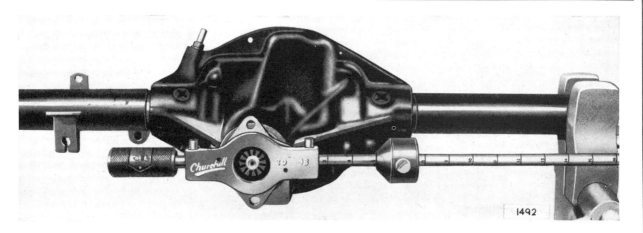

Fig. 25. Pre-Load gauge 20.SM.98

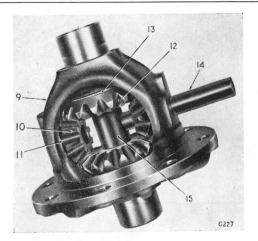

Fig. 26.   Fitting differential gears and thrust washers

Differential Gears (Fig. 26)

Assemble the thrust washer (13) to the sun gears (12) and insert them into the differential carrier (9).

Using grease to retain them, attach the planet thrust washers (11) on the thrust faces of the gears (10) and insert them through the side aperture in the differential carrier to mesh with the sun gears already positioned.

Align the gears with the holes in the casing ; insert the cross pin (14) and simultaneously feed the axle shaft thrust block (15) into position.

Fig. 27.   Fitting locking pin to differential cross-shaft

Align the locating hole in the cross pin and insert the lock pin (16). (Fig. 13).

Using a punch, peen the metal of the differential carrier over the end of the lock pin to prevent its working loose. (Fig. 27).

Fig. 28.   Using a dial gauge to measure total float

Differential—Measuring Total Float

Fit the differential bearings (7) without shims at this stage.

Pressing both outer rings towards the bearing, place the carrier into the casing.

Mount a dial gauge on the casing as shown in Fig. 28. Move the carrier AWAY from the gauge and zero the dial.

Move the carrier TOWARDS the gauge and note the dial reading. This indicates total side float and is referred to as dimension "A" (see Fig. 31) at a later stage.

Remove the differential carrier from the centre casing.

Crown Wheel—Measuring "In and Out" of Mesh

Clean, examine and remove any burrs from the gear mounting face of the carrier and the crown wheel.

Fit the crown wheel (17) to the carrier (9), and insert the bolts (18) with new spring washers (19). Tighten the bolts uniformly to the specified torque.

Fig. 29. Fitting the crown wheel to the differential carrier

Refit the differential unit in the axle casing and position the dial gauge as shown in Fig. 30.

Move the differential unit away from the gauge, to the "Full Mesh" position, and zero the dial.

Note the dial reading when the differential unit is moved towards the indicator gauge. This is the "in and out" of mesh dimension used in the following calculations and referred to as dimension "B" (see Fig. 31).

Lift the differential unit from the axle casing and remove the bearings (7), Fig. 16, taking care not to mix them.

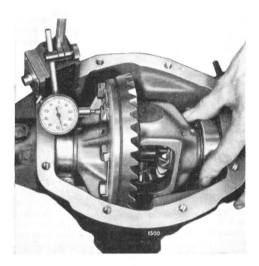

Fig. 30. Using a dial gauge to measure "in and out" of mesh

Differential Bearing Pre-load

To ensure that the differential bearings are correctly pre-loaded, the shim packs interposed between the carrier and each bearing must be of a precise thickness.

By substituting correct measurements in place of those used in the examples, the thickness of both shim packs may be calculated as follows :

Example

Total float "A" - - -	0·060″
Plus 0·003″ pre-load - - -	0·003″
Total thickness of shims required -	0·063″
Shim thickness at "Y"	
In/Out of mesh clearance "B" -	0·025″
Subtract specified backlash 0·004″/ 0·006″ - - - -	0·005″
Shim pack thickness required at "Y"	0·020″
Shim thickness at "X"	
Total shim thickness - - -	0·063″
Minus shim pack thickness at "Y" -	0·020″
Shim pack thickness required at "X"	0·043″

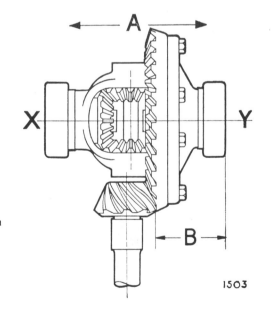

Fig. 31. Diagram for calculating shim thickness.

A. Total float

B. In and out of mesh

Fig. 32. Using
adaptor No.
S.100 with
Handle No. 550
to refit
differential
bearings

Crown Wheel Backlash

Using the axle spreading tool and observing the same precautions in respect of overspreading, re-insert the differential unit into the casing. Remove the axle spreader, assemble the caps and tighten the securing bolts (2) to the specified torque.

Check the crown wheel backlash by mounting the dial gauge and moving the crown wheel in alternative directions as shown on Fig. 33. Measure the backlash at several positions each of which should be within the limits of 0·004″ - 0·006″ (0·1 - 0·15 mm.).

Should the backlash be excessive, reduce the thickness of the shim pack at "X", Fig. 31, and add an equal amount to "Y". If the backlash is insufficient, reverse the procedure.

Fig. 33.
Measuring
crown wheel
backlash

Tooth Markings

After setting the backlash to the required figure, use a small brush to lightly smear eight or ten of the crown wheel teeth with engineer's blue. Move the painted gear in mesh with the pinion to obtain a good tooth impression.

Fig. 34. Painting
crown wheel
teeth to check
pinion marking

(a) **Correct Markings** (Fig. 35)

When the gear meshing is correctly adjusted, the markings obtained should closely approximate those shown in Fig. 35a, this being the ideal contact.

The area of contact is evenly distributed over the working depth of the tooth profile and is located slightly nearer to the TOE than the heel.

(b) High Contact

The markings shown at (35b) are those produced by high contact, i.e., when the tooth contact is heavy on the crown wheel face or addendum and caused by the pinion being too far out of mesh. To rectify, move the pinion deeper into mesh by adding shims under the pinion head bearing outer ring. To maintain the existing pinion bearing preload, an equal amount of shims must also be added between the tail bearing inner cone and the bearing distance piece.

(c) Low Contact

Fig. 35 (c) shows heavy markings on the crown wheel flank or dedendum, this being the opposite to that shown in (b). Rectification of this condition necessitates moving the pinion out of mesh by removing an equal amount of shims from the positions described in (b).

NOTE :-When correcting for (b), the new position will tend to move the tooth contact towards the toe on drive and the heel on coast, whilst correcting for (c) will tend to move the tooth contact towards the heel on drive and the toe on coast. In either case it may be necessary, after correcting the pinion mesh, to re-adjust the crown wheel as described in (d) and (e).

(d) Toe Contact

The markings shown in Fig. 35 (d) result when the tooth contact is concentrated at the small end of the tooth. To rectify this condition, move the crown wheel out of mesh, i.e., increase backlash by transferring shims from the crown wheel side of the differential to the opposite side.

(e) Heel Contact

Fig. 35 (e) shows the markings obtained when the tooth contact is concentrated at the large end of the tooth. This condition is rectified by reducing backlash, i.e., by transferring shims in the opposite direction as for (d).

IMPORTANT :-Whatever corrections are necessary, it is most important that the backlash at all times is within the specified limits.

(i) **Backlash** When adjusting for backlash, always move the crown wheel as this member has more direct influence on backlash.

(ii) **Crown Wheel Movement** Moving the gear out of mesh has the effect of moving the tooth contact towards the heel and raising it slightly towards the top of the tooth.

(iii) **Pinion Movement** Moving the pinion out of mesh raises the tooth contact on the face of the tooth and slightly towards the heel on drive, and towards the toe on coast.

ADDENDUM - upper part of tooth profile
DEDENDUM - lower part of tooth profile

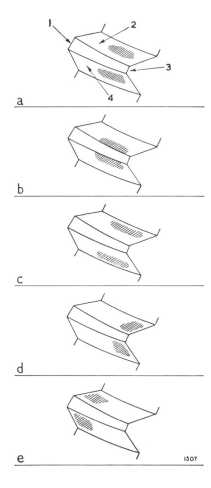

1 Heel (outer end)
2 Coast side (concave)
3 Toe (inner end)
4 Drive side (convex)

Fig. 35. Typical gear tooth markings

REAR AXLE DIMENSIONS

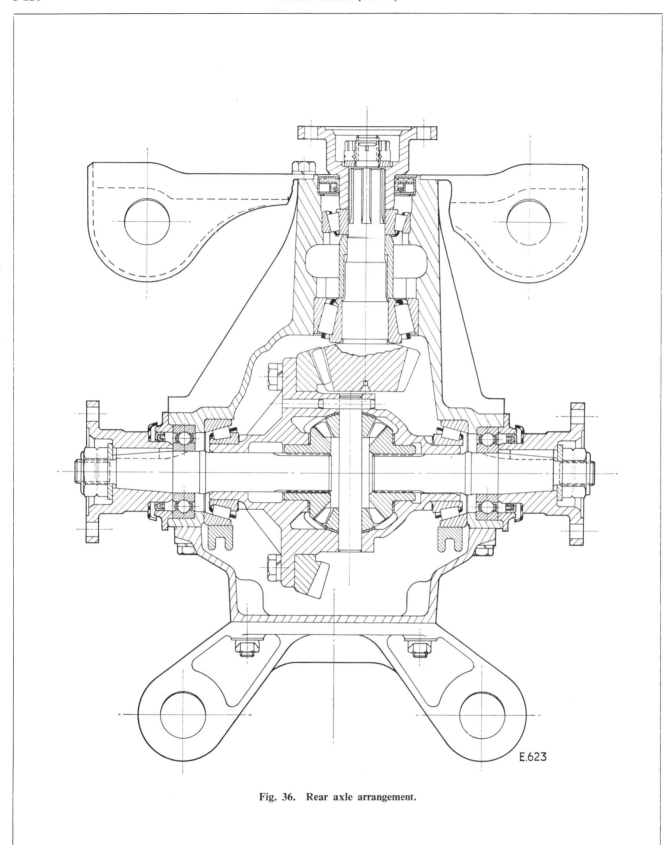

Fig. 36.   Rear axle arrangement.

REAR AXLE — DIMENSIONS AND TOLERANCES

PARTS AND DESCRIPTION	DIMENSIONS WHEN NEW		REMARKS
	ins.	mm.	
Axle ratio	4·1 : 1 or 3·7 : 1		
Crown Wheel			
Number of teeth	41		37 for 3·7 : 1 ratio
Location diameter	4·376/4·375	111·15/111·13	Clearance 0·001″—0·003″ (0·025—0·076 mm.)
Maximum permissible run-out	·003	·07	When mounted on differential cage
Fixing bolts	10		
Thread dimensions	⅜ U.N.F. 2A ·41 deep		
Pinion			
Number of teeth	10		
Journal diameter for:			
Pinion head bearing	1·2511/1·2506	31·78/31·77	Bearings press fit. Interference
Pinion tail bearing	1·0009/1·0004	25·42/25·41	0·0001″—0·0011″ (·002—·03 mm.)
Spline diameter — major	0·9916/0·9912	25·19/25·18	Clearance in driving sleeve
— root	0·8475/0·8460	21·53/21·49	Slide fit in driving sleeve
Key width	0·2485/0·2475	6·31/6·29	Slide fit in driving sleeve
Number of keys	6		
Thread dimensions	⅝ UNF. 2A		
Axle Casing			
Internal diameter for:			Bearings press fit. Interference
Pinion head bearing outer race	2·8588/2·8578	72·61/72·59	0·0005″—0·0021″ (0·013—0·053 mm.)
Pinion tail bearing outer race	2·4405/2·4395	61·99/61·96	Bearings press fit. Interference 0·0005″—0·0019″ (0·013—0·048 mm.)
Pinion oil seal	2·687/2·686	68·25/68·22	
Differential trunnion bearing outer race	2·8455/2·8445	72·28/72·25	With bearing caps tightened bearings transition fit. 0·0015″ clearance to 0·0001″ interference
Inner axle shaft journal bearing	2·5003/2·4993	63·51/63·48	Bearing transition fit 0·0002″ clearance to 0·0013″ interference
External diameter of spigot for mounting bracket	2·938/2·936	74·63/74·57	
Width between differential bearing abutments	7·263/7·255	184·48/184·28	
Diameter of rear cover dowel holes	0·3135/0·3131	7·96/7·95	
Level plug thread dimensions	⅜″ × 18 t.p.i. N.P.T.		
Pinion Setting Dimensions			
Offset of pinion below crown wheel centre line	1·001/0·999	25·43/25·37	Determined by axle casing
Centre line of pinion to crown wheel mounting face of differential cage	1·878/1·872	47·70/47·55	These dimensions are theoretical and may vary in practice when meshing is adjusted to correct backlash and tooth marking
Pinion head bearing abutment face to crown wheel centre line	3·4375	87·31	
Backlash	0·006/0·004	0·15/0·10	

REAR AXLE — DIMENSIONS AND TOLERANCES — continued

PARTS AND DESCRIPTION	DIMENSIONS WHEN NEW		REMARKS
	ins.	mm.	
Differential Unit			
Differential Sun Gears			Gears and shafts to be selected to
Number of teeth	16		give a push fit on the splines
Journal diameter	1·4993/1·4985	38·08/38·06	Clearance in cage
			0·002″—0·004″ (0·05—0·10 mm.)
Number of splines	24		
Internal diameter	0·979/0·975	24·87/24·77	
Thrust washer thickness	0·0495/0·0465	1·26/1·18	
Planet Gears			
Number of gears	2		
Number of teeth	10		
Internal diameter	0·6265/0·6250	15·91/15·88	Clearance on cross shaft
			0·0028″—0·0008″ (0·07—0·02 mm.)
Thrust washer thickness	0·0495/0·0465	1·26/1·18	Varying thicknesses available to
			reduce backlash
Cross Shaft			
Diameter	0·6242/0·6237	15·85/15·84	See Differential Cage
Length	4·20/4·18	106·68/106·17	
Differential Cage			
Location diameter for crown wheel	4·374/4·373	111·10/111·07	
Diameter of trunnions	1·5018/1·5012	38·15/38·13	Bearings press fit. Interference
			0·0006″/0·0018″ (0·015—0·046 mm.)
Internal diameter for sun gears	1·5025/1·5013	38·16/38·13	Clearance on gears
			0·002″—0·004″ (0·05—0·10 mm.)
Width between trunnion bearing			
abutments	5·317/5·312	135·05/134·92	
Bearing abutment to crown wheel			
mounting face	1·568/1·562	39·83/39·67	
Width between sun wheel thrust			
faces	2·366/2·362	60·10/60·00	
Diameter of cross shaft bores	0·6257/0·6245	15·89/15·86	Clearance on shaft
			0·0003″—0·002″ (0·007—0·05 mm.)
Differential bearing pre-load	0·004/0·002	0·10/0·05	Measured over both bearings
Inner Axle Shafts			
Overall length, left-hand	7·06	179·32	
Overall length, right-hand	6·19	157·23	
Top diameter of splines	1·0417/1·0377	26·46/26·36	Involute form keys
			Flank fitting; push fit
Number of splines	24		
Keyway width	0·250/0·249	6·35/6·32	
Shaft diameter for journal bearing	1·1258/1·1254	28·60/28·59	Shaft press fit in bearing
			Interference 0·0002″ to 0·0011″
			(0·005 to 0·028 mm.)
Thread dimensions	$\frac{5}{8}$ UNF. 2A		

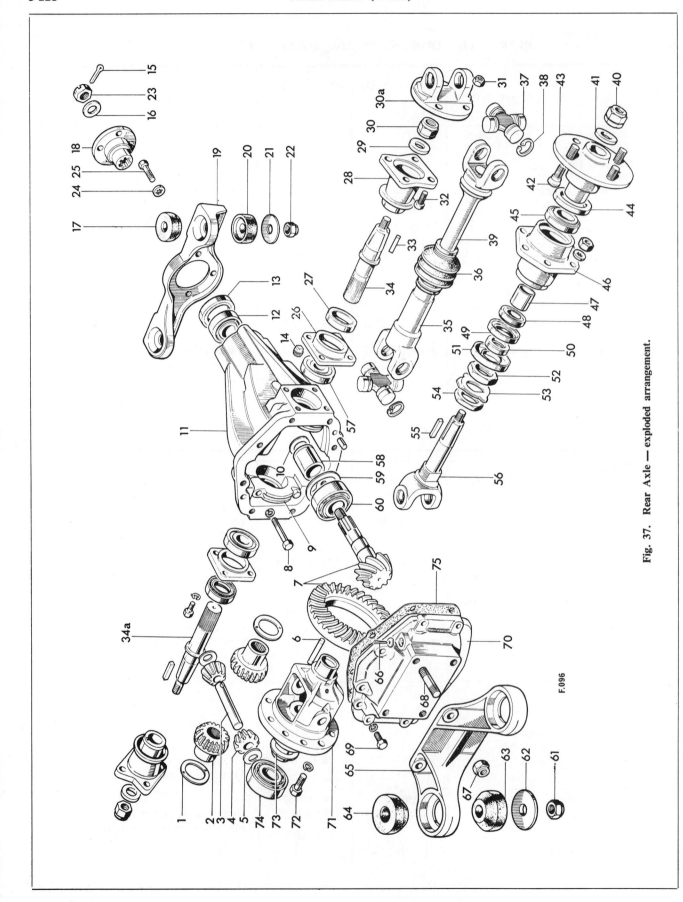

Fig. 37. Rear Axle — exploded arrangement.

F.096

Key to Fig. 37

REAR AXLE COMPONENTS

1. Thrust washer — sun wheel
2. Sun wheel
3. Cross shaft
4. Planet wheel
5. Thrust washer — planet wheel
6. Locking pin — cross shaft
7. Crown wheel and pinion
8. Bolt, bearing cap
9. Bearing cap
10. Shim, pinion pre-loading
11. Axle casing
12. Tail bearing, pinion
13. Oil seal, pinion
14. Filler plug — oil level
15. Split pin
16. Washer
17. Rubber buffer, upper
18. Companion flange
19. Mounting, front
20. Rubber buffer, lower
21. Backing plate
22. Nyloc nut
23. Castellated nut
24. Lockwasher
25. Bolt
26. Bearing retainer
27. Oil seal
28. Flange
29. Washer
30. Nut
30a. Yoke
31. Nut, nyloc
32. Bolt
33. Key
34. Axle shaft, inner, short
34a. Axle shaft, inner, long
35. Axle shaft, fixed, outer
36. Gaiter
37. Universal spider
38. Circlip
39. Axle shaft, sliding, outer
40. Nut
41. Washer
42. Wheel stud
43. Hub
44. Oil seal
45. Hub bearing, outer
46. Bearing housing
47. Bearing spacer, collapsible
48. Hub bearing, inner
49. Oil seal
50. Bearing spacer
51. Stone guard
52. Adjusting nut
53. Tab washer
54. Locknut
55. Key
56. Stub shaft
57. Bearing, inner axle shaft
58. Spacer, pinion bearing
59. Shim, pinion locating
60. Head bearing, pinion
61. Nut, nyloc
62. Backing plate
63. Buffer, lower
64. Buffer, upper
65. Mounting, rear
66. Split pin — breather
67. Nut, nyloc
68. Stud
69. Bolt
70. Rear cover
71. Differential cage
72. Bolt
73. Shim, crown wheel pre-load
74. Bearing, differential cage
75. Gasket, rear cover

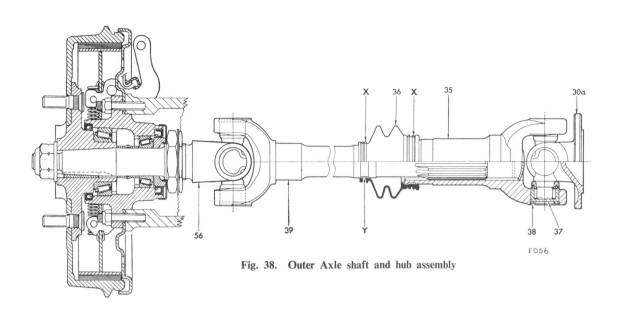

Fig. 38. Outer Axle shaft and hub assembly

TELESCOPIC SHAFTS, WHEEL BEARINGS,
SEALS AND DRIVING FLANGES

(Fig. 38)

Removal

These items are removed as a complete assembly. Proceed as follows:-

Chock the front wheels, slacken the rear wheel nuts and release the handbrake. With a trolley jack placed under the differential casing, raise the rear of the car onto stands positioned beneath the chassis frame. Remove the road wheels, the countersunk screws and the brake drums.

With a socket spanner passed through the holes in the driving flange, remove the six nuts securing the hub assembly to the suspension arm (Fig. 39).

Remove the four nuts and bolts from the inboard universal coupling on the axle shaft, wire the sliding portions of the axle shaft together as shown in Fig. 40, and withdraw the axle shaft through the boss in the trailing arm

The rear brake assembly need not be disturbed, but if it is necessary to remove it for other reasons, it may be withdrawn at this stage after draining the hydraulic system and disconnecting the brake pipe and handbrake cable from the brake backplate.

Fig. 39. Removing bearing housing retaining nuts

Fig. 40. Axle shaft companion flange bolt

**Fig. 41.
Axle shaft
and
hub assembly**

**Fig. 42.
Removing the
hub retaining nut**

**Fig. 43.
Extracting a
rear hub**

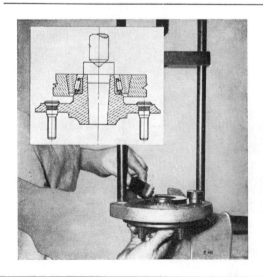

**Fig. 44.
Extracting an
outer
hub bearing cone**

To Dismantle (Fig. 37)

Mount the axle shaft in the holding fixture as shown on Fig. 42 and remove the nut (40), the washer (41) and extract the hub (43), see Fig. 43. The rear hub bearing housing assembly will be removed with the hub. Remove the key (55) and discard the collapsible spacer (47); remove the inner hub bearing cone (48), the bearing spacer (50) and the stone guard (51).

Release the tabs on the tabwasher (53) and wind the adjusting nut (52) and the locknut (54) one complete turn towards the universal joint.

With the bearing housing (46) supported under its mounting face, drive out the inner hub bearing outer race. The inner oil seal (49) will simultaneously be removed.

Lever out the outer oil seal (44) and drive out the outer hub bearing, outer race (45). Using Tool No. S4221A-16, extract the outer hub bearing cone (45) from the hub.

Inspection

Wash all dismantled components in clean paraffin and dry with an air jet. Examine the rollers and roller tracks of the bearings for wear, pitting or fractures.

Examine the key, keyways, and tapers in the stubshaft (56) and hub (43) for wear or damage. Examine the stubshaft for cracks and scores at the inner hub bearing seat and the surface of the bearing spacer (50) outer diameter (oil seal track).

To Re-assemble

Press the outer hub bearing cone (45) up to the shoulder on the hub (43). Press the outer and inner hub bearing outer races up to the shoulders in the bearing housing (46), followed by the inner and outer oil seals (49) and (44).

Feed the stoneguard (51), bearing spacer (50), the inner cone of the inner hub bearing and a new collapsible spacer (47) onto the stubshaft and fit the key (55) into the keyway in the stubshaft, with its inner end in line with the two indentations on the shoulders of the key way.

Pack the spaces between the bearing rollers and the recess in the bearing housing with grease.

Pass the bearing housing assembly over the stubshaft so that the inner hub bearing outer race engages with its mating cone. Avoid damage to the lip of the inner oil seal.

Feed the hub onto the stubshaft, followed by the washer (41) and the nut (40). Tighten the nut to the correct torque.

Bearing End Float — to Adjust

Wind the nut (52) up against the stoneguard (51) until it is finger tight.

Mount a dial indicator on the hub flange with the indicator stylus contacting the bearing housing flange (Fig. 46).

Pull the bearing housing as far as possible AWAY from the indicator, using a rocking motion to ensure proper contact between the bearing components. Zero the indicator dial.

Push the bearing housing as far as possible TOWARDS the indicator, again rocking the housing. Note the reading on the indicator. Tighten the nut (52) one flat at a time whilst an assistant checks the end float as described previously. When the total float is between 0·004″ and 0·002″ (0·10 and 0·05 mm.) secure the assembly with the locknut (54) and tabwasher (53).

NOTE: If the end float has been reduced below 0·002″ (0·05 mm.), the collapsible spacer must be replaced. Merely slackening back the nut (52) is NOT satisfactory.

To Refit

Reverse the removal instructions. If grease has leaked into the rear brake assembly, remove the brake shoes, wash off the backplate assembly and brake drum in clean petrol and dry with an air jet. If the brake linings have become contaminated with grease, the shoes must be replaced.

Fig. 45.
Fitting the outer hub bearing cone

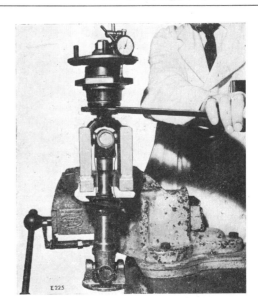

Fig. 46.
Adjusting the bearing end float

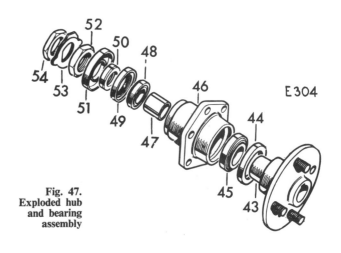

Fig. 47.
Exploded hub and bearing assembly

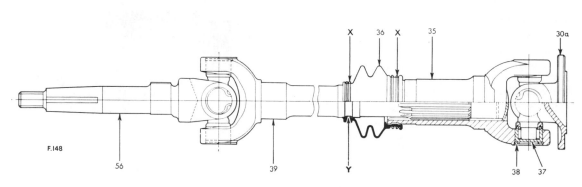

Fig. 48.   Outer Axle shaft assembly

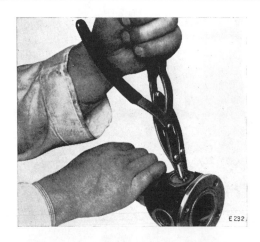

Fig. 49.
Removing a
circlip

Fig. 50.
Removing a
bearing cup
from the flange

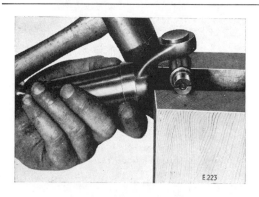

Fig. 51.
Removing a
bearing cup
from the shaft

Outer Axle Shafts (Fig. 48)

To Dismantle

Remove the axle shaft from the vehicle (see page 3·119) and remove the hub and bearing housing. Release the gaiter clip X from the fixed shaft (35) and disengage the gaiter (36). Discard the sealer strip (Y). Withdraw the sliding shaft (39) from the fixed shaft and remove the clip, gaiter and sealer strip from the sliding shaft.

Remove the circlips (38), support the forked end of the shaft (35) as shown, and by striking the flange (30a) with a mallet, drive out the needle bearing cap until it is sufficiently exposed to be removed with a pair of grips. Reverse the shaft and extract the opposite cup in a similar manner. Remove the seals (Fig. 52).

Support the two exposed trunnions of the spider (37) on wooden blocks (Fig. 51) and, by striking the radiused portion of the forked end of the shaft, drive out the needle bearing cup until it is sufficiently exposed to be removed. Repeat the operations to remove the remaining cup. Remove the spider from the forked end of the shaft.

Employ the same method for removing the stubshaft (56) from the sliding shaft (39).

Inspection

Examine the trunnions of the universal joint spiders and the needles and needle tracks in the cups. Examine the grease seals and the circlips and grooves.

Wash the sliding splines of the shafts (35) and (39) in paraffin and dry them with an air jet. Check the splines for wear or damage.

To Re-assemble (Fig. 48)

Pass two trunnions of the spider through the bearing bores in the forked end of the shaft (35). With the exposed trunnions supported as shown in Fig. 51, fit the grease seals and needle bearing assembly into the uppermost bearing bore; fit the circlip (38). Reverse the shaft and fit the opposite grease seal, needle bearing assembly and circlip.

Pass the remaining two trunnions into the bores in the flange (30a) and fit the grease seals, needle bearing assemblies and circlips.

Employing the same procedure, fit the universal joint to the stubshaft (56) and the sliding shaft (39). Wrap a length of Expandite Sealer Strip (Y) $\frac{1}{2}'' \times \frac{1}{16}''$ section round the groove in the shaft (39) so as to completely cover the groove. Fit the smaller end of the gaiter (36) over the sealer strip and double wrap the gaiter clip (X) round the gaiter; secure the clip.

Liberally coat the splined end of the sliding shaft with ROCOL MOLYTONE 320 or Duckham's Q5648 Grease and assemble the sliding shaft (39) into the fixed shaft (35). Ensure that the splines slide freely.

Fit a length of Expandite Sealer Strip round the groove in the fixed shaft, pull the larger end of the gaiter (36) over the sealer strip and secure by double wrapping the gaiter clip (X) round the gaiter.

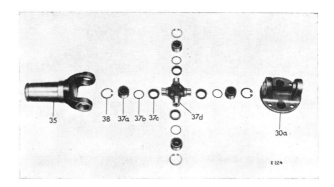

35	Outer shaft — fixed
38	Circlip
37a	Needle bearing assembly
37b	Seal spreader
37c	Grease seal
37d	Spider
30a	Companion flange

Fig. 52. Exploded universal coupling

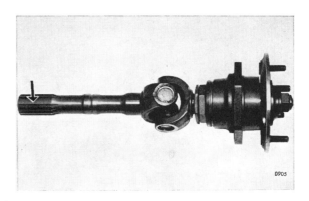

Fig. 53. Stubshaft, sliding outer shaft and hub bearing assembly

(The arrow indicates the master spline)

Fig. 54.   Location of chassis stands

Fig. 55.   Axle unit attachment to chassis

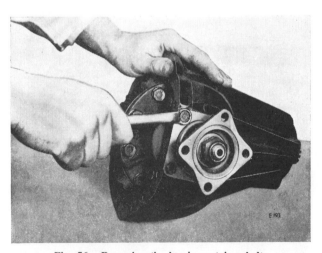

Fig. 56.   Removing the bearing retainer bolts

Rear Axle Casing and Differential Unit

Rear Axle Removal

Chock the front wheels, release the handbrake, and with a trolley jack placed under the differential casing, raise the rear of the car onto stands positioned beneath the chassis frame, as shown on Fig. 54.

Working underneath the car, remove the obstructing section of the exhaust system; disconnect the wheel shafts and the propeller shaft from the axle unit. Support the axle with the trolley jack, unscrew the four nuts, shown arrowed on Fig. 55, which suspend the axle in the chassis and lower the unit to the ground.

Rear Axle Installation

Reverse the removal procedure.

Differential Unit — To Remove (refer to Fig. 37 for component designations)

Remove the eight bolts (69) and spring washers and remove the rear cover (70) together with the mounting (65) and the joint (75).

Remove the inner axle shafts (34), by removing four bolts (Fig. 56) and spring washers from the bearing retainers (26) and withdrawing the shaft assemblies (Fig. 57). Remove the nut (30) and washer (29) and extract the flange (28); see Fig. 58.

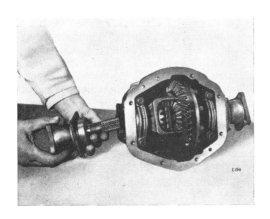

Fig. 57. Removing the inner axle shaft assembly

Fig. 59.
Extracting the
inner axle shaft
bearing

Remove the key (33), the bearing retainer (26) with the oil seal (27). Extract the bearing (57), see Fig. 59. Remove the oil seal (27) from the bearing retainer, see Fig. 60.

Fig. 60.
Removing the
inner axle shaft
seal

Remove the bolts (8) and spring washers, and lift out the bearing caps (9), see Fig. 62.

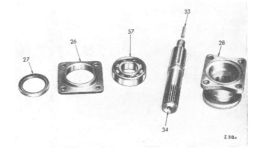

Fig. 61.
Exploded
inner axle
asembly

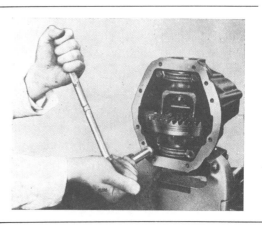

Fig. 62.
Removing the
differential
bearing caps

Fig. 58.   Extracting the inner axle shaft flange

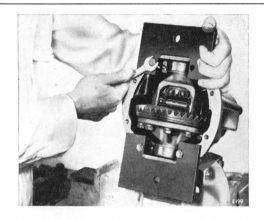

Fig. 63.
Fitting the
spreader adaptor
plates

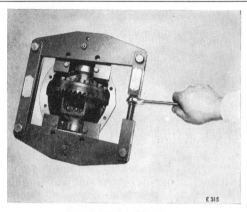

Fig. 64.
Spreading the
axle casing

Fig. 65.
Lifting out the
differential unit

Fig. 66.
Removing the
crown wheel

Fit the spreader tool adaptor plates to the axle casing and lightly nip them down with four ⅜″ U.N.F. bolts 2¼″ long (Fig. 63). Mount the spreader tool on the adaptor plates so that the pegs in the arms of the spreader fit into the large holes in the adaptor plates; turn the jacking screw until it is hand tight. A further HALF TURN with a spanner will spread the casing sufficiently to release the differential unit (Fig. 64).

IMPORTANT: OVERSPREADING WILL CAUSE IRREPARABLE DAMAGE TO THE AXLE CASING.

Lift the differential unit from the axle casing (Fig. 65) and ensure that the trunnion bearing cups and cones are kept in respective pairs.

Differential Unit — To Dismantle

With the differential cage (71) mounted in a vice, remove the bolts (72) and spring washers, and remove the crown wheel (7) from its location spigot on the cage (Fig. 66).

Preliminary Check for Run-out of the Differential Cage

Before removing the inner cones of the trunnion bearings from the differential cage, check the crown wheel mounting face of the differential cage for run-out as follows:—

Wash the oil from the trunnion bearings, assemble the cups onto their respective cones and install the differential assembly into the axle casing. Release all tension on the spreading tool and mount a dial gauge as shown in Fig. 67. Zero the dial of the gauge and rotate the differential cage.

Run-out must not exceed 0·003″ (0·08mm.). Greater run-out indicates defective bearings or a distorted differential cage.

Fig. 67.   Checking the differential cage for run-out

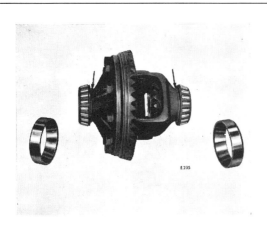

Fig. 68. Differential unit and bearings

Fig. 70.
Driving out the
cross shaft pin

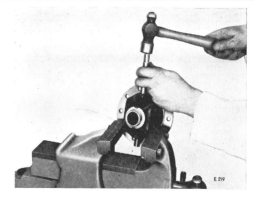

Fig. 71.
Drifting out the
cross shaft

Remove the cage from the casing and extract the bearings (74), see Fig. 69. Remove the shims (73) and note the thickness and location of each shim pack. The shims are shown on Fig. 68.

Remove the spreading tool.

Drive out the cross shaft locking pin (6), Fig. 70, and drift out the cross shaft (3), Fig. 71. Rotate both sun wheels (2) through 90°, thus bringing the planet wheels (4) in line with the apertures in the differential cage.

Remove the planet wheels (4) and thrust washers (5) and the sun wheels (2) and thrust washers (1).

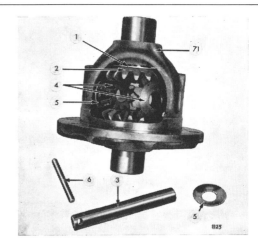

Fig. 72.
Removing the
differential gears

Fig. 69. Extracting the differential bearing cones

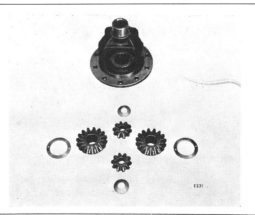

Fig. 73.
Exploded
differential   unit

Fig. 74.   Removing the pinion shaft nut

Fig. 75.   Driving out the pinion

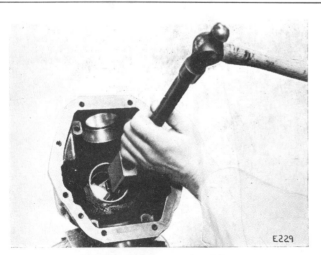

Fig. 76.   Driving out the pinion
bearing outer races

Removing the Pinion and Bearings

Withdraw the split pin, fit the peg spanner (Fig. 74) over the companion flange (18) and remove the castellated nut (23) and the washer (16).   Drive out the pinion (Fig. 75) taking care to avoid damaging the threaded end diameter.

Remove the spacer (58) and the shim pack (10).   Extract the pinion head bearing cone.

Drive out the seal (13) with the pinion tail bearing outer race (12) as shown in Fig. 76.   In a similar manner, drive out the pinion head bearing outer race (60) and remove the shim pack (59).

Inspection

Wash all dismantled components in clean paraffin and dry with a compressed air jet. Examine all bearings for wear, chips, or cracks; pay particular attention to the balls and rollers and replace the complete bearings where pitting of these components is evident.

ENSURE   BEARING   COMPONENTS REMAIN IN SETS.

Lubricate the bearings and wrap in clean paper until required.

Check all gear teeth for wear, chips and cracks, and ensure that all bearing seats are undamaged and free from burrs.

Check the threads on all bolts, nuts and studs and replace all doubtful components.

IMPORTANT: **Crown wheels and pinions are produced as matched pairs and etched with identical identification marks. These components must, if necessary, be replaced as a pair.**

Axle Re-assembly

Using tool No. M.70, pull the pinion bearing outer races (cups) into the axle casing without the shims (59) fitted (Fig. 77).

Fig. 77.
Pulling in pinion bearing outer races

Fit the pinion head bearing cone (60) on the dummy pinion (Fig. 78) and install the assembly into the axle casing. Fit the tail bearing cone (12), the companion flange (18) and the washer and nut (16) and (23) onto the pinion shaft. Do NOT at this stage fit the spacer (58) or the shims (10). Tighten the nut (16) to pre-load the bearings until a torque of 15-18 lb.ins. will just turn the pinion (Fig. 82).

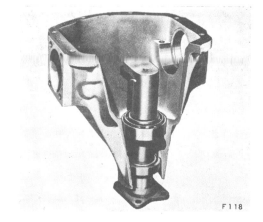

Fig. 78.
Dummy pinion installed

Zero the pinion setting gauge by fully depressing the stylus with the setting button (Fig. 79) and setting the zero mark on the dial in line with the indicator needle.

Fig. 79.
Zeroing pinion setting gauge

To determine the thickness of the shim pack (59) to be inserted under the pinion head bearing outer race (60), place the zeroed gauge in the axle casing with the stylus contacting the ground face of the dummy pinion (Fig. 80). Exerting downwards pressure on the gauge body, rock it in the differential trunnion bearing bores and observe the swing of the needle. The minimum reading is obtained when the gauge stylus is parallel to the pinion centre line and this value indicates the thickness of the shims required under the head bearing outer race.

Remove the gauge, dummy pinion and the head bearing outer race from the axle casing.

Fig. 80.
Measuring pinion height

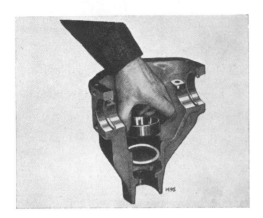

Fig. 81.　Pinion positioning shims in casing

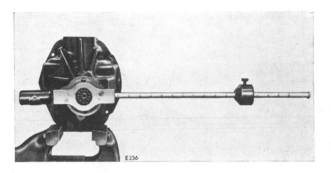

Fig. 82.　Pre-load gauge

Fig. 83.　Planet gear float measurement

Place the required shims (59) on the pinion head bearing abutment face in the casing and install the outer race (Fig. 81).

Assemble the inner cone of the head bearing (60), the spacer (58), and the shims (10) to the pinion shaft and install the assembly into the axle casing.

NOTE: Ensure that the chamfered end of the spacer is towards the tail bearing.

The thickness of the shim pack (10) may require adjustment to give the correct pre-loading of the pinion bearings.

Drive the tail bearing inner cone (12) onto the pinion shaft. Fit the companion flange (18), the washer (16) and the nut (23). Securely tighten the nut, whilst turning the companion flange to ensure that the pre-load does not become excessive.

Pinion Pre-load

Attach a pre-load gauge to the companion flange (Fig. 82).

Move the weight along the graduated rod until the pinion just begins to rotate. Read off the torque value at which this occurs. The value should be between 15 and 18. To increase pre-loading, subtract shims from the pack between the tail bearing inner cone (12) and the spacer (58); to decrease pre-loading, add shims.

When correct pre-loading has been achieved, remove the gauge and the companion flange. Fit the oil seal (13), refit the companion flange, securely tighten the slotted nut and lock with a new split pin.

Differential Gears (Fig. 72)

Assemble the thrust washers (1) to the sun gears (2) and insert them into the differential cage (71). Retain the thrust washers (5) with grease on the planet wheels (4) and insert the planet gears through the apertures in the cage to mesh with the sun gears.

Rotate both sun gears together to carry the planet gears into the cage. When the gear and cage bores are aligned, insert the cross shaft (3) through the cage bores, thrust washers and planet gears.

Check the planet gear backlash by measuring the sun gear end float with feeler gauges (Fig. 83). By selection from the range of thrust washers of differing thicknesses, adjust the backlash between the sun and planet gears to the minimum value consistent with freedom of rotation.

Differential Gears—(continued)

Align the locating hole in the cross shaft (3) with the drilling in the cage and fit the locking pin (6). Peen over the side of the locking pin hole to prevent dislodgement of the pin (Fig. 84).

Differential — Measuring Total End Float

Press the inner cones of the differential trunnion bearing (74) onto the journals of the differential cage. Do NOT fit the shims (73) at this stage. Fit the bearing outer races over the cones and place the assembly into the axle casing.

Mount a dial indicator as shown in Fig. 85, and zero the indicator when the differential assembly has been moved as far as possible AWAY from the indicator.

NOTE: Ensure that the trailing bearing outer race is not left behind, thus allowing the differential assembly to tilt and give a false indicator reading.

Move the differential assembly as far as possible TOWARDS the indicator and read off the total travel. This value gives DIMENSION "A" for later use (Fig. 87).

Crown Wheel—Measuring "In and Out of Mesh"

Remove all burrs and clean the gear mounting face of the differential cage. Check that the mounting face of the crown wheel is clean and free from burrs and fit the crown wheel to the differential cage. Fit the ten bolts (72) and new spring washers and tighten down uniformly to the specified torque.

Install the differential unit into the axle casing but do NOT fit the bearing caps (9). Mount a dial indicator as shown in Fig. 86 and move the differential unit away from the indicator until the crown wheel is hard in mesh with the pinion. Observe the precautions set out under "Measuring Total End Float". Zero the indicator. Move the differential unit towards the indicator until the bearing outer race is hard against the face of the bearing bore in the axle case and read off the total travel. This is the "In and out mesh" dimension ('B' in Fig. 87).

Fig. 84.
Securing the cross shaft locking pin

Fig. 85.
Measuring the total differential end float

Fig. 86.
Measuring the crown wheel "in and out of mesh"

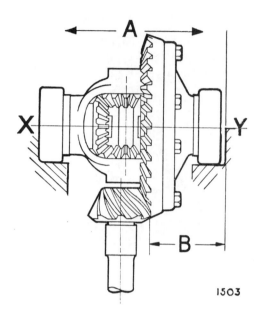

A Total float   B In and out of mesh

Fig. 87. Diagram for calculation of shim thickness

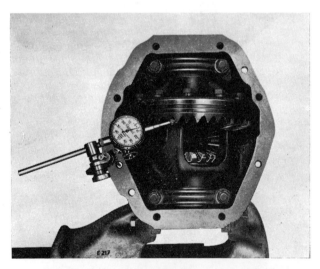

Fig. 88. Measuring crown wheel pinion backlash

Remove the differential unit from the axle casing and extract the bearings (74). Ensure that the bearings cups (outer races) and cones (roller assemblies) are not mixed and that they are fitted to the same sides of the cage when the axle is re-assembled.

Differential Bearing Pre-Load (Fig. 87)

Correct pre-load is achieved only by precise shimming.

Example

(i)	Total float 'A'	...	...	...	·060″
(ii)	Plus pre-load	...	...	...	·003″
(iii)	Total shims required ((i) plus (ii))				·063″

Shim thickness at 'Y':—

(iv)	In/out mesh 'B'	...	...	...	·025″
(v)	Specified backlash (·004″ to ·006″)				·005″
(vi)	Shims required at 'Y' ((iv) minus (v))				·020″

Shim thickness at 'X':—

(iii)	minus (vi)	...	...	...	·063″
					·020″
(vii)	Shims required at 'X'	...	...		·043″

Fit the appropriate shims to the differential cage trunnions and refit the bearings (74).

Crown Wheel/Pinion Backlash

Using the spreading tool, refit the differential unit to the axle casing. Remove the spreading tool; fit the caps (9). Use new spring washers and tighten the bolts (8) to the specified torque.

Check the backlash with a dial indicator mounted as shown in Fig. 88. With the pinion rigidly held, rock the crown wheel to the full possible extent and note the total indicator reading.

Measure the backlash at several positions and check that it is within the specified ·004/·006″ (·10/·15 mm.).

If the backlash is excessive, transfer shims to the equivalent value by which backlash is to be reduced from 'X' to 'Y'. To increase backlash, reverse the procedure.

Tooth Markings   Refer to Page 3·114.

Differential Unit—To Install

Refit the rear cover (70) and joint (75) to the correctly adjusted axle casing and bolt on the mounting (65).

Rear Axle Casing and Differential Unit

To refit, reverse the removal instructions given on page 3·124, fill the casing with one of the approved lubricants and road test the car.

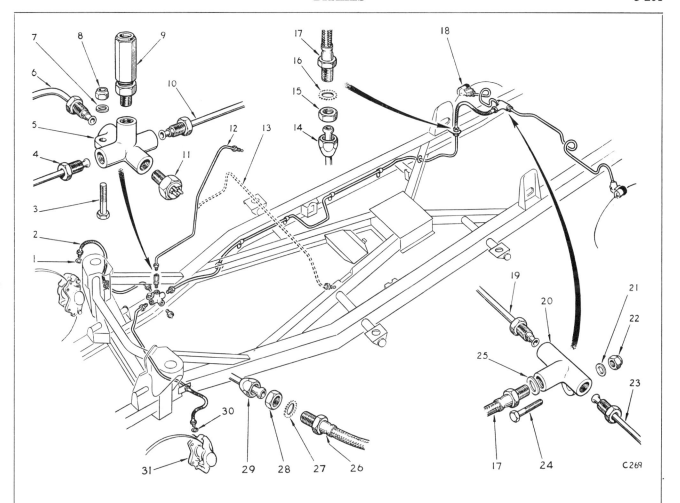

1	Copper washer	13	Pipe—five way union to master cylinder—L.H. drive	23	Pipe—three way union to L.H. rear brake
2	Flexible pipe R.H. front	14	Pipe—five way union to rear flexible pipe	24	Bolt
3	Bolt	15	Nut	25	Copper washer
4	Pipe—L.H. front brake	16	Shakeproof washer	26	Flexible pipe—L.H. front brake
5	Five way union	17	Flexible pipe	27	Shakeproof washer
6	Pipe—R.H. front brake	18	R.H. rear hydraulic cylinder	28	Nut
7	Washer	19	Pipe—three way union to R.H. rear brake	29	Pipe—L.H. front brake
8	Nyloc nut	20	Three way union	30	Copper washer
9	Restrictor valve	21	Washer	31	L.H. front caliper unit
10	Pipe—rear brakes	22	Nyloc nut		
11	Stop light switch				
12	Pipe—five way union to master cylinder—R.H. drive				

Fig. 1.   Hydraulic pipes and couplings

MASTER CYLINDER OPERATION (Fig. 2)

A. Brakes Released Condition

When the brake pedal is released, the push rod (9) is returned to its stop (12) by the pedal return spring. This permits the plunger (7) to move rearwards under pressure of the spring (5). The flange on the end of the valve shank (4) contacts the spring retainer (6) and as the plunger continues to move rearwards, the valve shank (4) lifts the seal (1) from its seat on the end of the cylinder bore and compresses the spring (2). Hydraulic fluid can then flow past the three legged distance piece (3) and seal (1) either to or from the reservoir.

B. Brakes Applied Condition

Initial movement of the push rod (9) and plunger (7) releases the valve shank (4) and permits the spring (2) to press the valve shank (4) and seal (1) against its seat. This cuts off communication between the cylinder and reservoir. Continued movement of the plunger displaces fluid through the hydraulic pipelines and applies the brakes.

Maximum stroke available—
       1·38″ (35·05 mm.).

Stroke position at maximum cut off—
       0·099″ (2·5 mm.).

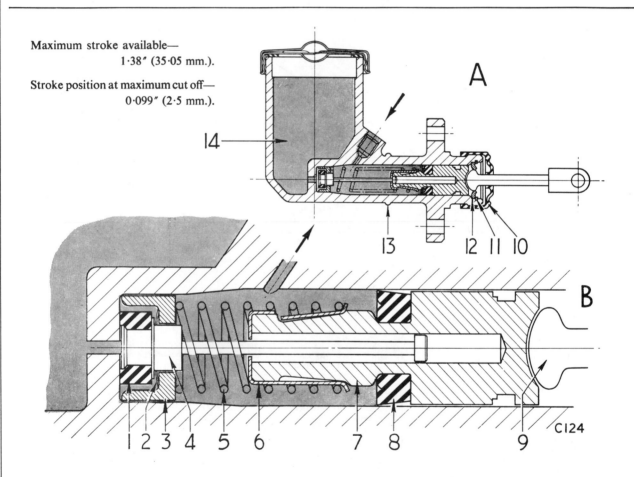

Fig. 2. Section through brake master cylinder

1 Valve seal	6 Spring retainer	11 Circlip
2 Spring (valve seal)	7 Plunger	12 Push rod stop
3 Distance piece	8 Plunger seal	13 Identification ring(s)
4 Valve shank	9 Push rod	14 Fluid reservoir
5 Plunger return spring	10 Dust cover	

Note.—A single ring (13) cast on the body indicates a bore of 0·75″ (19·05 mm.). Two rings indicate a bore of 0·7″ (17·78 mm.).

The smaller bore supersedes the larger from Commission Number CT.5783

Brake Master Cylinder

Removal (Fig. 3)

Clutch and brake master cylinders cannot be removed individually, but only as an assembly, therefore :—

1. Empty the clutch and brake hydraulic systems.
2. Detach the fluid pipes from the master cylinders.
3. Remove the brake and clutch pedal clevis pins (1).
4. Remove setscrews (4) and nuts (3) from the cylinder support bracket (11), and lift the bracket, complete with cylinders, from the scuttle.
5. Remove the master cylinders from the support bracket.

Dismantling (Fig. 2)

1. Remove the dust cover (10). Depress the push rod (9), remove the circlip (11) and withdraw the push rod (9) together with items (10), (11) and (12).
2. Shake out the plunger, spring and valve assembly. If necessary, apply low pressure compressed air to the outlet union to eject the plunger assembly.
3. Lift the locating clip on the spring retainer (6) and remove the retainer from the plunger (7) with the valve and spring assembly.
4. Detach the valve shank (4) by passing it through the offset hole in the retainer (6). Remove the spring (5), distance piece (3) and spring (2) from the valve shank (4). Using fingers, detach the seal (1) from item (4) and the seal (8) from item (7).

Inspection

Clean and examine all components for deterioration, renewing items as necessary.

Re-Assembly (Fig. 2)

1. Refit the seals (1) and (8) to items (4) and (7).
2. Fit the spring (2), distance piece (3) and spring (5) to the valve shank (4), attach the spring retainer (6) and fit the assembly to the plunger (7). Lubricate the components with clean hydraulic fluid and fit them to the master cylinder bore. Fit the push rod (9) with stop plate (12), circlip (11) and dust cover (10).

To Refit (Fig. 3)

Re-assemble the master cylinder to the bracket and secure this to the bulkhead. Re-connect the clutch and brake pedals to the push rods, using new split pins to secure the clevis pins (1). Refill and bleed the clutch and brake hydraulic systems as described on page 3·204.

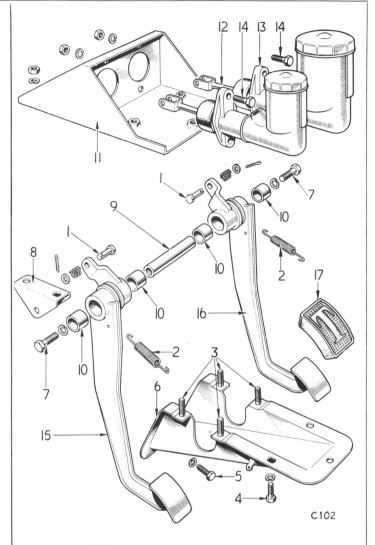

C.102

1 Clevis pin
2 Pedal return spring
3 Bolts ⎰ Pedal shaft cover assembly to
4 Bolts ⎱ master cylinder support bracket
5 Setscrew (pedal shaft cover assembly to bulkhead)
6 Pedal shaft cover assembly
7 Setscrew (pedal stay to pedal shaft support bracket)
8 Pedal shaft support bracket
9 Pedal shaft
10 Pedal pivot bush
11 Master cylinder support bracket
12 Push rod
13 Bracket master cylinder
14 Setscrew (master cylinder to support bracket)
15 Clutch pedal
16 Brake pedal
17 Pedal pad

Fig. 3. Master cylinder support and pedal details

1 Brake master cylinder   2 Clutch master cylinder

Fig. 4.   Position of master cylinders

Fig. 5.   Bleeding the brakes

Draining the Hydraulic System

Before a brake pipe is disconnected, drain the brake hydraulic system as follows :—

1. Attach a length of rubber tube to the bleed nipple nearest the pipe being disconnected.
2. Insert the opposite end of the tube in a clean jar. Unscrew the bleed nipple one turn and pump the brake pedal to drain the system.
3. Tighten the bleed nipple and remove the draining tube.

Bleeding Procedure

1. Fill the reservoir with fluid, check regularly and maintain the level during bleeding operations.
2. Remove the rubber dust cap from the bleed nipple on the wheel cylinder furthest from the master cylinder (N/S rear). Fit a flexible bleed tube over the nipple, with the free end immersed in a jar containing a little brake fluid.
3. Unscrew the nipple approximately ¾ of a turn and, giving fairly fast full strokes, pump the brake pedal until fluid entering the jar is free from air bubbles.
4. Hold the pedal fully depressed, tighten the bleed nipple, remove the bleed tube and refit the dust cap.
5. Repeat the procedure for the remaining three brakes, finishing with the wheel cylinder nearest the master cylinder (O/S front).
6. Adjust all the brakes in the normal manner and whilst applying pressure to the brake pedal, check for leaks at all pipe joints and unions, flexible hose connections, wheel cylinders and master cylinder.

NOTE : Should the fluid reservoir empty during bleeding operations, the whole process must be repeated from the beginning. When replenishing the system, use only new fluid that has been stored in a container sealed from atmosphere. Immediately bleeding is completed, re-seal residual fluid in the container, before it is again stored.

BRAKES

Front Brakes

Self-adjusting front brakes consist of Girling 11″ discs with cast iron double acting caliper units, each containing two quickly detachable friction pads.

Friction Pad Replacement

1. Jack up the car and remove the front road wheels.
2. Release two spring retainers (9) and remove the pad retainer pins (10).
3. Lift the friction pads (4) and the anti-squeal plates (5) from the caliper and renew them if worn. **Do not attempt to re-line worn pad assemblies.**
4. Before fitting new pads, push the pistons (6) back to the full extent of their travel. Refit the pads and anti-squeal plates, positioning the arrow in the direction of wheel rotation. Insert the retainer pins (10) and secure them with the spring retainer clips (9).

Caliper Cylinder Maintenance

To replace piston sealing rings or dust excluders, dismantle as follows :—

1. Release the rigid pipe and locknut at the support bracket. Unscrew the flexible hose from the caliper.
2. Remove two bolts securing the caliper to its support bracket.
3. Remove the caliper and withdraw the pistons from the body.
4. Carefully remove the rubber sealing ring from its recess.
5. Clean the piston, cylinder and rubbers with clean brake fluid ONLY.
6. Examine all components for serviceability and renew where necessary.

Re-Assembly

Lubricate the surfaces of the bore and piston with clean brake fluid.

1. Fit a new piston seal into the recess in the cylinder.
2. Locate the projecting lip of the rubber dust excluder in its recess in the cylinder.
3. Insert the piston, closed end leading, into the cylinder, taking care not to damage the polished surface. Push piston fully home and engage the outer lip of the dust excluder with the recess in the piston.
   Replace the friction pads.
4. Assemble the caliper over the disc, and refit shims between caliper and mounting bracket.
5. Refit the flexible brake hose and bleed the system.

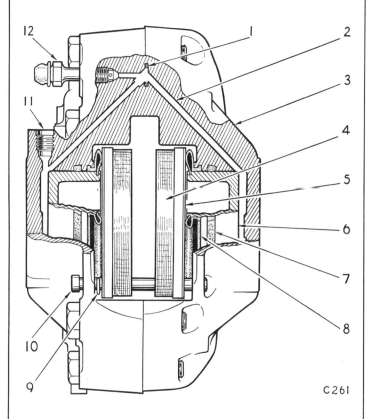

C 261

1 Rubber 'O' ring
2 Fluid transfer channels
3 Caliper body
4 Brake pad
5 Anti-squeal plate
6 Piston
7 Piston sealing ring
8 Dust cover
9 Retaining clip
10 Retaining pin
11 Flexible hose connection
12 Bleed nipple

Fig. 6. Details of caliper assembly

Fig. 7. Using a dial indicator to check disc run-out

Fig. 8. Removing the brake pads

Note.—The arrow on the anti-squeal plate pointing
in the direction of forward wheel rotation.

Discs

Maximum permissible run-out on the friction faces of the disc is ·002″ (0·0508 mm.).

The discs may be machined to a thickness of ·440″ (11·18 mm.) to rectify excessive run-out or scored faces. Minimum permissible finish of the disc machining :
15-30 micro inches measured circumferentially.
50 micro inches measured radially.

Disc and Hub Removal (Fig. 9)

1. Remove caliper assembly (24).
2. Remove the grease retaining cap (21) from the hub by screwing through it a No. 10 U.N.F. setscrew (supplied in tool kit).
3. Remove the split pin, slotted nut (19) and plain washer (18) from the stub axle (6).
4. Withdraw the hub (16) complete with the outer race (17) and the outer part of the inner race (14).
5. Detach the brake disc (15) from the hub (16) and degrease the hub components.

If new bearings are required, drift the old bearing outer rings and the oil seal (10) with retainer (11) from the hub.   New bearings should only be fitted as complete sets.

Re-Assembly

1. Fit the bearing outer rings (14) and (17) with their tapers facing outwards.   Refit the disc (15), securing with bolts (12) and washers (13).
2. Assemble the inner races (14) and (17) and fit the hub and disc to the stub axle.   Fit the washer (18) and slotted nut (19) and, whilst rotating the hub, tighten the nut (19) with finger pressure only.   Slacken the nut back to the nearest split pin hole and mark its position by centre punching the end of nut and stub axle.   The hub should have 0·003″ - 0·005″ (·076 mm. - 0·127 mm.) end float.   If slacking back the nut produces excessive end float, remove the nut and file the rear face so that when refitted the correct end float is provided.
3. Remove the nut (19), washer (18), hub (16) and races (14) and (17).   Pack the races and hub with an approved grease.
4. Secure a new hub sealing felt (10) to the seal retainer (11) with jointing compound. Allow the compound to dry, then soak the seal in engine oil and squeeze out surplus oil.
5. Fit the races (14) and (17) and seal retainer (11) to the hub, with the felt seal facing inwards.
6. Fit the hub assembly to the stub axle, securing it with the washer (18) and nut (19). Tighten the nut until the centre punch marks made in (2) correspond, and secure the nut with a new split pin (20).
7. Fit the cap (21). Secure the caliper assembly with bolts (1) and spring washers (2), refitting any shims originally fitted between the caliper and bracket.

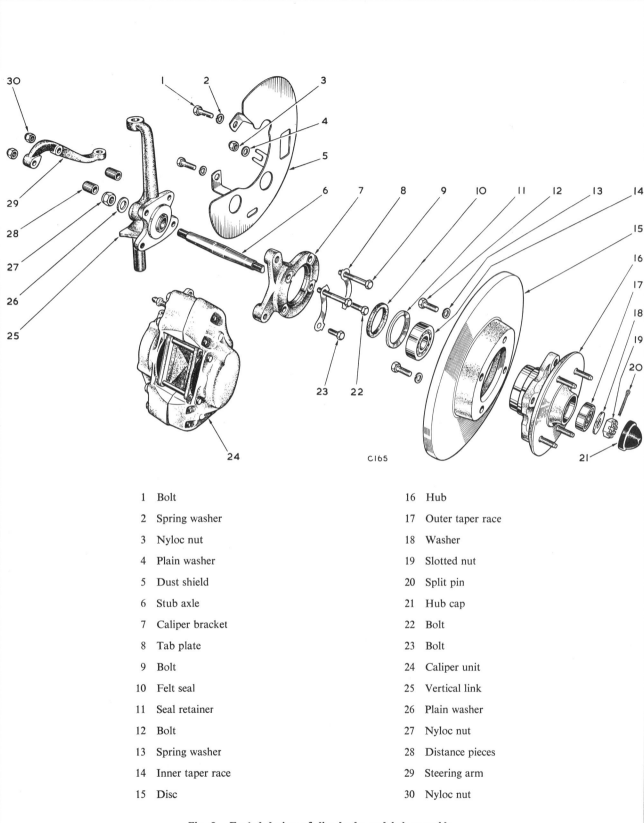

C165

1 Bolt	16 Hub
2 Spring washer	17 Outer taper race
3 Nyloc nut	18 Washer
4 Plain washer	19 Slotted nut
5 Dust shield	20 Split pin
6 Stub axle	21 Hub cap
7 Caliper bracket	22 Bolt
8 Tab plate	23 Bolt
9 Bolt	24 Caliper unit
10 Felt seal	25 Vertical link
11 Seal retainer	26 Plain washer
12 Bolt	27 Nyloc nut
13 Spring washer	28 Distance pieces
14 Inner taper race	29 Steering arm
15 Disc	30 Nyloc nut

Fig. 9. Exploded view of disc brake and hub assembly

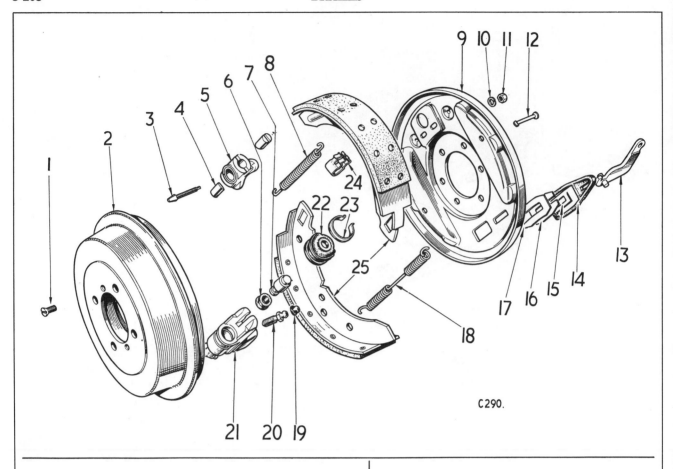

C290.

1 Screw	14 Dust excluder
2 Brake drum	15 Abutment plate
3 Tappet	16 Spring plate—retaining
4 Expander-adjuster	17 Spring plate
5 Adjuster housing	18 Spring
6 Piston seal	19 Dust cap
7 Piston	20 Bleed nipple
8 Spring	21 Hydraulic cylinder
9 Backplate	22 Dust excluders
10 Spring washer	23 Clip
11 Nut	24 Spring clip—steady pin
12 Steady pin	25 Brake shoes
13 Handbrake lever	

Fig. 10. Rear brake details

Brake Shoes

Removal

Should the brake linings be contaminated with grease or hydraulic fluid, trace the source of leakage and rectify. Saturated shoes cannot be satisfactorily cleaned and must, therefore, be renewed as follows :—

1. Chock the front wheels, jack up the rear and release the handbrake.
2. Remove the road wheel and brake drum.
3. Turn the adjuster back to the fully "OFF" position.
4. Press the spring plate (24), turn the anchor pin (12) 90 degrees and withdraw it from the rear of the backing plate.
5. Pull one of the brake shoes against spring load and lift it over the adjuster anchorage. Release the springs and remove the brake shoes.

Clean the backplate and inspect the operating cylinder for leaks and freedom of piston movement. Ensure that the cylinder slides laterally in the backplate slot and check the adjuster tappets and wedge for freedom of movement. Inspect the brake drums for scoring and grease contamination which, if present, must be removed with petrol or methylated spirits.

Assembly

The brake shoe linings are shorter in length than the platforms to which they are attached. The end of the shoe having the greater length of platform exposed is the "toe", whilst the other end is the "heel". When installed, the toe of the leading shoe is adjacent to the wheel cylinder piston, and its heel is located in a slot in the abutment. The heel of the opposite shoe locates in a slot at the closed end of the wheel cylinder body.

Lightly smear a thin film of white (Zinc base) grease over the six shoe contact pads and over the area on which the wheel cylinder and spring plate slide. Do not contaminate the shoe linings with grease or oil.

Assemble the brake shoes, pull-off springs and shoe anchor pins to the L.H. brake assembly as shown on Fig. 11. The R.H. side assembly is symmetrically opposite.

Refit the brake drum ; turn the adjuster fully "IN" and turn it back one notch to free the drum.

Refit the road wheel and lower the jack.

Wheel Cylinders

To Renew Piston Seal

Remove the brake shoes, drain the hydraulic system, uncouple the brake pipe, and disconnect the cable from the wheel cylinder lever.

Remove the dust cover (14), abutment plate (15), spring plate (16) and spring plate (17).

Withdraw the wheel cylinder and handbrake lever from the backplate.

Extract the piston (7) from the wheel cylinder body (21) and renew the piston seal (6). Examine the cylinder bore and renew if scored or damaged.

Re-assemble the brake components by reversing the removal procedure.

Brake Adjustment

Front

The front brakes are self-adjusting.

Rear

Each rear brake is provided with an adjuster protruding from the backplate (see Fig. 12).

The procedure for adjusting is as follows :—
1. Jack up the rear of the vehicle.
2. Screw in each adjuster until solid resistance is felt, then slacken back one notch, which should allow the drum to rotate freely.
   If excessive binding is felt, slacken the adjuster a further notch.

NOTE : Do not confuse binding with the normal drag caused by hub grease and the oil in the differential unit, particularly when cold.

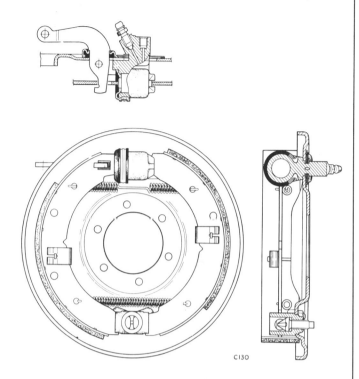

Fig. 11. Arrangement of brake shoes and wheel cylinder

Fig. 12. Rear brake adjuster shown arrowed

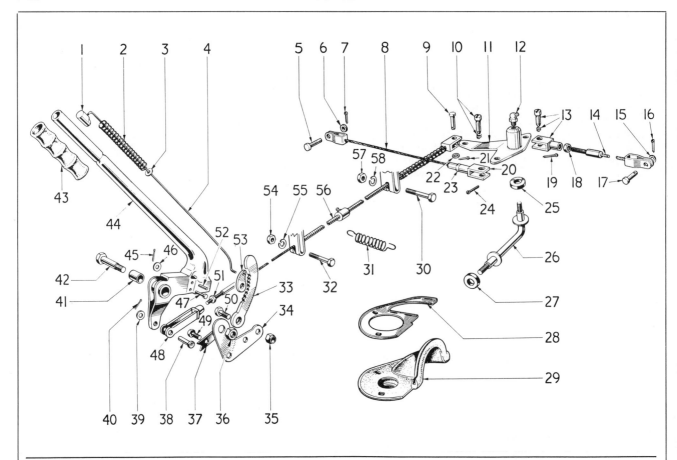

Fig. 13.　Details of handbrake and linkage

1 Push rod button	30 Bolt
2 Pawl release spring	31 Spring
3 Plain washer (between spring	32 Bolt
and lever)	33 Ratchet
4 Push rod	34 Attachment plate
5 Clevis pin	35 Nyloc nut
6 Plain washer	36 Nyloc nut
7 Split pin	37 Tab washer
8 Cable assembly (compensator	38 Clevis pin
to R.H. brake unit)	39 Plain washer
9 Clevis pin	40 Split pin
10 Clevis joint assembly	41 Lever pivot bush
11 Compensator lever	42 Pivot bolt
12 Grease nipple	43 Handbrake grip
13 Clevis joint assembly	44 Lever assembly
14 Cable assembly (compensator	45 Split pin
to L.H. brake unit)	46 Plain washer
15 Plain washer	47 Joint pin (pawl to lever)
16 Split pin	48 Fork end
17 Clevis pin	49 Setscrew (attachment plate to
18 Jam nut	frame bracket)
19 Split pin	50 Setscrew (ratchet to attach-
20 Clevis joint assembly	ment plate)
21 Split pin	51 Jam nut
22 Plain washer	52 Mills pin
23 Jam nut	53 Pawl
24 Split pin	54 Nut
25 Felt seal	55 Spring washer
26 Compensator bar assembly	56 Cable assembly (handbrake to
27 Felt seal	compensator lever)
28 Cover plate	57 Nut
29 Handbrake grommet	58 Spring washer

HANDBRAKE

Removal

1. Chock the wheels, jack up the rear of the car and release the handbrake.
2. Remove the moulded hand grip (43).
3. Withdraw the three self-tapping screws securing the draught excluder (28) to the floor. Remove the plate and the draught excluder (29).
4. Disconnect the fork end (48) from the handbrake lever (44).
5. Release the tabs of the locking plate (37) and withdraw two bolts (49), (50) securing the attachment plate (34) to its mounting bracket.
6. Remove the exhaust down pipe and the nyloc nut (36) locking the pivot bolt (42) to the chassis frame. Withdraw the pivot bolt.
7. Withdraw the handbrake lever (44) from beneath the car.

Dismantling

1. Detach the attachment plate (34) from the ratchet (33).
2. Withdraw the pawl pivot pin (47) whilst applying pressure to the press button (1). Withdraw the ratchet (33).
3. Remove press button (1), spring (2) and plain washer (3) from the push rod (4).
4. Withdraw the push rod (4) and pawl (53) from the lever (44).

Refitting

1. Fit the pivot bolt (42) through the lever assembly (44) and the attachment plate (34).

2. From beneath the car, feed the lever (44) through the floor assembly and attach it to the chassis with the pivot bolt (42). Do not tighten the bolt at this juncture.

3. Refit the lever attachment plate (34) to the chassis.

4. Tighten the pivot bolt (42), allowing the lever (44) sufficient freedom of movement, and attach the locking nut (36) from inside the cruciform.

5. Refit the exhaust down-pipe.

6. Secure the fork end (48) of the cable to the brake lever (44). Refit the draught excluder (29), its cover plate (28) and the moulded hand grip (43).

7. Lower the car and remove the chocks from the wheel.

Re-Assembly

1. Attach the pawl (53), pointing rearwards, to the push rod (4), and fit the rod into the lever (44) so that its shape corresponds with that of the lever.

2. Fit the plain washer (3), spring (2) and press button (1) to the push rod.

3. Hold the press button (1) down and fit the ratchet (33), teeth facing the pawl (53) into the lever (44). Manipulate the pawl (53) and insert the pivot pin (47) through both lever and pawl. Secure the pivot pin.

4. Secure the attachment plate (34) to the ratchet (33) and the nyloc nut (35), allowing sufficient freedom of movement for the plate to swing on the ratchet.

Handbrake

Under normal circumstances, adjustment of the rear brakes will automatically provide satisfactory handbrake adjustment. Stretched cables will necessitate further adjustment as follows :—

1. Jack up the rear wheels, release the handbrake and lock the brake drums by screwing each brake adjuster fully in.

2. Remove the clevis pin (2) and re-adjust the primary cable to position the compensator lever as shown on Fig. 15. Re-connect the cable.

3. Remove the clevis pins (1) and adjust the transverse cables to remove slackness. Re-connect the cables. The cables are too tight if the clevis pins cannot be easily inserted without straining the cables.

4. Turn each adjuster back one notch to release the brakes and lower the jack.

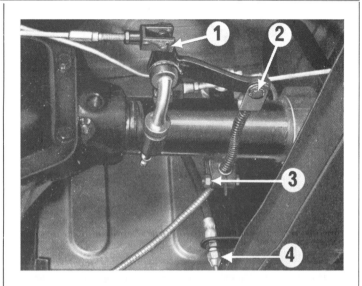

Fig. 14. Handbrake compensator

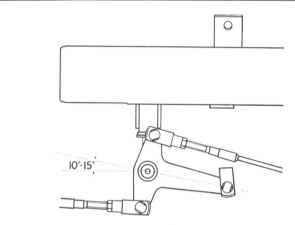

Fig. 15. Angle of handbrake compensator

Fig. 16. Stop light switch

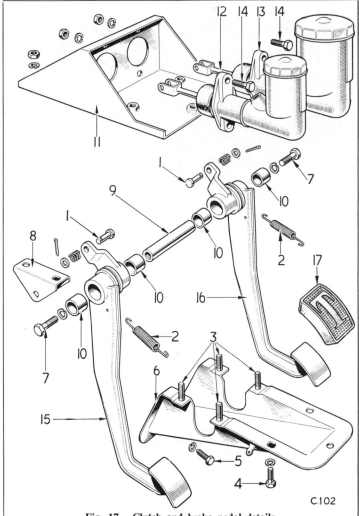

Fig. 17. Clutch and brake pedal details

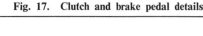
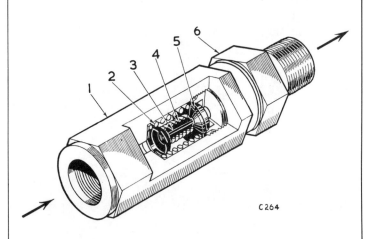

Fig. 18. Section through brake restrictor valve

Stop Light Switch (Fig. 16)

An electric stop light switch is now located directly in front of the brake master cylinder, and is operated by the action of the push rod (see (12) Fig. 3). When the brake pedal (16) is applied, the push rod is pulled away from the spring-loaded plunger of the stop light switch, and the light circuit is completed.

When the brake pedal is released, the push rod reasserts itself and the stop light circuit is broken.

Brake and Clutch Pedals (Fig. 17)

To Renew Bushes

1. Remove clevis pins (1).
2. Remove pedal return springs (2).
3. Remove four nuts from the studs (3) and three setscrews (4) and setscrews (5).
4. Detach the complete brake pedal assembly from beneath the bulkhead.
5. Detach the pedal shaft cover (6) from the pedal assembly.
6. Remove setscrews (7) and detach pedal shaft support brackets (8).
7. Detach pedals from pivot shaft (9).
8. Renew the pedal bushes and re-assemble the components by reversing the dismantling sequence.

Brake Restrictor Valve (Fig. 18)

A restrictor valve is fitted between the pipe-line from the brake master cylinder and the 5-way union. The restrictor maintains a low pressure in the hydraulic system to prevent the disc brake pads and pistons moving away from the disc and causing excessive brake pedal travel at the next application of the brakes.

The restrictor valve consists of a body (1) and end cap (6) containing a spring loaded valve assembly. Operation of the brake pedal causes the hydraulic fluid to compress the spring (4) and lifts the valve (3) from its seat against the disc (5). Fluid is then displaced through the pipe lines and applies the brakes.

When the brake pedal is released the resultant differential pressure acting on the disc (5) causes it to lift off its seat, compressing the spring (2). When the differential pressure falls to a point when the spring pressure (2) is greater than the force applied to the disc (5) by the returning fluid, the disc returns to its seat and maintains a low pressure in the hydraulic system.

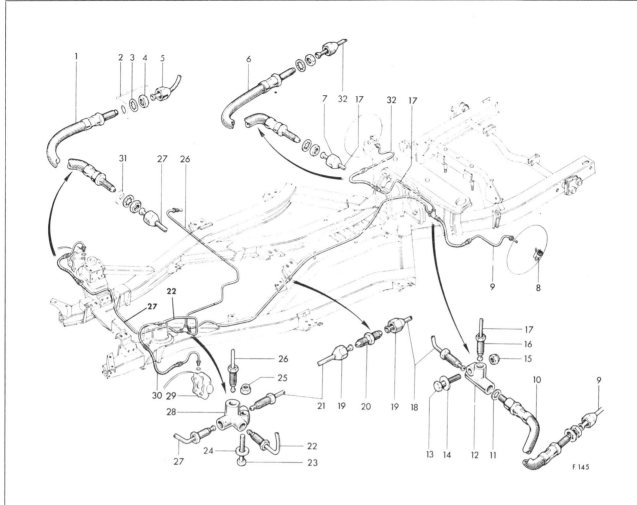

Fig. 19. Hydraulic Pipes and Couplings
(TR.4A I.R.S. — R.H.D.)

1	R.H. front flexible hose	17	Pipe — three-way to R.H. rear hose
2	Support bracket — hose to caliper	18	Pipe — three-way to connector
3	Shakeproof washer	19	Tube nut — female
4	Nut	20	Pipe connector
5	Tube nut — female	21	Pipe — connector to four-way union
6	R.H. rear flexible hose	22	Pipe — four-way to L.H. front hose
7	Tube nut — female	23	Bolt
8	Wheel cylinder — L.H. rear	24	Washer
9	Pipe — hose to L.H. rear cylinder	25	Nyloc nut
10	L.H. rear flexible hose	26	Pipe — four-way to master cylinder
11	Copper washer	27	Pipe — four-way to R.H. front hose
12	Three-way union	28	Four-way union
13	Bolt	29	Disc brake caliper — L.H. front
14	Washer	30	L.H. front flexible hose
15	Nyloc nut	31	Bracket welded to chassis
16	Tube nut — male	32	Pipe — hose to R.H. rear cylinder

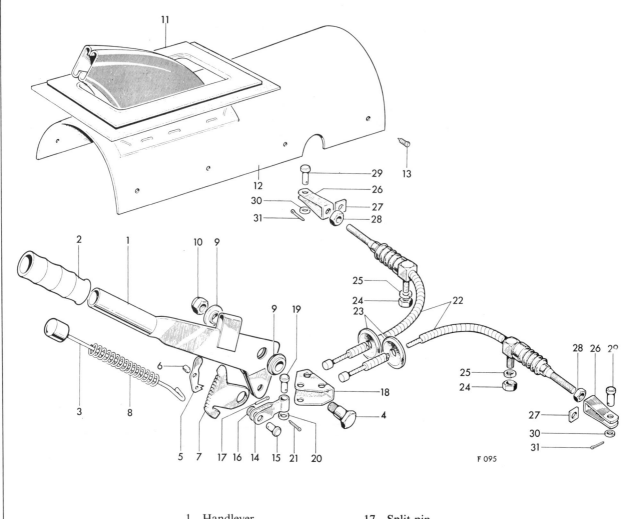

F 095

1	Handlever	17	Split pin
2	Rubber grip	18	Compensator
3	Operating rod, pawl	19	Clevis pin
4	Fulcrum pin, handlever	20	Washer
5	Pawl	21	Split pin
6	Pivot pin, pawl	22	Cable assembly
7	Ratchet	23	Rubber grommet
8	Spring	24	Nut
9	Nylon washer	25	Lockwasher
10	Nyloc nut	26	Fork end
11	Carpet trim	27	Nut
12	Cardboard cover	28	Locknut
13	Screw	29	Clevis pin
14	Link	30	Washer
15	Clevis pin	31	Split pin
16	Washer		

Fig. 20.   Exploded Handbrake Components

HANDBRAKE

Handlever Removal

Unclip the small section of carpet around the hand lever. Unscrew four screws from each side of the central tunnel to remove the cardboard handbrake cover. This reveals the lever and its mounting bracket which also houses the compensator.

Unscrew the fulcrum pin (4, Fig. 21) and detach the cables as shown in Fig. 22 to release the lever assembly.

Refitting

Reverse the removal procedure.

Renewing the Ratchet and Pawl

File or grind off the protruding ends of the pawl pivot pin. Tap out the pin and remove the pawl and the ratchet.

Insert the new ratchet first, followed by the pawl, and rivet the new pawl pin to the side of the handlever by peening over the reduced end of the pin.

Renewing Cables

Detach the cables from the compensator, as shown in Fig. 22.

Referring to Fig. 23 detach the cable cover holder (1) from the suspension arm and remove the clevis pin (2). Slacken nut (3), screw off the fork and remove the rubber shield and the holder (1). Withdraw the cable and its cover. Reverse this procedure to fit the new cable and adjust the handbrake.

Adjustment of the Handbrake

Under normal circumstances, adjustment of the rear brakes will also adjust the handbrake. Stretched cables will necessitate further adjustment as follows:—

Chock the front wheels in the straight-ahead position, prise off the rear nave plates and slacken the rear wheel nuts. Release the handbrake, and with a trolley jack placed under the differential casing, raise the rear of the car onto stands positioned beneath the chassis frame.

Remove the road wheels and slacken each locknut (3). Remove each clevis pin (2) and screw each fork along the cable to bring the compensator level and the handlever tight on the fifth notch.

Tighten the locknuts (3), refit the clevis pins (2) using new split pins, and re-check the handlever setting and the compensator. Refit the road wheels and lower the car to the ground. Apply the handbrake, remove the chocks and tighten the wheel nuts.

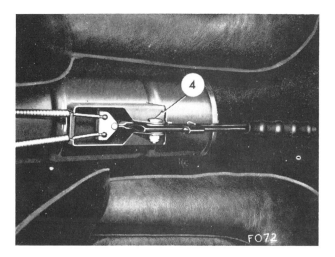

Fig. 21. Handlever fulcrum pin

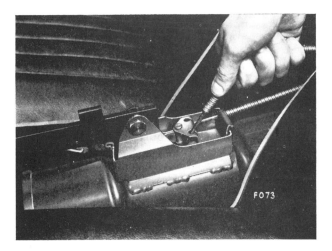

Fig. 22. Detaching cable from compressor

Fig. 23. Handbrake adjustment mechanism

THE MOT-A-VAC UNIT

DESCRIPTION (Fig. 2)

The Mot-A-Vac is a vacuum-hydraulic unit which supplements the manual effort required to apply the brakes. The unit is totally enclosed and is so designed that vacuum failure will not affect normal operation of the brakes. The unit comprises three major assemblies, namely, a vacuum chamber, hydraulic slave cylinder and hydraulically-actuated control valve.

Two aluminium castings form the vacuum chamber which contains a diaphragm (3) separating the power chamber (1) from the constant vacuum chamber (22). The diaphragm is biased to the "off" position by a return spring (2).

A non-return valve, in a port (21) connected to the engine inlet manifold, maintains vacuum in the chamber (22) when the engine is running. A push rod assembly (4), attached to the diaphragm (3), passes through two seals to operate the slave cylinder. A port (15) connects the slave cylinder (16) with the wheel brake cylinders. A port (20) connected to the hydraulic master cylinder, communicates via the passage (5) with the reaction valve hydraulic piston (6), which contacts the diaphragm (9) separating the chambers (8) and (10). The chamber (8) communicates with the constant vacuum chamber (22) and the chamber (10) is connected via the passage (7) with the power chamber (1).

The diaphragm assembly (9) is biased by a return spring (11) so that in the "off" position the vacuum valve seat (12) does not contact the atmosphere valve (13). Air is admitted into the valve cover through the air filter (14).

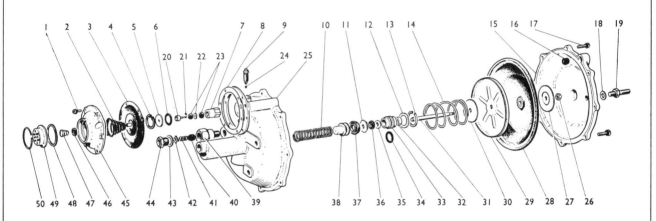

B126

1	Setscrew	14	Spring	27	Washer	40	Valve seating rubber
2	Spring	15	Rear casing	28	Diaphragm	41	Spring
3	Diaphragm	16	Rubber sleeve	29	Diaphragm plate	42	Abutment washer
4	Circlip	17	Setscrew	30	Washer	43	Sealing washer
5	Washer	18	Plain washer	31	Push rod	44	Union
6	Rubber ring	19	Stud	32	Seal	45	Cover
7	Valve adaptor	20	Valve	33	Sleeve	46	Rubber sealing cup
8	Gasket	21	Circlip	34	Sealing ring	47	Spring
9	Bleed nipple	22	Washer	35	Bush	48	Sealing ring
10	Spring	23	Rubber sealing cups	36	Rubber sealing cup	49	Air filter
11	Spacer	24	Seating	37	Rubber sealing cup	50	Circlip
12	Plain washer	25	Front casing	38	Piston		
13	Circlip	26	Nut	39	Adaptor		

Fig. 1. Exploded view of Mot-A-Vac Unit

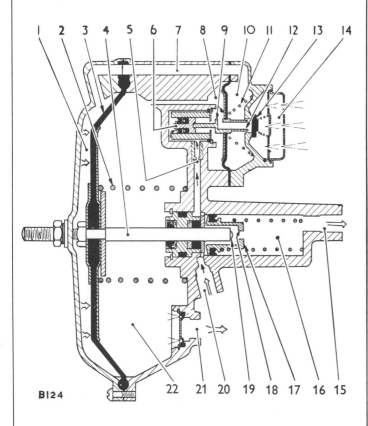

B124

1   Power diaphragm variable vacuum chamber
2   Power diaphragm return spring
3   Power diaphragm
4   Power diaphragm push rod
5   Communicating port to reaction valve hydraulic piston (with restrictor orifice)
6   Reaction valve hydraulic piston
7   Variable vacuum communicating port
8   Reaction valve diaphragm constant vacuum chamber
9   Reaction valve diaphragm assembly
10 Reaction valve diaphragm variable vacuum chamber
11 Reaction valve diaphragm return spring
12 Vacuum valve seat
13 Atmospheric valve
14 Air filter
15 Slave cylinder hydraulic output port
16 Slave cylinder hydraulic
17 Slave cylinder hydraulic piston
18 Slave cylinder piston push rod ball valve seat
19 Power diaphragm push rod ball valve
20 Hydraulic input port—from pedal master cylinder
21 Vacuum inlet port with non-return valve—from manifold
22 Power diaphragm constant vacuum chamber

Fig. 2.   Sectioned view of Mot-A-Vac unit

Brake Application (Fig. 2)

Initial brake application increases the fluid pressure to the left of the piston (6), causing it to move to the right, overcoming the pressure of the spring (11). The valve (13) contacts a seat (12), cutting off communication between the valve chambers (8) and (10) and between the diaphragm chambers (20) and (1). Further piston movement (6) lifts valve (13) from its seat to admit air via filter (14) into chamber (10) and passage (7) to chamber (1). Pressure differential between chambers (20) and (1) moves the diaphragm to the right, against the spring (2), closing the seat (18) and preventing the flow of fluid into cylinder (16).

The push rod (4) continues to push the piston (17) to the right, increasing pressure on the cylinder (16), which is transmitted to the wheel cylinders. The pressure of air acting on the diaphragm (9) opposes the force of the fluid pressure to the left of the piston (6) to provide sensitive brake control.

When the reactive force on the diaphragm (9) equals that to the left of the piston (6) the valve assumes a holding position. Contact of the valve seat (12) on valve (13) is maintained whilst the valve (13) is returned to its seat in the valve cover. Thus, with vacuum connections closed, pressure differential between chambers (1) and (20) is maintained until pedal effort is increased or decreased.

If the brake pedal effort causes pressure left of piston (6), to overcome the force on diaphragm (9), this assembly moves fully right, destroying vacuum and allowing diaphragm (3) to exert maximum effort.

From this point greater braking application can only be achieved by heavier pressure on the pedal.

Releasing Brakes

Less pedal effort reduces pressure at the left of piston (6) and allows reactive force on diaphragm (9), plus spring load (11) to move the piston left. This re-seals valve (13) and prevents air entering chambers (10) and (1). The valve seat (12) moves away from valve (13) and re-establishes vacuum connection to chambers (10) and (1), causing the push rod to move left, so reducing the braking effort.

In the event of vacuum failure, the servo returns to the released position, where the open port (18) in piston (17) allows free passage of fluid from the hydraulic master cylinder to the wheel cylinders to provide normal braking.

Fitting the Unit — R.H.D. and L.H.D. Models

Mark-off and drill two $\frac{5}{16}$" (8 mm.) diameter clearance holes in the bulkhead, as shown on Fig. 3.

Fit the unit to the vertical face of the bulkhead using a stiffening washer (18) Fig. 1 on L.H.D. only.

Reset the support bracket as shown on Fig. 5 and attach it to the unit and bulkhead shelf.

Fitting the Hydraulic Pipes — R.H.D. and L.H.D. Models

Depress the brake pedal approximately 1" (25 mm.) and fix it in this position to avoid unnecessary loss of fluid.

Disconnect the pipe from the master cylinder at the four-way connector, and re-form the pipe at this end to fit into the input adaptor.

Connect a new 24" (61 cm.) long pipe to the four-way connector and shape the pipe to the contour of the wing panel, looping the top end to fit the unit output banjo as shown.

Drill a $\frac{7}{32}$" (5·556 mm.) diameter hole and use a push-in type clip to secure the pipe to the wing panel.

Release the brake pedal.

Bleeding the System—R.H.D. and L.H.D. Models

NO VACUUM in unit for this operation.

Remove the cap from the fluid reservoir and fill the reservoir with clean fluid. Check regularly and maintain the level throughout the bleeding operation.

Slacken the nut securing the pipe to the four-way connector, and withdraw the pipe from its seating.

Operate the brake pedal until fluid, free of air bubbles, flows from the loosened connection and tighten the pipe nut immediately. Use a piece of cotton waste to absorb waste fluid.

Apply pressure at the brake pedal and slacken the bleed screw at the top of the unit to expel air from the valve chamber. Tighten up the bleed screw when fluid is ejected and slowly release the pedal.

Starting with the wheel having the shortest pipe run and finishing with the longest, bleed all wheel cylinders.

Finally, bleed the unit by using the bleed screw at the top.

NOTE : When bleeding, apply the pedal sharply and allow to return slowly with a five second pause after each return stroke. Tighten bleed screws with pedal released.

Top up the reservoir and replace the cap.

Check all pipes and connections for leaks whilst pressure is applied to the brake pedal.

| 1 | $\frac{3}{4}$" (19 mm.) | 3 | $\frac{1}{2}$" (12·7 mm.) |
| 2 | $4\frac{3}{4}$" (120 mm.) | 4 | $4\frac{1}{4}$" (108 mm.) |

Fig. 3. Showing the position of two holes drilled in the bulkhead

Fig. 4. Installation of the Mot-A-Vac unit

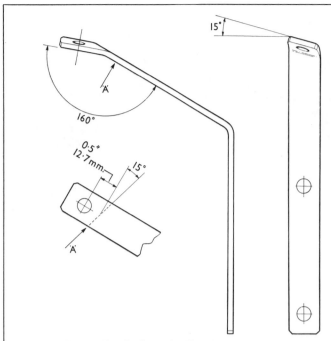

Fig. 5.   Details for re-bending the support bracket

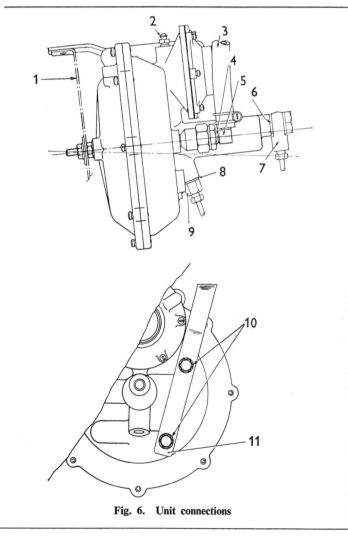

Fig. 6.   Unit connections

Fitting the Vacuum Pipe—R.H.D. and L.H.D. Models

Drill and tap the engine induction manifold, ⅛″ N.P.T.F. (Taper Thread) at the top of the balance pipe midway between the two carburettors and at an angle of approximately 45° from the vertical pointing towards the rear of the car. Where the balance pipe has cast-on bosses, drill and tap the rear angled boss. Use a letter 'R' tapping drill and ensure that all swarf is removed from the manifold after this operation.

Screw the dual-purpose hose connection into the manifold and fit the vacuum hose (3), (Fig. 6) on to the main branch of the connection. Cut off surplus hose and fit the other end on to the unit elbow connection, securing both ends with the wire clips.

Seal off the secondary branch of the manifold connection with the rubber dust cap unless required for other vacuum operated equipment.

Road test the vehicle.

1	Bulkhead
2	Bleed nipple
3	Vacuum hose to manifold
4	Plain washer
5	Elbow
6	Copper washer
7	Banjo—pipe to 4-way connector
8	Copper washer
9	Adaptor—pipe to master cylinder
10	Setscrews
11	Stay to bulkhead shelf

ROAD WHEELS AND TYRES

Pressed Steel Wheels (Fig. 2)

Removal — Using the combination tool supplied in the kit, remove the nave plate (hub cap) by levering at a point adjacent to one of the attachment studs.

Progressively slacken and detach the wheel nuts (R.H. thread) with the wheel brace, then remove the road wheel.

Refitting — Smear the attachment studs with oil or grease to prevent corrosion, fit the wheel and secure it by fitting and progressively tightening the nuts. Refit the nave plate by engaging its rim over two of the attachment studs and springing it over the third stud by giving it a sharp blow with the palm of the hand.

Wheel Tolerances

S.M.M. and T. Standard tolerances are :
(a) Wobble.
   The lateral variation measured on the vertical inside face of a flange should not exceed $\frac{3}{32}''$ (2·4 mm.).
(b) Lift.
   The difference between the high and low points of a rotating wheel measured at any location on either tyre bead seat should not exceed $\frac{3}{32}''$ (2·4 mm.).

Radial and lateral eccentricity outside these limits contribute to static and dynamic unbalance respectively. Severe radial eccentricity imposes intermittent loading on the tyre, which cannot be rectified by static or dynamic balancing. Irregular tyre wear will result from this defect.

In the interests of safety, renew wheels having damaged or elongated stud holes, and as there is no effective method of correcting pressed steel wheels which do not conform to the above tolerances, these should also be renewed.

Ensure that rim seatings and flanges in contact with the tyre beads are maintained free from rust and dirt.

Wire Wheels

Removal — A copper faced hammer is provided with cars fitted with wire spoked (knock-on) wheels to facilitate hub cap removal. Turn the hub caps, on the right-hand side of the car, clockwise and the hub caps on the left-hand side of the car, anti-clockwise, to remove them. Detach the wheel by pulling it straight off the splined hub.

Refitting — When refitting the road wheels, smear the hub splines with oil or grease to prevent corrosion and possible difficulty with wheel removal. Ensure that the hub caps are fully tightened by striking the "ears" in the appropriate direction with the copper-faced hammer.

Fig. 1. Removing a wire-spoked wheel

**Fig. 2. Using special tool to remove nave plate
from pressed steel wheel**

WARNING. If the vehicle is fitted with wire-spoked wheels, the splined hubs, when removed, must be refitted to the correct side of the vehicle, i.e. the knock-on hub cap must tighten in the opposite direction to road wheel rotation. Failure to ensure this may result in a road wheel coming off its splined hub.

Fig. 3.
Truing a wire-spoked wheel

Fig. 4.
Checking the dynamic balance of road wheel and tyre assembly

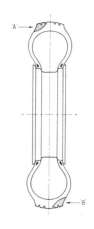

Fig. 5.
Showing equal masses at "A" and "B" which result in dynamic unbalance

Spokes

If a car fitted with wire-spoked wheels is used for competition driving, clean the wheels regularly and examine the spokes for looseness, and the splines for wear. When tightening loose spokes or removing damaged spokes, avoid disturbing rim concentricity. Maintain an equal load on all spokes and do not over-tighten.

If the tension is too high the wheel becomes rigid and easily damaged by shock loads. If too loose, undue. bending stresses placed on the spokes also result in breakage.

Spoke tensioning is best carried out with the tyre and the tube removed and any protruding spoke heads filed off flush to the nipple.

Tyre and Wheel Balance

The original degree of balance is not necessarily maintained, and it may be affected by uneven tread wear, by repairs, by tyre removal and refitting or by wheel damage and eccentricity. The vehicle may also become more sensitive to unbalance due to normal wear of moving parts.

If roughness or steering troubles develop and mechanical investigation fails to disclose a possible cause, wheel and tyre balance should be suspected. Static unbalance can be measured when the tyre and wheel assembly is stationary. Dynamic unbalance can be detected only when the assembly is revolving.

There may be no heavy spot—that is, there may be no natural tendency for the assembly to rotate about its centre due to gravity, but the weight may be unevenly distributed each side of the tyre centre line (Fig. 5). Laterally eccentric wheels give the same effect. During rotation the offset weight distribution sets up a rotating couple which tends to steer the wheel to right and left alternately. Dynamic unbalance of tyre and wheel assemblies should be measured on a Balancing Machine and suitable corrections made when vehicle shows sensitivity to this form of unbalance. Where it is clear that a damaged wheel is the primary cause of severe unbalance it is advisable to renew the wheel.

Tyre Interchanging

Uneven tyre wear may be caused by road conditions, traffic conditions, driving methods and certain features of design which are essential to the control, steering and driving of a vehicle. Close attention to inflation pressures and the mechanical condition of the vehicle will not always prevent irregular wear. It is therefore recommended that front tyres be interchanged with rear tyres at least every 3,000 miles. Diagonal interchanging between near front and off rear and between off front and near rear provides the most satisfactory first change because it reverses the direction of rotation.

Subsequent interchanging of front and rear tyres should be as indicated by the appearance of the tyres, with the object of keeping the wear of all tyres even and uniform.

FACTORS AFFECTING TYRE LIFE

Inflation Pressures

There is an average loss of 13% tread mileage for every 10% reduction in inflation pressure below the recommended figure.

Severe and persistent under-inflation produces unmistakable evidence on the tread (Fig. 6). It also causes structural failure due to excessive friction and temperature within the casing.

Pressures higher than those recommended reduce tread life by concentrating the load on a small tread area. Excessive pressures overstrain the casing cords, cause rapid wear, and make the tyres more susceptible to impact fractures and cuts.

Effect of Temperature

Air expands with heating and tyre pressures increase as the tyres warm up. Pressures increase more in hot weather than in cold weather and as result of high speed.

Pressures in warm tyres should not be reduced to standard pressure for cold tyres. "Bleeding" the tyres increases their deflections and causes their temperatures to climb still higher. The tyres will also be under-inflated when they have cooled.

The rate of tread wear may be twice as fast at 50 m.p.h. as at 30 m.p.h.

High speed causes increased temperatures due to more deflections per minute and a faster rate of deflection and recovery. The resistance of the tread to abrasion decreases with increased tyre temperature.

Camber, Castor and King Pin Inclination

These angles normally require no attention unless they have been disturbed by a severe impact or abnormal wear of front end bearings. It is always advisable to check them if steering irregularities develop.

Wheel camber, usually combined with road camber, causes a wheel to try to turn in the direction of lean, due to one side of the tread attempting to make more revolutions per mile than the other side. The resulting increased tread shuffle on the road and the off centre tyre loading tend to cause rapid and one-sided wear. Unequal cambers introduce unbalanced forces which try to steer the car one way or the other. This must be countered by steering in the opposite direction which increases tread wear.

Castor and king pin inclination by themselves have no direct bearing on tyre wear but their measurement is often useful for providing a general indication of the condition of the front end geometry and suspension.

Fig. 6. Tyre wear resulting from under-inflation.

Under-inflation causes fast wear, excessive heating, and can bring about tyre failure through blow-out.

Fig. 7 Tyre wear resulting from over-inflation.

This causes the fabric to be easily damaged, and seriously shortens tyre life by rapidly wearing the centre of the tread.

Fig. 8. The results of excessive front wheel camber.

Possibly caused by wear or impact damage to the suspension unit.

Fig. 9. Spotty tread wear.

Resulting from mechanical front end faults such as inefficient suspension, out of balance wheel assembly or grabbing brakes.

Braking

Braking factors not directly connected with the method of driving can affect tyre wear. Correct balance, lining clearances, and freedom from binding, are important. Braking may vary between one wheel and another.

Tyre wear may be affected if shoes are relined with non-standard material having unsuitable characteristics or dimensions. Front tyres, and particularly near front tyres, are very sensitive to any conditions which add to the severity of front braking in relation to the rear.

Local "pulling up" or flats on the tread pattern can often be traced to brake drum eccentricity (Fig. 9). The braking varies during each wheel revolution as the minor and major axes of the eccentric drum pass alternatively over the shoes.

Fig. 10. Tyre wear resulting from front wheel misalignment.

Excessive toe-in or toe-out will cause a feather edge of rubber on the tread design.

Wheel Alignment and Road Camber

An upstanding sharp "fin" on the edge of each pattern rib is a sure sign of misalignment and it is possible to determine from the position of the "fins" whether the wheels are "toed in" or "toed out" (Fig. 10).

"Fins" on the inside edges of the pattern ribs indicate toe in. "Fins" on the outside edges, indicate toe out.

Sharp pattern edges may be caused by road camber even when wheel alignment is correct. In such cases it is better to make sure by checking with an alignment gauge.

Tyre pressure data

is given on page 7

Road camber affects the direction of the car by imposing a side thrust and if left to follow its natural course the car will drift towards the nearside. This is instinctively corrected by steering towards the road centre.

TRIUMPH TR4
WORKSHOP MANUAL

GROUP 4

Comprising:

TR4 WORKSHOP MANUAL

GROUP 4

_____

CONTENTS

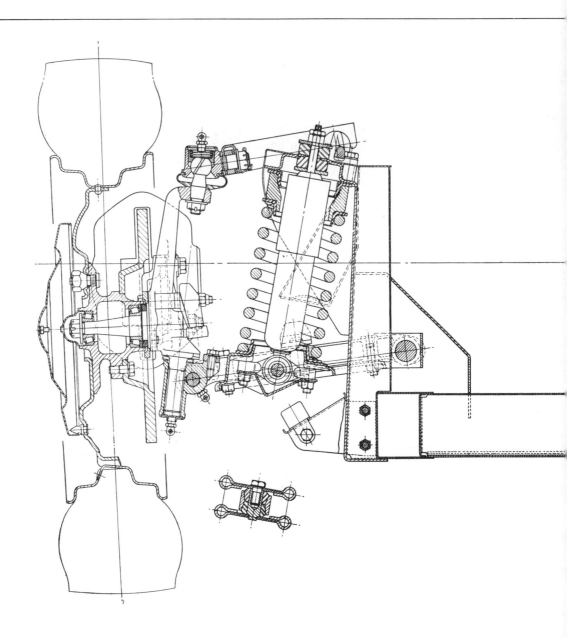

Fig. 1. STEERING AND FRONT SUSPENSION

Steering axis inclination (static laden) .. .. 7°.
Camber angle (static laden) .. .. .. 2° positive.
Turning circle .. .. 33 ft. (10·058 metres).
Maximum back lock .. .. 30½°.
Maximum front lock .. .. 29°.
20° back lock gives 19·25° front lock.
Front wheel alignment .. .. ⅛″ (3·175 mm.) toe-in (normal tyres).
                                    ¹⁄₁₆″ (1·59 mm.) toe-in (Michelin X or (
End float of outer shackle pin .. .. .. 0·004″—0·012″ (0·1016—0·305 mm.).
Length of tie rods (centre to centre) .. .. 8·55″ (21·7 cm.).
Distance between outer ball joints .. .. 43·0″ (109·22 cm.).

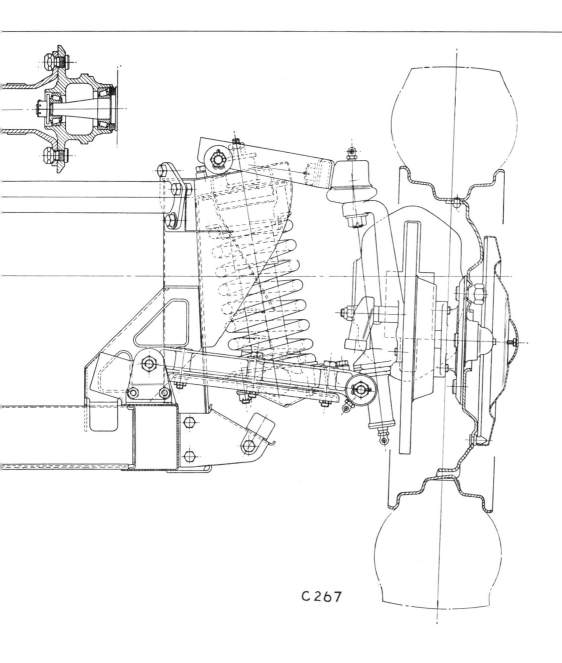

C 267

Track at ground level (static laden).
    Disc wheels ..   ..   49″ (124·46 cm.).
    Wire wheels   ..   ..   50″ (127 cm.).

Castor angle (static laden).
    Up to Commission Numbers CT. 6344   ..   0° (Wire wheels).
                              CT. 6390   ..   0° (Disc wheels).
    From Commission Numbers CT. 6345   ..   3° positive.
                                CT. 6391   ..   3° positive.

ROAD SPRINGS AND DAMPERS

Road springs and dampers are available for the Triumph TR4 in the following combinations to suit the conditions listed below :

(a) Normal Equipment

	Rear	
	Up to Commission No. CT.23382	From Commission No. CT.23383
Road springs	208636	209964*
Dampers	209494 L.H. 209495 R.H.	209494 L.H. 209495 R.H.

(b) Export

	Rear	
	Up to Commission No. CT.23382	From Commission No. CT.23383
Road springs	208636 L.H. ⎫ (L.H. Steering 208637 R.H. ⎬ cars)	209964*
Dampers	202388 R.H. ⎫ U.S.A. 202389 L.H. ⎬ market only	202388 R.H. ⎫ U.S.A. 202389 L.H. ⎬ market only

(c) Competition work

	Rear
Road springs	304008
Dampers	202390 R.H. 202391 L.H.

Interchangeability is not affected. An identical damper must be fitted when a single replacement is necessary.

* Part Number 209964 is used in conjunction with Distance Pieces R.H. and L.H., Part Numbers being 209962 and 209963 respectively.

NOTE: Re-cambered Rear Road Springs (Part Number 209964) are fitted. together with Distance Pieces, under axle in order to reduce or minimise roll steer.

FRONT ROAD SPRINGS

	NORMAL AND EXPORT		COMPETITION
	Up to Commission No. CT29984	After Commission No. CT29985	
Wire Dia.	0·5″ ±0·002″ (12·7 mm. ±0·0508 mm.)	0·48″ ±0·002″ (12·3 mm. ±0·0508 mm.)	0·52″ ±0·002″ (13·2 mm. ±0·0508 mm.)
No. of coils	6¾	5¾	6¾
Rate	310 lb/in. (3·595 mkg.)	312 lb/in. (3·595 mkg.)	380 lb/in. (4·386 mkg.)
Free length	9·75″ (247·65 mm.)	11·1″ (approx.) (281·1 mm.)	9·19″ (233·43 mm.)
Fitted length	6·75″ ±0·094″ (171·5 mm. ±2·38 mm.)	8·12″ ±0·094″ (206·4 mm. ±2·38 mm.)	6·75″ ±0·094″ (171·5 mm. ±2·38 mm.)
Fitted load	925 lb. (419·57 kg.)	925 lb. (approx.) (419·57 kg.)	925 lb. (419·57 kg.)
Part Number	201898 (Old)	210903 (New)	201899

NOTE: Service with latest condition in Sets. Where only one Spring is called for, it will be necessary to discard the Packing Piece and Rubber Gaiter when fitting the new Spring.

ROAD SPRINGS AND DAMPERS

(a) Normal Equipment	**Front** Up to Commission No.	**Front** After Commission No.	**Rear**
Road springs	201898	210903	208636
Dampers	134101	134101	209494 L.H. 209495 R.H.

(b) Export	**Front** Up to Commission No.	**Front** After Commission No.	**Rear**
Road springs	201898	210903	208636 Driver's side 208637 Passenger's side (L.H. Steering cars only)
Dampers	113624	113624	202388 R.H. ⎱ U.S.A. 202389 L.H. ⎰ Market only

(c) Competition work	**Front**		**Rear**
Road springs	201899		304008
Dampers	113556		202390 R.H. 202391 L.H.

REAR ROAD SPRINGS

	NORMAL AND EXPORT		COMPETITION
	Up to Commission No. CT.23382	From Commission No. CT.23383	
Blade thickness ...	Master 0·219″ (5·56 mm.) Nos. 2-6. 0·188″ (4·76 mm.)	Master 0·219″ (5·56 mm.) Nos. 2-6. 0·188″ (4·76 mm.)	Master and No. 2 0·219″ (5·56 mm.) Nos. 3-6. 0·203″ (5·16 mm.)
No. of blades ...	6	6	6
Rate	128±5% lb/in. (1·5 mkg.)	128±5% lb/in. (1·5 mkg.)	155±5% lb/in. (1·8 mkg.)
Laden camber ...	0·38″—0·63″ Negative (9·65—16·0 mm.)	3·00″—3·255″ Positive (76·2—82·68 mm.)	0·75″—1″ Negative (19·05—25·4 mm.)
Fitted load	515 lb. (233·6 kg.)	515 lb. (233·6 kg.)	515 lb. (233·6 kg.)
Part Number ...	208636	209964*	304008

On L.H. drive vehicles, spring Part Number 208637, identical to Part Number 208636 but with two packings on the centre pin above the master blade, is fitted to the passenger's side of the car.

* Part Number 209964 is used in conjunction with Distance Pieces R.H. and L.H. Part Numbers 209962 and 209963 respectively.

NOTE: Re-cambered Rear Road Springs (Part Number 209964) are fitted together with Distance Pieces under axle, in order to reduce roll steer.

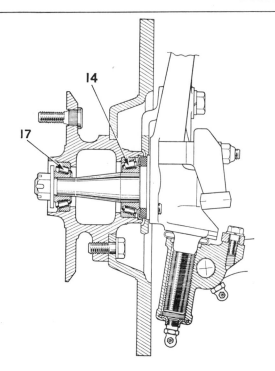

Fig. 2.   Section through front hub

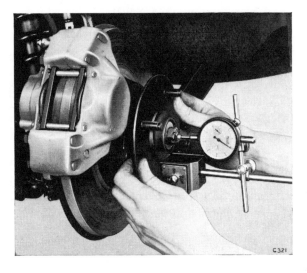

Fig. 3.   Measuring front hub end-float

FRONT SUSPENSION

General

Before disturbing any part of the front suspension assembly, jack up the front of the vehicle and lower it on to stands placed under the chassis side members, rearward of the front cross-member. Remove the road wheels and dismantle either the right or left-hand front suspension unit, as follows :

Front Hubs

Removal (Fig. 4)

Unscrew the bolts (1) and remove the caliper assembly. Note the number and position of shims fitted between the caliper and bracket (7). They are used to align the caliper relative to the disc. Support, or tie-up the caliper assembly to prevent its weight being taken by the flexible hydraulic brake hose.

Screw a No. 10 N.F. setscrew into the grease cap (21) and force the cap from the hub. Extract the split pin (20), unscrew the slotted nut (19) and withdraw the hub assembly from the stub axle. Remove the inner member of the bearing (14) from the stub axle.

Dismantling

Remove the bolts (12) with lockwashers (13) and detach the disc from the hub. Using a soft drift, drive the outer rings of the bearings (14), (17), and the grease seal retainer (11), from the hub.

Re-assembly

Fit the outer rings of the bearings (14), (17) to the hub, placing the tapered faces outwards, and refit the disc (15), securing it with the bolts (12) and washers (13).

Assemble the inner members of the bearings (14), (17) to the hub (16) and fit the assembly to the stub axle (6). Fit the washer (18), the slotted nut (19), and whilst rotating the hub, tighten the nut only sufficiently to remove slackness. Slacken the nut back to the nearest split pin hole and mark its position by centre punching the nut and stub axle. Remove the hub assembly and pack the bearings with grease.

Attach a new hub sealing felt (10) to the seal retainer (11) with jointing compound. When the compound is dry, soak the seal in engine oil and squeeze out surplus oil. Fit the seal retainer to the hub, placing the felt face towards the centre of the car.

Refit the hub assembly, washer (18) and nut (19) to the stub axle, tightening the nut until the centre punch marks correspond. Secure the nut with a new split pin (20) and refit the cap (21).

Re-attach the caliper assembly, repositioning any shims previously fitted between the caliper and bracket. Refit the road wheel and nave plate, remove the axle stands and lower the vehicle to the ground.

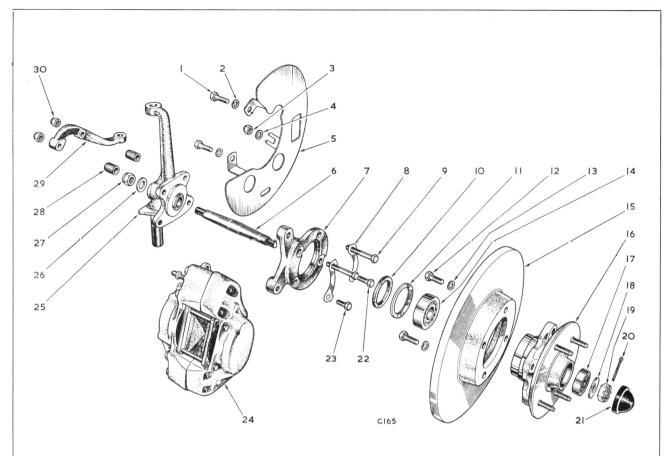

C165

1	Bolt	16	Hub
2	Spring washer	17	Outer taper race
3	Nyloc nut	18	Washer
4	Plain washer	19	Slotted nut
5	Dust shield	20	Split pin
6	Stub axle	21	Hub cap
7	Caliper bracket	22	Bolt
8	Lock plate	23	Bolt
9	Bolt	24	Caliper unit
10	Felt seal	25	Vertical link
11	Seal retainer	26	Plain washer
12	Bolt	27	Nyloc nut
13	Spring washer	28	Distance pieces
14	Inner taper race	29	Steering arm
15	Disc	30	Nyloc nut

Fig. 4. Arrangement of Disc Brake and Hub Details

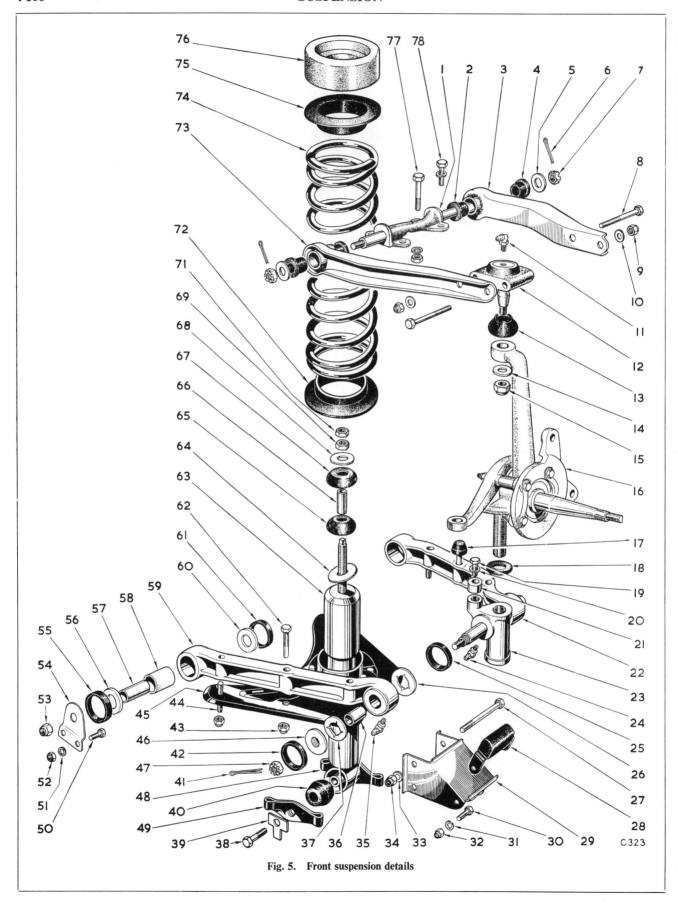

Fig. 5. Front suspension details

KEY TO FIG. 5

1	Upper inner fulcrum	40	Rubber bush
2	Rubber bush	41	Split pin
3	Upper wishbone arm– rear	42	Rubber seal
4	Rubber bush	43	Nyloc nut
5	Washer	44	Stud
6	Split pin	45	Spring pan
7	Slotted nut	46	Serrated washer
8	Bolt	47	Slotted nut
9	Nyloc nut	48	Damper attachment bracket—rear
10	Plain washer	49	Damper attachment bracket—front
11	Grease nipple	50	Bolt
12	Upper ball joint	51	Spring washer
13	Rubber gaiter	52	Nut
14	Plain washer	53	Nyloc nut
15	Nyloc nut	54	Fulcrum bracket
16	Caliper bracket and vertical link	55	Rubber seal
17	Bump rubber	56	Thrust washer
18	Rubber seal	57	Steel sleeve
19	Bolt	58	Nylon bush
20	Spring washer	59	Lower wishbone—front
21	Lock stop collar	60	Thrust washer
22	Lower wishbone arm—rear	61	Rubber seal
23	Lower trunnion bracket	62	Bolt
24	Grease nipple	63	Damper
25	Rubber seal	64	Washer
26	Thrust washer	65	Rubber bush
27	Bolt	66	Sleeve
28	Rebound rubber	67	Rubber bush
29	Bracket	68	Washer
30	Bolt	69	Nut
31	Spring washer	71	Locknut
32	Nyloc nut	72	Rubber collar
33	Plain washer	73	Upper wishbone arm—front
34	Nyloc nut	74	Spring
35	Grease nipple	75	Rubber collar
36	Bush—nylon	76	Distance piece
37	Thrust washer	77	Bolt
38	Bolt	78	Bolt
39	Tab washer		

Front Spring Damper

Removal (Fig. 6)

Release the lower attachment by removing the nuts (79) and spring washers (80). Remove the locknut (71), nut (69), plain washer (68) and rubber bush (67) from the upper attachment and withdraw the damper unit downwards.

Check the condition of rubber bushes and renew them if required.

Testing

The servicing of telescopic dampers is not generally practicable. Therefore, if a damper unit shows any of the following defects, it should be scrapped and replaced by a new one :

— damage or dented body,
— bent piston rod,
— loosened mounting,
— fluid leakage.

If none of these defects is apparent, hold the unit vertically in a vice and perform the following manual operations :

Slowly extend and compress the damper approximately 10 times, moving it to the limit of its stroke in both directions. **There should be appreciable and constant resistance in both directions.**

Reject damper units having the following defects :

— none, or only slight resistance in one or both directions,
— excessive resistance ; cannot be operated manually,
— pocket of no resistance when reversing direction.

Refitting

After pumping the damper as previously described, keep the damper upright and in the extended condition whilst passing it upwards through the aperture in the spring pan. Secure the upper end by fitting the washer (64), rubber bushes (65) and (67), sleeve (66), washer (68), nut (69) and locknut (71) as shown on Fig. 6.

Insert the rubber bushes (40) into the lower damper eye and push the screwed sleeve, attached to the mounting bracket (48), through the bushes. Fit the bracket (49) and secure it with the bolt (38) and lockplate (39).

Locate the brackets (48) and (49), and the rebound stop plate (81) on the studs (82) and secure the assembly with the washers (80) and nuts (79).

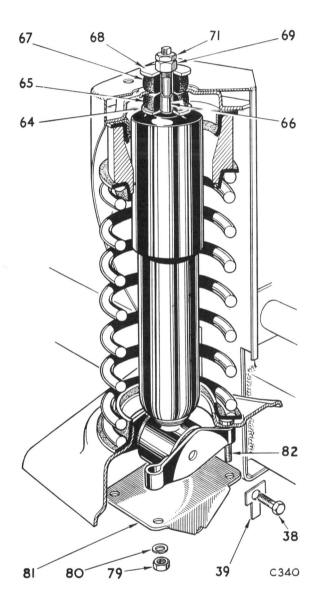

Fig. 6. Attachment of front damper

Fig. 7.   Front spring compressor tool and adaptor S.112-1

Fig. 8.   Releasing the front spring

Fig. 9.   Position of collar at the upper end of the spring compressor

FRONT ROAD SPRINGS

Removal (Fig. 5)

Remove the front dampers as described on page 4·107.

Jack up under the spring pan to release the spring load from the rebound rubber. Remove the bolts (27) and detach the bracket (29) with rebound rubber (28). Remove the jack.

Assemble the spring compressor tool No. S.112/1 (Fig. 7), by first passing the screwed shaft with adaptor up through the spring pan, spring and turret. Fit the collar to the shaft (Fig. 9) and assemble the adaptor, hemi-spherical thrust piece and wing nut to the lower end of the shaft.

Compress the spring by tightening the wing nut until the lower wishbone arms are horizontal. Remove the bolts (62) and fit two $\frac{3}{8}$″ × 6″ (9·5 mm. × 152 mm.) guide rods as shown on Fig. 8.

Whilst supporting the suspension unit by inserting a block of wood between the upper wishbone arms and the spring housing, unscrew the wing nut to release the spring tension. Dismantle the spring compressor and remove the spring pan (45), pads (72) and (75), the spring (74), and packing (76).

Re-assembly

Lift the suspension unit and insert, between the upper wishbone arms and spring housing, a block of wood sufficiently thick to bring the lower wishbone arms to a horizontal position.

Assemble the spring (74), pads (72), (75), packing (76), spring pan (45) and guide pins to the suspension unit and install the spring compressor tool as described for removal.

Tighten the wing nut until the spring pan seats against the lower wishbone arms. Refit two bolts (62), remove the guide pins, and refit the remaining attachments and nuts (43).

If necessary, renew the rebound rubber (28) and assemble the bracket (29) with rubber to the chassis, securing with the bolts (27). Remove the spring compressor and refit the damper unit as described on page 4·107.

Refit the road wheels, remove the chassis stands and lower the vehicle to the ground.

Vertical Link Ball Joint

Vehicles from Commission Number CT.6390 (disc wheels) and CT.6344 (wire wheels) are fitted with a modified upper wishbone and ball joint assembly.

Early Type (Fig. 10)

To Remove

Support the spring pan with a jack and remove the split pin, slotted nut and plain washer securing the ball joint to the vertical link. Use extractor tool No. S.166 to separate the ball joint from the vertical link as shown.

Remove the split pin, slotted nut, plain washer and detach the ball joint and distance piece from the upper wishbones.

To refit, reverse the removal procedure.

Fig. 10.　Using tool No. S.166 to separate early type ball joint

Later Type (Figs. 5 and 11)

To Remove

Support the spring pan with a jack and remove the nyloc nut (15). Using extractor tool No. S.166, separate the ball joint (12) from the vertical link as shown on Fig. 11. Release the ball joint from the upper wishbones by removing the nyloc nuts (9), plain washers (10) and bolts (8).

To refit, reverse the removal procedure.

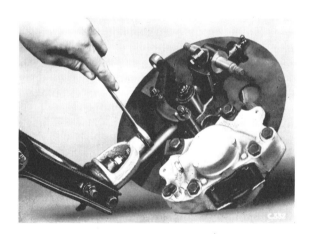

Fig. 11.　Showing the later type ball joint

Upper Wishbones

To Remove (Figs. 5 and 12)

Remove the ball joint as described previously. Extract the split pins (6), unscrew the slotted nuts (7) and remove the washers (5), wishbone arms (3), (73) and the rubber bushes (2), (4).

To refit, reverse the removal procedure and ensure that the wishbone arm having the larger amount of "offset" is positioned at the front of the assembly.

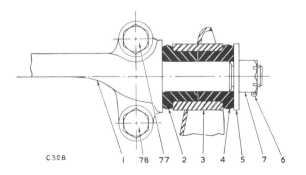

Fig. 12.　Section through upper inner fulcrum

Fig. 13.   Removing tie rod

Fig. 14.   Lower wishbone arm

Fig. 15.   Upper wishbone and inner fulcrum

Wishbone and Vertical Link Assembly (Fig. 5)

To Remove Lower Wishbones

Detach the brake caliper unit or, alternatively, empty the hydraulic system and disconnect the flexible brake hose at the chassis bracket.

Remove the damper and road spring as described on pages 4·107 and 4·108.

Unscrew the nyloc nut and separate the outer tie-rod ball joint from the steering arm.

Release the lower inner fulcrum pin end brackets by removing the nyloc nut (53), nuts (52), bolts (50) and washers (51).

Withdraw the split pins (41), unscrew the nuts (47) and remove the retainer washers (46), seals (42) and the lower wishbone arms (59) and (22).

To Remove Upper Inner Fulcrum

Remove the nuts, spring washers, bolts (77) and plain washers from the fulcrum inner fixings. Unscrew the setscrews (78) from the outer fixings and lift the assembly from the vehicle.

To Dismantle (Fig. 4)

Remove the caliper and hub assemblies as described on page 4·104. Detach the dust shield (5) by removing the nut (3), and plain washer (4).

Unscrew the nuts (30), bolts (9) and setscrews (22 and 23) to remove the steering arm (29), distance tubes (28), and caliper mounting bracket (7).

Referring to Fig. 5, remove the setscrew (19), spring washer (20) and steering lock stop (21). Unscrew the bottom trunnion assembly (23) and remove the oil seal (18).

Detach the top ball joint (12) from the vertical link and separate the upper wishbone arms (3), (73) as described on page 4·109.

Referring to Fig. 4, remove the nyloc nut (27), washer (26) and press the stub axle (6) from the vertical link (25).

Re-assembly

Fig. 4. Fit the stub axle (6) to the vertical link (25) and secure it with a plain washer (26) and nyloc nut (27).

Assemble the caliper mounting bracket (7), distance tube (28) and steering arm (29) to the vertical link. Tighten the nyloc nuts and secure the bolts (9) by turning up the ends of the lockplates (8) against the bolt heads.

Fig. 5. Screw the lower trunnion (23) with rubber seal (18) on to the vertical link (16). Secure the lock stop collar (21) with a setscrew (19) and spring washer (20). Ensure that the trunnion will swivel easily from stop to stop.

Fig. 4. Fit the dust shield (5), securing the slotted lug beneath the nut (3). Assemble the hub and disc and adjust as described on page 4·104.

Fig. 5. Assemble the top inner fulcrum (1), the rubber bushes (2), (4), both upper wishbone arms (73), (3) and ball joint (12) as shown on Fig. 5 and attach the assembly to the vertical link (16).

Fig. 4. If the hydraulic hose has been disconnected, refit the caliper unit and shim pack, securing with the bolts (1) and spring washers (2).

Offer up the suspension unit and secure the upper inner fulcrum to the spring turret.

Fig. 5. Assemble the lower wishbone arms (22), (59), to the bottom inner fulcrums and trunnion as shown on Figs. 5, 16 and 17. Fit the support brackets (54) and secure them with bolts (50) and nuts (52 and 53).

The outer lower fulcrum bosses must have 0·004″—0·012″ (0·1—0·3 mm.) end float. This is obtained by tightening both slotted nuts to a torque of 5 lbs. ft. (0·69 kilogrammetres); then slackening each slotted nut 1 to 2 flats before inserting the split pins (41). Ensure that the suspension is free to move from bump to rebound.

Refit the outer tie-rod ends and secure them with plain washers and nyloc nuts.

Refit the caliper unit with shims (if not already fitted) and if necessary, bleed the hydraulic system.

Refit the road spring, spring pan and damper unit as described on pages 4·107 and 4·108.

Refit the road wheels and nave plates, remove the chassis stands and lower the vehicle to the ground.

Rear Road Springs (Fig. 22)

Removal

Jack up the rear of the vehicle and support it on chassis stands.

Remove the road wheels and take the road spring load with a jack placed beneath the spring blades.

Remove the damper link (22) and remove the nuts (15), plain washers (14), spring plate (13), and 'U' bolts (3). Lower the jack to release the road spring tension.

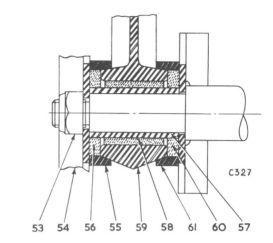

Fig. 16. Section through bottom inner fulcrum

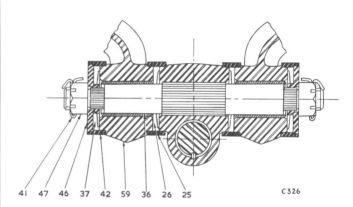

Fig. 17. Section through bottom outer fulcrum

Fig. 18. Front suspension assembly

Fig. 19.   Rear spring attachments

Fig. 20.   Removing the rear spring

Fig. 21.   Axle spring distance piece

Remove the nuts (4), spring washers (5) and detach the shackle plates (6), (8) and rubber bushes (7) from the spring and chassis bracket.

Remove the split pin (18), slotted nut (19), washer (20) and withdraw the bolt (24) to release the spring (9) from the vehicle.

To Refit

Offer up the spring and fit the pin (24), plain washer (20) and nut (19) leaving the nut slack.

Assemble the rear shackle (6) and (8), with bushes (7), spring washers (5) and nuts (4), leaving the nuts slack.

Jack up the spring blades until they contact the axle pad and fit the 'U' bolts (3), spring plate, (13), plain washers (14) and nuts (15).

Note that on L.H. drive vehicles, two packings are fitted between the R.H. spring and axle pad.

Tighten the nuts (4) and (19) and fit the split pin (18).

Rear Dampers (Fig. 22)

To Remove

Jack up the rear of the vehicle and support on chassis stands. Remove the rear road wheels.

Remove the nuts (11) and (16), washers (12) and (17) and detach the damper links (22).

Remove the bolts (23), washers (26), nuts (27) and detach the damper (25).

To Refit

Hold the damper vertical in a vice, and move the arm through its full arc to expel air from the damper cylinder. Remove the filler plug, top up with oil and refit the plug. Maintaining the damper in a vertical position, offer it up to the chassis bracket and secure with bolts (23), washers (26) and nuts (27).

Refit the damper link (22), securing it with nuts (11) and (16) and washers (12) and (17).

Refit the road wheels, remove axle stands and lower the vehicle to the ground.

SUSPENSION

Distance pieces, approximately $3\frac{1}{2}''$ in height, are located between the bottom of the rear axle and each rear spring centre, and secured by 'U' bolts. A shoulder on the rear edge of each distance piece bears against the rear 'U' bolt of each spring to prevent movement.

A flat base at the bottom of each side of the rear axle casing accommodates a dowel which locates and prevents displacement of each distance piece.

Rear shock absorber links (lower mounting points) locate in the centre of each distance piece extension arm at the front leading inner edge.

Tendency to roll steer is minimised by fitting Re-cambered Rear Road Springs, Part Number 209964, with distance pieces, Part Number R.H. 209962 and L.H. 209963.

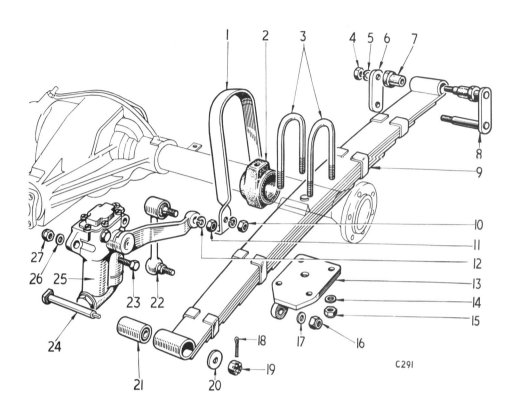

C291

1	Bump strap	14	Plain washer
2	Bump and rebound rubber	15	Nyloc nut
3	'U' bolts	16	Nyloc nut
4	Nut	17	Plain washer
5	Spring washer	18	Split pin
6	Shackle plate	19	Slotted nut
7	Rubber bush	20	Washer
8	Shackle	21	Bush
9	Spring	22	Damper link
10	Nut	23	Bolt
11	Nut	24	Shackle pin
12	Spring washer	25	Damper
13	Spring plate	26	Plain washer
		27	Nyloc nut

Fig. 22.   Rear suspension details

ASSESSMENT OF ACCIDENTAL DAMAGE

The following dimensioned illustrations assist in the assessment of accidental damage.

It is suggested that any components which have sustained damage or are suspect in any way, should first be removed from the vehicle as instructed, then cleaned and accurately measured on a surface table.

The measurements obtained should then be compared with those given in the appropriate illustration and a decision made relative to the serviceability of the components.

0° Castor

Rear R.H. and Front L.H. (Part No. 132632)

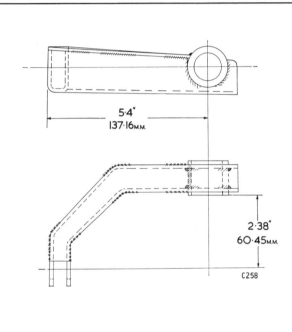

Front R.H. and Rear L.H. (Part No. 132633)

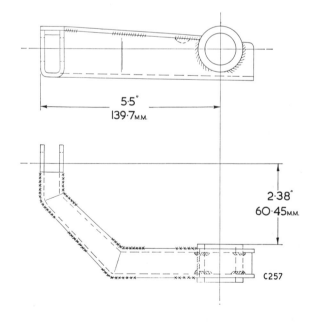

Fig. 23.   Upper wishbone dimensions

3° Castor

Front R.H. and L.H. (Part No. 133504).

Dimension	In.	cm.
1	1·687	4·285
2	5·66	14·38
3	1·115	2·832
4	2·03	5·156
5	1·034	2·626

Rear R.H. and L.H. (Part No. 133507).

4	0·98	2·489

All other dimensions are identical to Part No. 133504.

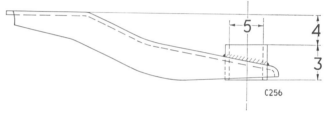

Fig. 24. Upper wishbone dimensions

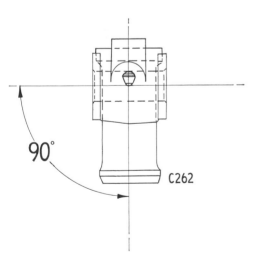

Fig. 25. Lower trunnion bracket 0° Castor

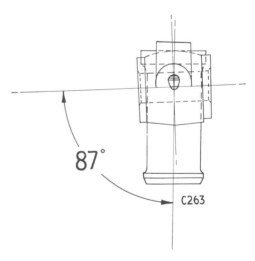

Fig 26. Lower trunnion bracket 3° Castor

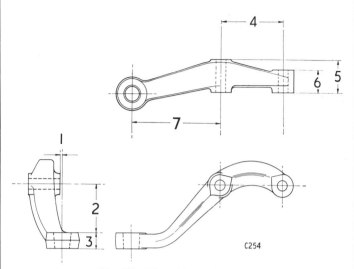

Fig. 27. Tie-rod lever dimensions

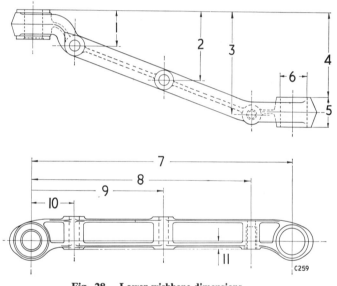

Fig. 28. Lower wishbone dimensions

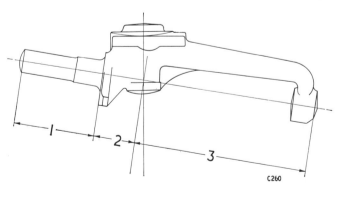

Fig. 29. Vertical link dimensions

0° Castor

Part Number 127830 (R.H.) and 127831 (L.H.).

Dimension	In.	cm.
1	0·06	0·1524
2	1·75	4·445
3	0·56	1·422
4	2·345	5·956
5	1·19	3·023
6	0·81	2·057
7	3·33	8·458

3° Castor

Part Number 129836 (R.H.) and 129837 (L.H.)

Dimension	In.	cm.
2	1·97	5·004

All other dimensions are identical to those given for 0° castor.

0° and 3° Castor

L.H. (Part No. 106577).
R.H. (Part No. 106578).

Dimension	In.	cm.
1	1·38	3·505
2	2·66	6·756
3	3·94	10·080
4	3·31	8·407
5	1·12	2·845
6	1·034	2·626
7	10·25	26·035
8	8·63	21·92
9	5·13	13·03
10	1·63	4·14
11	0·31	0·787

Part Number 201803 R.H. and L.H.

Dimension	In.	cm.
1	2·59	6·579
2	1·53	3·886
3	6·50	16·51

SUSPENSION AND STEERING DATA

The following dimensions apply to the vehicle only when it is static laden; this condition is obtained by placing a 150 lb. (68 kg.) weight on each front seat.

Wheel base	7′ 4″ (2235 mm.)
Front track	
Disc wheels	4′ 1″ (1245 mm.)
Wire wheels	4′ 1$\frac{3}{4}$″ (1263 mm.)
Rear track	
I.R.S. $\left\{\begin{array}{l}\text{Disc wheels}\\\text{Wire wheels}\end{array}\right.$	
Disc wheels	4′ $\frac{1}{2}$″ (1232 mm.)
Wire wheels	4′ 1$\frac{1}{4}$ (1251 mm.)
Live $\left\{\begin{array}{l}\text{Disc wheels}\\\text{Wire wheels}\end{array}\right.$ axle	
Disc wheels	4′ 0″ (1220 mm.)
Wire wheels	4′ $\frac{3}{4}$″ (1239 mm.)
Toe-in (front and rear for I.R.S.)	0″ to $\frac{1}{16}$″ (1·6 mm.)
Ground clearance	6″ (152 mm.)
Turning circle (between kerbs)	33 ft. (10 m.)
Front wheel camber	0° ± $\frac{1}{2}$°
I.R.S. Rear wheel camber	1° negative ± $\frac{1}{2}$°
Castor angle	2°40′ ± $\frac{1}{2}$°
K.P.I.	9° ± $\frac{3}{4}$°
Maximum back lock	31$\frac{1}{2}$°
Maximum front lock	26$\frac{1}{2}$°

    20° front lock gives 21$\frac{1}{2}$° back lock.

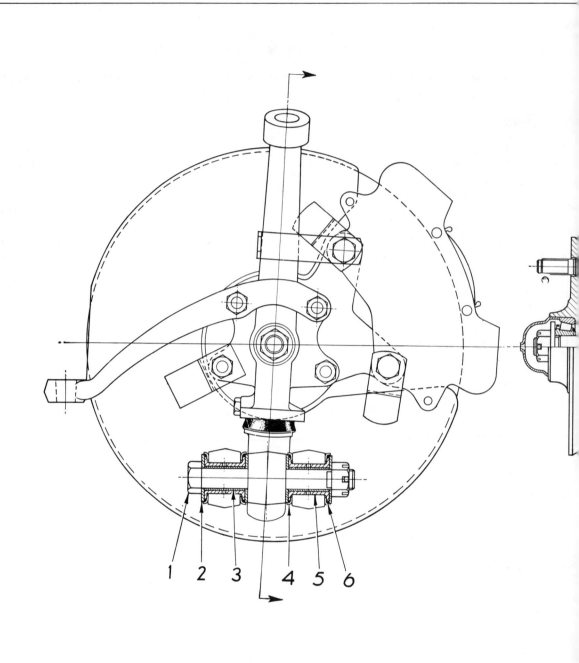

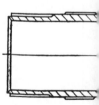

Fig. 29a.   Steering and front suspension

1   2   3   4   5   6

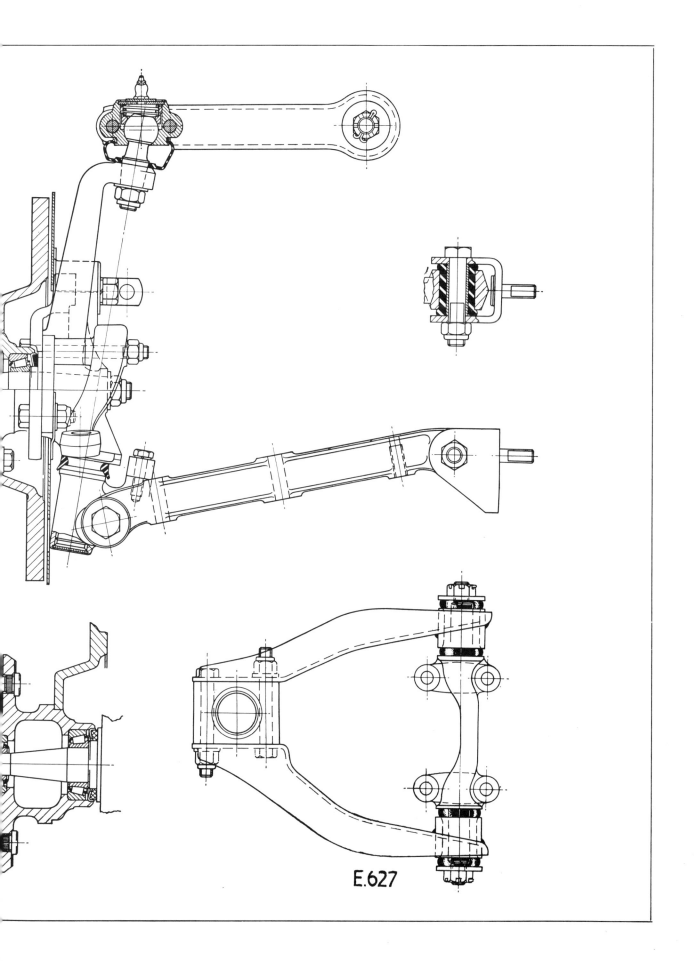

E.627

Fig. 30.   Location of shims behind fulcrum brackets

FRONT SUSPENSION

Lower Wishbone

Removal

Firmly apply the handbrake and remove the road spring as described on page 4·108. Proceed as follows to remove and dismantle the lower wishbone:-

Note the number and position of shims (Fig. 30) between the chassis frame and front and rear inner fulcrum brackets. Remove the nyloc nut and washer (Fig. 31) securing each fulcrum bracket to the chassis. Remove the outer fulcrum bolt (1, Fig. 29) to detach both lower wishbone arms.

Servicing

Refer to page 4·122 to check for damage to each component. If necessary fit new inner fulcrum bushes as instructed on page 4·120. Check the outer fulcrum and if necessary fit new nylon bushes (5), steel sleeves (3), thrust washers (2), dust excluders (6) and retainers (4) (see Fig. 29a).

Refitting

Reverse the removal procedure and fit the road spring as instructed on page 4·108. Roll the car forwards a few feet in order that the suspension assumes its straight-ahead running position. Accurately check and, if necessary, re-set the Castor and Camber angles by means of the shims between the inner fulcrum brackets and the chassis. Check the toe-in and, if necessary, re-adjust (see pages 4·201 and 4·212).

Fig. 31.   Fulcrum bracket securing nuts

Fig. 32.   Position of disc brake caliper

Fig. 33.   Removal of rear road spring

Fig. 34.   Suspension pivot attachment nuts

Fig. 35.   Rear suspension semi-trailing arm

REAR SUSPENSION

Chock the front wheels back and front in the straight-ahead direction.

Road Spring Removal

Prise off the nave plate and slacken the wheel nuts.   Release the handbrake, and with a trolley jack placed under the differential casing, raise the rear of the car onto stands positioned beneath the chassis frame.

Raise the suspension arm with the jack under the spring well; remove the wheel, uncouple the drive shaft and disconnect the damper from the suspension arm.   Taking care to avoid straining the brake hose, lower the arm until the spring is just free.   Do not disconnect any part of the hydraulic brake system.

Rear Dampers

As in the TR.4, the damper body is secured to the chassis by two bolts.

Renewal of Rubber Bushes

Position the suspension arm above a spacer block resting on the table of a hand press and force out the bush.   Thoroughly clean the eye of the suspension arm and, using a liberal amount of Castrol rubber grease, press in a new bush by its centre tube (protecting the end of the tube with a bolt).   If available, a tapered guide-in will facilitate the entry of the bush.

Suspension Arm Removal

Remove the road spring as described previously, and temporarily re-connect the damper.

Drain the brake system and disconnect the brake hose.   Disconnect the handbrake cable from the backplate and from the suspension arm. Support the suspension arm with a jack under the spring well and disconnect the damper. Release the suspension arm from the chassis by removing the four nuts (Fig. 34), noting the number and location of shims removed.

Installing Suspension Arm

Check that the grooves in the edges of the mounting brackets are uppermost.   The bracket having four grooves is the outside pivot and the bracket with only two grooves is the inside pivot.

Reverse the removal procedure and load the vehicle before tightening the bolts which secure the rubber bushes.

Set the rear wheel alignment as described on page 4·212.

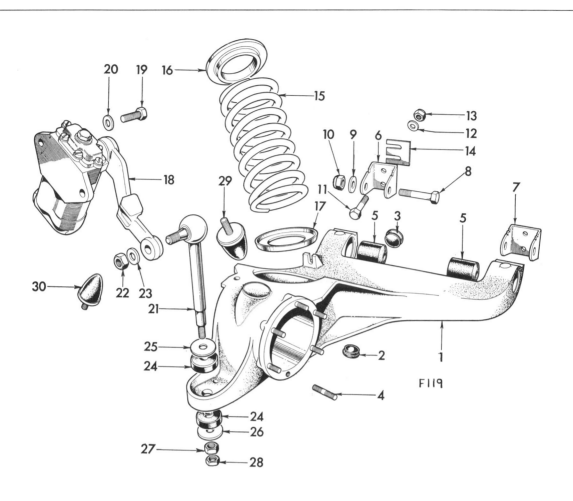

F119

1	Suspension arm	16	Rubber insulator
2	Rubber plug	17	Rubber insulator
3	Rubber plug	18	Damper arm
4	Stud	19	Bolt
5	Metalastik bush	20	Washer
6	Fulcrum bracket, inner	21	Damper link
7	Fulcrum bracket, outer	22	Nut
8	Bolt	23	Washer
9	Plain washer	24	Rubber buffer
10	Nyloc nut	25	Backing plate
11	Bolt	26	Backing plate
12	Plain washer	27	Nut
13	Nyloc nut	28	Locknut
14	Shim	29	Bump stop
15	Road spring	30	Rebound rubber

Fig. 36. Rear suspension exploded

ASSESSMENT OF ACCIDENTAL DAMAGE

The following dimensioned illustrations assist in the assessment of accidental damage.

It is suggested that any components which have sustained damage or are suspect in any way, should first be removed from the vehicle as instructed, then cleaned and accurately measured on a surface table.

The measurements obtained should then be compared with those given in the appropriate illustration and a decision made relative to the serviceability of the components.

± 0·005″ (0·127 mm.) except where otherwise stated.

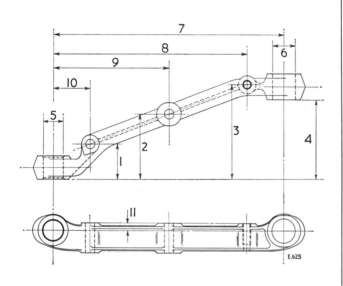

Fig. 37. Lower Wishbone Arm

R.H. rear/L.H. front — as drawn
             Part Number 307209.
       — opposite hand
             Part Number 307210.

Dimension	in.	cm.
1	1·523	3·87
2	2·803	7·12
3	4·083	10·37
4	3·453	8·77
5	0·8750	2·222
	0·8762	2·225
6	1·031	2·619
	1·037	2·634
7	10·25	26·035
8	8·63	21·92
9	5·13	13·03
10	1·63	4·14
11	0·31	0·787

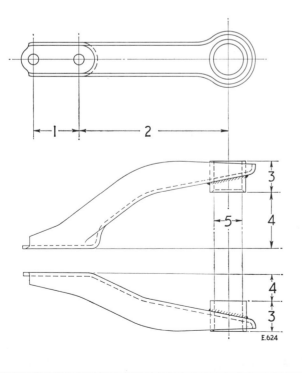

Fig. 38. Upper Wishbone

Front R.H. and L.H. (Part No. 133504).

Dimension	in.	cm.
1	1·687	4·285
2	5·66	14·38
3	1·115	2·832
4	2·03	5·156
5	1·034	2·626

Rear R.H. and L.H. (Part No. 133507).

4	0·98	2·489

All other dimensions are identical to Part No. 133504.

Fig. 39. Vertical Link
    Part Numbers R.H. 307215
                 L.H. 307216

± 0·005″ (0·127 mm.) except where otherwise stated.

Dimension	in.	mm.
1	1·96	49·78
2	0·38	9·65
3	0·63	16·0
4	0·25	6·35
5	6·5	165·1
6	1·1736	29·81
	1·1716	29·76
7	1·0005	25·413
	0·9995	25·387
8	1·125	28·57
9	1·7	43·18
10	4·38	111·25
11	3·25	82·5
12	0·687	17·45
13	9 degrees	

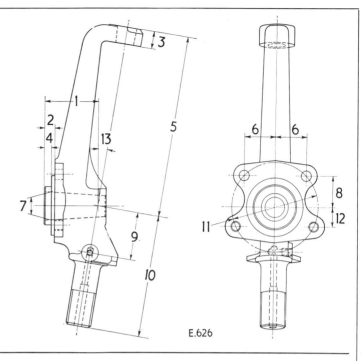

E.626

Fig. 40. Tie-rod Lever
    Part Numbers R.H. 307211
                 L.H. 307212

Dimension	in.	mm.
1	3 degrees	
2	1·53	38·86
3	4·81	122·17
4	2·347	59·62
	2·343	59·52
5	0·88	22·35
6	0·17	4·32

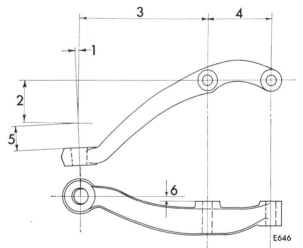

E646

Fig. 41. R.H. Rear Spring Eye Bracket (Live Axle)
    Part Numbers R.H. 142427
                 L.H. 142426

Dimension	in.	mm.
1	32 degrees	
2	1·97	50·04
3	1·53	38·86
4	0·192	4·88
5	2·25	57·15
6	0·94	23·88
7	2·75	69·85
8	1·50	38·1
9	0·25	6·35
10	0·651	16·53
	0·641	16·28

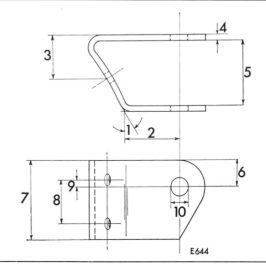

E644

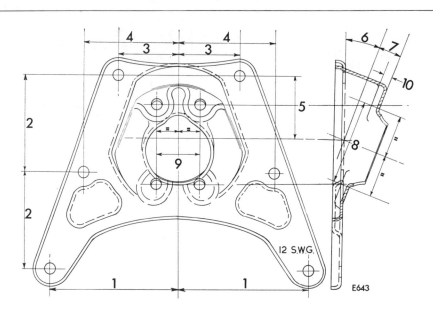

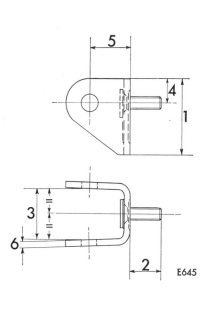

Fig. 42. Lower Spring Pan
Part Number 211811

Dimension	in.	mm.
1	4·81	122·17
2	3·5	88·9
3	2·25	57·15
4	3·53	89·66
5	2·25	57·15
6	20½ degrees	
7	0·81	20·57
8	3·06	77·72
9	1·66	42·16
10	0·324	8·23

Fig. 43. Lower Wishbone Inner Fulcrum Bracket
Part Number 139715

Dimension	in.	mm.
1	2·38	60·45
2	1·0	25·4
3	1·523	38·68
	1·508	38·30
4	0·75	19·05
5	1·34	34·04
6	0·192	4·88

STEERING MEASUREMENTS AND ADJUSTMENTS

Before carrying out measurements and adjustments on the front suspension and steering, position the vehicle on a smooth level surface, inflate the tyres to the correct pressures and place a load of 150 lb. (68 kg.) on each seat.

At Commission Numbers CT.6344 (wire wheels) and CT.6390 (disc wheels) the castor angle was changed from 0° to 3° positive. This was achieved by the incorporation of modified upper wishbone arms, ball joints and vertical link trunnions.

Lock Stop Adjustment

Run the front wheels onto Weaver or similar wheel turning radius gauges as shown on Fig. 4 and place wood blocks of equivalent thickness to that of each gauge under the rear wheels. Turn the front wheels to the straight ahead position and zero the gauges.

Slacken the setscrews (19) Fig. 5. Adjust the positions of the eccentricity drilled collars (21) to provide 31° back lock and 28½° front lock. Re-tighten the setscrews (19).

Check that the wheels and tyres do not foul the chassis when on full lock and that the steering unit rack teeth are not at the end of their travel.

Track Adjustment

Centralise the steering unit by turning the steering wheel, counting the number of turns necessary to move the steering from lock to lock and turning the steering wheel back half the number of turns. In this position, the steering wheel spokes should assume a horizontal position.

Using Weaver or similar wheel alignment equipment as shown on Fig. 2, measure the front wheel alignment. If adjustment is required, slacken the tie-rod end lock nuts, the outer gaiter clips and rotate the tie-rods until the correct alignment is obtained. Take one reading, roll the vehicle forward so that the wheels rotate 180°; then obtain a second reading and adjust the tie-rods to a mean of the two readings. This allows for wheel rim run out.

When correct adjustment has been obtained, tighten the tie-rod lock nuts and gaiter clips.

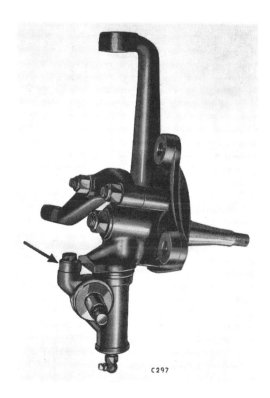

C297

Fig. 1. Vertical link assembly. The eccentric collar for lock stop adjustment is arrowed.

C243

Fig. 2. Checking front wheel alignment.

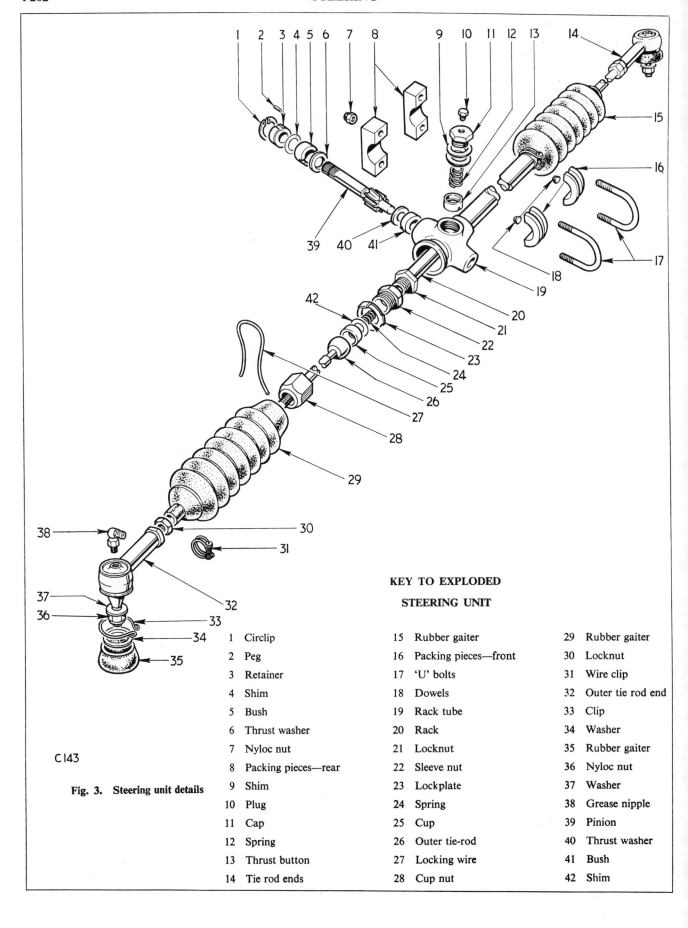

C 143

Fig. 3. Steering unit details

KEY TO EXPLODED
STEERING UNIT

1	Circlip	15	Rubber gaiter	29	Rubber gaiter
2	Peg	16	Packing pieces—front	30	Locknut
3	Retainer	17	'U' bolts	31	Wire clip
4	Shim	18	Dowels	32	Outer tie rod end
5	Bush	19	Rack tube	33	Clip
6	Thrust washer	20	Rack	34	Washer
7	Nyloc nut	21	Locknut	35	Rubber gaiter
8	Packing pieces—rear	22	Sleeve nut	36	Nyloc nut
9	Shim	23	Lockplate	37	Washer
10	Plug	24	Spring	38	Grease nipple
11	Cap	25	Cup	39	Pinion
12	Spring	26	Outer tie-rod	40	Thrust washer
13	Thrust button	27	Locking wire	41	Bush
14	Tie rod ends	28	Cup nut	42	Shim

Castor and Camber Measurement

The following instructions for measuring castor and camber are applicable to the Weaver instrument. Other types of measuring equipment may, however, be equally effective.

Run the front wheels on to Weaver or similar wheel turning radius gauges as shown on Fig. 4 and place wood blocks of equivalent thickness to that of each gauge under the rear wheels. Zero the gauges with the front wheels in the straight ahead position.

Using the No. 10 UNF setscrew supplied in the tool kit, remove the hub cap from the hub.

Ensuring that the split pin does not foul it, place the spacer washer (4) Fig. 5, with flange outwards, and engage the claws of the adaptor (3) on the stub axle thread between two of the nut slots. Secure the spirit level unit (1) to the adaptor and tighten the knurled nut (2).

With the wheels in the straight ahead position, measure the camber from the L.H. scale.

Turn the wheel to 20° back lock and zero the bubble on the R.H. scale.

Turn the wheel to 20° front lock and read the castor angle from the R.H. scale.

Repeat the operations on the opposite wheel. Compare the camber and castor angles with those given on page 4·102. Appreciable differences indicate distorted suspension components, worn suspension bushes or settled front springs.

Fig. 4. Measuring castor and camber angles

STEERING UNIT

Removal (Fig. 3)

Jack up the front of the vehicle, support it on chassis stands, and remove the front road wheels. Drain the cooling system and remove the bottom radiator hose.

Remove the bolt (1) from the steering coupling Fig. 6. Remove the nyloc attachment nuts (36) and separate the outer tie rod ball joints from the tie rod levers, as shown on Fig. 3.

Remove the nyloc nuts (7) 'U' bolts (17), aluminium packing pieces (16) and release the steering unit by moving it forwards, to disengage the pinion shaft from the splined coupling. Remove the unit by withdrawing it through the wheelarch.

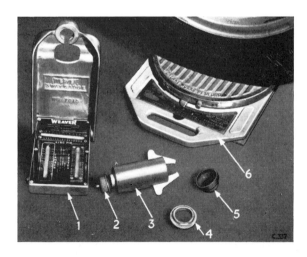

Fig. 5. Weaver measuring equipment

Fig. 6. Steering unit attachment

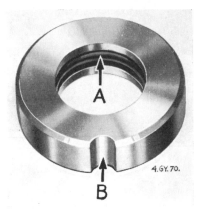

Fig. 7. Pinion retainer showing the seal "A" and dowel recess "B"

Fig. 8. Measuring pinion end float

Steering Unit (Fig. 3)

Dismantling

Release the clips (31) and (27), and slide both bellows towards the outer ball joints. Slacken the locknuts (21) and unscrew both outer tie rod assemblies from the rack (20). Withdraw the coil spring (24) from each end of the rack.

Release the tabwasher (23), unscrew the sleeve nut (22), and remove the tabwasher (23) shims (42) and thrust pad (25). Slacken the locknuts (30) and unscrew the outer ball joint assemblies (14) and (32) from their respective tie rods.

Remove the locknut (30), rubber bellows (15) and (29), clips (31) and cup nut (28) from each outer tie rod (26).

Remove the locknuts from the ends of the rack. Unscrew the cap (11) and remove the shims (9), spring (12) and pressure pad (13) from the housing.

Remove the circlip (1) and withdraw the pinion assembly, taking care not to lose the dowel peg (2). Remove the retaining ring (3), shims (4), bush (5) and thrust washer (6). Detach the rubber 'O' ring from the annular groove in the retaining ring (3).

Withdraw the rack (20) from the tube (19) and remove the thrust washer (40) and bush (41) from the pinion housing.

Inspection

Clean and examine all components for wear and damage, renewing parts as required.

If necessary, renew the bush in the end of the rack tube by drifting out the old bush and pressing in a new one.

Assembly

Insert the rack (20) into the tube (19) and place the bush (41) and thrust washer (40) into the pinion housing.

Adjust the pinion end float as follows :—

1. Assemble the thrust washer (6), bush (5) and retaining ring (3) to the pinion (39). Insert the assembly into the pinion housing and secure the pinion with the circlip (1).

2. Mount a dial gauge on the tube as shown on Fig. 8. Push the pinion down to its limit and zero the dial gauge. Lift the shaft until the retaining ring contacts the circlip and note the dial reading which represents the total pinion shaft end float. Remove the circlip (1) and withdraw the pinion shaft assembly. Remove the retaining ring (3) and renew its rubber 'O' ring if required.

3. Make up a shim pack to give the minimum end float consistent with free rotation of the pinion shaft. Shims are available in 0·004″ (0·102 mm.) and 0·010″ (0·254 mm.) thickness.

4. Assemble the shim pack (4) and retainer ring (3) to the pinion. Re-insert the assembly into the housing and finally secure it by fitting the dowel (2) and circlip (1).

Adjust the pinion pressure pad as follows :—

1. Fit the pressure pad (13) and cap nut (11) to the rack tube (19). Tighten the plug to eliminate all end float and using feeler gauges, measure the clearance between the plug and rack tube faces as shown on Fig. 10. Remove the cap nut (11) and pad (13).

2. Make up a shim pack equal to the cap/housing clearance plus 0·004″ (0·1 mm.) nominal end float.

3. Pack the unit with grease and assemble the cap nut (11), shim pack (9) spring (12) and plunger (13) to the housing (19) and tighten the cap nut.

4. When the unit is correctly adjusted, a force of 2 lb. (0·91 kg.) is required to rotate the pinion shaft at a radius of 8″ (20·3 cm.). If correction is needed, adjust the unit by adding or subtracting shims from beneath the cap nut (10).

Refitting

Having checked that the steering unit conforms to the dimensions given on Fig. 19, count the number of pinion shaft revolutions required to move the rack from lock to lock. Turn the shaft back to centralise the rack, and move the steering wheel to the straight ahead position.

Fit the steering unit by entering the splined pinion shaft into the splined coupling. Assemble the two aluminium packing pieces (8) behind the rack and the two front aluminium blocks (16), entering their dowels (18) into the holes in the rack tube (19). Fit the 'U' bolts (17) and nyloc nuts (7).

Enter the taper pins of the outer tie rod ball joints (32) into the steering levers and fit washers (37) and nyloc nuts (36). Refit the bolt (1) Fig. 6, and nyloc nut to the steering coupling.

Refit the road wheels, lower the vehicle to the ground and check the front wheel alignment as described on page 4·201.

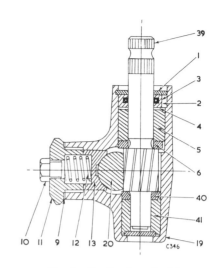

Fig. 9. Section through pinion

Fig. 10. Using feeler gauges to establish the thickness of shims required under the cap nut

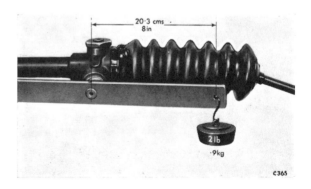

Fig. 11. Measuring the load required to turn the pinion

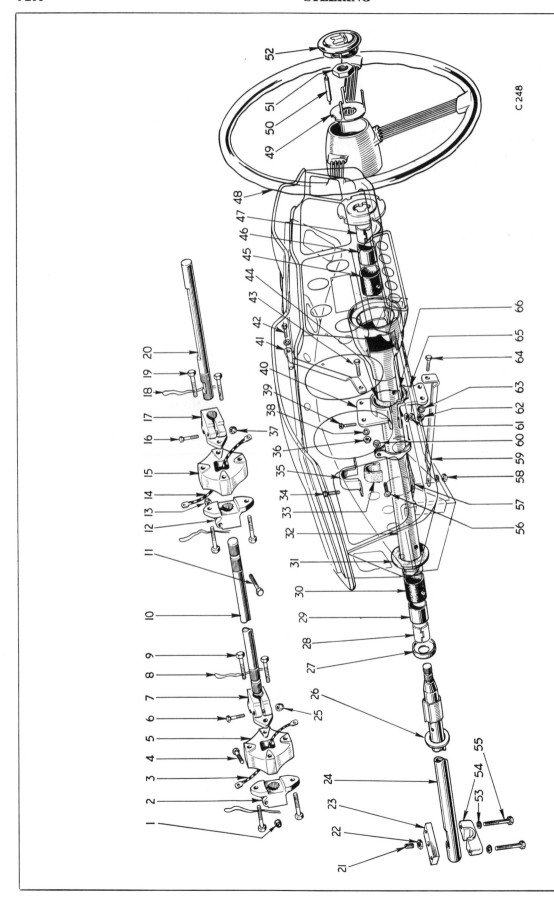

C 248

Fig. 12. Steering Column Details

KEY TO FIG. 12

1   Nyloc nut
2   Adaptor
3   Earthing cable
4   Pinch bolt
5   Rubber coupling
6   Pinch bolt
7   Adaptor
8   Locking wire
9   Bolt
10 Lower steering column
11 Pinch bolt
12 Adaptor
13 Nut
14 Earthing cable
15 Rubber coupling
16 Pinch bolt
17 Adaptor
18 Locking wire
19 Bolt
20 Lower column
21 Allen screw
22 Locknut

23 Impact clamp plate
24 Upper inner column
25 Nyloc nut
26 Washer
27 Cap
28 Nylon bush
29 Steel bush
30 Rubber bush
31 Rubber grommet
32 Upper outer column
33 Felt
34 Bolt
35 Clamp
36 Nut
37 Nyloc nut
38 Spring washer
39 Bolt
40 Upper clamp
41 Stay
42 Bolt
43 Bolt
44 Felt

45 Rubber bush
46 Steel bush
47 Nylon bush
48 Steering wheel
49 Clip
50 Horn brush
51 Nut
52 Horn push
53 Spring washer
54 Impact clamp
55 Bolt
56 Screw
57 Felt
58 Nut
59 Stay
60 Nut
61 Nut
62 Nut
63 Spring washer
64 Bolt
65 Bracket
66 Cable trough

STEERING COLUMN

Removal (Fig. 12)

Disconnect the battery, and remove the bolt (4) securing the adaptor (2) to the steering unit pinion shaft. Remove the impact clamp (54) and push the column (20) into the upper inner column (24), to disengage the coupling (2) from the pinion shaft. Move the coupling to one side, pull the assembly from the column (24), and detach the nylon washer (26).

Working inside the car, remove the nuts (58) to release the clamp (35), with felt (33). Remove the stay (41), the upper bracket (40), and felt (44).

Disconnect the horn and direction indicator cables at their snap connectors. Remove the bolt (56) and open the cable trough clip. Pull the steering column and wheel assembly up through the bulkhead grommet (31) and facia aperture, allowing the cable trough (66) to slide off the column.

Dismantling

If necessary, dismantle the universal couplings.

Detach the retaining screws and switch covers from head of the outer column (32). Remove the direction indicator switch, pulling the cables through the apertures in the column head. Withdraw the column (24) and steering wheel assembly from the outer column (32).

Remove the horn button (52), brush (50) and nut (51) ; then press the inner column (24) from the wheel boss (48).

Remove the end cap (27) and whilst depressing the protrusions on the rubber bush (30), eject the lower bush from the column, using a long shaft. Remove the metal sleeve (29) and nylon bush (28) from the flexible end of the rubber bush (30). Similarly, remove the upper bushes (45), (46) and (47).

Re-assembly

Assemble the nylon bush (28) and steel sleeve (29) to the rubber bush (30) as shown on Fig. 14.

Push the bush assembly into the bottom of the outer column (32), engaging the locating lugs with the holes as shown on Fig. 14. Ensure that the metal reinforcement ring at the end of the bush is positioned towards the lower end of the column. Repeat the upper bush assembly.

Fit the metal cup (27) to the lower end of the column (32).

Fit the steering wheel (48) to the inner column (24), aligning the direction indicator cancelling lugs on the column to correspond with the steering wheel spokes as shown on Fig. 15, and tighten its attachment nut (51). Peen the metal of the nut to the inner column to prevent it unscrewing.

Fig. 13. Using tool No. S. 3600 to remove steering wheel

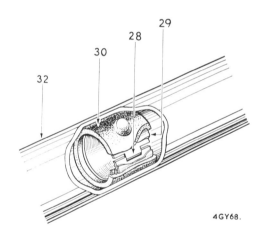

Fig. 14. Section through steering column bush assembly

Fig. 15. Showing the direction indicator cancelling lugs at the top of the inner column aligned with the steering wheel spokes

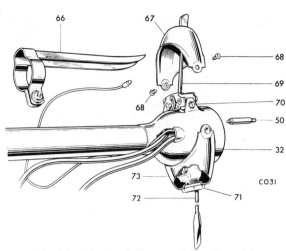

Fig. 16. Direction indicator switch and overdrive switch attachment

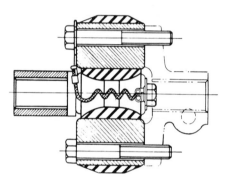

Fig. 17. Section through steering coupling

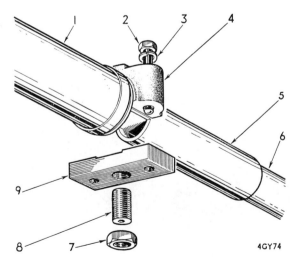

Fig. 18. Impact clamp details

Insert the inner column (24), into the outer column (32) taking care not to dislodge the bushes.

Feed the cables of the overdrive and direction indicator switches through the apertures in the upper end of the outer column, and retain the switches in position by fitting the attachment screws (70) and lock-ring (71). Fit the switch covers and retaining screws (68).

Insert the horn contact plunger (50) into the steering wheel boss and fit the horn button assembly (52) (Fig. 12).

Fit the adaptors (2), (7), (12) and (17) with earthing cables (3) and (14) to the joints (5) and (15) and secure with bolts (9) and (19). Wire-lock each pair of bolts together.

Refitting

Fit the steering column to the vehicle, passing it through the facia and rubber grommet in the bulkhead. Fit the cable trough (66), securing with the screws (56), spring washer and nut (60).

Fit the upper half of the upper support clamp (40) with felt (44), the tie rod (59), bolts (39), washers and nuts (61) (leave the nuts slack). Secure the stay (41) with spring washer (38) and nut (36).

Attach the lower clamp (35) felt (33) and (50), bolts (34), washers (57) and nuts (58) (leave the nuts slack).

Fit the lower column (10) to the coupling adaptors (7) and (12) and secure with the bolts (6) and (11) and nyloc nuts (25) and (13).

Refit the washer (26) to the column (24).

Insert the lower column assembly into the inner column (24).

Refit the impact clamp as follows :—

(a) Slacken the locknut (22) and using a $\frac{1}{8}''$ A/F Unbrako hexagon wrench, unscrew the Allen screw (21) two complete turns.

(b) Turn the column (20) to bring the machined flat in line with that machined aperture in the column (24).

(c) Fit the impact clamp (54) and (23), retaining bolts (55) and washers (53).

With the road wheels and steering wheel (48) in the straight ahead position fit the lower coupling adaptor (2) to the steering unit pinion shaft. Fit and tighten the retaining bolt (4) and nut (1).

Move the steering column to the desired height. To lower, push down on the steering wheel. To raise, pull on the outer column.

Tighten the upper and lower clamp nuts (58) and (61) and bolts (34) and (39).

Using the $\frac{1}{8}''$ A/F Unbrako hexagon wrench, tighten the Allen screw (21) as much as possible without bending the wrench, then tighten the locknut (22).

Refit the horn and direction indicator cables at their snap connectors, and reconnect the battery.

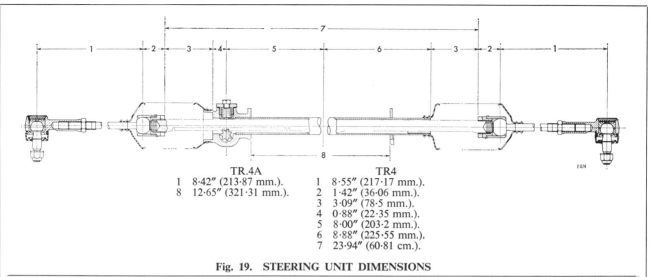

TR.4A
1	8·42″ (213·87 mm.).
8	12·65″ (321·31 mm.).

TR4
1	8·55″ (217·17 mm.).
2	1·42″ (36·06 mm.).
3	3·09″ (78·5 mm.).
4	0·88″ (22·35 mm.).
5	8·00″ (203·2 mm.).
6	8·88″ (225·55 mm.).
7	23·94″ (60·81 cm.).

Fig. 19. STEERING UNIT DIMENSIONS

Inner Ball Joints

Assembly and Adjustment

Slide the cup nut (28) over the tie-rod (26) and insert the thrust ring (25) into the cup (28). Position the lockplate (23) over the sleeve nut (22) and screw this fully into the cup nut.

With the cup nut held in a vice, pull and push the tie-rod to estimate the approximate amount of "ball-lift". Prepare a shim pack (42) slightly thicker than the estimated "ball-lift" and insert this between the thrust ring (25) and the sleeve nut (22).

Add or remove shims to obtain the requisite ·002″ (·05 mm.) ball-lift when the sleeve nut is firmly screwed into the cup nut.

IMPORTANT. The ball should now move freely in the joint. If tightness occurs at any point, increase the shim thickness sufficiently to overcome this.

When adjustment is satisfactory, lock the assembly by bending the lockplate (23) over the sleeve nut (22) and the cup nut (28). Assemble the opposite tie-rod by repeating the foregoing procedure.

Fit a locknut (21) and spring (24) to each end of the rack (20), and screw on each outer tie-rod assembly. Adjust the position of the tie-rod assemblies on the rack (20) to dimension 7 Fig. 19. Tighten the locknut to maintain this position.

Fit the bellows (15) and (29) securing them with clips (27) and (31). Assemble the locknuts (30) and tie-rod ends (14) and (32) to the tie-rods.

Fig. 20.
Tie-rod coupling details

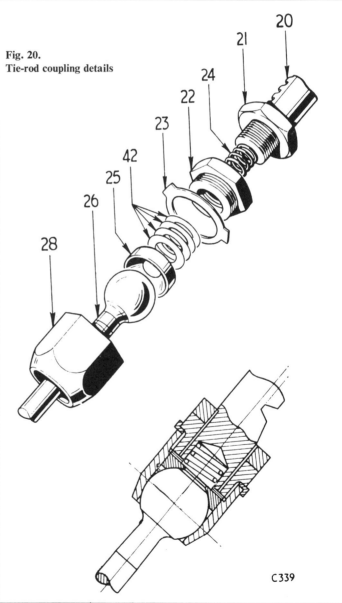

C339

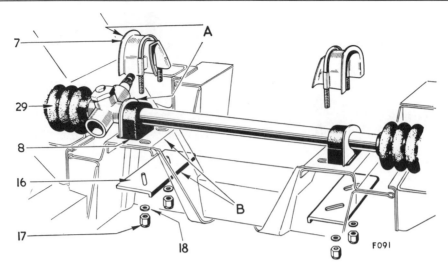

A   Distance between flanges must be ⅛″ (3·17 mm.)
B   Flange of item (16) must contact innermost flange of frame

7	"U" bolt	17	Nyloc nut
8	Rubber bush	18	Plain washer
16	Locating plate	29	Rubber gaiter

Fig. 21.   Steering unit attachments

**Fig. 22.   Expander fitted to compress rack mounting
rubbers**

**Fig. 23.   Expander tool for use when fitting steering
rack**

STEERING   UNIT

Removal of Steering Rack (Fig. 21)

Raise the front of the car onto stands, remove the road wheels and take out the pinch-bolt which retains the universal fork on the rack pinion.

Remove the engine cooling fan and detach the tie-rod ends from the steering arms.

Remove nuts (17), washers (18), locating plates (16) and "U" bolts (7). Bring the rack forwards and manoeuvre the unit from the vehicle.

Refitting

Fit new rubber bushes (8) and manoeuvre the rack onto the crossmember brackets. Fit the "U" bolts (7), plates (16) and washers (18), loosely securing them with the nuts (17).

Move one "U" bolt outwards to the ends of the elongated holes in the crossmember bracket. Slide the locating plate inwards until the flanged edge of the plate completely contacts the side of the bracket. If necessary, further elongate the holes in the locating plate. Tighten the two nyloc nuts to the correct torque. Avoid overtightening.

Compress the rubbers to give a clearance of ⅛″ (3·175 mm.) between the flange plates on the rack tube and the retainers welded to the "U" bolts whilst securing the other locating plate.

Refit the tie-rod ends to the steering arms, refit the wheels and remove the stands. Tighten the wheel nuts and refit the wheel trim and nave plates. Refit the engine cooling fan and check the front wheel toe-in.

Set the front wheels in the straight-ahead position and secure the steering couplings with the upper column and the steering wheel in the straight-ahead position.

Steering

Steering geometry and Suspension geometry

The term "steering geometry" refers to the lay-out of the steering mechanism and any of its dimensions, linear or angular, which contribute to the required behaviour of the steering system. The steering system is always designed to comply with the specification of the front suspension, in order that the best possible steering behaviour is obtained under all conditions.

For example, Toe-in and Camber are classed as suspension geometry K.P.I.; and Castor are classed as steering geometry.

Departure from any steering/suspension dimensions may result in unsatisfactory steering and/or abnormal wear of tyres, steering and suspension components.

NOTE: Poor steering and tyre wear is often caused by unbalance of the tyres themselves.

To avoid using jigs for rear wheel alignment, it is recommended that optical equipment (e.g. Optiline, Optoflex, etc.) be used, enabling the front and rear wheels to be aligned simultaneously. This equipment projects a beam of light in a plane at right angles to each individual wheel axle, on to a graduated screen. The various angles and dimensions may be read directly and accurately off the screens.

Steering Axis Inclination (Fig. 24)

This is the angle in front elevation between the steering axis 'A' and the vertical line 'B'. The steering axis is the continuation of the lower trunnion centre line through the centre point of the upper ball swivel, and it is about this axis that the wheel pivots as it is turned for control of vehicle direction.

Camber (Fig. 24)

Positive camber is the amount in degrees that the front wheels are tilted outwards at the top 'C', from the vertical line 'B'.

Castor (Fig. 25)

Castor is the angle in side elevation between the steering axis 'A' and the vertical line 'B'. It is considered positive when the steering axis is inclined rearwards.

Wheel Alignment

To ensure parallel tracking when the vehicle is moving, the recommended static setting is parallel to $\frac{1}{16}''$ (1·6 mm.) toe-in.

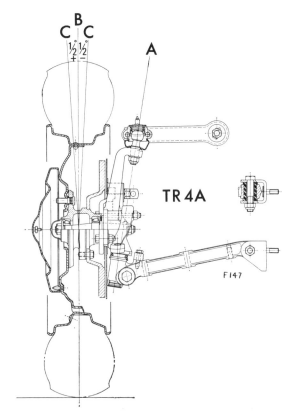

Fig. 24. Steering axis inclination and camber angle

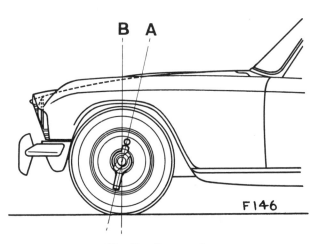

Fig. 25. Castor angle

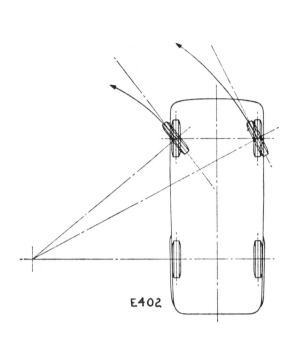

E402

Fig. 26.   Showing the relative angles of the front wheels when making a turn

TR.4A Turning Radius Angles (Fig. 26)

Outside wheel	Inside wheel
20 degrees	21½ degrees
26½ degrees max.	31½ degrees max.

Toe-out on Turns (Fig. 26)

This is the alignment of the front wheels relative to each other as they are turned to the left or right.

To eliminate scuffing when the vehicle is making a turn, each front wheel must be at right angles to the radius from its point of contact with the road to the centre of the returning circle. Thus the inner wheel toes-out relative to the outer wheel.

Unfortunately, using simple steering mechanisms, it is not possible to obtain the exact toe-out at every position through the complete turn from straight-ahead to full lock. However, scuffing can be minimised by careful positioning of the steering components.

Static Laden

The steering dimensions illustrated on Figs. 24 and 25 apply to a vehicle when static laden.

This condition is obtained by placing a 150 lb. (68 kg.) weight on each front seat and two similar weights on the rear seat.

OPTICAL ALIGNMENT EQUIPMENT
General Recommendations

To obtain the greatest accuracy from optical alignment equipment, it is necessary to comply with the following instructions:

(a) Assemble the equipment in accordance with the manufacturers' instructions.

(b) Set the screen parallel and at right angles to a level floor.

(c) Set the car square to the screen with the centre of the front wheels 5 ft. 7 in. from the face of the screen.

(d) Adjust the tyre pressures and load the vehicle to the static laden condition.

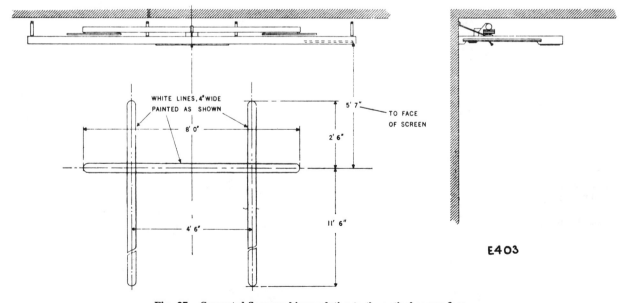

E403

Fig. 27.   Suggested floor markings relative to the optical screen face

Attaching the Projectors

Attach the wheel clamps by resting the lower support (6) on the edge of the wheel rim and pushing the upper support (4) until the cut-screws touch the inside of the upper wheel rim. Whilst pressing the upper support against the wheel rim edge, turn the cam lock (3) to secure the clamp.

Jack up the front wheels and ensure that the wheel clamp is clear of obstructions when rotating the wheel. Loosen the projector cam lock (5) centre the projector pivot (7) on the rods and retighten the cam lock (5). Slide the projector on to its pivot and tighten the clamping bolt (9). Repeat the procedure on the opposite front wheel.

Compensating for Wheel Run-out

The projector pivot mountings are provided with three large diameter milled edged compensating screws (2) for adjusting the projector beams to the true axis of the road wheels. Compensation for wheel run-out is effected as follows:

Connect the projectors to the control panel and, by sliding the telescopic projector lens (8) backwards or forwards, focus the light beam on the vertical line trueing scale immediately above the mirror hole in the screen.

Slacken the projector clamp screw (9) and, holding the projector (10) to keep the light image within the trueing scale, slowly rotate the road wheel. Note the extent of movement made by the light image across the scale and stop turning the wheel when the image reaches one extreme position.

Adjust the rearmost compensating screw (2) to bring the image to the centre of its movement. If two screws point to the rear, adjust both evenly. Repeat as necessary until the light image remains laterally stationary during wheel rotation.

Lower the wheels on to the centre of the turntables and apply the brake pedal depressor. Take hold of the bumper and jolt the car up and down a few more times. Unlock the turntables and jolt the car a few more times.

Fig. 28. Projector attachment

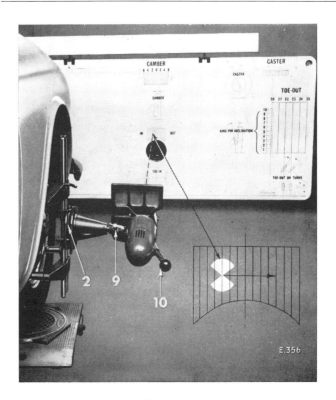

Fig. 29. Checking wheel run-out

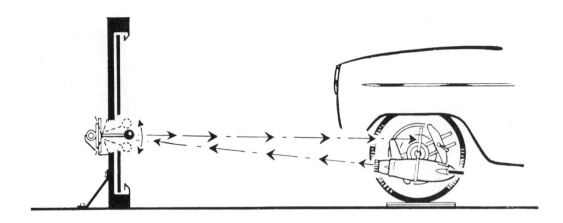

Fig. 30.   Aligning mirrors to re-direct light image to the toe-in scale

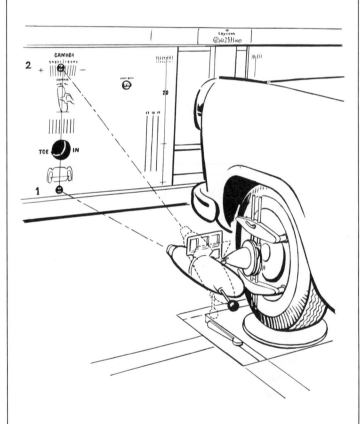

Fig. 31.   Checking front wheel camber angle

TAKE CARE TO ENSURE THAT THE SCREENS REMAIN IN THIS POSITION FOR ALL FURTHER OPERATIONS.

Toe-in

To check toe-in condition, aim the light image at the centre of the mirror and, by tilting the mirror up or down, re-direct and focus the image on to the toe-in scale (1), Fig. 28, attached to the top of the projector.   Turn the steering to align the light image with the zero line on the scale.   In this position the road wheel is at right angles to the mirror.

Aim the opposite projector at the centre of its mirror and focus the reflected image on the toe-in scale.   A direct reading of the toe-in condition can now be read from this scale.

Centre Steering

When the toe-in checks have been completed, turn the steering to equalize the readings on both projector toe-in scales and check the position of the steering wheel spokes.   These should be perfectly horizontal.

Camber—Straight-ahead position

IMPORTANT: Before taking a camber reading it is essential that the wheel is in the straight-ahead position (this applies for both L.H. and R.H. front wheels).

To check the camber of either front wheel, aim the light image at the centre of the mirror and, by tilting the mirror up or down, re-direct and focus the image on to the toe-in scale attached to the top of the projector.   Turn the steering to align the light image with the zero line on the scale.   In this position the road wheel is at right angles to the mirror.

By traversing the screen horizontally and tilting the projector, aim and refocus the light image on the measuring cross below the mirror. Tilt the projector to bring the image into the camber scale and note the reading.

Repeat the procedure on the opposite wheel.

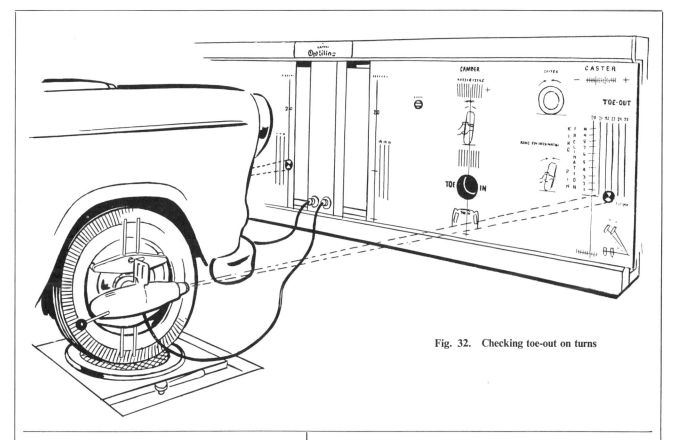

Fig. 32.   Checking toe-out on turns

King Pin Inclination and Castor (Fig. 33)

Turn the wheel inwards and tilt the projector to focus the light image on the lower measuring cross (Position 1). Tilt the projector to bring the image into Position 2 **and note the reading on the Castor index scale.**

Tilt the projector to focus the image on the measuring cross (Position 3) and tighten the projector clamping screw. Turn the wheel 20° outwards and **note the reading on the K.P.I. scale** (Position 4).

Slacken the projector clamping screw and, by turning the road wheels and tilting the projector as necessary, focus the light image on the lower Castor index scale (Position 5) to the same value noted in Position 2.

Tilt the projector to bring the image into Position 4 **and note the reading on the Castor scale.**

Toe-out on Turns (Fig. 32)

Turn the L.H. wheel inwards and focus the light image on the mean measuring cross on the 20° line nearest the inner edge of the L.H. screen. Tilt the projector on the opposite wheel and focus the light image on the base line of the Toe-out scale, nearest to the outer edge of the R.H. screen.

This will indicate R.H. wheel toe-out on turns.

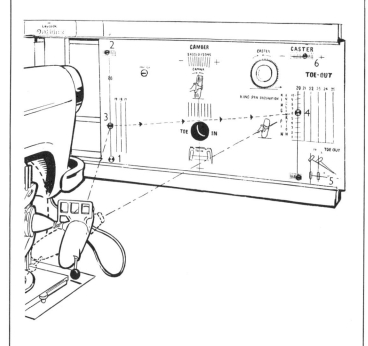

Fig. 33.   Measuring castor and king pin inclination

Fig. 34.   Scales fitted to the rear wheels

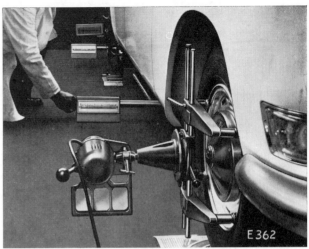

Fig. 35.   Centralising the front measuring rod

Fig. 36.   Centralising the rear measuring rod

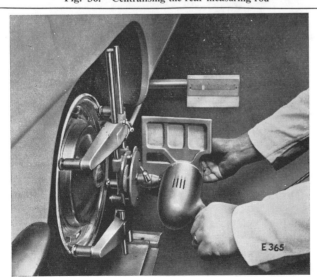

Fig. 37.   Checking rear wheel toe-in

Rear Wheel Toe-in

Attach wheel clamps and scales to the rear wheels by following the procedure on page 4·213, for "attaching the projectors", but substituting scales for projectors.

Turn the projectors on the front holders through 180° until the beams of light appear on the scales mounted on the rear holders. Turn the steering wheel until the same reading is obtained on both right and left rear wheel scales.

Mount the distance rods onto the measuring rods; place the assemblies on the floor in front and behind the rear axle with the distance rod plates resting against the wheels.

Focus both beams of light onto the front measuring rod scales, move measuring rods sideways until the same reading is obtained on the right- and left-hand scales; repeat this operation for setting the rear measuring rod.

Remove the projectors from the front holders and fit them in place of the rear wheel scales on the rear holders. Focus the beam of light on both front and rear measuring rods in turn, taking note of the readings obtained; by subtracting one from the other a toe-in value is obtained from each rear wheel.

Rear Wheel Camber (Fig. 38)

1. With the projectors mounted on the rear holders, focus the beam of light onto the main screens and, by traversing the screens horizontally, focus the light image on the measuring cross (Position 1).

2. Tilt the projector to bring the image into the camber scale (Position 2) and note the reading. Repeat the procedure on the opposite side.

Chassis Alignment

When the rear end check is completed, check chassis alignment by placing the wheel indicator scales on the front holders (without disturbing the wheels, as they are set in the straight-ahead position). Readings taken direct from the wheel indicator scales will give an indication of the chassis and axle condition.

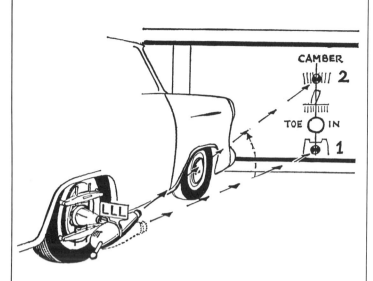

Fig. 38. Checking rear wheel camber

TRIUMPH TR4

WORKSHOP MANUAL

GROUP 5

Comprising:

TR4 WORKSHOP MANUAL

GROUP 5

CONTENTS

CHASSIS FRAME DIMENSIONS

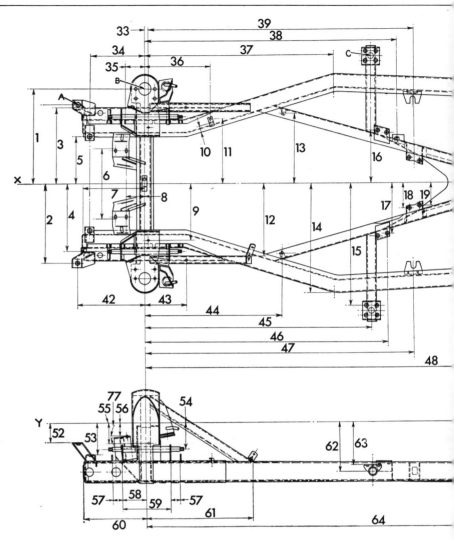

Fig. 1.   Chassis Frame Dimensions

	Inches	Centimetres		Inches	Centimetre
1	15·19	38·58	21	5·13	13·03
2	12·63	32·08	22	8·50	21·59
3	12·19	30·96	23	16·41/16·35	41·68/41·5
4	10·77	27·36	24	12·94	32·87
5	7·50	19·05	25	1·06	2·69
6	11·06/11·00	28·09/27·94	26	6·50	16·51
7	10·00	25·40	27	13·50	34·29
8	3·00	7·62	28	30·69	77·95
9	8·46	21·49	29	16·81/16·75	42·70/42·5
10	1·00	2·54	30	9·75	24·76
11	10·25	26·03	31	15·00	38·10
12	11·56	29·36	32	15·88	40·33
13	11·13	28·27	33	0·50	1·27
14	17·50	44·45	34	9·00	22·86
15	21·13	53·67	35	3·23	8·20
16	8·34	21·18	36	10·78	27·38
17	7·94	20·17	37	31·00	78·74
18	3·97	10·08	38	41·25	104·77
19	3·53	8·97	39	43·78/43·72	111·10/111·
20	2·44	6·20			

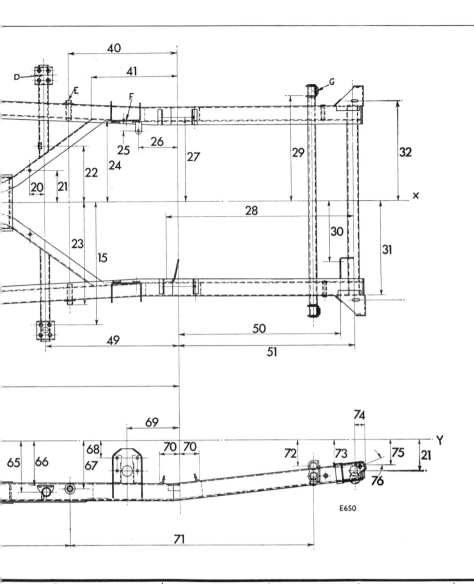

E650

	Inches	Centimetres		Inches	Centimetres
40	18·00	45·72	59	7·96	20·22
41	14·25	36·19	60	10·38	26·36
42	11·00	27·94	61	17·40	44·20
43	6·80	17·27	62	8·00	20·32
44	22·50	57·15	63	6·94	17·63
45	37·00	93·98	64	70·06	177·95
46	39·56	100·48	65	8·19	20·80
47	44·00	111·76	66	7·13	18·11
48	88·00	223·62	67	7·78/7·72	19·76/19·61
49	22·00	55·88	68	2·88	7·31
50	26·50	67·31	69	8·63	21·92
51	28·75	73·02	70	3·25	8·25
52	3·13	7·95	71	39·90/39·60	101·35/100·58
53	4·92	12·50	72	4·28/4·22	10·87/10·06
54	4·19	10·64	73	4·50	11·43
55	3·69	9·37	74	1·50	3·81
56	2·25	5·71	75	4·09	10·39
57	1·67	4·24	76	23°	
58	3·98	10·01	77	5°	

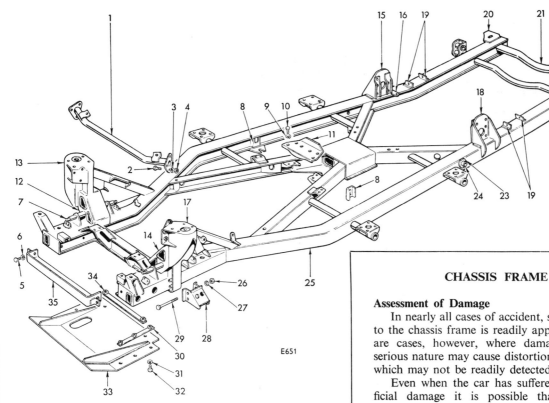

E651

Fig. 2.　Chassis Frame Details

1	Front cross tube	18	Shock absorber mounting
2	Bolt		bracket
3	Lock washer	19	Anchor bracket
4	Nut	20	Body mounting bracket
5	Bolt	21	Rear cross tube
6	Lock washer	22	Body mounting bracket
7	Fulcrum pin	23	Washer
8	Jacking bracket	24	Spring anchor tube
9	Lock washer	25	Chassis frame
10	Bolt	26	Nut
11	Crossmember	27	Plain washer
12	Engine mounting bracket	28	Rebound stop bracket
13	Spring abutment bracket	29	Bolt
14	Engine mounting bracket	30	Support strip
15	Shock absorber mounting	31	Lock washer
	bracket	32	Bolt
16	Brake pipe support bracket	33	Skid shield
17	Spring abutment bracket	34	Support strip
		35	Crossmember

CHASSIS FRAME

Assessment of Damage

In nearly all cases of accident, severe damage to the chassis frame is readily apparent. There are cases, however, where damage of a less serious nature may cause distortion of the frame which may not be readily detected visually.

Even when the car has suffered only superficial damage it is possible that the frame members may have been displaced, causing misalignment of the road wheels.

It is recommended that a check is made on the alignment of the front and rear suspension attachment points. This preliminary examination should include a check on wheelbase dimensions, castor and wheel camber angles. A decision may then be taken as to whether the frame can be repaired *in situ*, or whether body removal is necessary to permit fuller examination.

Fig. 1, which is a plan and side elevation of the chassis frame, gives all the required dimensions for carrying out chassis repairs and alignment. Figs. 5 and 6 are chassis checking diagrams.

To enable certain dimensions to be measured whilst assessing damage, all components, including front suspensions and rear road springs must be removed to provide access to the checking points.

It is essential that all checks for distortion are carried out on a surface table or a perfectly level floor.

Checking for Distortion

Place bottle jacks under the jacking points and raise frame to any convenient height which can be measured accurately.

From the side elevation shown on Fig. 1, it will be seen that points (52) are 3·13″ (7·95 cm.) and points (75) are 4·09″ (10·39 cm.) below the datum line. Once this level has been established it becomes a simple matter to measure all other points in relation to the datum line, and so establish the exact amount of distortion.

CHASSIS FRAME DIMENSIONS
(TR4A)

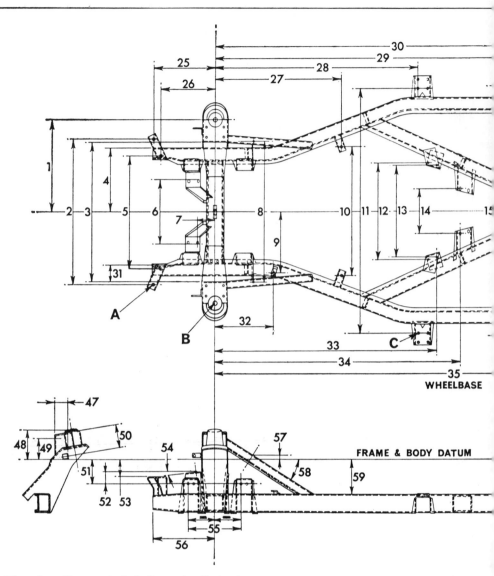

Fig. 3.   Chassis Frame Dimensions (Common to both Suspension Systems).

	Inches	Centimetres		Inches	Centimetres		Inches	Centimetres
1	15·04	38·2	9	10·56	26·8	17	10·31	26·2
2	25·31	64·3		10·44	26·5		10·19	26·0
	25·19	63·9	10	22·31	56·7	18	20·36	51·7
3	24·03	61·0		22·19	56·4		20·30	51·6
	23·97	60·9	11	42·31	107·5	19	10·56	26·8
4	11·06	28·1		42·19	107·2		10·44	26·5
	10·94	27·8	12	16·71	42·4	20	16·13	41·0
5	19·56	49·7		16·65	42·3		16·00	40·6
	19·44	49·4	13	15·91	40·4	21	7·56	19·2
6	11·06	28·1		15·85	40·3		7·44	19·0
	11·00	27·9	14	7·81	19·8	22	31·81	80·8
7	3·03	7·7		7·69	19·5		31·69	80·4
	2·97	7·5	15	43·14	109·6	23	33·50	85·1
8	24·44	62·1		43·02	109·3	24	36·62	93·0
	24·31	61·7	16	11·94	30·3		36·50	92·7
				11·81	30·0			

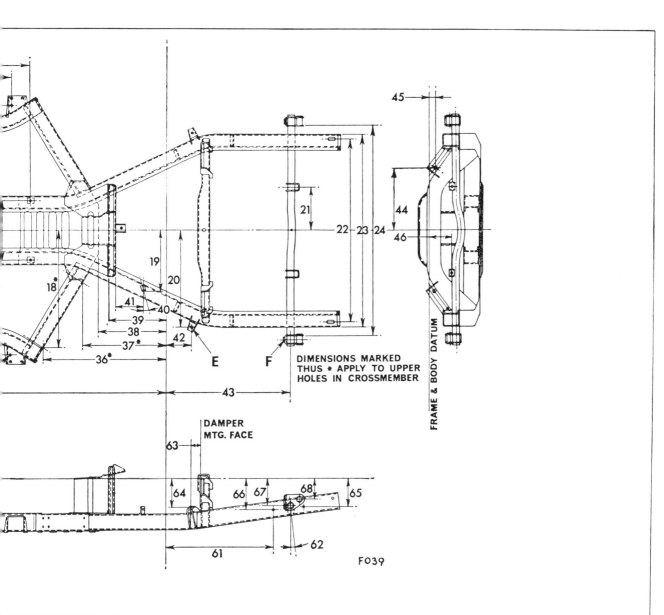

DIMENSIONS MARKED
THUS * APPLY TO UPPER
HOLES IN CROSSMEMBER

FRAME & BODY DATUM

DAMPER
MTG. FACE

F039

	Inches	Centimetres		Inches	Centimetres		Inches	Centimetres
25	11·06	28·1	33	39·59	100·5	41	5·06	12·8
	10·94	27·8		39·53	100·3		4·94	12·5
26	9·78	24·8	34	43·91	111·6	42	4·38	11·1
	9·66	24·5		43·85	111·2		4·25	10·8
27	22·56	57·3	35	88·13	223·9	43	21·81	55·4
	22·44	56·9		87·88	221·5		21·69	55·0
28	36·25	92·1	36	21·92	55·7	44	10·72	27·2
	36·13	91·8		21·87	55·5		10·66	27·0
29	60·06	152·4	37	14·71	37·3	45	1·00	2·5
	59·94	152·3		14·65	37·2		0·94	2·4
30	63·63	161·8	38	12·31	31·2	46	4·00	10·2
	63·50	161·4		12·19	30·9		3·88	9·8
31	2·97	7·5	39	10·63	27·0	47	2·44	6·2
	2·91	7·4		10·56	26·8		2·31	5·9
32	10·69	27·1	40	15°		48	4·97	12·6
	10·56	26·8						

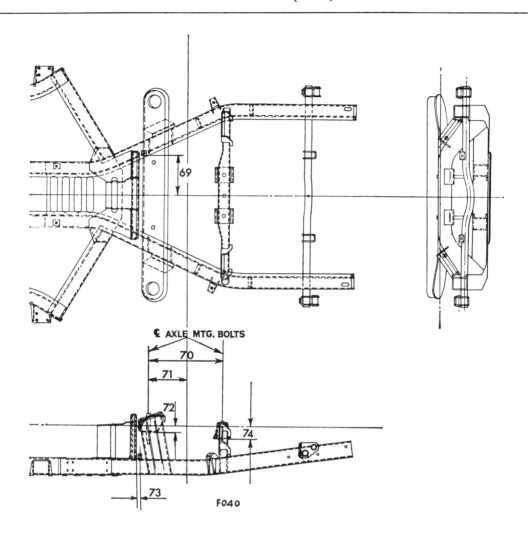

Fig. 4. Extra Dimensions for Independent Rear Suspension.

	Inches	Centimetres		Inches	Centimetres		Inches	Centimetres
49	3·59	9·1	57	0·69	1·8	67	4·75	12·1
	3·53	9·0		0·56	1·4	68	3·34	8·5
50	3·94	10·0	58	32° 7'			3·28	8·3
	3·81	9·7	59	6·06	15·4	69	7·44	18·9
51	4·28	10·9	60	6·53	16·6		7·31	18·6
	4·22	10·7		6·47	16·4	70	13·23	33·6
52	2·03	5·2	61	18·75	49·2		13·17	33·4
	1·97	5·0	62	8°		71	6·76	17·2
53	3·25	8·2	63	1·70	4·3		6·70	17·0
	3·13	7·9		1·64	4·2	72	1·34	3·4
54	5°		64	5·25	13·3		1·28	3·3
55	9·53	24·2		5·13	13·0	73	0·75	1·9
	9·47	24·0	65	4·94	12·6		0·63	1·6
56	11·19	28·4		4·81	12·4	74	2·22	5·6
	11·06	28·2	66	5·38	13·7		2·16	5·5

Checking for Squareness

Reference to Figs. 1 and 3, plan view of chassis, shows the location of body mounting, spring and spring damper points. Using a plumb-bob and line, transfer these points to the floor and letter them as shown in Fig. 5. Connect the letters in pairs, e.g., AA, BB together by drawing a line between them using a straight edge.

Measure from each point in turn to the centre and join up all centres, thus producing the centre datum line X - X. The diagram on the floor should be similar to that shown in Fig. 5.

A further check on squareness must be made by joining up all the diagonals as shown in Fig. 6. The length of diagonal lines must be equal and bisect each other on the datum line.

In general, chassis distortion is assessed by the amount and direction of any transverse or diagonal lines from the datum line. All dimensions not within the tolerances shown in Figs. 1 and 3 must be rectified.

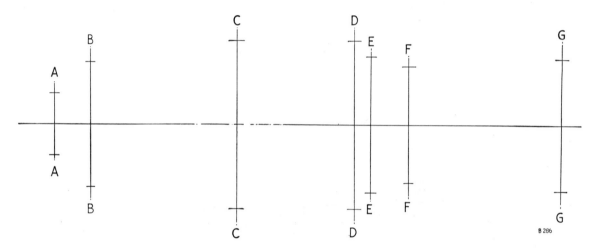

Fig. 5. Body mounting, spring and major checking points transferred to floor to establish datum line

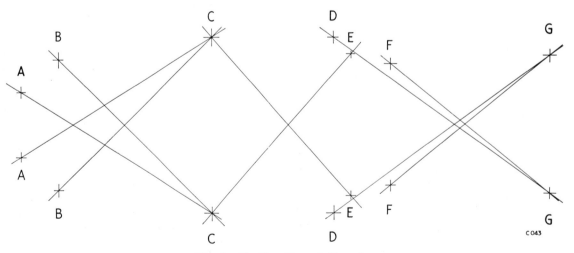

Fig. 6. Checking diagonal dimensions

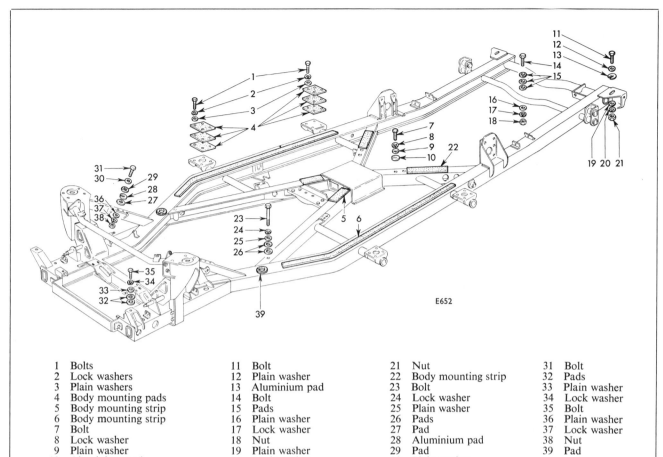

1	Bolts	11	Bolt	21	Nut	31	Bolt
2	Lock washers	12	Plain washer	22	Body mounting strip	32	Pads
3	Plain washers	13	Aluminium pad	23	Bolt	33	Plain washer
4	Body mounting pads	14	Bolt	24	Lock washer	34	Lock washer
5	Body mounting strip	15	Pads	25	Plain washer	35	Bolt
6	Body mounting strip	16	Plain washer	26	Pads	36	Plain washer
7	Bolt	17	Lock washer	27	Pad	37	Lock washer
8	Lock washer	18	Nut	28	Aluminium pad	38	Nut
9	Plain washer	19	Plain washer	29	Pad	39	Pad
10	Aluminium pad	20	Lock washer	30	Plain washer		

Fig. 1. Body mounting details

BODY

To Remove Complete Unit

Remove battery, drain cooling, fuel and hydraulic systems.

Remove :
    Bonnet.
    Front bumpers and bumper support brackets.
    Rear bumpers and bumper support brackets.
    Spare wheel and tool kit.

Disconnect :
    Oil pressure pipe from engine.
    Revolutions counter from base of distributor.
    Clutch fluid pipe at flexible pipe.
    Brake fluid pipe from top of three-way connector.
    Heater water hoses.
    Heater control cable.
    Choke and accelerator control.
    Cables from transmitter, distributor/SW, generator, starter motor and stop lamp.
    Fuel pipe at tank union.

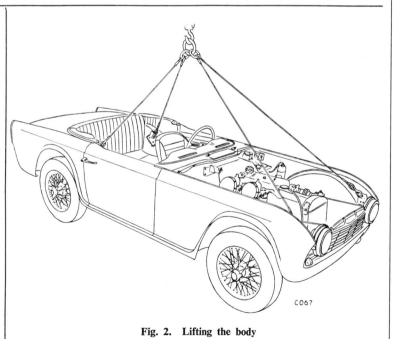

Fig. 2. Lifting the body

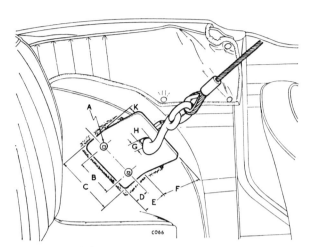

**Fig. 3.   Lifting plate attached to safety harness
securing screws**

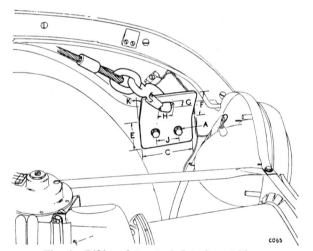

**Fig. 4.   Lifting plate attached to bonnet hinge
securing screws**

DIMENSIONS OF LIFTING PLATES

A 0·438″ (1·11 cm.)	F. 4·00″ (10·16 cm.)
B. 3·25″ (8·26 cm.)	G. 0·75″ (1·93 cm.)
C. 5·00″ (12·7 cm.)	H. 1·00″ (2·54 cm.)
D. 1·25″ (3·17 cm.)	J. 1·81″ (4·60 cm.)
E. 2·25″ (5·72 cm.)	K. 40°

Remove :
    Screws securing starter solenoid and move
solenoid clear of engine.
    Water control valve.
    Water pipe from left-hand side of engine.
    Upper pinch bolt from lower steering
coupling.   Slacken impact coupling and
push the steering shaft upwards clear of
lower coupling.
    Carburettors.
    Both seats.
    Knob and grommet from change speed
lever.
    Change speed lever.
    Grommet from base of handbrake lever.
    Four bolts securing facia support bracket
to floor.
Remove 27 body mounting bolts from the
following locations :
    Front of Car :
        2 on front crossmember, one in each down
        member.
    Inside Car :
        Four groups of four bolts, forward and
        rearward of door apertures.
        Two each side transmission tunnel in line
        with front end of gearbox.
        Two each side of the rear edge of seat
        runner.
    Rear of Car :
        One at each side rear end of frame.
        One bolt through centre of spare wheel
        panel.
    The method of lifting the body from the
chassis will be determined by the equipment
available to the repairer.
    In the example illustrated, four plates are
made from 10SWG. mild steel to the dimensions
shown under Figs. 3 and 4.
    One plate is secured to each rear wheelarch
utilizing the safety harness anchorage screws,
Fig. 3.
    The remaining plates are secured to the front
wing valance utilizing the bonnet to valance
hinge securing bolts.   See Fig. 4.

To Refit
    Secure body mounting pads in position using
Bostik 1261 or similar compound.   Using two
¼″ diameter rods, line up the holes in the body
with those in the chassis as the body is lowered
into position.   Apply sealing compound between
washers and main floor panel before fitting body
mounting bolts inside the car.
    Re-assemble by reversing the removal pro-
cedure and bleed the brake and clutch hydraulic
systems.

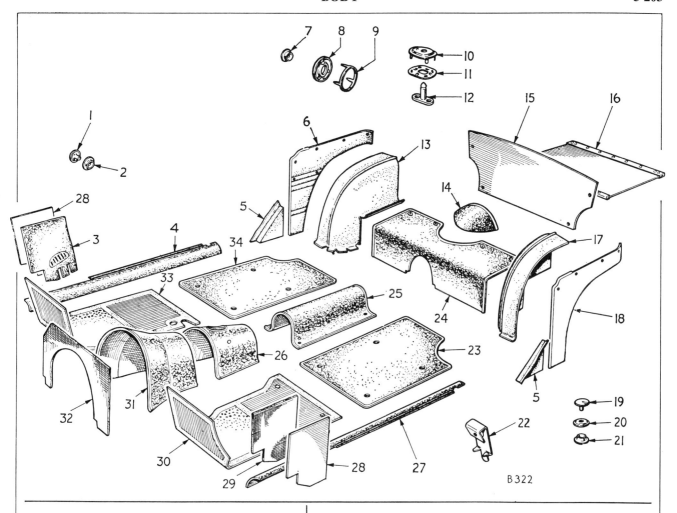

Fig. 5. Exploded arrangement of Trim Panels and Carpets

REAR SQUAB AND QUARTER TRIM PANELS

To Remove

If the car is provided with a soft top, remove this and fold the frame down as described on page 5·217.

Referring to Fig. 42 remove the screws securing the studs (1) and (2) and mouldings (7), (11) and (12) to the body. Lift the mouldings away.

On some early models, rivets may have been used in lieu of screws.

Referring to Fig. 5 pull the squab (15) and trim panels (6) and (18) from the body (secured by rubber adhesive).

To Refit

Apply a thin coating of adhesive to the areas of contact on the body, rear squab and trim panels.

Starting with one of the quarter trim panels, fasten the lower edge and sides to the fastener studs, pull the panel into position and press the upper edge firmly into contact with the body.

Repeat this operation on the opposite side of the car and then finally the squab.

Refit the mouldings and studs.

1 Press stud	18 Quarter trim panel
2 Fastener	19 Button
3 Kick pad carpet	20 Socket
4 Sill carpet	21 Stud
5 'B' post reinforcement	22 Clip
6 Quarter trim panel	23 Rear floor carpet
7 Stud	24 Heelboard carpet
8 Socket	25 Carpet
9 Pronged ring	26 Gearbox cover carpet
10 Socket	27 Sill carpet
11 Clinch plate	28 Kick pad mill board
12 Stud	29 Kick pad carpet
13 Wheelarch trim pad	30 Floor rubber mat
14 Differential cover carpet	31 Gearbox cover carpet
15 Trim panel	32 Centre dash carpet
16 Spare wheel cover	33 Floor rubber mat
17 Wheelarch trim pad	34 Rear floor carpet

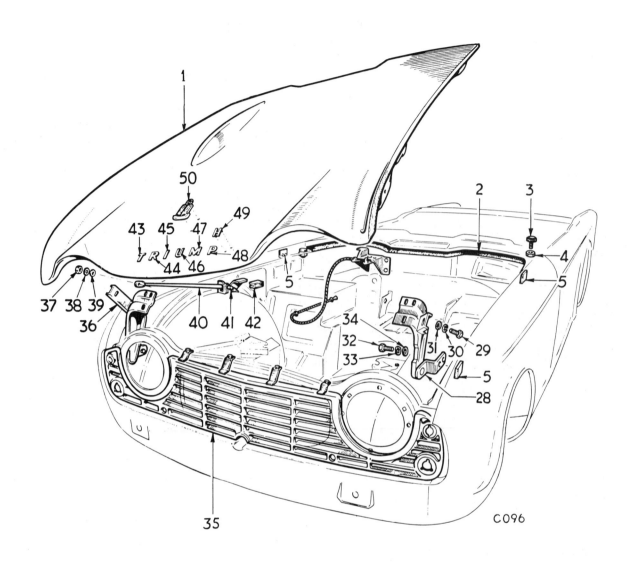

KEY TO FIGS. 6, 7 AND 8

1	Bonnet	18	Bracket	35	Grille
2	Sealing rubber	19	Bolt	36	Bonnet hinge
3	Bonnet stop	20	Washer	37	Nut
4	Locknut	21	Washer	38	Washer
5	Rubber buffer	22	Lever	39	Washer
6	Bonnet catch (early models only)	23	Screw	40	Bonnet support stay
7	Bolt	24	Inner cable	41	Bonnet stay bracket
8	Washer	25	Outer cable	42	Rubber buffer
9	Washer	26	Grommet	43	'T'
10	Bonnet fastener assembly	27	Cable clip	44	'R'
11	Bolt	28	Bonnet hinge	45	'I'
12	Washer	29	Bolt	46	'U'
13	Washer	30	Washer	47	'M'
14	Spring retaining cup	31	Washer	48	'P'
15	Striker pin	32	Bolt	49	'H'
16	Spring	33	Washer	50	Medallion
17	Nut	34	Washer		

Fig. 6.   Exploded arrangement of Grille and Bonnet Details

BONNET

To Remove

Remove two bolts securing each hinge to the wing valance and lift the bonnet away. The hinges are secured to the bonnet with four bolts in each ; the long bolt is used in the outer position.

To Refit

Refit the hinges to the bonnet and the bonnet to the body, tightening the bolts only sufficiently to prevent the bonnet from moving under its own weight.

Test the opening and closing action.

Elongated holes in the bonnet fixings permit limited adjustment in all directions.

An adjustable rubber buffer (3) fitted to rear corners of the engine compartment restricts unnecessary bonnet movement.

When correctly positioned, fully tighten all hinge securing bolts.

Bonnet Lock Adjustment

Slacken the clamping ferrule screw (23), push the bonnet lock control inside the car to within $\frac{1}{8}''$ of its 'fully in' position, and re-tighten the screw.

Dovetail Adjustment

If the bonnet is loose at the catch plate, slacken off the locknut and turn the dovetail bolt in a clockwise direction until satisfactory adjustment is attained. Re-tighten locknut. Rectify excess dovetail spring pressure by turning the dovetail bolt counter-clockwise.

FRONT GRILLE

To Remove

Remove the parking and direction indicator lamps. (See page 5·227).

Remove both over-riders. (See page 5·213).

Remove grille (four screws in upper edge and four in lower edge).

To Refit

Reverse the above instructions and refer to the circuit diagram before re-connecting the lamps.

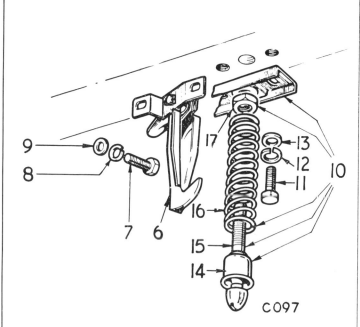

Fig. 7. Bonnet striker mechanism

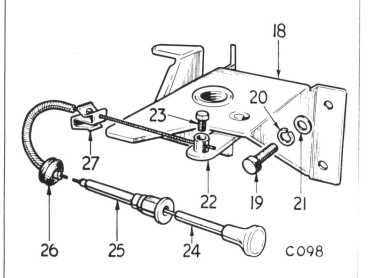

Fig. 8. Bonnet lock

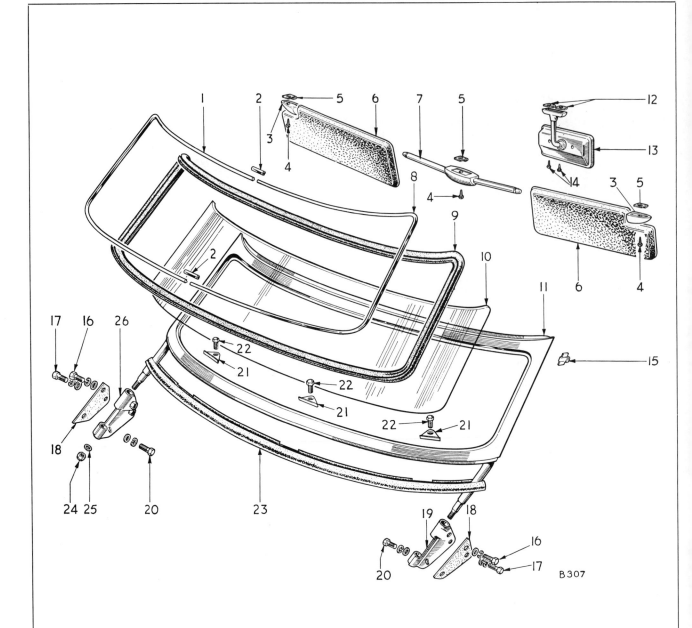

1	Moulding	8	Moulding	15	Bracket
2	Cover plate	9	Rubber weatherstrip	16	Bolt
3	Mounting	10	Windscreen glass	17	Bolt
4	Screw	11	Frame	18	Packing piece
5	Spire fix	12	Packing piece	19	Mounting bracket
6	Visor	13	Mirror	20	Bolt
7	Mounting	14	Screws	21	Cover plate

22	Bolt
23	Seal
24	Nut
25	Washer
26	Mounting bracket

Fig. 9. Exploded arrangement of Windscreen

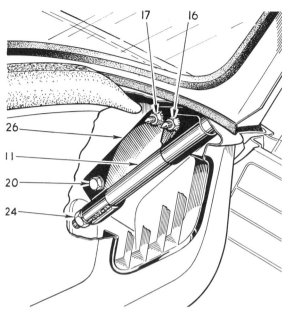

Fig. 10.   Screen pillar fixing

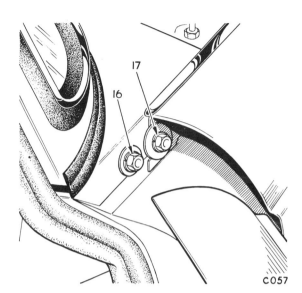

Fig. 11.   Screen pillar upper fixing

Windscreen (Fig. 9)

To Remove

Pull off the draught welting from the screen pillars.

Remove three bolts (22) with cover plates (21), one nut (24) with washer (25) from the bottom of each screen pillar (11). These nuts are accessible under the facia, Fig. 10.

Slacken bolts (16) and (17) which are accessible when the door is opened.

Lift out the windscreen assembly (11).

Remove the rubber weatherstrip (23) from the back of the windscreen assembly.

To Refit

Remove old sealing compound from the contacting surfaces of the windscreen weatherstrip and the scuttle panel.

Apply a fresh piece of Seal-a-strip along the underside of the rubber and refit the windscreen assembly.

There is provision for limited adjustment between the windscreen frame and door glass.

If adjustment is required, slacken the bolts (16), (17) and (20) on both sides of the car, raise both door glasses, and move the top of the windscreen to provide a uniform clearance between the glass and the windscreen. Re-tighten the bolts.

Seal the windscreen frame to the rubber with Seelastik.

Fig. 12.   Removing the windscreen

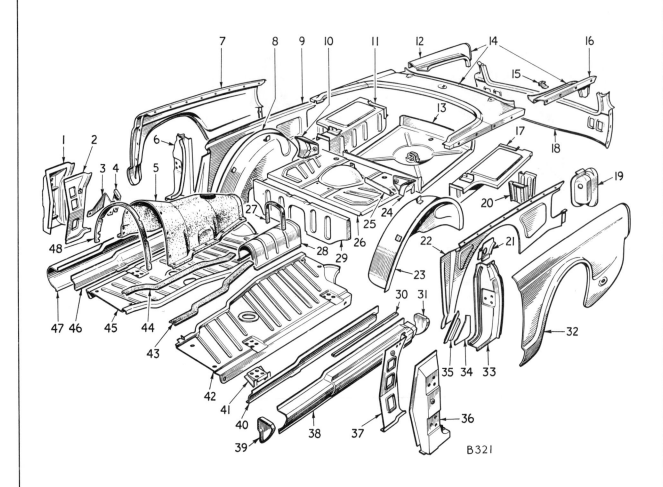

B 321

1	'A' post outer panel	13	Spare wheel panel	25	Squab support bracket	37	'A' post inner panel
2	'A' post inner panel	14	Rear deck assembly	26	Seat panel	38	Outer sill panel
3	Foot rest bracket	15	Locker lid stay bracket	27	Rubber seal	39	Filler panel
4	Foot rest rubber	16	Tonneau side panel	28	Propeller shaft tunnel	40	Inner sill panel
5	Gearbox cover	17	Floor panel	29	Heelboard	41	Bracket
6	'B' post panel	18	Rear valance	30	Seal retainer	42	Floor panel
7	Rear wing	19	Lamp housing	31	Filler panel	43	Rubber seal
8	Inner wheel arch panel	20	Bracket	32	Rear wing	44	Rubber seal
9	Wheel arch closing panel	21	Gusset	33	'B' post panel	45	Floor panel
10	Support bracket	22	Wheel arch closing panel	34	'B' post reinforcement	46	Inner sill panel
11	Floor panel	23	Inner wheel arch panel	35	'B' post gusset	47	Outer sill panel
12	Tonneau side panel	24	Support bracket	36	'A' post outer panel	48	Rubber seal

Fig. 13.   Exploded arrangement of Floor, Side Panels and Rear Wing Details

REAR WINGS

To Remove

Disconnect :

Cables from battery.

Brake stop/tail lamp.

Flasher lamp and number plate lamps at the snap connectors in the upper corners of luggage locker.

Remove :

Brake stop/tail lamp (four nuts accessible) from inside locker.

Rear bumpers.

Trim panel from rear of fuel tank (four screws).

Soft top and hoodstick assembly (Soft Top models only).

Quarter trim panel (six screws).

15 screws securing wing to body. The location and type of screws are shown in Fig. 14.

To Refit

Remove old sealing compound.

Straighten the retaining lugs on the chromium beading.

Refit rear wing and press beading firmly down as the screws (A) are tightened along its top edge.

Bend the retaining lugs to secure beading.

Seal the joint between the wing and the body with Supradedseal sealing compound, from underneath the wing.

Refit brake stop lamp, rear bumpers, trim panel and quarter trim panel.

Soft Top Models Only

Refit hoodstick assembly and soft top.

FRONT WINGS

To Remove

Remove front bumper and over-rider.

The location of the 19 screws which secure the wing to the body are shown in Fig. 15.

Remove bonnet side buffer rubbers (two screws in each).

To Refit

Remove all trace of old sealing compound.

Straighten the retaining lugs on the chromium beading.

Refit the wing and press the beading firmly into position as the securing screws (A) are tightened.

Bend the retaining tags to secure the wing beading firmly in position.

Seal the joint between the wing and the body with Supradedseal or similar compound, from underneath the wing.

Refit bonnet buffer rubbers and front bumper.

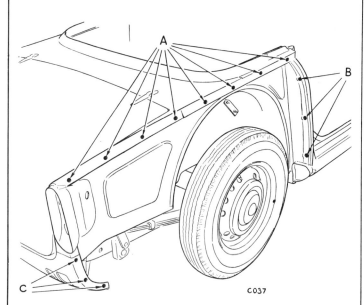

C037

A. Acme spire fixings ; located inside waistline.
B. U.N.F. bolts ; located under wheel arch.
C. U.N.F. bolts ; located under rear edge of wing.

Fig. 14. Rear wing attachment points

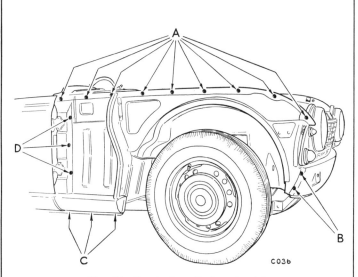

C036

Fig. 15. Front wing attachment points

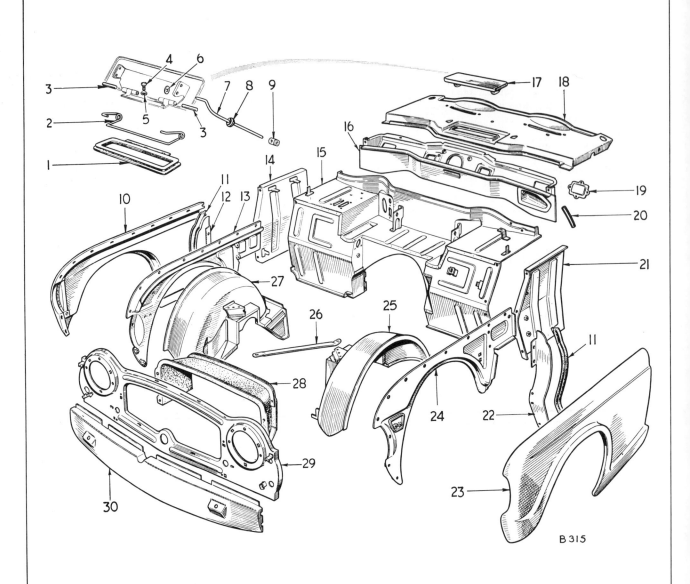

Fig. 16.　Exploded arrangement of Front End Panels

1	Rubber seal	9	Clamp	17	Ventilator lid	25	Inner wheelarch
2	Spring	10	Front wing	18	Scuttle panel	26	Radiator stay rod
3	Hinge pin	11	Sealing rubber	19	Wheelbox cover plate	27	Inner wheelarch
4	Bolt	12	Baffle plate	20	Drain tube	28	Duct
5	Washer	13	Outer wheelarch	21	Bulkhead end panel	29	Upper valance
6	Retainer	14	Bulkhead end panel	22	Baffle plate	30	Front valance
7	Rod	15	Bulkhead	23	Front wing		
8	Grommet	16	Plenum assembly	24	Outer wheelarch		

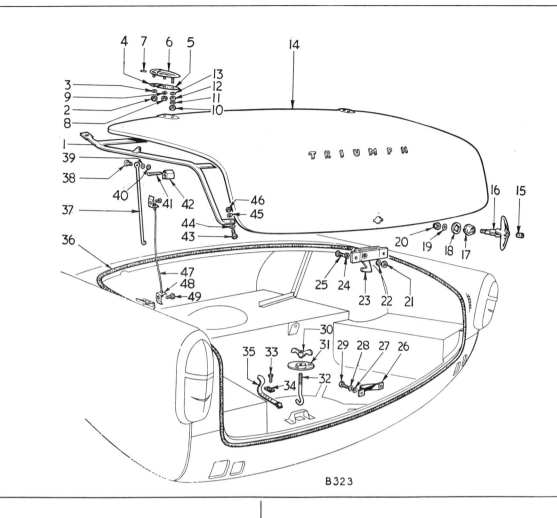

B323

LUGGAGE LOCKER LID

To Remove

Take out one screw (49) and disconnect the restrainer (47).

Remove one nut (2) securing each hinge (6) to the body and lift the lid (14) away.

Note the position of the seating washer (4).

If required, remove the hinge (6) and seating washer (13) from the locker lid (four nuts (8) and (10) from back hinge).

The lid reinforcement tubing (1) is secured in position utilizing nuts (10) at its forward edge and two bolts (43) at the rear edge.

To Refit

Loosely refit the hinges (6) to the body with seating washers (4).

Loosely refit the locker lid to the hinge.

Adjust the lid and fully tighten the nuts.

Limited adjustment of the position of the lid relative to the body is available.

Re-connect the restrainer (47).

1	Lid reinforcement tube	18	Washer	35	Strap
2	Nut	19	Washer	36	Sealing rubber
3	Washer	20	Nut	37	Lid support
4	Fibre washer	21	Nut	38	Pivot pin
5	Fibre washer	22	Washer	39	Washer
6	Hinge	23	Lock	40	Clip
7	Hinge pin	24	Washer	41	Split pin
8	Nut	25	Screw	42	Retainer
9	Washer	26	Striker	43	Screw
10	Nut	27	Washer	44	Washer
11	Washer	28	Washer	45	Washer
12	Washer	29	Screw	46	Nut
13	Washer	30	Wing nut	47	Restrainer
14	Locker lid assembly	31	Disc plate	48	Bracket
15	Lock cylinder	32	Hook bolt	49	Screw
16	Handle	33	Screw		
17	Escutcheon	34	Plate		

Fig. 17.   Exploded arrangement of Luggage Locker components

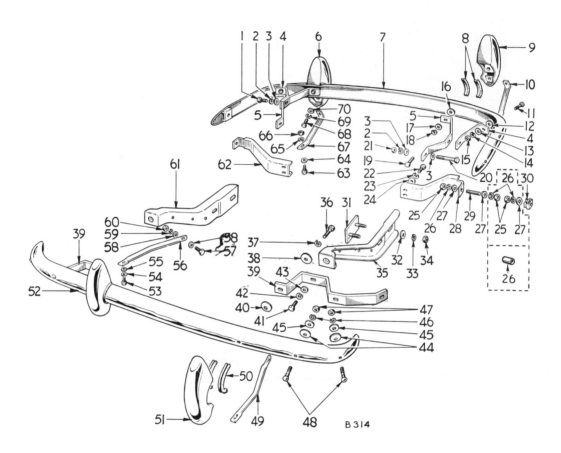

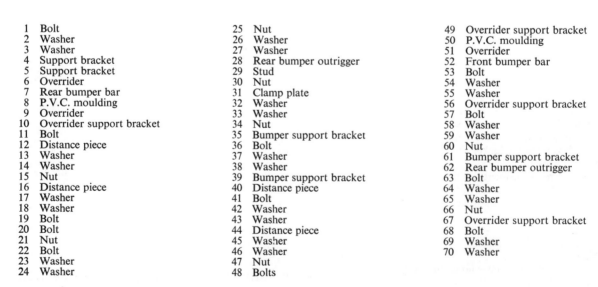

B 314

1	Bolt	25	Nut	49	Overrider support bracket		
2	Washer	26	Washer	50	P.V.C. moulding		
3	Washer	27	Washer	51	Overrider		
4	Support bracket	28	Rear bumper outrigger	52	Front bumper bar		
5	Support bracket	29	Stud	53	Bolt		
6	Overrider	30	Nut	54	Washer		
7	Rear bumper bar	31	Clamp plate	55	Washer		
8	P.V.C. moulding	32	Washer	56	Overrider support bracket		
9	Overrider	33	Washer	57	Bolt		
10	Overrider support bracket	34	Nut	58	Washer		
11	Bolt	35	Bumper support bracket	59	Washer		
12	Distance piece	36	Bolt	60	Nut		
13	Washer	37	Washer	61	Bumper support bracket		
14	Washer	38	Washer	62	Rear bumper outrigger		
15	Nut	39	Bumper support bracket	63	Bolt		
16	Distance piece	40	Distance piece	64	Washer		
17	Washer	41	Bolt	65	Washer		
18	Washer	42	Washer	66	Nut		
19	Bolt	43	Washer	67	Overrider support bracket		
20	Bolt	44	Distance piece	68	Bolt		
21	Nut	45	Washer	69	Washer		
22	Bolt	46	Washer	70	Washer		
23	Washer	47	Nut				
24	Washer	48	Bolts				

Fig. 18. Exploded arrangement of Front and Rear Bumpers

BUMPER

Front (Figs. 18 and 19)
To Remove

Remove two bolts (57) securing over-rider support stay (56) to the inner valance.

Remove two bolts (41) and lift the front bumper (52) away complete with over-riders (51) and support stays (49) and (56).

Remove over-riders from the bumper and the support stay from the over-rider.

Note the position of the curved distance piece (40) between the bumper and support bracket (39).

If required, remove two nuts (34) securing each bumper support bracket (35) and (61) to the chassis and lift the bracket away.

To Refit

Loosely refit the bumper support brackets (35) and (61), two nuts and washers.

Refit the bumper.

Assemble the sealing strips (50) to the over-riders and refit over-riders (51) and (52) complete with the support brackets (49) and (56).

Rear (Figs. 18 and 20)
To Remove

Disconnect the plate illumination lamp cables at the connectors in the luggage locker and pull the cables through the locker to the underside of the car. See Plate Illumination Lamp, page 5·229.

Remove bolts (63) securing the over-rider support bracket (10) and (61) to the chassis.

Slacken the nuts (25) and remove stud (29). A slot is provided for this purpose on the inner end of the stud. On later models the nuts and washers shown in the dotted square are superseded by a distance piece (26).

Remove two bolts (68) securing the over-riders (6) and (9) to the bumper and support brackets (5).

Remove two nuts (15) securing the bumper to the support brackets (4) and lift the bumper away.

Note the position of the distance pieces (12) and (16).

If required, remove four bolts (1) and withdraw the support brackets (4) and (5) from the body.

Remove four bolts (22) and lift away the outrigger support (28) and (62).

To Refit

Loosely refit outrigger support (28) and (62), and bumper support brackets (4) and (5).

Refit bumper with distance pieces (12) and (16) to support brackets.

Refit studs (29) with nuts (25) and washers (26) and (27) or distance piece (26).

Adjust the clearance between the bumper, body and wings to approximately 0·75″ (1·9 cm.) and re-tighten the support and outrigger brackets.

Refit the over-riders with support brackets and re-connect the plate illumination lamp cables.

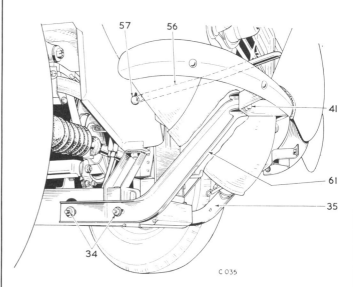

Fig. 19. Location of front bumper attachments

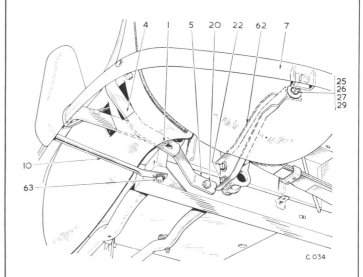

Fig. 20. Location of rear bumper attachments

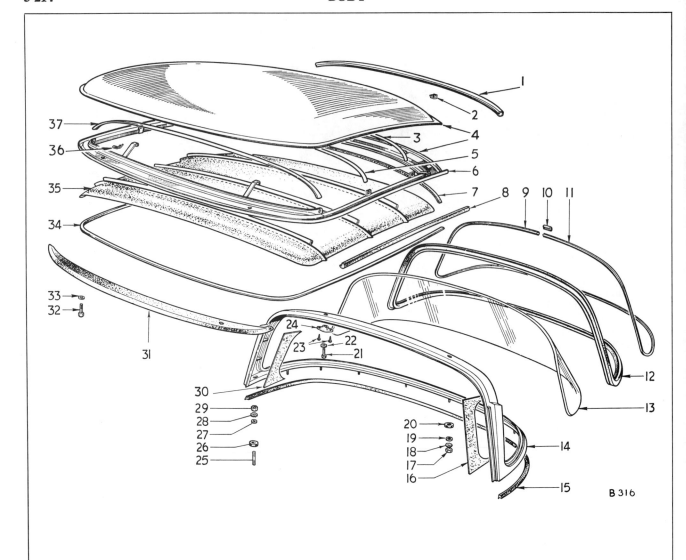

1	Roof capping	11	Backlight moulding	21	Bolt	31	Sealing rubber
2	Capping clip	12	Backlight weatherstrip	22	Washer	32	Bolt
3	Lining listing rail	13	Backlight glass	23	Screw	33	Washer
4	Hard top roof components	14	Backlight frame	24	Cover plate	34	Finisher
5	Lining listing rail	15	Sealing rubber	25	Stud	35	Roof lining
6	Cantrail stiffeners	16	Trim panel	26	Washer	36	Clip
7	Sealing rubber	17	Nut	27	Washer	37	Listing rail
8	Sealing rubber	18	Washer	28	Washer		
9	Backlight moulding	19	Washer	29	Nut		
10	Moulding coverplate	20	Rubber washer	30	Trim panel		

Fig. 21. Exploded arrangement of Detachable Hard Top and Backlight

HARD TOP AND BACKLIGHT (Fig. 21)

Hard Top

To Remove

Remove two bolts (32) securing the front end of the hard top to the windscreen header rail and two shorter bolts (21) which secure the rear end to the backlight frame, and lift the roof panel away.

To Refit

Place the roof panel in position. Refit and progressively tighten the bolts.

Backlight Frame Assembly

To Remove

Remove roof panel as above.

Pull the draught welting from the backlight frame to below the waist-line.

Remove rear seat cushion, if fitted, and the quarter and rear squab trim panels.

Using a screwdriver, as shown in Fig. 23, lift the edge of the backlight weatherstrip and remove the trim panels concealing the nuts (29) and studs (25) shown on Fig. 24.

Remove seven nuts (17), washers (18) and (19) located inside the body waist-line flange below the backlight frame.

Slacken the nut (29), the right-hand side nut is shown in Fig. 24.

Break the sealing between the rubber and the body, using a small screwdriver from which all sharp edges have been removed.

Progressively slacken the nuts (29) as the backlight frame is raised clear of the stud (25).

Note the location of the rubber washers (20) and (26) between the backlight and body.

To Refit

Clean all trace of sealing compound from the contacting surfaces of the rubber seal (15) and the body.

Secure the rubber washers (20) and (26) in position with Seelastik.

Seal the contacting surfaces of the rubber to the body and backlight frame with Seelastik.

Refit the rubber weatherstrip (15).

Lower the backlight frame into position.

Lift the front edge slightly and refit the nuts (29) with washers (28) and (27).

Refit the remaining nuts.

Refit trim panels and draught welting.

Fig. 22.   Inserting screw securing roof panel to header rail

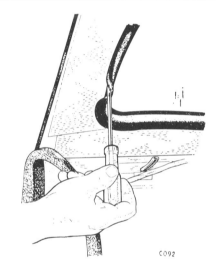

Fig. 23.   Removing trim panel

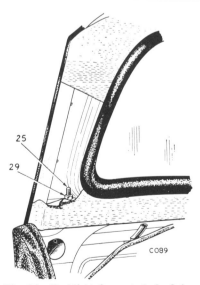

Fig. 24.   Backlight frame to body fixing

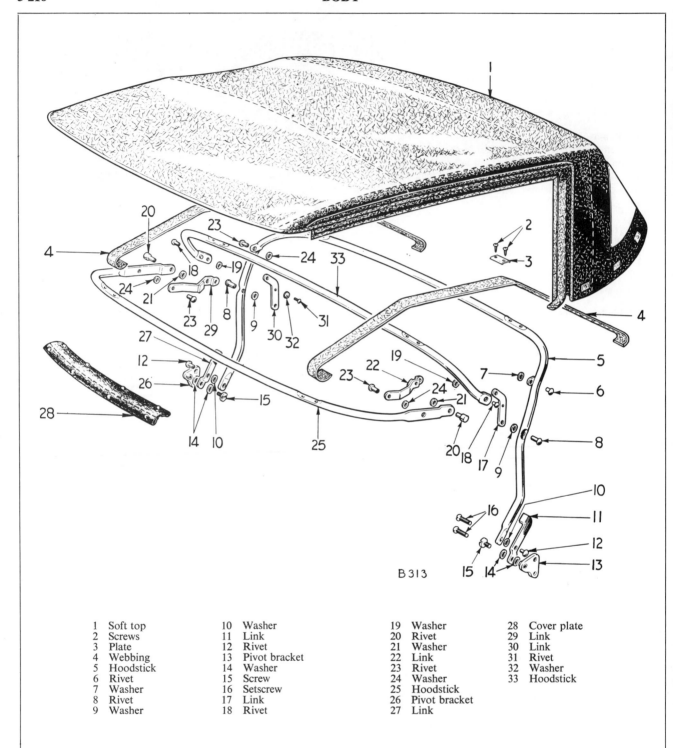

B 313

1	Soft top	10	Washer	19	Washer	28 Cover plate
2	Screws	11	Link	20	Rivet	29 Link
3	Plate	12	Rivet	21	Washer	30 Link
4	Webbing	13	Pivot bracket	22	Link	31 Rivet
5	Hoodstick	14	Washer	23	Rivet	32 Washer
6	Rivet	15	Screw	24	Washer	33 Hoodstick
7	Washer	16	Setscrew	25	Hoodstick	
8	Rivet	17	Link	26	Pivot bracket	
9	Washer	18	Rivet	27	Link	

Fig. 25.　Soft top and hoodstick details

SOFT TOP

To Remove

Move the driver's seat forward and fold down the back of the passenger seat.

Release the clips securing the soft top to the forward rail of the hoodstick assembly.

Fig. 26.

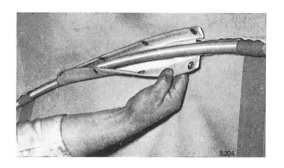

Release the quarter trim panel from the hoodstick assembly and pull the locking lever forward which releases the tension on the material.

Fig. 27.

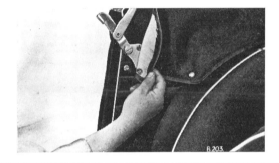

Release the valance tensioners from the rear hoodstick.

Fig. 28.

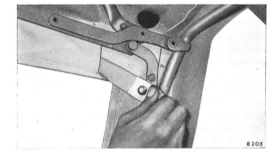

Lift the fasteners securing the rear edge of the top to the body.

Fig. 29.

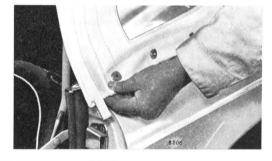

Release the fastener on the top outer edge of the top.

Fig. 30.

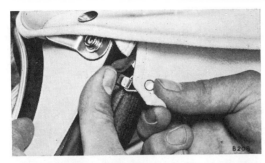

Fig. 31.

Fig. 32.

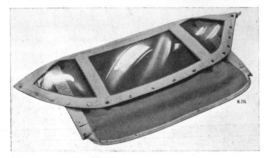

Fig. 33.

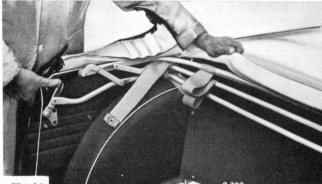

Fig. 34.

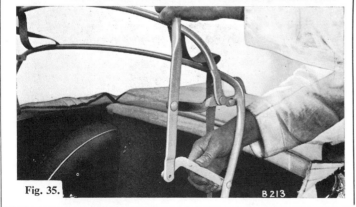

Fig. 35.

Turn back the top corner of the draught rubber on the screen pillar and unhook the soft top from the pillar.

Pull the soft top forward and disengage the front retainer from the top of the windshield header rail.

Lift the top away from the car and fold it at the seam above the back window. Fold the side windows inward to rest on the back window. The surplus material is then folded over to form a neat pack.

Stow the folded top into the luggage locker.

Release both webbing straps from the rear of the car.

Release the fasteners securing the carpet and rear squab trim to the floor and lift the quarter and rear trim pads over the upper edge of the car.

Push the front rail rearward and at the same time pull the connecting link forward and fold the hoodstick assembly into the rear of the car.

Push the locking lever back to lock the assembly in its folded condition.

Pull the quarter trim into position and press the fasteners.

Refit the rear trim and carpet.

To Raise

Move the driver's seat forward and fold down the back of the passenger's seat.

Unclip the carpet, rear and quarter trim pads and pull the trim onto the rear edge of the body.

Pull the locking lever upwards.

Raise the hoodstick assembly.

Push the quarter and trim panel loosely into position and attach the two webbing straps to the upper and rear edge of the body.

Unfold the soft top and lay it loosely on the frame.

Engage the retaining strip on the forward edge of the soft top with the windshield header rail.

Commencing at the two centre fasteners, attach the top to the rear of the car.

Lift the weatherstrip at the top edge of the screen pillars and hook the soft top to the pillar.

Attach the top to the upper end of screen pillar.

Push the locking lever into position.

Attach the valance tensioner to the hoodstick.

Place the quarter trim into position and re-connect the fasteners.

Refit the rear trim and carpet.

Refit the soft top to the front hoodstick.

Adjust the position of the driving seat.

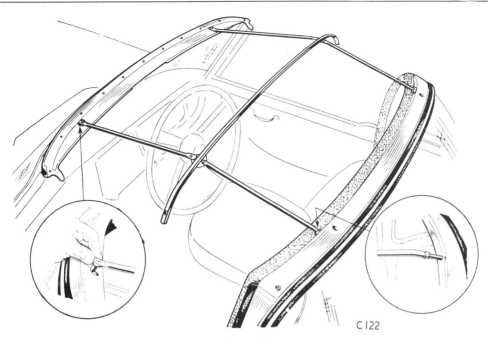

Fig. 36. Surrey Top Frame

SURREY TOP

To Fit (Fig. 36)

Open out the surrey top frame and enter the rear ends of the frame into the holes in the top backlight surround.

Press the rubber covered studs, attached to the front end of the frame, into the holes in the screen header rail.

Adjust the nuts on the rear end of the frame to provide rigidity without stressing the front rubbers, or making frame removal difficult.

Once the nuts have been correctly adjusted, no further adjustments should be required when the frame is subsequently removed or refitted.

Fit the front end of the surrey top by folding its stiffened edge under the retainer strip attached to the top of the screen as shown in Fig. 37.

Enter the two nylon studs, attached to the rear edge of the surrey top, in to the top of the backlight frame as shown in Fig. 38 and secure them with the small wing nuts provided in the conversion kit.

Fit one press stud, shown in Fig. 39, on each upper side of the backlight frame as follows—

1. Apply marking blue to the press button, attached to the rear corner of the surrey top, pull the fabric taut and transfer the marking to the backlight frame.
2. Drill the frame and fit the press stud.
3. Engage each valance tensioner with a hook revealed by turning back the weatherstrip at each side of the door.
4. Secure the press studs.

Fig. 37.

Fig. 38.

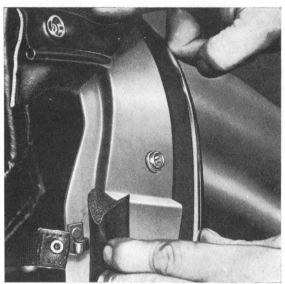

Fig. 39.　Fitting press stud to the backlight frame.
Note the position of the valance tensioner hook

Fig. 40.　Window lowered to show inner backing strip

Fig. 41.　Attachment of the rubber retainer

Surrey Top (cont'd.)

When closing the door, ensure that the top edge of the cover shown held in Fig. 40 is to the outside, and the backing strip to the inside of the window in the raised position.

TO CONVERT SOFT TOP TO HARD TOP

Remove and discard :
　— soft top and hinged frame.
　— quarter trim panels.
　— rear squab, door seals, draught welts and squab boards.

Spray the roof panel back frame and retainers to colour.

Fit the rubber retainer using four rivets in each, Fig. 41.

Trim the roof and backlight frame.

Fit the rubber to the lower edge of the roof panel.

Seal the contacting surfaces between the rubber and frame and body.

Fit the backlight frame assembly.

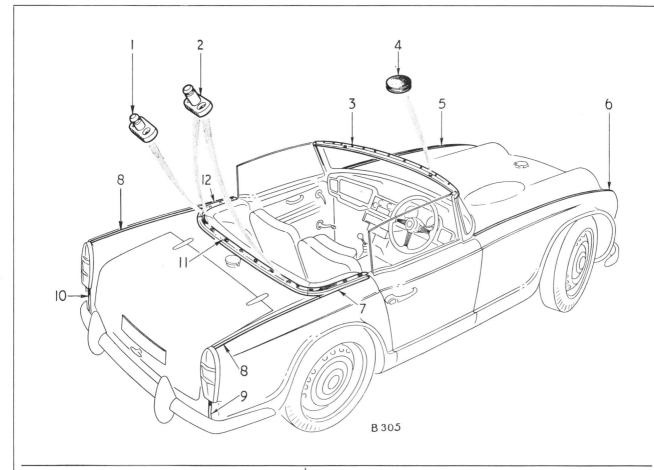

B 305

Fit backlight glass as follows :—

> Assemble the rubber weatherstrip to the glass with the vulcanised joint at the lower edge.
>
> Fit the beading. This operation is facilitated using soft soap in the channel.
>
> Insert a piece of strong cord in channel in the rubber.
>
> Position the glass and rubber assembly into position on the outside of the car with the ends of the cord inside the body, and withdraw the cord.
>
> Seal the glass to rubber and the rubber to the frame with Seelastik.

Fit — "B" post trim panel, Fig. 23.

- — The hard top roof panel (four screws).
- — New draught rubbers to door aperture and roof panel.
- — New draught welt.
- — New squab board and quarter trim panels.

1	Stud	* 7	Moulding
2	Stud	8	Rear wing beading
3	Windscreen capping	9	Rear wing beading
†4	Rubber plug	10	Rear wing beading
5	Front wing beading	*11	Moulding
6	Front wing beading	*12	Moulding

† Not fitted on Soft Top models

* Not fitted on Hard Top models

Fig. 42. General arrangement of Beadings, Capping and Mouldings

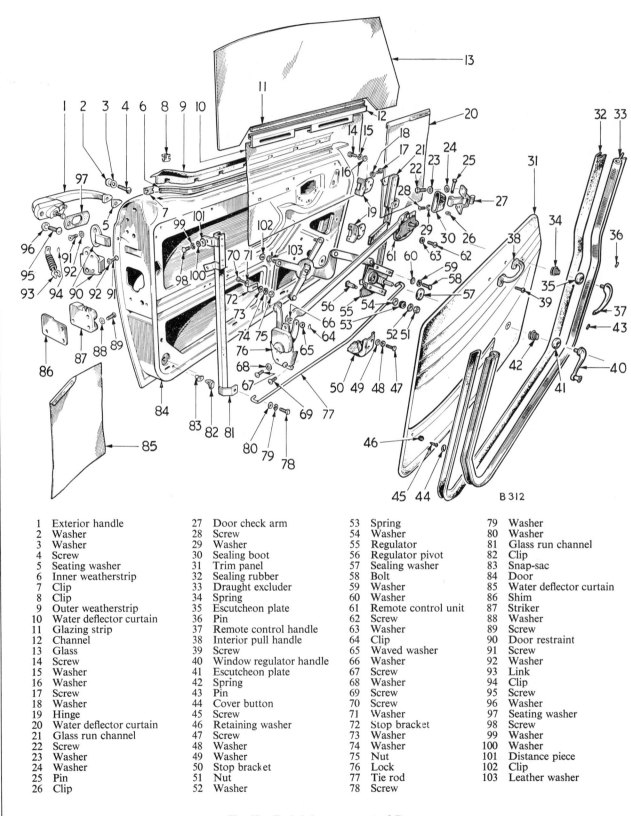

Fig. 43.   Exploded arrangement of Door

1 Exterior handle	27 Door check arm	53 Spring	79 Washer
2 Washer	28 Screw	54 Washer	80 Washer
3 Washer	29 Washer	55 Regulator	81 Glass run channel
4 Screw	30 Sealing boot	56 Regulator pivot	82 Clip
5 Seating washer	31 Trim panel	57 Sealing washer	83 Snap-sac
6 Inner weatherstrip	32 Sealing rubber	58 Bolt	84 Door
7 Clip	33 Draught excluder	59 Washer	85 Water deflector curtain
8 Clip	34 Spring	60 Washer	86 Shim
9 Outer weatherstrip	35 Escutcheon plate	61 Remote control unit	87 Striker
10 Water deflector curtain	36 Pin	62 Screw	88 Washer
11 Glazing strip	37 Remote control handle	63 Washer	89 Screw
12 Channel	38 Interior pull handle	64 Clip	90 Door restraint
13 Glass	39 Screw	65 Waved washer	91 Screw
14 Screw	40 Window regulator handle	66 Washer	92 Washer
15 Washer	41 Escutcheon plate	67 Screw	93 Link
16 Washer	42 Spring	68 Washer	94 Clip
17 Screw	43 Pin	69 Screw	95 Screw
18 Washer	44 Cover button	70 Screw	96 Washer
19 Hinge	45 Screw	71 Washer	97 Seating washer
20 Water deflector curtain	46 Retaining washer	72 Stop bracket	98 Screw
21 Glass run channel	47 Screw	73 Washer	99 Washer
22 Screw	48 Washer	74 Washer	100 Washer
23 Washer	49 Washer	75 Nut	101 Distance piece
24 Washer	50 Stop bracket	76 Lock	102 Clip
25 Pin	51 Nut	77 Tie rod	103 Leather washer
26 Clip	52 Washer	78 Screw	

DOORS

To Remove (Fig. 43)

Remove — five screws securing the kick pad to the 'A' post and turn the pad forward.

— the pin (25) from the check arm (27). This pin is retained in position with a small spring clip (26).

— six bolts securing the hinges (19) to the body and lift the door away.

If required, remove the hinges (19) from the door.

The check arm (27) may be renewed without prior removal of the door, but it is necessary to release the kick pad described above to gain access to the attachment bolts.

To Refit

Refit hinges to the door and then refit the door to the car.

Reconnect the check arm using the pin (25) and clip (26).

Vertical adjustment of the door is by means of the bolts securing the hinges to the 'A' post. In and out adjustment of the leading edge of the door is by means of the hinge to door securing bolts.

Slacken the bolts securing the section requiring adjustment and move the door to provide uniform appearance between the contours of the door and the wing.

Striker Dovetail and Door Restraint Device

The striker dovetail (87) should not normally require attention, but when adjustment or renewal is required it must be carried out in conjunction with adjustments to the door restraint device (90).

Never slam a door when adjusting the dovetail or door restraint as any misalignment may damage the components.

Window Regulator Mechanism

To Remove (Figs. 43 and 48)

The numbers shown in brackets are shown in Fig. 43.

Remove interior handles and trim panel.

Loosely refit regulating handle and partially raise the window to gain easy access to operating arms (L).

Disconnect the arms (L) from the channel (M) at the base of the door glass by taking off the spring clips (102) with leather washers (103) and spring the arms (L) clear of the channel.

Lift the glass to the highest position and loosely secure it using a small wedge of wood.

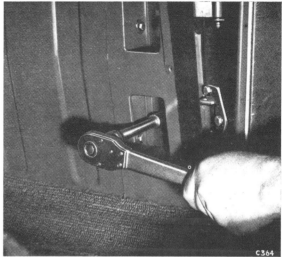

Fig. 44.   Location of kick pads

Fig. 45.   Striker dovetail and door restraint

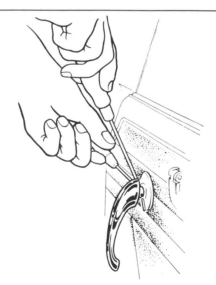

Fig. 46.   Removing interior handles

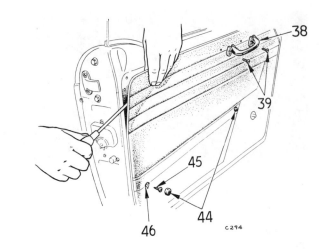

Fig. 47. Removing trim panel

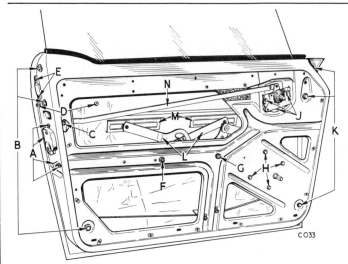

Fig. 48. Door assembly

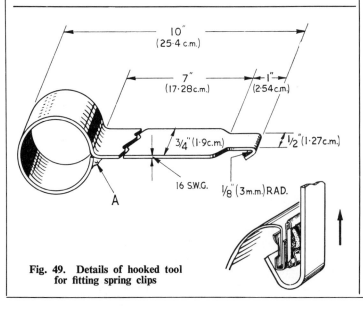

Fig. 49. Details of hooked tool for fitting spring clips

Remove the nut (F) with spring washers securing the pivot (56) to the door inner panel. Remove the pivot (56) and the double coil spring washer (53) which is fitted between the regulator and the inner panel of the door.

Take out four screws (H) and remove the regulator mechanism assembly (55) through the large cut-out in the door inner panel.

To Refit

Pass the regulator mechanism through the large cutout in the inner panel and loosely secure it using four screws (H).

Apply a thin coating of grease to all moving parts.

Engage the lower arms of the regulator in the fixed channel which is rivetted to the inner side of the door inner panel.

Refit the pivot (56) with the plain washer (54) and double coil spring washer (53) between the regulator and the inner panel.

Fully tighten securing screws (H).

Reconnect the arms (L) to the channel (M).

Refit trim panel and interior handles.

Door Glass

To Remove (Figs. 43 and 48)

The numbers in brackets are illustrated in Fig. 43.

Remove trim panel.

Loosely refit handle and lower the glass.

Remove the inner weatherstrip (6) by pushing its lower edge upward from inside the door using a screwdriver. This weatherstrip is retained in position by seven small spring clips (7).

Partially raise the glass and remove two clips (102) and leather washer (103) and disconnect the regulator arms (L) from the channel (M).

Lift the glass out of the door, taking care not to damage the water deflector panel which is attached to the glass by the channel.

To Refit

Fold the deflector flat against the inner side of the glass and place the glass into the door.

Reconnect the regulator and lower the glass. Reposition the deflector panel.

Using the hooked tool (Fig. 49), hold the spring clips in position and push the inner weatherstrip back into place. The hooked tool may be used to fit any clip which may require renewing.

Refit the trim panel.

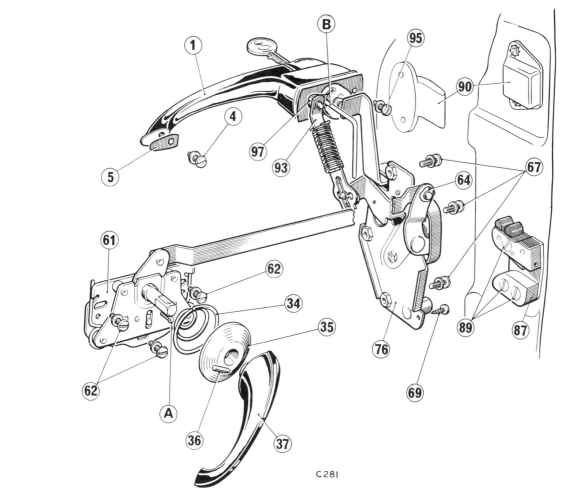

Fig. 50. Door lock details

Door Locks

Lock—To Remove (Figs. 43, 50 and 51)

Fully raise glass and remove the interior handle and trim panel.

Take off the retaining spring clip (64) and waved washer (65) and disconnect the remote control link (61).

Disconnect the link (93) between the exterior handle and the lock at the lock.

Remove glass run channel (81) from the rear of the lock (three screws) (98 and 78).

Take out four screws (67 and 69) and remove the lock (76) from the door.

To Refit

Reverse the above instructions. No adjustment of the lock is provided.

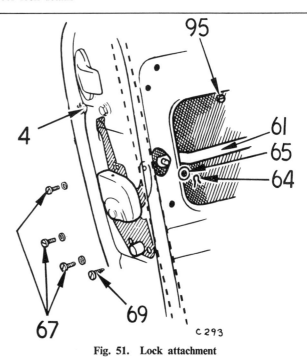

Fig. 51. Lock attachment

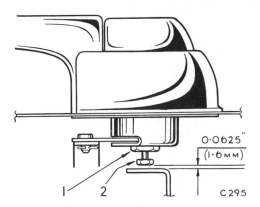

Fig. 52.   Lock plunger adjustment

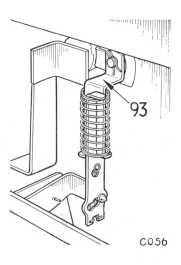

Fig. 53.   Lock connecting link

Remote Control

To Remove

Remove interior handles, trim panel and disconnect remote control link by taking off the spring clip and waved washer securing it to the lock.

Take out three screws (62) and lift the remote control away.

To Refit

Pass the remote control link into the door and loosely secure the unit.

Reconnect remote control link to the lock and loosely refit the handle. Turn the control into the locked position and pin it in this condition using a $\frac{1}{8}$″ split pin as shown "A" Fig. 50, or a piece of $\frac{1}{8}$″ wire rod.

Move the control towards the lock to take up all free play in the link and fully tighten the securing screws.

Refit trim panel and interior handles.

Exterior Handle

To Remove (Figs. 53 and 50)

Raise window, remove trim panel and disconnect the connecting link (93) between the lock and the exterior handle at the lock.

Remove two screws (4 and 95) and take off the handle (1) with its seating washers (97 and 5).

To Refit and Adjust

Hold handle with its two seating washers firmly in position on the door panel and check the clearance between the push button plunger and the lock contactor through the aperture in the inner door panel. Do not check the clearance by depressing the push button as this may be deceptive. The clearance should be $\frac{1}{16}$″. Turn the plunger operating lever to the unlocked position so that depression of the push button moves the plunger through its housing.

In this position release the locknut (Fig. 52) (1), screw the plunger bolt (2) in or out as required, and re-tighten the locknut before releasing the push button.

Before finally fitting the handle to the door, the connecting link (93) should be fitted to the plunger operating lever and retained by a circlip. Fit the link so that the bent portion at the top is inclined away from the handle.

Turn the plunger operating lever to the locked position, i.e. until the location holes in the operating lever and plunger housing are in line, and insert a short length of $\frac{1}{8}$″ diameter rod (B) cranked to a right angle.

Manoeuvre the connecting link (93) and the locating rod (B) through the handle aperture so that they hang downwards inside the door when the handle with its seating washers are finally secured to the door with two screws (95 and 4).

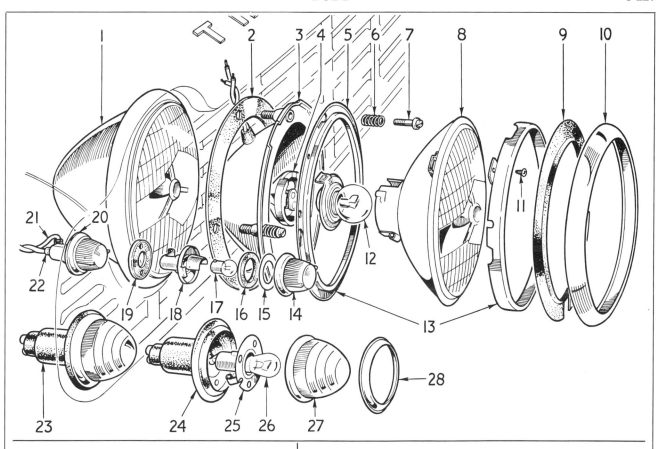

Fig. 54. Exploded arrangement of Lamps

1	Headlamp	16	Seal
2	Seal	17	Bulb
3	Lamp body	18	Lamp
4	Bulb and adaptor	19	Seal
5	Retainer rim	20	Parking lamp
6	Spring	21	Earth cable
7	Screw	22	Sleeve
8	Light unit	23	Direction indicator
9	Dust seal		lamp assembly
10	Rim	24	Lamp body
11	Screw	25	Housing
12	Bulb	26	Bulb
13	Retainer plate and rim	27	Lens
14	Lens	28	Rim
15	Ring		

LAMPS

Headlamp (Fig. 54)

To Remove

Isolate the battery and disconnect the cables from the headlamp at the cable connectors located under the lower centre flange of the grille. Insert the special tool provided with the car or a broad bladed screwdriver between the rim (10) and the rubber (9) and turn it to lever the rim away.

Remove the light unit (8), detach the adaptor (4) and take out the bulb (12).

Remove lamp housing (3) and sealing rubber (2) (three screws).

To Refit

Clean off old sealing compound from the contacting surfaces of the wing, sealing rubber and lamp housing (3).

Apply sealing compound to the wing, both sides of the rubber and to housing.

Refit the lamp housing, lamp and rim.

Refer to circuit diagram for colour coding and re-connect the cables.

Clean off surplus compound using petrol or white spirit.

Fig. 55. Removing the headlamp rim

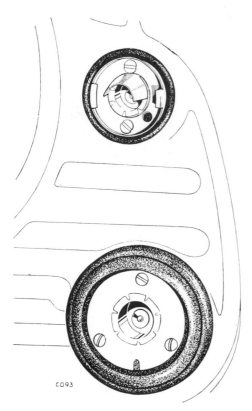

**Fig. 56.   Parking and direction indicator lamps
with lenses removed**

**Fig. 57.   Showing lens removed from stop/tail
flasher lamp**

Parking Lamp (Fig. 54)

To Remove
   Isolate the battery.
   Disconnect the cables from the lamp at the cable located under the lower centre of the grille.
   Turn the lens counter-clockwise for approximately 25° and withdraw the lens.
   Remove the plastic and rubber washers (15) and (16) respectively.
   Take out two screws and remove the lamp housing (18) and sealing rubber (19).

To Refit
   Reverse the above instructions.

Direction Indicator Lamps (Fig. 54)

To Remove
   Isolate the battery and disconnect the cables at the snap connector located at the lower centre of the grille.
   Remove — the rim (28) and lens (27).
            — three screws and withdraw the
              lamp body (24) complete with
              housing (25).

To Refit
   Clean off old sealing compound and re-seal with fresh sealing compound.
   Refit — the lamp with locating slot at the
             bottom.
            — lens and rim.
   Re-connect the cables.

Stop/Tail Flasher Lamp (Fig. 58)

To Remove
   Isolate the battery and disconnect the lamp cables at the cable connectors located in the upper and inward corner of the luggage locker.
   Remove the four nuts securing the lamp to the car and lift the lamp away. These nuts are accessible from inside the locker.

To Refit
   Reverse the above instructions. Refer to the circuit diagram for cable colour coding.

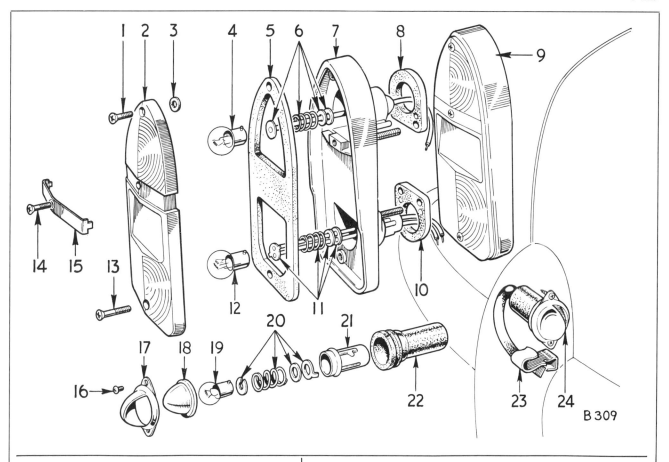

Fig. 58. Rear lamp details

Plate Illumination Lamp (Fig. 58)

To Remove

Isolate the battery and disconnect the cables to the lamp at the cable connectors located in the upper forward corner of the luggage locker.

Release the cable from the clip (23).

Tie a length of cord to the lamp cables to facilitate refitting.

Take out two securing screws and withdraw the lamp from the over-rider, leaving the cord in position.

To Refit

Connect the cord to the lamp cables. Refit the lamp to the over-rider using the cord to pull the cables back into position.

Re-connect the cables.

1	Screw	13	Screw
2	Lens	14	Screw
3	Washer	15	Bezel
4	Flasher bulb	16	Screw
5	Seal	17	Bezel
6	Cable and spring contacts	18	Lens
7	Housing	19	Bulb
8	Seal	20	Spring and contacts
9	Stop/tail and direction indicator lamp	21	Housing
10	Seal	22	Lamp body
11	Cable and spring contacts	23	Cable clip
12	Stop/tail bulb	24	Plate illumination lamp

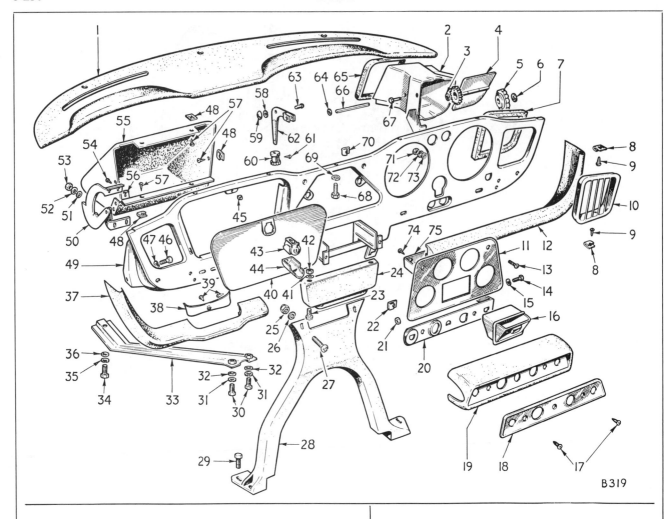

B 319

Fig. 59. Exploded facia panel

1 Scuttle top crash	26 Washer	51 Washer
pad	27 Bolt	52 Washer
2 Air duct	28 Facia support	53 Nut
3 Washer	bracket	54 Screw
4 Air control valve	29 Bolt	55 Locker box
5 Air control	30 Bolt	56 Spirefix
6 Spire fix	31 Washer	57 Screw
7 Seal	32 Washer	58 Washer
8 Spire nut	33 Reinforcement	59 Nut
9 Screw	bracket	60 Knob
10 Grille	34 Bolt	61 Screw
11 Instrument panel	35 Washer	62 Lever
12 Crash pad	36 Washer	63 Screw
13 Screw	37 Crash pad	64 Spirefix
14 Screw	38 Finisher	65 Seal
15 Washer	39 Screw	66 Spindle
16 Ash tray	40 Locker lid	67 Screw
17 Screw	41 Washer	68 Bolt
18 Switch plate	42 Nut	69 Washer
19 Switch plinth	43 Lock	70 Spire nut
20 Switch reinforce-	44 Finger pull	71 Nut
ment	45 Rubber buffer	72 Washer
21 Nut	46 Screw	73 Washer
22 Spire nut	47 Washer	74 Screw
23 Screw	48 Spire nut	75 Ash tray retainer
24 Facia board	49 Facia panel	
25 Nut	50 Hinge	

FACIA PANEL (Fig. 59)

To Remove

Disconnect — cables from battery.
— drive cables from speedometer and tachometer.
— choke control cable from carburettor.

Remove — steering column and cowl (see Group 4).
— facia reinforcement (33) by unscrewing two screws (30) with washers (31) and (32) located in line with the centre of the locker box (55), and move the reinforcement (33) outward.
— locker box (55), six screws (57).
— speedometer and tachometer.
— facia board (24) (four bolts with nuts and washers).

Remove— control panel. This panel comprises ignition/starter, lighting and wiper switches and the choke control. The panel is removed as follows :

Remove the screw (14), washer (15) and nut (21) which secures the choke control side of the panel to the facia. Take out two screws (17) and withdraw the panel comprising items (18), (19) and (20) from the facia sufficient to gain access to the back of the switches. Disconnect the cables from the switches, noting the cable coding relative to the terminals, and remove the control panel complete with choke control.

Slacken the trunnion screw (63) securing the scuttle ventilator rod to the control lever (62).

Remove — instrument panel.

— five bolts (68) with washers (69) securing the upper edge of the facia panel to the scuttle top. The bolts are located as follows :

One in each upper corner of locker box aperture, one in the centre of facia and one in the apertures of speedometer and tachometer.

Take out two bolts (46) one at each side, and lift the facia panel away.

To Refit

Assemble the facia to the car and loosely secure it in position (two bolts (46) and washers (47)).

Push the upper edge of the panel into position and secure it (five bolts).

Fully tighten the two outer bolts (46).

Refit speedometer and tachometer.

Re-connect the cables to the instruments and the oil pipe to the pressure gauge.

Refit — instrument illumination bulb holders.

— instrument panel.

Re-connect the cables to the switches on the control panel.

Pass the choke control cable through the grommet in the dash panel and refit the control panel.

Re-connect the choke control cable to the carburettor. See Group 1.

Refit cubby box, centre panel and all remaining components.

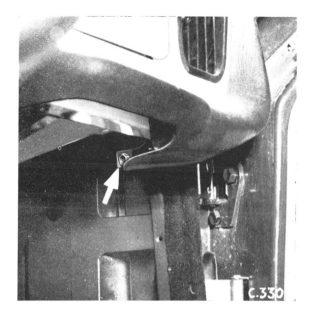

Fig. 60. Facia outer attachment

Fig. 61. Ventilator control

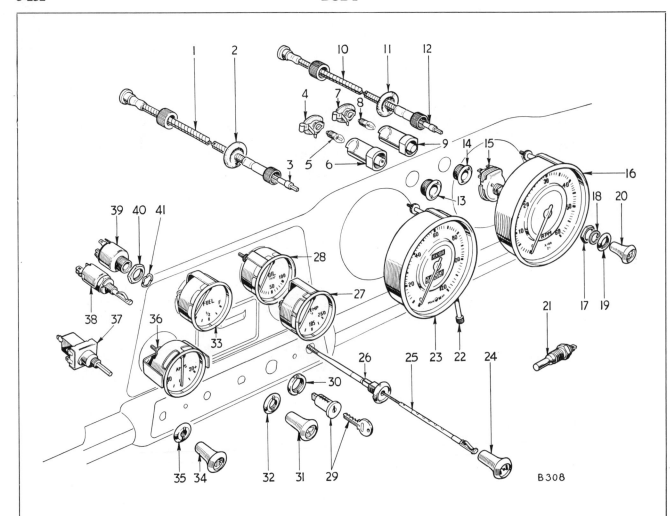

1	Speedometer drive cable — outer	15	Rheostat	29	Key and lock
2	Grommet	16	Tachometer	30	Nut
3	Speedometer drive cable — inner	17	Nut	31	Knob
4	Bulbholder	18	Washer	32	Nut
5	Bulb	19	Nut	33	Fuel gauge
6	Housing	20	Knob	34	Knob
7	Bulbholder	21	Temperature transmitter	35	Nut
8	Bulb	22	Trip cancelling cable	36	Ammeter
9	Housing	23	Speedometer	37	Lighting switch
10	Tachometer drive cable — outer	24	Knob	38	Wiper switch
11	Grommet	25	Choke control inner cable	39	Starter ignition switch
12	Tachometer drive cable — inner	26	Choke control outer cable	40	Nut
13	Bezel	27	Temperature gauge	41	Washer
14	Bezel	28	Oil pressure gauge		

Fig. 62. Exploded arrangement of Instruments and Switches

INSTRUMENT SWITCHES AND CONTROLS

All instruments, switches and controls may be removed and refitted with only minor displacement of adjacent equipment.

Speedometer and Engine Revolution Counter

Each instrument is secured to the facia with a bridge clamp and two knurled nuts and may be removed independently.

Oil Pressure Gauge, Fuel Gauge, Temperature Gauge and Ammeter

The oil pressure, fuel and temperature gauges and ammeter are grouped together and mounted on a single panel which is secured to the facia with two screws.

The method of gaining access to the rear of the instrument panel is as follows :

Isolate the battery.

Referring to Fig. 59, take out two screws (17) securing the front side of the switch panel assembly (18), (19) and (20) to the facia.

Remove the nut (21) and screw (14) from the choke control side of the panel and withdraw the panel sufficiently to provide clearance at the base of the instrument panel.

Take out two screws (13) from the front of the panel and withdraw the panel from the facia sufficiently to gain access to the back of the instruments.

If required, disconnect the pipe from the oil pressure gauge, noting the position of the leather sealing washer between the pipe and the gauge.

At this stage the panel can be withdrawn approximately 4″ (10 cm.).

All instruments are secured to the panel with bridge clamps and knurled nuts.

On early cars these instruments have rim lighting and on later models individual illumination of instruments is employed.

Where the later type of illumination is used the bulb holders must be withdrawn from the sockets before an instrument is removed from the panel.

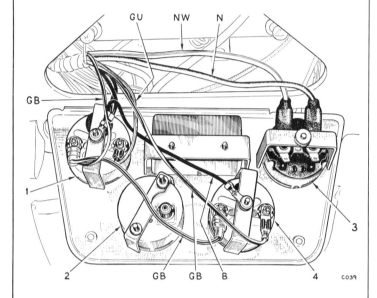

GU.	Green/Blue	1	Temperature gauge
GB.	Green/Black	2	Oil pressure gauge
NW.	Brown/White	3	Ammeter
B.	Black	4	Fuel gauge
N.	Brown		

Fig. 63. Rear view of the instrument panel

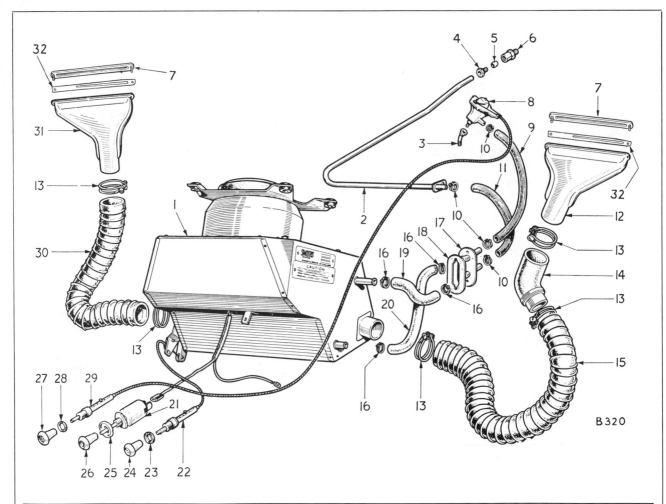

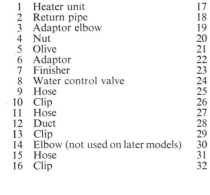

Fig. 64. Exploded arrangement of Heater Unit

1	Heater unit	17	Bulkhead adaptor
2	Return pipe	18	Seal
3	Adaptor elbow	19	Hose
4	Nut	20	Hose
5	Olive	21	Switch
6	Adaptor	22	Air distribution control
7	Finisher	23	Nut
8	Water control valve	24	Knob
9	Hose	25	Nut
10	Clip	26	Knob
11	Hose	27	Knob
12	Duct	28	Nut
13	Clip	29	Heat control
14	Elbow (not used on later models)	30	Hose
15	Hose	31	Duct
16	Clip	32	Deflector

HEATER INSTALLATION

Isolate battery and drain cooling system.

Remove facia support stay.

Cut the forward edge of the trim concealing the outlets of the demister aperture.

Apply adhesive to the end of the trim and turn it back under facia.

Fit the finisher (7) to the top of facia.

Remove locker box and lid.

Fit the nozzle assembly to the underside of the facia with the deflector panel (32) between the nozzle and facia. The wide section of the slot in the deflector is positioned nearer the centre of the car.

Disconnect and remove the drive cables from tachometer and speedometer.

Fit the demister nozzle and deflector panel (two nuts).

Assemble the hoses (15) and (3) to nozzles. These will screw on to the nozzles. Longer hose fitted left-hand side of car.

Secure the hoses to the nozzles with hose clips (13).

Refer to Fig. 59.

Disconnect the choke control from carburettor and pull the inner and outer cables back into car.

Remove three screws (17 and 14) and withdraw switch and control panel.

Remove two screws (13), withdraw instrument panel and disconnect oil pressure pipe from gauge.

Refer to Fig. 64.

Remove blanking plate (3 bolts) from the underside of the facia and discard the plate.

Assemble the heater unit to the underside of facia and secure it commencing with R.H. side of heater (four bolts), three underside and one inside bracket on heater. The three bolts have plain washers and steel bush.

Remove the blanking plate and grommet located below bonnet locking mechanism (two screws) and fit the bulkhead adaptor (17) after applying sealing compound between the contacting surfaces.

Disconnect cables from sparking plugs.

Remove square plug from rear of water pump and loosely fit adaptor (6). Apply Wellseal or similar compound to the threads.

Loosely fit water pipe (2) to adaptor (6) using sealing compound on threads.

Remove nut from rearmost exhaust manifold stud, and fit water pipe to bracket stud. It will be necessary to spring the bracket, which is welded to the pipe, over the stud. Refit the nut.

Tighten adaptor (6) into the water pump and then the pipe (2) into the adaptor.

Re-connect H.T. cables to sparking plugs.

Remove the plug from the elbow (3) on rear and left-hand side of cylinder head and fit water control valve (8), applying sealing compound to the threads.

Fit hoses (11) and (9) between bulkhead adaptor (17) and water pipe (2) and control valve (8) respectively.

Connect short hoses (19) and (20) between bulkhead adaptor (17) and heater unit (1).

The return pipe (19) is connected to lower position of adaptor and to upper position on heater.

Fit hoses (15) and (30) between demister nozzle and heater unit.

Refit instrument and control panels.

Cut the trim concealing the holes for heater controls in facia support bracket and fit heater controls.

The heat control takes up left-hand position, the distribution air control right-hand and the blower switch in the centre.

Remove blanking plug and fit grommet to hole in dash panel above bulkhead adaptor, and push the cable from heat control (29) through the grommet and connect it to water control valve.

Adjust heat control as follows :

Push in heat control knob to within $\frac{1}{8}''$ of fully closed position.

Turn water control fully clockwise (closed position) and tighten trunnion screw.

1 Bulkhead adaptor   5 Return pipe
2 Bonnet release control   6 Rear manifold nut
3 Water return hoses   7 Heat control valve
4 Water hose   8 Choke control

Fig. 65. Heater installation

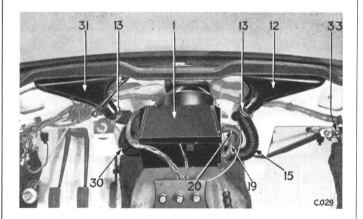

 1 Heater unit
12 Demister nozzle
13 Clip
15 Hose
19 Hose
20 Hose
30 Hose
31 Demister nozzle
33 Voltage stabilizer

Fig. 66. Heater connections

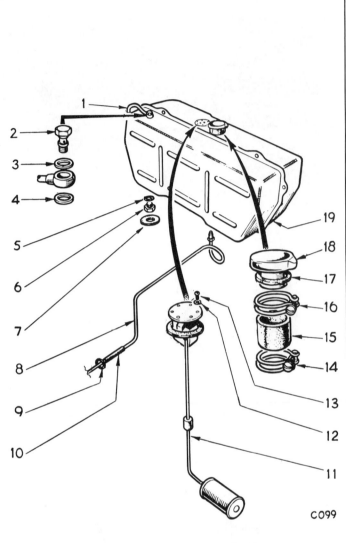

1	Vent pipe	11	Fuel tank gauge
2	Vent pipe union	12	Spring washer
3	Fibre washer	13	Screw
4	Fibre washer	14	Hose clip
5	Fibre washer	15	Hose
6	Drain plug	16	Hose clip
7	Seal	17	Grommet
8	Fuel feed pipe	18	Filler cap
9	Grommet	19	Tank
10	Connector		

Fig. 67. Fuel tank details

Connect the air distribution control and adjust as follows :

Push in air distribution knob to within ⅛″ of fully in position.

Close flap valve and tighten trunnion on heater.

Refit cubby box, lid and facia support bracket.

Refit speedometer and rev. counter.

Refill cooling system.

Electrical Connections

Connect earth cable from motor to the steering column to facia reinforcement bracket securing bolt.

Connect white cable with lucar connector from blower to switch.

Connect spare (green cable) in harness with lucar connector to switch.

Connect spare (green cable) with unprotected lucar connector in harness adjacent to voltage stabilizer to the stabilizer.

Re-connect the battery and test blower. The voltage stabilizer is located under the facia on the right-hand side of the car adjacent to the bonnet release cable, Fig. 66 (33).

FUEL TANK

To Remove

Isolate the battery.

Drain the fuel tank at the drain plug (6) and disconnect the fuel pipe (8). Both items are in the base of the tank.

Remove the trim panel from the forward side of the tank (12 screws).

Disconnect the vent pipe (1) from the upper right-hand side of the tank.

Remove — spare wheel and tool kit.
　　　　　— trim panel from forward side of luggage locker.

Release both clips (14 and 16) and remove filler pipe (18) and rubber hose (15).

Disconnect both cables from the tank unit (11).

Take out six securing screws and remove the tank (19) from the luggage locker.

To Refit

Insert the rubber hose (15) into the body from inside.

Refit the tank. The earthing cables are secured to the body using the right-hand side bolt.

Push the rubber hose (15) on to the tank (19) and refit the filler pipe (18). Fully tighten the clips (14 and 16).

Refit — drain plug (6) with washer (5) and re-connect pipe (8) to the underside of fuel tank.
　　　　— vent pipe (1).

Re-connect both trim panels.

Replace spare wheel and tool kit.

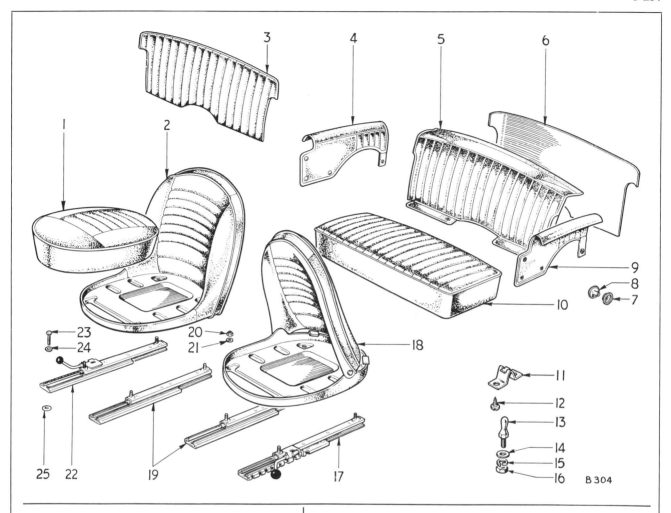

B 304

SEATS

To Remove

Lift out the seat cushion.

'Move the seat panel (2) and (18) rearward and remove the bolts (23) with washers (24) securing the front end of the runners to the floor.

Move the seat forward, remove the rearmost bolts and lift the seat frame away complete with the runners (22) and (19) or (19) and (17).

Note the location of the distance piece (25).

If required, remove the runners from the frame by taking off four nuts (20) with washers (21).

To Refit

Reverse the above instructions.

1	Seat cushion	14	Washer
2	Driver's seat frame	15	Washer
3	Trim panel	16	Nut
4	Quarter trim panel	17	Seat runner
* 5	Rear squab trim	18	Passenger's seat frame
6	Back board	19	Seat runner
7	Fastener	20	Nut
8	Fastener	21	Washer
† 9	Quarter trim panel	22	Seat runner
†10	Occasional seat cushion	23	Screw
11	Spring latch	24	Washer
12	Screw	25	Washer
13	Ball stud		

* Not used on Hard Top Models   † Special accessory

Fig. 68. Exploded Seating Arrangements

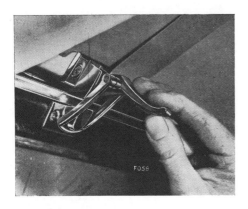

Fig. 69.

Fig. 70.

Fig. 71.

Fig. 72.

SOFT TOP

Hood Lowering

Release the toggles clamping the hood to the windscreen header rail.

Release three fasteners at each side, rearwards of the door. Push the hood frame upwards and rearwards until the hoodstick assembly begins to fold. Pull the hood fabric clear of the end of the centre rail (arrowed Fig. 70).

Pull the hood fabric rearwards to lie flat over the boot lid as the hoodsticks are pushed fully down. Ensure that the fabric is not trapped in the folded hoodsticks (arrowed Fig. 71).

Ensuring that the hoodstick assembly is fully down, fold the hood forward over the hoodsticks.

Fold the quarter lights inwards to lie flat upon the folded hood.

Keep the Vybak rear window free from distortion and fit the cover provided.

NOTE: Particular care is needed if the hood is folded in temperatures below freezing. The Vybak windows stiffen and are liable to shatter if subjected to sudden or sharp bending.

To Remove the Soft Top

With the hood in the half-folded position (Fig. 70), remove five hexagon headed bolts securing the hood back rail to the rear deck. Support the hood frame and remove three screws in each hoodstick pivot bracket.

To Fit

Reverse the above procedure.

DUST AND WATER SEALING

The following notes on dust and water sealing have been extracted from the production schedules. The notes and illustrations are not instructions but issued to assist dealers in rectifying any breakdown in the sealing compounds whenever applied to the joints between panels during production.

A full list of sealing compounds with their application is given below and on page 5·302.

NOTE. Plastisol compounds require curing and in consequence are not suitable for application in service. Docker's Compound or Hermetal "Double Bond" or Hermetal Plastic Metal Filler should be used when correcting a sealing failure at joints using this compound.

SEALING COMPOUNDS

COMPOUND	MANUFACTURER	COMPOUND	MANUFACTURER
Glasticon Glasticord Kelseal 3/315M.	Kelseal Limited, Vogue House, Hanover Square, London, W.1.	Seelastik Seelastik Auto 'B' Seelastrip.	Expandite Limited, Cunard Road Works, London, N.W.10.
Docker's Compound	Docker's Brothers Ltd. Rotton Park Street, Birmingham, 16.	Boscoseal B.B. Plastisol Putty S.106.46.	B.B. Chemicals Ltd. Ulverscroft Road, Leicester.
Supra Dedseal.	Supra Chemical & Paint Ltd. Hainge Road, Tipton, Staffs.	Hermetal 'Double Bond' Hermetal Plastic Metal Filler.	The Kenilworth Mfg. Co. Ltd., West Drayton, Middlesex.

SEALING COMPOUNDS

	APPLICATION	MATERIAL	CLASSIFICATION
BODY IN WHITE	Spotweld Sealer.	Expandite Seelastik (Natural)	Mastic.
	Plugging. Small Holes.	Expandite Seelastrip LS.105. Alternative Glasticon 303	Strip Sealer.
PAINT SHOP	Plugging. Small Holes.	Glasticon 303. BB Plastisol Putty S.106.46.	Putty. Plastisol.
	Internal Joints.	Expandite Seelastik Auto B.	Gun applied Sealer.
	External Joints.	Expandite Plastisol 53. Alternative Kelseal 3/315M.	Plastisol. Plastisol. Low temperature cure at 300°F. for 30 mins. after application.
	Sound Deadening.	Berry Wiggins Kingsnorth.	
BODY AFTER PAINT (TRIM & FINISH)	Windscreen Sealers—Rubber W'Strips, Plugs & Grommets.	Expandite Seelastik SR.51.	Mastic.
	Bolted-Metal to Metal Joints Metal moulding Small Holes Screw Fixings, etc.	Expandite Seelastik M.1.	Mastic.
	Special Purpose Paper to Metal.	Glasticord 400.	Strip Sealer.
	Body Underside Protectors.	Supra Dedseal Boscoseal 9010.	Solvent based.
AFTER PAINT REPAIRS	External Joints	Hermetal Double Bond. Alternative Dockers Compound.	

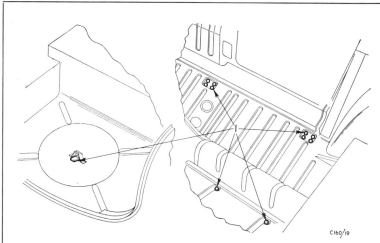

C160/19

1 Body mounting bolts, washers and floor.
   (Seelastik)

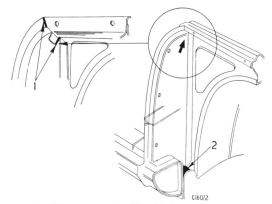

C160/2

1 Plug corner using Plastisol putty.
2 'B' post filler panel and outer sill panel.
   (Seelastik)

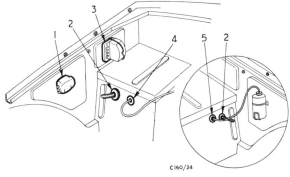

C160/24

1 Fuse unit and inner valance.
   (Seelastik)
2 Cable harness, grommet and bulkhead.
   (Seelastik)
3 Control box and inner valance.
   (Seelastik)
4 Heater control cable, grommet and bulkhead.
   (Seelastik)
5 Windscreen washer tube, grommet and bulkhead.
   (Seelastik)

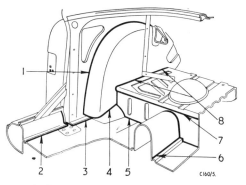

C160/5.

1 Inner wheelarch and closing panel.
   (Seelastik)
2 Floor panel and inner sill.
   (Seelastik)
3 Around base of 'B' post.
   (Seelastik)
4 Wheelarch and floor.
   (Seelastik)
5 Heelboard and floor.
   (Seelastik)
6 Transmission tunnel and floor.
   (Seelastik)
7 Heelboard and seat panel.
   (Seelastik)
8 Seat panel and inner wheelarch.
   (Seelastik)

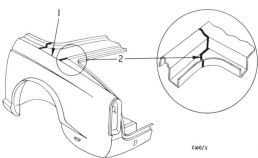

C160/11

1 Rear deck and tonneau side.   (Plastisol 53)
2 Rear deck and filler panel.   (Plastisol 53)

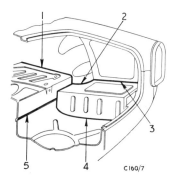

C160/7

1 Wheelarch inner panel and seat panel.
   (Seelastik)
2 Wheelarch inner panel and filler panel.
   (Seelastik)
3 Side floor and tonneau inner panel.
   (Seelastik)
4 Side floor and spare wheel pan.
   (Seelastik)
5 Seat panel and spare wheel pan.
   (Seelastik)

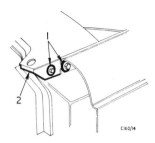

C160/14

1   Under washers and dash panel.
       (Seelastik)
2   Scuttle and 'A' post.
       (Seelastik)

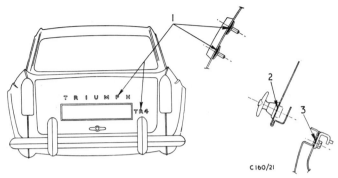

C160/21

1   Name plate fixings and luggage locker lid.
       (Glasticon 303)
2   Locker lid handle escutcheon and lid.
       (Prestik)
3   Locker lid striker and spare wheel pan.
       (Seelastik)

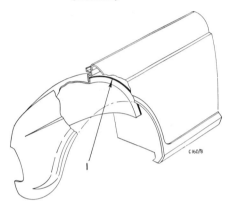

C160/8

1   Wheelarch panel and closing panel.
       (Plastisol 53)

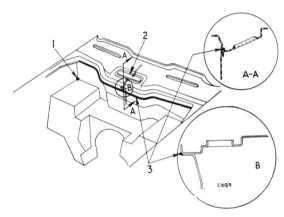

C160/9

1   Plug corner hole.
       (Plastisol Putty)
2   Upper bulkhead and plenum.
       (Seelastik)
3   Scuttle and bulkhead.
       (Plastisol Putty)

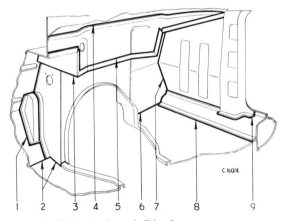

C.160/4.

1   Pocket to lower bulkhead.
       (Seelastik)
2   Bulkhead and floor panel.
       (Seelastik)
3   Dash shelf and centre bulkhead.
       (Seelastik)
4   Dash shelf and upper bulkhead.
       (Seelastik)
5   Dash shelf and bulkhead.
       (Seelastik)
6   Bulkhead and floor.
7   Bulkhead and panel and front bulkhead.
       (Seelastik)
8   Floor and inner sill.
       (Seelastik)
9   Sill and 'A' post.
       (Seelastik)

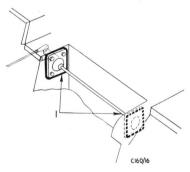

C160/16

1   Accelerator relay and bulkhead.
       (Seelastik)

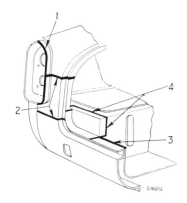

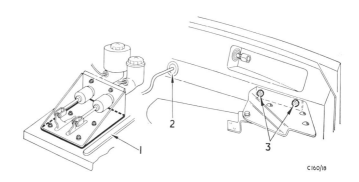

1 Tail lamp housing and tonneau panel.
   (Plastisol)
2 Upper and lower tonneau panel and rear valance.
   (Plastisol)
3 Spare wheel panel and rear valance.
   (Plastisol)
4 All round closing panel.
   (Plastisol)

1 Master cylinder mounting bracket and dash shelf.
   (Seelastik)
2 Grommet and bulkhead.
   (Seelastik)
3 Wiper motor mounting bracket. Seelastik under
   washers from inside the car.

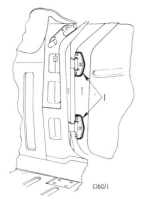

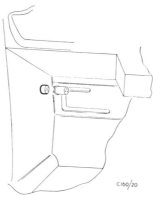

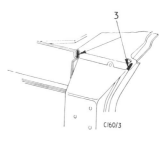

1 Door hinges and 'A' post.
   (Seelastik)

1 Flasher socket and bulkhead.
   (Seelastik)

3 Plug holes in corners of 'A'
   post from inside body.
   (Plastisol)

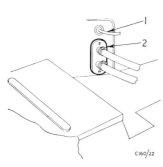

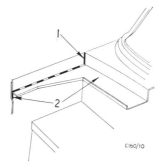

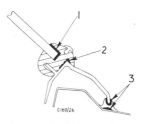

1 Choke control grommet and
   bulkhead.
   (Seelastik)
2 Adaptor plate and bulkhead.
   (Seelastik)

1 Wheelarch closing panel and
   scuttle and drip channel.
   (Plastisol 53)
2 Wheelarch closing panel and
   underside of drip channel
   for not less than 12".
   (Plastisol 53)

1 Glass and rubber weatherstrip.
   (Seelastik M1)
2 Rubber weatherstrip and frame.
   (Seelastik M1)
3 Backlight frame and sealing
   rubber and sealing
   rubber and rear deck.
   (Seelastik M1)

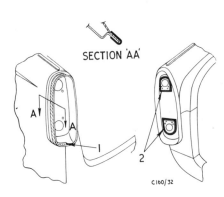

SECTION 'AA'

C 160/32

1   Tape round outer edges of tail lamp socket.
2   Tail lamp rubber and filler panel.
        (Seelastik)

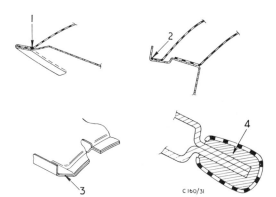

C 160/31

1   Front of roof.   (Plastisol)
2   Roof and drip channel.   (Plastisol)
3   Tear end of drip channel.   (Plastisol)
4   Roof rear finisher.   (Seelastik)

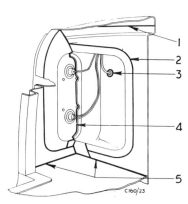

C 160/23

1   Tonneau side and wheelarch closing panel.
        (Seelastik)
2   Pocket and wheelarch closing panel.
        (Seelastik)
3   Grommet and tonneau side.
        (Seelastik)
4   All round lamp housing.
        (Seelastik)
5   Floor to lower tonneau and closing panels.
        (Seelastik)

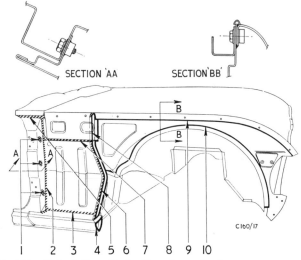

SECTION 'AA'   SECTION 'BB'

C 160/17

1   Wing fixing bolts.   (Seelastik under washers)
2   'A' post and side panel.   (Supra Dedseal)
3   Sill and side panel.   (Supra Dedseal)
4   Sill end filler panel and sill.   (Supra Dedseal)
5   Scuttle and 'A' post.   (Supra Dedseal)
6   Stoneguard baffle, front wing and closing panel.   (Supra Dedseal)
7   Upper and lower side panel.   (Supra Dedseal)
8   Wing fixing bolts.   (Seelastik under washers)
9   Wing and closing panel.   (Boscoseal)
10   Closing panel to wheelarch.   (Supra Dedseal)

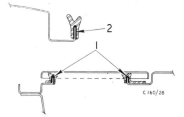

C 160/28

1   Ventilator sealing rubber.
        (Plus product 6/63)
2   Luggage locker sealing rubber.
        (Plus product 6/63)

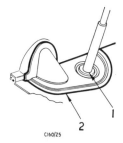

C160/25

1   Handbrake lever and rubber seal.
        (Seelastik M1)
2   Rubber seal and floor.
        (Seelastik)

C 160/30

Tail lamp rubber and body.
        (Seelastik)

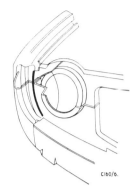

1 Upper valance and filler piece.
(Seelastik)

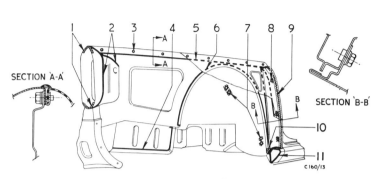

1 Edge of rear lamp housing.
(Seelastik)
2 Rear lamp housing and closing panel.
(Supra Dedseal)
3 Wing fixing bolts. (Seelastik under washers)
4 Spare wheel pan and tonneau side.
(Supra Dedseal)
5 Outer wing and side panel.
(Boscoseal)
6 Inner wheelarch and closing panel.
7 Safety harness holes.
(Seelastik)
8 Wing fixing bolts. (Seelastik under washers)
9 'B' post filter panel, rear wing and closing panel.
10 Plug corner hole.
(Plastisol Putty)
11 Sill end filler panel and sill.
(Supra Dedseal)

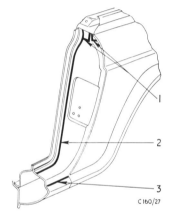

1 Rear deck filler and outer 'B' post panels.
(Plastisol 53)
2 Outer edge of door seal retainer channel.
(Plastisol 53)
3 'B' post and sill.
(Plastisol 53)

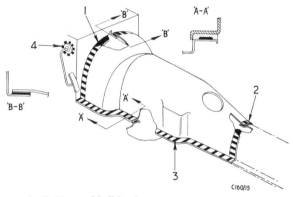

1 Rubber and bulkhead.
(Seelastik)
2 Rubber and transmission tunnel.
(Seelastik)
3 Rubber and floor.
(Seelastik)
4 Accelerator relay bracket, gaskets and bulkhead.
(Seelastik)

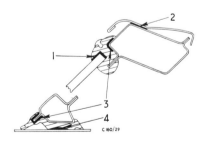

1 Glass and rubber weatherstrip.
(Seelastik M1)
2 Header capping and windscreen frame.
3 Rubber weatherstrip and windscreen frame.
(Seelastik M1)
4 Rubber and scuttle panel. Seel-A-Strip $\frac{1}{8}$" diameter.

TRIUMPH TR4

WORKSHOP MANUAL

GROUP 6

Comprising:

Electrical Section

TR4 WORKSHOP MANUAL

GROUP 6

CONTENTS

SPECIFICATIONS

Battery
Type BT.9A. (Home).	
Supplied dry and uncharged, or filled and charged	Lead acid.
Type BTZ.9A. (Export).	
Supplied dry but with plates charged ..	Lead acid.
Voltage	12.
Terminal earthed	Positive.
Capacity—at 10 hour rate	51 ampere hours.
—at 20 hour rate	58 ampere hours.
Plates per cell	9.
Electrolyte capacity (per cell)	1 pint imperial; 1·2 pints U.S.A.; 570 c.c.
Specific gravity charged—Climates below 32°C. ..	1·270—1·290.
—Climates above 32°C. ..	1·130—1·150.
Initial charging current for BT.9A	3·5 amperes.
Recharging current (both types)	5·0 amperes.

Generator
Model	C40—1.
Type	Two brush, two pole, compensated voltage control.
Rotation	Clockwise.
Field resistance	6 ohms. approximately.
Maximum output at 13·5 volts	22 amperes at 2,050—2,250 r.p.m. (connected to a load of 0·61 ohms).
Brush tension	22—25 ozs. (0·62—0·71 Kgs.).
Minimum brush length	$\frac{11}{32}''$ (9 mm.).

Control Box
Type	RB.106/2.
Cut-in voltage	12·7—13·3.
Drop-off voltage	11—8·5.
Open circuit settings—*Ambient temperatures* ..	*Open circuit voltages.*
10°C. (50°F.)	16·1—16·7
20°C. (68°F.)	16·0—16·6
30°C. (86°F.)	15·9—16·5
40°C. (104°F.)	15·8—16·4

Starter Motor
Model	M.418.G.
Type	Four pole, four brush, series wound.
Brush tension	32—40 ozs. (0·9—1·1 Kgs.).
Minimum brush length	$\frac{5}{16}''$ (8 mm.).
Number of teeth on ring gear	90.
Number of teeth on pinion	10.
Ratio	9 : 1.
Performance data	

ARMATURE SPEED	TORQUE		CURRENT CONSUMPTION	
	lbs.ft.	Kgms.	Amperes	Volts
Locked	17	2·35	440—460	7·4—7
1,000 r.p.m.	8	1·11	250—270	9·4—9
7,400—8,500 r.p.m. ..	No load		45	12

SPECIFICATIONS

Distributor

Model .. .. 25.D4.

Part Numbers

Compression Ratio	Lucas Service No.	Standard-Triumph Part No.
9	40795	208972
7	40842	209092

Design Data

Firing angles	$0°$, $90°$, $180°$, $270°$, $\pm 1°$.
Closed period	$60° \pm 3°$.
Open period	$30° \pm 3°$.
Contact breaker gap	$0·015''$
Rotation (viewed on rotor arm)	Anti-clockwise.

Centrifugal Timing Advance Tests

9 : 1 Compression Ratio

1. Set at $0°$ at a speed of less than 100 r.p.m.
2. Run distributor up to 1,200 r.p.m.—advance to be $9°$—$11°$.
3. Check at following decelerating speeds:—

7 : 1 Compression Ratio

1. Set at $0°$.
2. Run distributor up to 2,500 r.p.m.—advance to be $9°$ maximum.
3. Check at following decelerating speeds:—

Speed R.P.M.	Advance Degrees	Speed R.P.M.	Advance Degrees
800	9—11	1900	7—9
600	5—7	1350	4—6
350	0—2	700	$\frac{1}{2}$—$2\frac{1}{2}$
		400	0—1
No advance below 225 r.p.m.		No advance below 250 r.p.m.	

VACUUM ADVANCE TESTS CHECK ON RISING

Inches H.G.	Advance Degrees	Inches H.G.	Advance Degrees
2	0	2	0
3	1	3	$1\frac{1}{2}$
4	$1\frac{3}{4}$	5	$4\frac{1}{2}$
5	$2\frac{1}{2}$	7	$7\frac{1}{2}$
Maximum 6	$2\frac{3}{4}$	Maximum 8	10

Windscreen Wiper Motor

Lucas Model DR.3A	Shunt wound single speed.
Light running speed	44 to 48 cycles per minute of wiper blades.
Stall current	13—15 amps.
Light running currents	2·7—3·4 amps. (Measured less cable and rack).
Resistance of field winding at 20°C. (68°F.) ..	8·0—9·5 ohms.
Resistance of armature winding at 20°C. (68°F.) ..	0·29—0·352 ohms. (Measured between adjacent commutation segments).
Brush tension	125—140 grammes.
Maximum permissible force to move rack in protective tubing with wiper motor disconnected and wiper arms removed	6 lbs. (2·7 kgs.).

BULBS

Lamp	Lucas No.	Wattage	Cap
Headlamps			
R.H.D. Home	404	60/36	Pre-focus.
Export	414	50/40	Pre-focus.
L.H.D.	301	36/36	Pre-focus.
L.H.D.	370	45/40	Pre-focus.
L.H.D. Special order. European	410	45/40	3 lug.
L.H.D. Special order. (France)	411	45/40	3 lug.
Norway and Sweden only	350	35/35	Pre-focus.
Front parking (except Belgium and Switzerland) ..	222	4	M.B.C.
Flashing · Direction. Front. (Except Belgium and Switzerland)	382	21	S.C.C.
Front Parking and Flasher. (Belgium and Switzerland only)	380	21/6	S.B.C.
Brake Stop and Tail	380	21/6	S.B.C.
Number Plate Illumination	207	6	S.C.C.
Flasher Warning	987	2·2	M.E.S.
Ignition Warning	987	2·2	M.E.S.
Main Beam Warning	987	2·2	M.E.S.
Instrument Illumination	987	2·2	M.E.S.

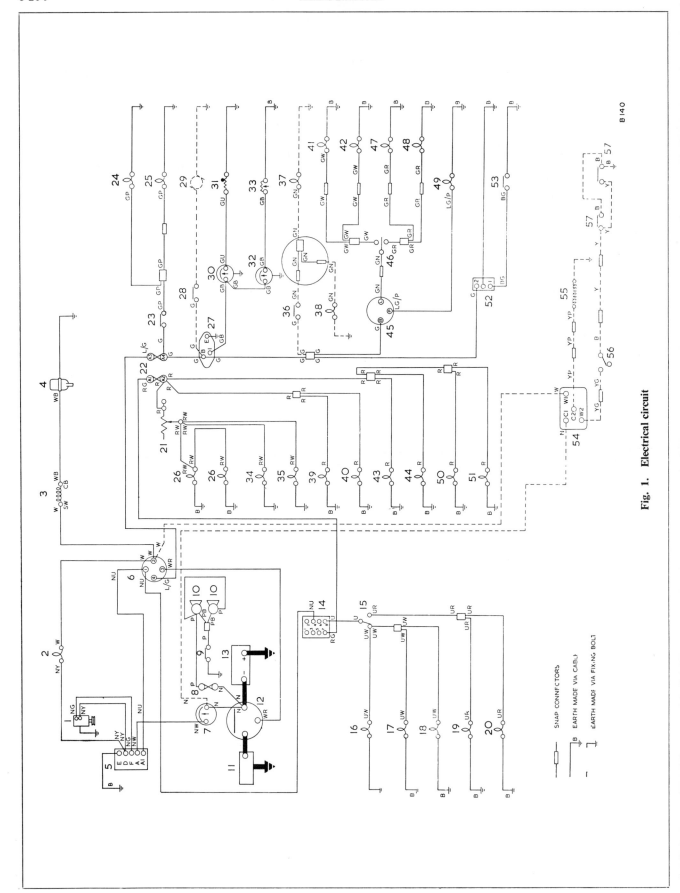

Fig. 1. Electrical circuit

KEY TO FIG. 1

1 Generator
2 Ignition warning lamp
3 Ignition coil
4 Distributor
5 Control box
6 Ignition switch
7 Ammeter
8 Horns fuse
9 Horn push
10 Horns
11 Starter motor
12 Starter solenoid
13 Battery
14 Lighting switch
15 Dipper switch
16 High beam indicator lamp
17 Headlamp high beam, R.H.
18 Headlamp high beam, L.H.
19 Headlamp dip beam, R.H.
20 Headlamp dip beam, L.H.
21 Instrument illumination rheostat
22 Fuse unit
23 Stop lamp switch
24 Stop lamp, R.H.
25 Stop lamp, L.H.
26 Ammeter and gauges illumination
27 Voltage stabilizer
28 Heater blower motor switch } Optional Extra
29 Heater blower motor } Optional Extra
30 Temperature indicator gauge
31 Temperature transmitter
32 Fuel gauge
33 Tank unit
34 Speedometer illumination
35 Tachometer illumination
36 Reversing lamp switch } Optional Extra
37 Reversing lamp } Optional Extra
38 Reversing lamp } Optional Extra
39 Parking lamp, R.H.
40 Parking lamp, L.H.
41 Direction indicator, R.H. Front
42 Direction indicator, L.H. Front
43 Tail lamp, R.H.
44 Plate illumination lamp, R.H.
45 Flasher unit
46 Direction indicator switch
47 Direction indicator, R.H. Rear
48 Direction indicator, L.H. Rear
49 Direction indicator monitor lamp
50 Tail lamp, L.H.
51 Plate illumination lamp, L.H.
52 Windscreen wiper motor
53 Windscreen wiper motor switch
54 Relay } Overdrive Optional Extras
55 Solenoid } Overdrive Optional Extras
56 Column control } Overdrive Optional Extras
57 Transmission switches } Overdrive Optional Extras

CABLE COLOUR CODE

B	Black	**S**	Slate
U	Blue	**W**	White
N	Brown	**Y**	Yellow
G	Green	**D**	Dark
K	Pink	**L**	Light
P	Purple	**M**	Medium
R	Red		

1 Battery
2 Voltage regulator relay coil
3 Split series coil
4 Voltage regulator contacts
5 Resistor
6 Main frame
7 Cutout contacts
8 Series winding
9 Cutout relay coil
10 Generator
11 Ignition switch
12 Ignition warning lamp
Nos. 2-9 are incorporated in the control box

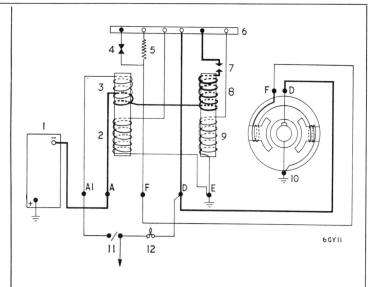

Fig. 2. Circuit diagram of generating system

1 To battery via terminal 'A' on control box
2 Ignition switch
3 Ignition coil primary winding
4 Ignition coil secondary winding
5 Distribution cap
6 Contact breaker
7 Capacitor
8 Rotor arm
9 To sparking plug

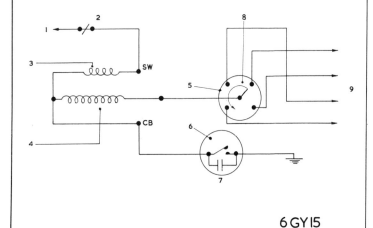

Fig. 3. Circuit diagram ignition system

6 GY 15

1 Control switch
2 Relay
3 Isolator switch
4 Isolator switch
5 Solenoid
6 To ignition switch
7 To ammeter

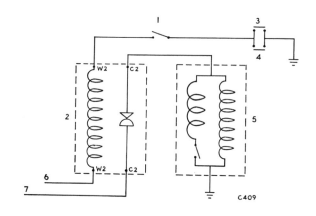

Fig. 4. Overdrive circuit

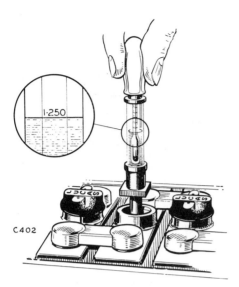

Fig. 5. Using a hydrometer to measure the specific gravity

TABLE 1. SPECIFIC GRAVITY OF ELECTROLYTE

Battery Condition	Climates below 90°F. (32°C.)	Climates over 90°F. (32°C.)
Fully charged.. ..	1·270—1·290	1·210—1·230
Half discharged ..	1·190—1·210	1·130—1·150
Completely discharged	1·110—1·130	1·050—1·070

TABLE 2
SPECIFIC GRAVITY OF ACID REQUIRED FOR FILLING

Quantity to half-fill each 2-volt cell	Specific gravity of electrolyte corrected to 60°F. (15·5°C.)	
	Climates below 90°F. (32°C.)	Climates over 90°F. (32°C.)
½ Pint	1·270 (30·83° Baume)	1·210 (25·16° Baume)

TABLE 3. PROPORTIONS OF ACID AND WATER

To obtain specific gravity when cooled to 60°F. (15·5°C.)	Add one part by volume of Acid (1·835 S.G.) to distilled water by volume as below.
1·210	4·0 parts
1·215	3·9 ,,
1·260	3·1 ,,
1·270	2·9 ,,
1·275	2·8 ,,
1·290	2·7 ,,
1·320	2·3 ,,
1·340	2·0 ,,

BATTERY

If the battery is subjected to long periods of discharge without suitable opportunities for re-charging, a low state of charge can be expected. A defect in the charging system can also result in a discharged battery.

There are two reliable methods of assessing battery conditions. (1) Checking the specific gravity of the electrolyte, and (2) high rate discharge test.

1. Hydrometer Test

The specific gravity of the electrolyte varies with battery conditions (see table 1), and also with temperature, which should be corrected to the standard of 60°F. (15·6°C.) as outlined in table 4.

If it is necessary to top up the electrolyte, do not attempt to take a reading until the battery has been on charge for at least one hour. There should be little variation in the specific gravity readings between one cell and another of a battery in reasonably good condition.

A large variation, which is not the result of electrolyte loss, is probably an indication of an internal short circuit. If the electrolyte is very dirty, or contains small particles in suspension, it is possible that the plates are in bad condition.

2. Discharge Test

The high rate discharge test gives an indication of the condition and capacity of the battery. On test, the battery should maintain 100 amp. flow for 10 seconds with no appreciable fall in voltage.

Where a hand instrument (incorporating a low resistance device) is used for checking the individual cells of a battery, the actual reading obtained will depend upon the exact type of instrument used, but the cell voltage on a 5 to 6 seconds test should remain steady between 1·2 and 1·7 volts.

Variations in individual cell readings can indicate faults, but if all cells in any one battery fall below standard, recharge and again test before rejecting the battery.

Never make a high rate discharge test on a battery known to be low in charge.

Re-Charging from an external supply

If the above tests indicate that the battery is merely discharged and is otherwise in a good condition, it should be re-charged until the specific gravity and voltage show no increase over three successive hourly readings.

Preparing New, Unfilled, Uncharged Batteries

Batteries should not be filled with electrolyte until required for initial charging. Approximately one pint (570 c.c.) of electrolyte is needed for each cell.

Electrolyte of the specific gravity is prepared by mixing distilled water and concentrated sulphuric acid, usually of 1·835 S.G. either in a lead-lined tank or in suitable glass or earthenware vessel. Slowly add the acid to the water, stirring with a glass rod. Never add the water to the acid, as the resulting chemical reaction causes violent and dangerous spurting of the concentrated acid.

The approximate proportions of acid and water are indicated in table 3.

Heat is produced by the mixture of acid and water. Allow the electrolyte to cool before taking hydrometer readings, or pouring it into the battery.

Filling the cells

The temperature of the electrolyte, battery and filling in room must not be below 32°F. (0°C.) freezing.

Break the seals in the filling holes or remove the moulded pegs from the vent plugs and half-fill each cell with electrolyte of the appropriate specific gravity. Allow the battery to stand for six hours and fill to the top of the separators. Allow to stand for a further two hours and then proceed with the initial charge.

Initial Charge

Charge at a constant 3·5 amperes for 40 to 80 hours until the voltage and specific gravity readings show no increase over five successive hourly readings.

If the temperature of any cell rises 20°F. (11·1°C.) above the ambient temperature, interrupt the charge until the temperature has fallen at least 10°F. (5·6°C.) below that figure. Keep the electrolyte level with the top of the separator guard by adding electrolyte of the same specific gravity as the original filling. Continue the charge until specific gravity and voltage readings remain constant for five successive hourly readings.

At the end of the charge, check and if necessary, adjust the specific gravity in each cell when corrected to 60°F. (15·6°C.). To adjust, siphon off some of the electrolyte and replace it either by distilled water or by electrolyte of the strength originally used for filling. Continue the charge for an hour or so to ensure adequate mixing of the electrolyte.

Preparing New, Dry-Charged Batteries

Break the seals in the filling holes and fill each cell with electrolyte of correct specific gravity to the top of the separators. The temperature of the filling room, battery and acid should be maintained at between 60°F. (15·6°C.) and 120°F. (48·8°C.). If the battery has been stored in a cool place, allow it to warm up to room temperature before filling.

Batteries filled in this way are up to 90% charged. When time permits, a freshening charge may be given at normal charging rate of 5 amps. for not more than 4 hours. Check the specific gravity of the electrolyte at the end of the charge; if 1·270 electrolyte was used, the specific gravity should now be between 1·270 and 1·290; if 1·210 electrolyte between 1·210 and 1·230.

TABLE 4
SPECIFIC GRAVITY TEMPERATURE CORRECTION

Electrolyte Temperature		Correction required to obtain true specific gravity at 60°F. (15·5°C.).
Degrees F.	Degrees C.	
50	10·0	Deduct ·004 from observed reading
55	12·7	,, ·002 ,, ,, ,,
60	15·5	Normal
65	18·3	Add ·002 to ,, ,,
70	21·1	,, ·004 ,, ,, ,,
75	23·8	,, ·006 ,, ,, ,,
80	26·6	,, ·008 ,, ,, ,,
85	29·4	,, ·010 ,, ,, ,,
90	32·2	,, ·012 ,, ,, ,,
95	35·0	,, ·014 ,, ,, ,,
100	37·7	,, ·016 ,, ,, ,,
110	43·3	,, ·020 ,, ,, ,,
120	48·8	,, ·024 ,, ,, ,,

TABLE 5. MAXIMUM PERMISSIBLE ELECTROLYTE TEMPERATURE DURING CHARGING

Climates below 80°F. (26·6°C.)	Climates between 80–100°F. (26·6—37·7° C.)	Climates above 100°F. (37·7°C.)
100°F. (37·7°C.)	110°F. (43·3°C.)	120°F. (48·8°C.)

C4 04

Fig. 6. Using a heavy discharge tester

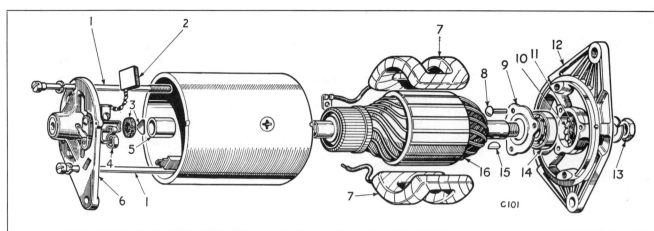

1   Bolts
2   Brush
3   Felt ring and aluminium sealing disc
4   Brush spring
5   Bearing bush
6   Commutator end bracket
7   Field coils
8   Rivet
9   Bearing retainer plate
10   Corrugated washer
11   Felt washer
12   Driving end bracket
13   Pulley retainer nut
14   Bearing
15   Woodruff key
16   Armature

Fig. 7.   Dismantled generator

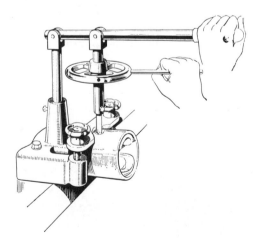

Fig. 8.   Removing the pole pieces from the yoke

GENERATOR

To Dismantle

Remove the generator from the engine, extract the driving pulley and take out the woodruff key (15). Remove two bolts and withdraw the commutator end bracket (6) from the yoke. Note the fibre thrust washer adjacent to the commutator.

Withdraw the armature (16) and drive end bracket (12) complete with bearing. Support the bearing retaining plate (9) and press the shaft from the drive end bracket.

Field Coils

Renew as follows:

1. Drill out the rivet securing the field terminal assembly to the yoke and unsolder the field coil connections.
2. Remove the insulation piece which prevents the junction of field coils from contacting the yoke.
3. Mark the yoke and pole shoes so that they can be refitted to their original positions.
4. Unscrew the pole shoe retaining screws, remove the pole shoes and lift off the coils.
5. Fit the new field coils over the pole shoes and re-position them inside the yolk.
6. Locate the pole shoes and field coils by lightly tightening the retaining screws; fully tighten them by using a wheel operated screwdriver. Lock the screws by caulking.
7. Replace the insulation piece between the field coil connections and the yoke.
8. Re-solder the field coil connections to the field coil terminal tags and rivet the assembly to the yoke.

Commutator

Burned commutator segments may be caused by an open-circuit in the armature windings. If armature testing facilities are not available, test the armature by substitution.

The commutator should be smooth and free from pits or burned spots. Slight burning may be rectified by careful polishing with a strip of fine glass paper while rotating the armature. To remedy a badly worn commutator, mount the armature, with or without the drive end bracket, in a lathe. Rotate the armature at high speed and take a light cut with a very sharp tool, removing as little metal as is necessary to clean up the commutator. Polish the commutator with very fine glasspaper and undercut the insulators between segments to a depth of $\frac{1}{32}$" (0·8 mm.), using a hacksaw blade ground to the thickness of the insulator (Fig. 9).

Brushes

Check that the brushes move freely in their holders, by holding back the tension springs and pulling gently on the flexible connectors. If a brush is inclined to stick, remove it from its holder and clean its sides with a petrol-moistened cloth.

Replace the brushes in their original position or renew those which are less than $\frac{11}{32}$" (8·7 mm.) in length.

Test the brush spring tension using a spring scale. Fit new springs if the tension is below 15 ozs.

Bearings

Replace the bearing bush in a commutator end bracket as follows:

Remove the old bearing bush from the end bracket by screwing a $\frac{5}{8}$" tap squarely into the bush for a few turns and pulling out the bush with the tap.

Insert the felt ring and aluminium disc (3) in the bearing housing and using a shouldered mandrel press the new bearing bush into the end bracket until the bearing is flush with the inner face of the bracket.

Replace the ball bearing at the driving end as follows:

1. Drill out the rivets (8) and remove the plate (9).
2. Press the bearing (14) from the end bracket (12) and remove the corrugated washer (10), felt washer (11) and oil retaining washer.
3. Clean and pack the replacement bearing with high melting point grease, such as Energrease RBB.3 or equivalent.
4. Place the oil retaining washer, felt washer and corrugated washer in the bearing housing and press in the bearing housing and press in the bearing.
5. Fit and rivet the retaining plate to the end bracket.

Re-assembly

1. Supporting the inner journal of the bearing to prevent damage, press the armature through the bearing assembled in the drive end bracket.
2. Assemble the armature and end bracket to the yoke.
3. Hold the brushes up by positioning each brush spring at the side of its brush.
4. Fit the commutator end bracket on the armature shaft until the brush boxes are partly over the commutator. Press each brush down on the commutator and move its spring to the operating position.
5. Fit the commutator end bracket to the yoke and refit the bolts (1).

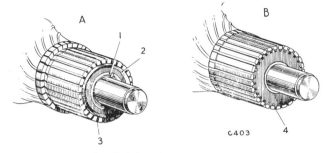

A. Fabricated commutator
B. Moulded commutator
1   Metal roll-over
2   Insulating cone
3   Slot depth - 0·032" (0·81 mm.) maximum
4   Slot depth - 0·02" - 0·035" (0·508—0·89 mm.)

Fig. 9.   Commutator details

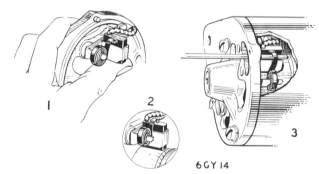

1   Method of trapping brush in raised position with spring
2   Normal working position
3   Method of releasing brush on to commutator

Fig. 10.   Fitting commutator end bracket to "windowless" yoke generator

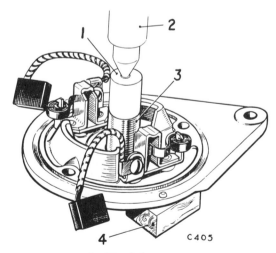

1   Mandrel
2   Press
3   Bush
4   Wood blocks

Fig. 11.   Fitting a new bearing to the commutator end bracket

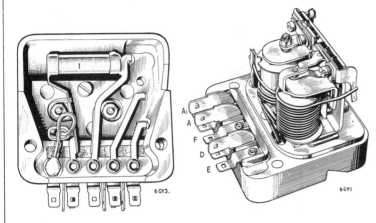

Fig. 12.   **The voltage regulator and cut-out**

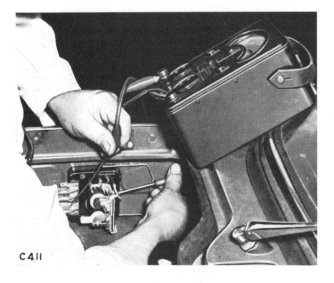

Fig. 13.   **Using a moving coil voltmeter to adjust the voltage regulator**

CONTROL BOX

The control box shown in Fig. 12 contains two units — a voltage regulator and a cut-out. Although combined structurally, the regulator and cut-out are electrically separate.

The regulator is set to maintain the generator terminal voltage between close limits at all speeds above the regulating point, the field strength being controlled by the automatic insertion and withdrawal of a resistor in the generator field circuit.

Cleaning Contacts

(i) Regulator Contacts — use fine carborundum stone or silicon carbide paper.

(ii) Cut-out Relay Contacts — use a strip of fine glasspaper — never carborundum stone or emery cloth.

Voltage Regulator—Electrical Setting

It is important that only a good quality MOVING COIL VOLTMETER (0·20 volts) is used when checking the regulator.

Remove the cover and insert a thin piece of cardboard between the armature and the core face of the cut-out to prevent the contacts from closing.

Start the engine and slowly increase its speed until the generator reaches 3,000 r.p.m., when the open circuit voltage reading should be between the appropriate limits given on page 6·102, according to the ambient temperature.

If the voltage, at which the reading becomes steady, occurs outside these limits, adjust the regulator by turning the adjusting screw clockwise to raise the voltage or counter clockwise to lower.

Adjustment of regulator open-circuit voltage should be completed within 30 seconds otherwise heating of the shunt windings will cause false settings to be made.

Remove the cardboard.

Voltage Regulator — Mechanical Setting

A copper separator, in the form of a disc or square, is welded to the core face of the voltage regulator, and affects the gap setting between the core-face and the underside of the armature as follows:—

Where a round separator is used, the air gap should be 0·015″ (0·38 mm.).

Where a square separator is used, the air gap should be 0·021″ (0·53 mm.).

To adjust the air gap:—

Slacken the fixed contact locking nut and unscrew the contact screw until it is well clear of the armature moving contact.

Slacken the voltage adjustment spring-loaded screw until it is well clear of the armature tension spring.

Slacken the two armature assembly securing screws.

Insert a gauge of sufficient width to cover the core face, and of the appropriate thickness, between the armature and copper separator.

Press the armature squarely down against the gauge and re-tighten the two armature assembly securing screws. Without removing the gauge, screw in the fixed contact adjustment screw until it just touches the armature contact. Re-tighten the locking nut.

Re-check the electrical setting of the regulator.

CUT-OUT

Electrical Setting

If the regulator is correctly set but the battery is still not being charged, the cut-out may be out of adjustment. To check the voltage at which the cut-out operates, remove the control box cover and connect the voltmeter between the terminals D and E. Start the engine and slowly increase its speed until the cut-out contacts are seen to close, noting the voltage at which this occurs. This should be 12·7-13·3 volts.

If operation of the cut-out takes place outside these limits, it will be necessary to adjust. To do this, turn the adjusting screw in a clockwise direction to raise the voltage setting or in a counter clockwise direction to reduce the setting. Turn the screw only a fraction of a turn at a time and test after each adjustment by increasing the engine speed and noting the voltmeter readings at the instant of contact closure. Electrical settings of the cut-out, like the regulator, must be made as quickly as possible, because of temperature rise effects. Tighten the locknut after making the adjustment. If the cut-out does not operate, there may be an open circuit in the wiring of the cut-out and regulator unit, in which case the unit should be removed for examination or replacement.

Cut-out Relay

Slacken the adjustment screw until it is well clear of the armature tension spring.

Slacken the two armature securing screws.

Press the armature squarely down against the core face (copper sprayed in some units, fit with a square of copper in others) and re-tighten the armature securing screws. No gauge is necessary.

With the armature still pressed against the core face, adjust the gap between the armature stop arm and the armature tongue to 0·032″ (0·81 mm.) by bending the stop arm.

Adjust the fixed contact blade so that it is deflected 0·015″ (0·38 mm.) by the armature moving contact when the armature is pressed against the core face.

Re-check the electrical setting of the cut-out.

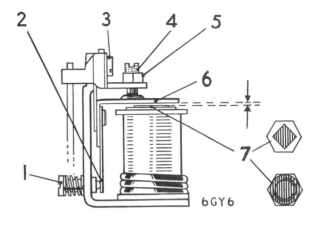

1 Voltage adjusting screw
2 Armature tension spring
3 Armature securing screws
4 Fixed contact adjustment screw
5 Lock nut
6 Armature
7 Core face and shim

Fig. 14. Regulator air gap settings

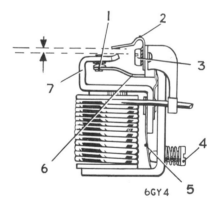

1. Follow through 0·010″ - 0·020″ (0·254 - 0·508 mm.)
2 Stop arm
3 Armature securing screws
4 Cut-out adjusting screw
5 Armature tension spring
6 Fixed contact blade
7 Armature tongue and moving contact

Fig. 15. Cut-out air gap settings

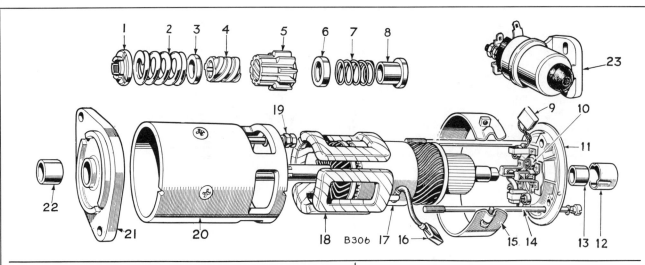

Fig. 16.   Dismantled starter motor

1	Starter drive nut	13	Bush
2	Starter drive spring	14	Bolt
3	Thrust washer	15	Brush cover
4	Screwed sleeve	16	Brush
5	Pinion	17	Field coil connection
6	Thrust washer	18	Field coil
7	Spring	19	Terminal
8	Collar	20	Yoke
9	Brush	21	Drive end cover
10	Brush spring	22	Bush
11	Commutator end bracket	23	Starter solenoid
12	Cover		

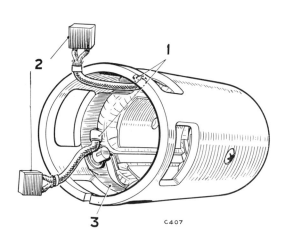

1   Field coil connections
2   Brushes
3   Yoke

Fig. 17.   Brush connections

STARTER MOTOR MODEL M.418G

To Remove

1. Disconnect the cables from the battery and the starter motor.
2. Remove two bolts, nuts and spring washers securing the starter motor to the cylinder block and clutch housing flanges.
3. Withdraw the starter motor from the clutch housing and manoeuvre it upwards between the carburettors and wing valance.

To Refit

Reverse the removal procedure, ensuring that the shoulder on the starter motor bolting face registers correctly with the cylinder block flange face.

Re-connect the cables to the battery and starter motor terminals.

Dismantling

Loosen the brush cover screw and slide the cover (15) from the unit. Lift the brush springs (10) and withdraw the brushes (9) from their holders.

Unscrew the terminal nuts (19), the two bolts (14) and remove the end bracket (11). Withdraw the drive end bracket (21) and armature from the yoke (20).

Extract the split pin, unscrew the nut (1), remove items 2—8 and slide the drive end bracket (21) from the shaft.

Reassembly — reverse the dismantling procedure.

Field Coils

To renew:

Unscrew the four-pole-shoe retaining screws, using a wheel operated screwdriver and pole expander tool for obstinate cases.

Mark the yoke and pole-shoes so that they can be refitted to their original positions.

Take out the pole-shoes, lift off the coils and unsolder the field coil tappings from the terminal post.

Fit new field coils by reversing the procedure, and replace the insulating pieces used to prevent the inter coil connectors from contacting the yoke.

To Reassemble

Assemble the components 1 to 8 in order shown on Fig. 16 and secure the retaining nut (1) with a split pin.

Bearings

To renew:

Using a shouldered mandrel of the same diameter as the shaft, drive out the old bush and press the new bearing bush into the end bracket.

The bronze bushes are porous and must not be opened out after fitting, otherwise the porosity of the bush may be impaired.

Commutator

A commutator in good condition is clean, smooth and free from pits or burned spots. If cleaning with a petrol-moistened cloth is ineffective, carefully polish the commutator with very fine glasspaper while the armature is rotating. Do not use emery cloth.

To rectify a badly worn commutator, mount the armature in a lathe, rotate at high speed and take a light cut with a sharp tool, removing the minimum of metal to obtain a clean finish. Finally, polish with very fine glasspaper.

Note:—Do not undercut the mica insulators between segments.

Brushes

Check that the brushes move freely on their holders by holding back the brush springs and pulling gently on the flexible connectors. If a brush is inclined to stick, remove it from its holder and release its sides with a smooth file.

Replace the brushes in their original positions or renew excessively worn brushes as follows:

Cut off the original brush flex $\frac{1}{8}''$ (3 mm.) approximately from the aluminium and tin the brazed joint. Open out the loop, taking care not to allow solder to run towards the brush.

Place the original joint within the loop, squeeze up and solder. The brushes are pre-formed so that bedding to the commutator is unnecessary.

Starter Drive

When the starter motor is removed from the engine, check the pinion for cleanliness and freedom of action. If necessary wash the drive assembly in paraffin to remove dirt and grease, which is the usual cause of a sticking pinion. Do not lubricate the components.

To Dismantle

Extract the split pin, unscrew the retaining nut (1), and slide the components 2—8 from the starter armature shaft.

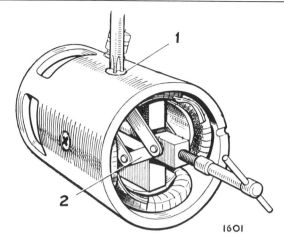

Fig. 18. Using a pole shoe expander to refit the field coils and retainer screws

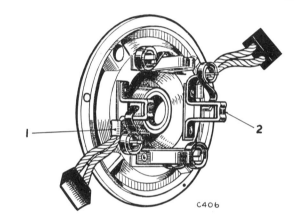

1 Brush connections
2 Brush boxes

Fig. 19. Commutator end bracket

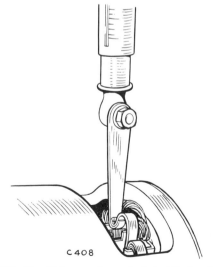

Fig. 20. Using a spring scale to test the brush spring tension

Fig. 21.   Distributor contacts

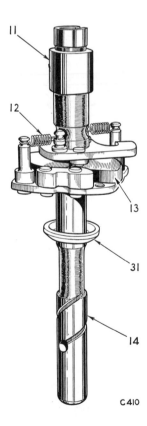

Fig. 22.   Assembly of centrifugal weights and springs to the action plate

IGNITION DISTRIBUTOR

The distributor is mounted on a pedestal at the L.H. side of the engine and driven by the camshaft, via a helical gear, which also drives the oil pump and tachometer. The degree of ignition advancement is controlled mechanically, according to engine speed, by two centrifugal weights mounted between a driving and driven plate within the body. Additional vacuum control, according to the effect of load on manifold depression, is provided by a diaphragm acting directly on the contact breaker plate.

Contact Breaker Adjustment (Fig. 21)

Take off the distributor cap, remove the rotor arm and turn the engine until the contact breaker heel is on the highest point of the cam.

Slacken the screw (28), insert the blade of a screwdriver into the slots (31), and twist the screwdriver to adjust the gap between the contact breaker points, which should be 0·014″—0·016″ (0·356—0·406 mm.) measured with a feeler gauge.

Tighten the locking screw (28), re-check the gap and, if satisfactory, refit the rotor arm and cap.

Contact Breaker Renewal

Slight pitting or discolouration of the points may be rectified by use of a fine carborundum stone. Do not use emery cloth unless the points are removed first and thoroughly cleaned before re-assembly. Renew burned or deeply pitted contacts as follows:—

1. Remove the nut (3), insulating sleeve (2) and lift the black and green cables from the terminal pillar.
2. Lift the spring contact (1) from the pivot post and remove the fibre washers (29) and (30).
3. Take out the lock screw (28) and lift off the fixed contact (27).

To Refit

Reverse the above instructions and adjust the gap between the contact breaker points.

Distributor Capacitor

A short circuit, resulting from the breakdown of the dielectric between the electrodes of the capacitor, which is parallel connected across the contact breaker points, will prevent the interruption of the low tension circuit and cause ignition failure.

An open circuit in the capacitor is more difficult to diagnose without the aid of special equipment, but may be suspect when the points are excessively burnt and difficult starting is experienced.

Renew the capacitor, or in case of doubt, substitute the existing one as follows:—

1. Remove the distributor cap and rotor arm, unscrew the nut (3) from the spring contact terminal post, and lift off the capacitor lead.
2. Take out the capacitor retainer screw and remove the capacitor.
3. Secure the new capacitor in place, reconnect the lead to the terminal post and refit the nut (3). Refit the rotor arm and distributor cap.

Overhauling the Distributor
To Remove

Disconnect the low tension cable from the side of the distributor, disconnect the high tension cable from the coil and release the high tension cables from the spark plugs.

Uncouple the vacuum pipe from the distributor, unscrew two nuts at the base of the distributor and lift it from the engine.

To Dismantle

Remove the distributor cover and rotor arm. Disconnect the vacuum control (26) from the contact plate (7), take out two screws (8) and remove the contact breaker assembly.

Release the circlip (19) and remove the adjusting nut (18) and spring (17), taking care not to lose the ratchet spring (16). Withdraw the vacuum control unit (25) from the distributor body.

Release both springs (12) from the base of the cam (11) and the action plate (14). Take out the screw (10) and lift the cam (11) from the shaft (14).

At this stage, check the shaft (14) for end float which should not exceed $\frac{1}{32}''$ (0·8 mm.). Drive out the pin (21), take off the collar (22) and the washer (23), and withdraw the shaft (14) from the distributor body.

Substituting a new shaft, or a test bar of 0·490″ (12·45 mm.) diameter check the bearing sleeve (24) for wear, and renew the sleeve if required.

To reduce excessive end float, renew the nylon spacer beneath the action plate (14), and the washer (23) between the driving dog and distributor body.

To Reassemble

Refit the nylon spacer under the action plate (14), reassemble the weights (13), spring (12) and cam (11) to the action plate (14) and secure the cam with the screw (10). Lubricate the shaft and insert the assembly into the distributor body.

Refit the washer (23) and, placing the offset driving collar (22) as shown on Fig. 23, secure the collar by inserting and swelling the ends of the pin (21).

Assemble the contact plate (7) to the fixed base plate (9) by springing the spring clip over the base plate slot edge, inserting the peg of the contact plate into a slot in the base plate and moving it slightly clockwise. Secure the assembly to the distributor body, using two screws (8).

Insert the vacuum unit (25) into the distributor body and assemble the ratchet spring (16), the coiled spring (17), adjusting nut (18) and the circlip (19). Hook the vacuum connecting spring (26) on to the pin attached to a cranked lug on the contact plate.

Assemble the capacitor and the contact breaker to the contact plate (7) and adjust the contact breaker points as described previously.

Refit the complete distributor to the engine, re-connect the vacuum pipe, the high and low tension cables, and adjust the ignition timing as instructed on page 1·131.

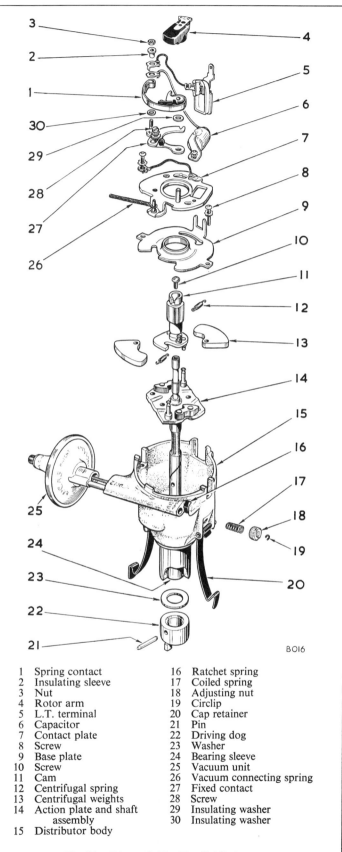

1	Spring contact	16	Ratchet spring
2	Insulating sleeve	17	Coiled spring
3	Nut	18	Adjusting nut
4	Rotor arm	19	Circlip
5	L.T. terminal	20	Cap retainer
6	Capacitor	21	Pin
7	Contact plate	22	Driving dog
8	Screw	23	Washer
9	Base plate	24	Bearing sleeve
10	Screw	25	Vacuum unit
11	Cam	26	Vacuum connecting spring
12	Centrifugal spring	27	Fixed contact
13	Centrifugal weights	28	Screw
14	Action plate and shaft assembly	29	Insulating washer
15	Distributor body	30	Insulating washer

Fig. 23.   Dismantled ignition distributor

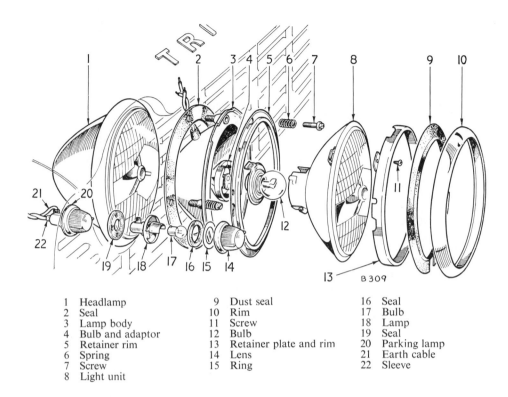

1	Headlamp	9	Dust seal	16	Seal
2	Seal	10	Rim	17	Bulb
3	Lamp body	11	Screw	18	Lamp
4	Bulb and adaptor	12	Bulb	19	Seal
5	Retainer rim	13	Retainer plate and rim	20	Parking lamp
6	Spring	14	Lens	21	Earth cable
7	Screw	15	Ring	22	Sleeve
8	Light unit				

Fig. 24. Dismantled headlamp and parking lamp

Fig. 25. Removing the headlamp rim

LAMPS

Headlamp Bulb Replacement

Remove the Snap-on rim by inserting the end of the special tool (provided in the kit) behind the lower edge of the rim and levering sideways as shown on Fig. 25. Press in the lamp unit against the tension of the adjusting screw springs and turn in an anti-clockwise direction until the key-slot holes in the rim line up with the screw heads. The lamp unit can then be drawn off. Do not rotate any of the screws, as this will affect the alignment of the reflector when assembled.

Rotate the adaptor anti-clockwise and pull off, then the headlamp bulb can be removed. Care should be taken to see that the bulb does not drop out.

Note:—Headlamp bulbs cannot be removed from the sealed beam units fitted to cars which are exported to the U.S.A. Bulb failure will necessitate unit replacement.

Headlamp Unit Replacement

Remove the lamp unit and bulb as described above. Unscrew three screws (11) and separate the inner and outer rims (5) and (13) from the light unit (8).

Fit a new unit by reversing the procedure and ensure that the locating clips at the edge of the light unit fit into corresponding slots in the rim.

Headlamp Alignment

The main beam is aligned in the vertical plane by turning the screw at the top of the lamp and in the horizontal plane by turning the screw on the side. Alignment of the beam on one lamp is best carried out with the other lamp covered.

Maximum illumination is obtained, and discomfort to other road users is prevented, by ensuring that the lamp beams do not project above the horizontal when the vehicle is fully laden.

Where adjustment is required, one of the following methods may be employed, subject to minor variations which may be necessary to meet varying conditions in different countries.

Method 1.
Lucas Beamsetter.

Remove the front rim and dust excluding rubber to gain access to the adjusting screws.

Roll the alignment bar into contact with the front wheels.

Wheel the beamsetter forward so that the two projecting arms butt against the alignment bar.

Adjust the height of the beamsetter unit to the level of the headlamp.

If the vehicle is not carrying its normal complement of passengers the height of the screen at the forward end of the setter may be adjusted to compensate for beam depression. The adjustment is calibrated in degrees and in inches per hundred feet and is effected by moving the lever to the appropriate angle of dip. This angle is dependent on the normal loading of the car. $0.5° = 2$ ft. 7 ins. in 100 yards (0·787 metres in 91·44 metres).

Switch on the lamp under test and adjust the screws to bring the beam image between the marker lines on the screen with the highest meter reading.

Method 2.
Wall Chart.

Position the car on level ground with the front facing squarely the screen or wall at a distance of $12\frac{1}{2}$ ft. (3·8 metres) from the screen.

Adjust the spheres (B) $\frac{7}{8}$″ (22·2 mm.) below the centre line of the lamps and to an equal distance either side of the centre line of the car.

Where the screen is not available, a wall may be marked to correspond with the adjustments given with the screen.

With one lamp covered adjust the screws on the other lamp to provide the pattern shown in Fig. 27.

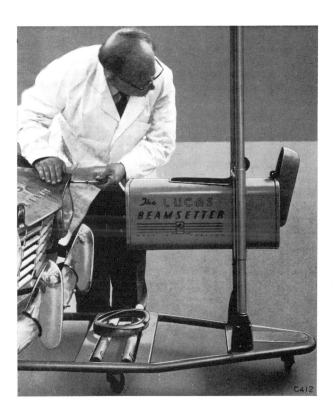

Fig. 26.   Using Lucas Beamsetter

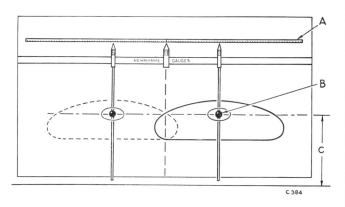

Fig. 27.   Showing the light pattern projected on to a Newnhams Gauge

Fig. 28.   Removing the lens from the direction indicator flashing lamp

Direction Indicator Flashing Lamps (Fig. 28)

With the aid of a thin screwdriver turn back the rubber and remove the rim. This then permits the glass lens to be similarly removed. When re-assembling the components fit the glass lens first.

Fig. 29.   Removing a bulb from the parking lamp

Parking Lamps (Fig. 29)

Twist the lens counter-clockwise and withdraw the lamp front to gain access to the bulb.

Fig. 30.   Removing the lens from the tail, brake stop and direction indicator flashing lamp

Tail/Brake Stop and Direction Indicator Flashing Lamps (Fig. 30)

Remove three screws and lift off the lens, which is in two sections, to gain access to the bulbs. The pins on the tail/brake stop lamp bulb are offset and cannot be fitted incorrectly.

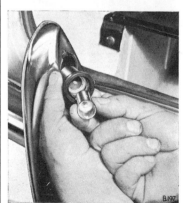

Fig. 31.   Removing a bulb from plate illumination lamp

Plate Illumination Lamps (Fig. 31)

Remove the two screws securing the rim and cowl to the over-rider, withdraw the lamp approximately 2″ (5 cm.) and renew the bulb.

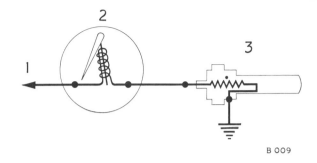

1 To "B" terminal on voltage stabilizer
2 Gauge unit
3 Transmitter

Fig. 32. Circuit diagram of temperature indicator

TEMPERATURE INDICATOR

The temperature indicator, comprising a temperature transmitter and a gauge unit, operates on a 10 volts system which is controlled by a voltage stabilizer.

Temperature Transmitter

The temperature transmitter which is mounted in the right-hand side of the thermostat housing, consists of a temperature sensitive resistance element contained within a brass sleeve. The resistance element is a semi-conductor which has a high negative temperature co-efficient of resistance and its electrical resistance therefore decreases rapidly with an increase in temperature. As the temperature of the engine coolant increases, the resistance of the semi-conductor increases the flow of current through the indicator, similarly a decrease in coolant temperature will reverse the procedure.

Gauge Unit

The gauge unit comprises a heater winding round a bimetal strip which is linked to the pointer of the gauge unit. The flow of current through the heater winding is controlled by the temperature transmitter which reacts to any change in engine coolant temperature by varying the current drawn through the heater windings. This affects the bimetal strip which in turn causes the pointer to indicate the temperature of the coolant. The slow movement of the pointer is caused by the time taken to heat or cool off the bimetal strip.

Voltage Stabilizer

The voltage stabilizer is a small sealed unit, located under the facia on the right-hand side of the car, and is used to provide a constant current of 10 volts for the operation of the fuel contents gauge and the Temperature Indicator.

Since it is not possible to repair any of the units described above, a defective unit must, therefore, be renewed.

Testing

To establish which unit is defective, test for circuit continuity using an Ohmmeter or by substituting a known unit.

Do not connect any unit direct to the battery.

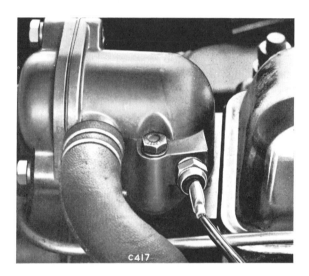

Fig. 33. Location of temperature transmitter

Fig. 34. Location of voltage stabilizer

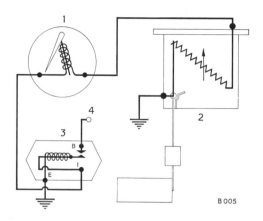

1 Fuel indicator gauge
2 Tank unit
3 Voltage stabilizer
4 To "A4" on fuse unit

Fig. 35. Circuit diagram of fuel contents gauge

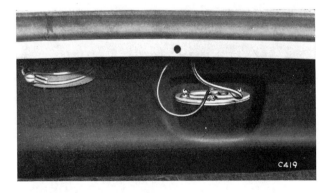

Fig. 36. Location of fuel tank unit

FUEL CONTENTS GAUGE

The fuel contents gauge operates on a stabilized 10 volts and comprises:
1. Indicator Gauge.
2. Tank Unit.

The units may be renewed independently of each other.

1. Indicator Gauge

The construction and operation of the contents indicator is identical to the temperature indicator gauge unit.

2. Tank Unit

The tank unit is virtually a variable resistor, with the sliding member controlled by the arm to which the float is attached.

The flow of current through the indicator will vary as the float rises or falls with the level of fuel in the tank.

Fault Finding

1. No reading on fuel indicator.
(a) Check the fuse between A3 and A4.
(b) Check the input and output voltages at the stabilizer. These should be set at battery voltage and 10 volts respectively.
   If the input voltage is correct then the coil between the fuse unit and stabilizer is in order.
   If an incorrect or no-volts reading is obtained at the output terminal "T" on the stabilizer then the stabilizer is faulty and must be renewed.
(c) Remove the tank unit and test by substituting it with a "known" unit.
2. High or Low Reading on Fuel Indicator.
(a) Check the voltage stabilizer as described in 1 (b) above.
(b) Check the instrument by substituting "known" components.
(c) Check condition of insulation of interconnecting cables between the units for lead to earth.
3. Intermittent reading
(a) Check for loose connections.
(b) Substitute voltage stabilizer.
(c) Substitute indicator and tank unit in turn with similar type.

WIND TONE HORNS
MODEL 9H

Lucas miniature wind tone horns, model 9H, operate on the principle of a resonating air column vibrated by a diaphragm, actuated electro-magnetically by a self-interrupting circuit. The horns are intended to be sounded in matched pairs, each pair consisting of a high note and a low note horn — the notes differing by a definite musical interval.

Maintenance

If a horn fails to sound or its performance is unsatisfactory, check the following and rectify as necessary:

1. Battery condition.
2. Loose or broken connection in the horn circuit.
3. Loose fixing bolts.

If the above points are in order, adjust the horn as follows:

Adjustment

Adjustment does not alter the pitch of the note but merely takes up the wear of moving parts.

Disconnect one horn whilst adjusting the other, and take care to avoid earthing disconnected live wires. Connect a first grade moving-coil O-10A ammeter in series with the horn and adjust the small serrated adjustment screw on the side of the horn at which the cables terminate.

Turn the adjusting screw clockwise to increase the current, or anti-clockwise to decrease it, until the best performance is obtained with the least current.

If adjustment is being made without an ammeter, turn the adjusting screws anti-clockwise until the horn just fails to sound; then turn it back one quarter of a turn.

WARNING

Do not disturb the central slotted stem and locking nut.

FUSES

The fuse carrier is located at the side of the control box and houses two operating and two spare fuses. The left-hand fuse (25 amp.) protects the side and number plate illumination lamps, while the right-hand fuse (25 amp.) protects those items which can only operate when the ignition is switched on, i.e. direction indicators, windscreen wipers, brake lamp, fuel gauge, reverse lamp, screen washer and heater.

When replacing a fuse, it is important to use the correct replacement; the fusing value is marked on a coloured paper slip inside the tube.

The horns are protected by an in-line fuse (35 amp.) located below the fuse unit, adjacent to the main harness.

A blown fuse will be indicated by the failure of all units protected by it and is confirmed by examination of the fuse. If the new fuse blows immediately, locate the cause of the trouble.

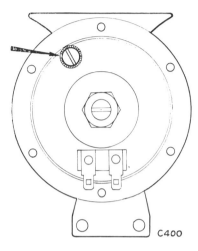

Fig. 37. Horn adjusting screw (indicated by arrow)

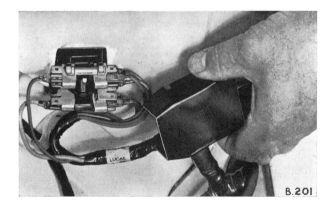

Fig. 38. Fuse unit

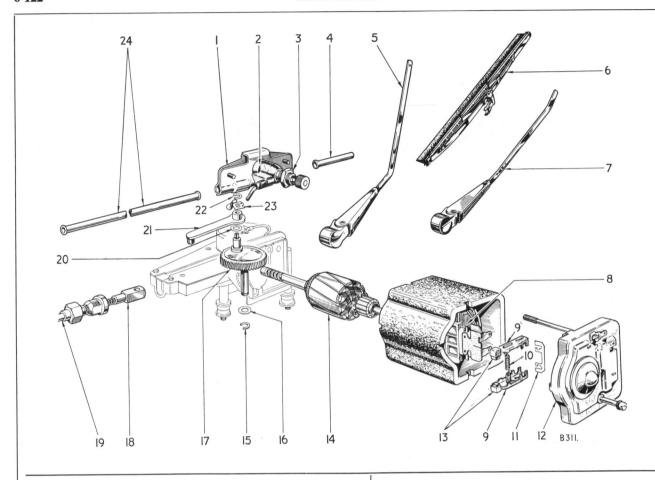

1   Wheel box
2   Jet and bush assembly
3   Nut
4   Rigid tubing—right-hand side
5   Wiper arm
6   Blade
7   Wiper arm
8   Field coil assembly
9   Brushgear
10 Tension spring and retainers
11 Brushgear retainer
12 End cover
13 Brushes
14 Armature
15 Circlip
16 Washer
17 Final drive wheel
18 Cable rack
19 Rigid tubing—left-hand side
20 Spacer
21 Connecting rod
22 Circlip
23 Parking switch contact
24 Rigid tubing—centre section

**Fig. 39. Exploded arrangement of
windscreen wiper mechanism**

WINDSCREEN WIPER

General

The motor and gearbox unit is mounted on three pillars cast integral with the unit body and is located on the right-hand side of the dash panel in the engine compartment. Rotary motion of the motor armature is converted to a reciprocating movement by a single stage worm and nylon gear to which a connecting rod is attached. This actuates the cable rack which consists of a flexible core of steel wire wound with a wire helix to engage with a gear in each wheelbox for transmitting the reciprocating motion to the wiper arm spindles.

A parking switch is incorporated in the domed cover of the gearbox. On switching off at the wiper control switch, the motor continues to run until the moving contact of the parking switch reaches the insulated sector portion and so interrupts the earth return circuit and stops the motor. The domed cover is adjustable to give the correct park position of the wiper blades.

Dismantling

Remove the wiper arms and blades.

Unscrew the large nut securing the outer tubing (19) to the gearbox.

Remove three bolts securing the motor mounting bracket to the dash panel and withdraw the motor complete with inner cable rack.

Note:—The force required to withdraw the rack from the inner tubing should not exceed 6 lbs.

Mark the dome limit switch cover in relation to the gearbox lid, and remove the lid (four screws).

Release the circlip (22) and lift off the limit switch wiper (23).

Lift off the connecting rod (21) from the final drive wheel (17) and cable rack (18). Note the spacer (20) between the connecting rod (21) and final drive wheel (17).

The cable is now free to be removed.

Push the rack back into the tubing and wheelboxes and withdraw the rack from the tubing using a spring balance. The force required should not exceed 6 lbs.

Remove two bolts and lift off the end cover (12).

Check brush tension. This should be between 125 and 140 grammes.

Lift out the brush gear retainers (11).

Release the spring (10) and remove the brush gear (9) complete with brushes and spring retainers (12).

Remove the body complete with field coil; the red earth cable is long enough to permit the body to be lifted clear of the armature.

Remove the armature.

If further dismantling is required, remove the circlip (15) with washers (16). Use a fine file and remove any burrs from around the circlip groove.

Remove the final drive wheel (17).

Clean the wheel and associated parts and examine for wear or damage.

Mark the yoke and field coil in relation to each other.

Remove two screws and withdraw the field coil pole piece and field coil.

Re-assembly

Re-assembly is a reversal of the dismantling procedure.

The adjusting screw in the side of the gearbox should be set and firmly locked to permit 0·008″ to 0·012″ (0·203 — 0·305 mm.) end play of the armature.

Lubrication

The commutator and brush gear must be free of oil or grease. Apply Oilene, B.B.B. or engine oil to the bearings and bushes of the shafts of the final drive wheel and armature.

If the gearbox has been washed clean, use 25 to 35 cubic centimetres of Ragosine Listate grease to refill.

Fig. 40. Location of wiper motor

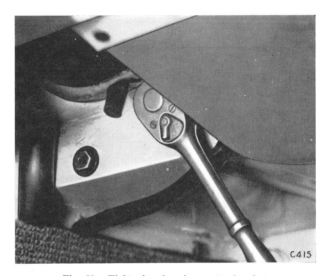

Fig. 41. Tightening the wiper motor bracket attachment bolts

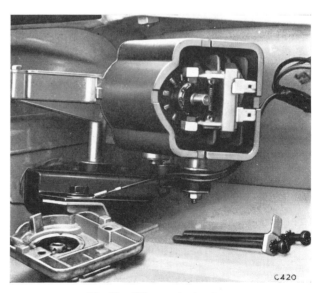

Fig. 42. Wiper motor brushgear

Fig. 43. Wiper arms in the "Parked" condition
(RHD cars)

1 Lamps
2 Pilot lamp
3 Battery

Fig. 44. Location of flasher unit socket

Wiper Wheel Boxes

To Remove (Fig. 39)

Remove wiper motor and working under the facia, remove:
— demister nozzles
— cover plate, located beneath each wheel box (two screws in each).

Remove the nut (3) from each wheel box.

Withdraw the jet and bush assembly (2) for approximately 2″ (5·1 cm.) and disconnect the water pipes.

Pass a piece of thin wire around the right-hand rigid tubing (4) to retain it in position.

Remove the back plate of the wheel box (two screws) and move the rigid tubing outward.

Grip the back of the wheel box with long nose pliers and withdraw it through the aperture.

To Refit

Clean all trace of old sealing compound from the body jet and bush assembly using petrol or white spirit.

Push the wheel box back into position and re-connect the assembly with Seelastik.

Re-connect the water pipes and the securing nut (3).

Clean the contacting surfaces of the cover plate and the underside of the facia. Apply fresh sealing compound to the surfaces and refit the cover plates.

Refit the wiper motor.

FLASHER UNIT DIRECTION-INDICATOR MODEL FL. 5

Housed in a small cylindrical container, the FL 5 Flasher Unit incorporates an actuating wire which heats and cools alternately to operate the main armature and associated pair of contacts in the flasher lamp supply circuit. Simultaneously a secondary armature operates the pilot contacts which cause a warning light to flash when the system is functioning correctly.

Defective Flasher Units cannot be dismantled for subsequent reassembly and must therefore be renewed. Handle the Flasher Unit with care, otherwise the delicate setting may be disturbed and the unit rendered unserviceable.

Trace the cause of faulty operation as follows:

(i)   Check the bulbs for broken filaments.
(ii) Check all flasher circuit connections.
(iii) Switch on the ignition and check the voltage at terminal "B" (12 volts).
(iv) Connect terminals "B" and "L" together and operate the direction-indicator switch. If the flasher lamps light, the Flasher Unit is defective. If the flasher lamps do not light, check the direction-indicator switch.

CABLE CONNECTORS

Servicing

Connectors which are similar in design to those fitted in production are available as service replacements. The new connectors may be fitted as shown in Fig. 45.

1. Push the rubber sleeve clear of the end of the cable and strip the insulation from the conductor for approximately $\frac{5}{16}$″ (8 mm.) for 12 ampere connector or $\frac{7}{16}$″ (11 mm.) for 35 ampere connector.
2. Pass the conductor through the aperture and secure the cables with the tags.
3. Bend the conductors back over the connector and spread flat.
4. Solder the conductors neatly to the connector. Do not allow the solder to run freely through the aperture. Re-tighten the rubber insulating sleeve.

Wiring Harness Loom

The electrical components are connected as shown on Fig. 1 by a single loom, extending from the front end of the car and terminating in the luggage locker. The loom is secured by small clips welded to the body.

Commencing at a group of snap connectors located at the top side of the air intake duct, the loom passes along the right-hand side valance to the fuse unit and control box and into the body to the instrument panel. At this point, a section branches out and re-enters the engine compartment with connections for the wind-screen wiper motor; and on earlier models, this branch of the loom connects the generator and the left-hand side horn. On later models, connections to the left-hand side horn, ignition and generator are provided for in the loom at the side of the right-hand valance.

From the instrument panel the loom passes along the floor to the top of the fuel tank and terminates at the upper forward corner of the locker with connectors for the tail and plate illumination lamps.

INSTRUMENTS
See Group 5.

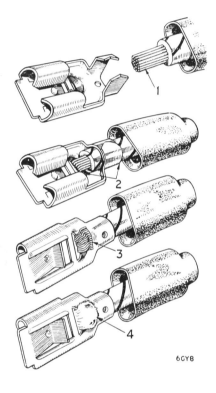

6GY8

Figure 45.   Cable connectors

Printed and distributed by Brooklands Books Ltd., PO Box 146, Cobham, Surrey
KT11 1LG, England Phone: 01932 865051 Fax: 01932 868803

ISBN 0 948207 95 7   Ref: B -T142WH